POETRY as EPITAPH

POETRY as
EPITAPH

REPRESENTATION AND POETIC LANGUAGE

Karen Mills-Courts

LOUISIANA STATE UNIVERSITY PRESS   BATON ROUGE AND LONDON

99 98 97 96 95 94 93 92 91 90   5 4 3 2 1

Designer: Amanda McDonald Key
Typeface: Bembo
Typesetter: G&S Typesetters, Inc.
Printer and binder: Thomson-Shore, Inc.

Library of Congress Cataloging-in-Publication Data

Mills-Courts, Karen.
    Poetry as epitaph : representation and poetic language / Karen
  Mills-Courts.
        p.   cm.
    Includes bibliographical references.
    ISBN 0-8071-1568-1 (alk. paper)
    ISBN 0-8071-1657-2 (pbk.: alk. paper)
    1. English poetry—History and criticism.   2. Epitaphs in
  literature.   3. Mimesis in literature.   4. Death in literature.
  5. Ashbery, John—Criticism and interpretation.   I. Title.
  PR508.E55M5   1990
  821.009'354—dc20
                                                    89-13533
                                                    CIP

The author gratefully acknowledges permission to reprint the following excerpts and selections:
Robert Alter's translation of Tuvia Rubner's poem, from *The Art of Biblical Poetry*. Copyright ©
1985 by Robert Alter. Reprinted by permission of Basic Books, Inc., Publishers, and Georges
Borchardt, Inc., for the author.
    Reprinted by permission of Viking Penguin Inc., New York, and Carcanet Press Ltd., Man-
chester, England: *Selected Poems* by John Ashbery. (These selections originally appeared in *Three
Poems, Houseboat Days, As We Know,* and *A Wave.*) Copyright © 1985 by John Ashbery. All
rights reserved; excerpts from *Self-Portrait In A Convex Mirror* by John Ashbery. Copyright ©
1973, 1974 by John Ashbery. All rights reserved. "Fear of Death" originally appeared in the *New
Yorker.*
    Reprinted by permission of Georges Borchardt, Inc., for the author: Excerpts from *The
Double Dream of Spring* by John Ashbery. Copyright © 1966, 1967, 1968, 1969, 1970 by John
Ashbery; excerpts from *Three Poems* by John Ashbery. Copyright © 1970, 1971, 1972 by John
Ashbery; excerpts from *Some Trees* by John Ashbery. Copyright © 1956 by John Ashbery.
    Reprinted by permission of the Oxford University Press: Excerpts from *The Works of George
Herbert,* edited by F. E. Hutchinson. Copyright © 1945 by the Oxford University Press; ex-
cerpts from *The Prelude* by William Wordsworth, edited by Ernest De Selincourt. Copyright ©
1975 by the Oxford University Press.
    Reprinted by permission of The University of Chicago Press: Excerpts from *Margins of Phi-
losophy* by Jacques Derrida, translated by Alan Bass. Copyright © 1982 by The University of
Chicago Press; excerpts from *Writing and Difference* by Jacques Derrida, translated by Alan Bass.
Copyright © 1978 by The University of Chicago Press.
    Excerpts from *The Confessions of St. Augustine,* translated by Rex Warner. Copyright © 1963
by Rex Warner. Reprinted by arrangement with New American Library, A Division of Penguin
Books USA Inc.; excerpts from *Speech and Phenomena and Other Essays on Husserl's Theory of
Signs* by Jacques Derrida, translated by David B. Allison. Copyright © 1973 by the Northwestern University Press. Reprinted by permission of the Northwestern University Press; excerpts from *Of Grammatology* by Jacques Derrida, translated by Gayatri Spivak. Copyright ©
1976 by The Johns Hopkins University Press. Reprinted by permission of The Johns Hopkins
University Press; brief quotations from *Poetry, Language, Thought,* by Martin Heidegger. Trans-
lated by Alfred Hofstadter. Copyright © 1971 by Martin Heidegger. Reprinted by permission of
Harper & Row, Publishers, Inc.; selections from *The Complete Works of Shelley,* edited by Roger
Ingpen and Walter Peck. Copyright © 1965 by Gordian Press, Inc. Reprinted by permission of
Gordian Press; "Ars Poetica" from *New and Collected Poems, 1917–1982* by Archibald MacLeish.
Copyright © 1985 by The Estate of Archibald MacLeish. Reprinted by permission of Houghton
Mifflin Company.

AJQ3154

I dedicate this book to the memory of
Jeanette Wheeler Mills
and to the loving presence of
my family

CONTENTS

ACKNOWLEDGMENTS

I am unable to discover the exact origins of this book in my intellectual history. Hence my desire to acknowledge all of those who have made it possible forces me to encounter, firsthand and in a very personal way, the problems of incarnating truth and presence with which *Poetry as Epitaph* is concerned. Whose presence do I wish to unveil here? How do I identify their traces in this text? Whose book is this, anyway? I feel certain that it belongs to every text that has taught and delighted me, that it belongs to every person in the familial and intellectual communities that have so generously and warmly embraced me, challenged me, created me. The desire to write down all the names is both overwhelming and impossible; hence, those which follow are representative of all of those who remain unspoken forces haunting my thoughts. They know, I hope, who they are.

I am consciously and constantly aware of the influence of extraordinary teachers: Robert Deming, who first showed me the elegance of theory, Malcolm Nelson, who first showed me the beauty of poetry, and James Shokoff, who taught me the depths and value of "words which speak of nothing more than what we are." I am grateful, also, to my teachers at the State University of New York at Buffalo who planted so many new ideas in the rich ground provided by these first three. I owe a special debt to Gale Carrithers, who read an early version of the manuscript and assured me that I had, indeed, written a book. Minda Rae Amiran, Diana Hume George, and George Sebhouian, friends and colleagues, patiently read sections of the manuscript, freely giving me the gifts of their own excellent minds. Penelope Deakin gave me daily contact with her unique poetic vision, a gift beyond price. I am indebted to others of my colleagues in the English Department at The State University of New York at Fredonia whose support never wavered while I was writing this book during professionally difficult times. They have taught me the best meanings of the phrase "intellectual community."

Kim, Ingrid, and Patrick have taught me that only children can "bring back the hour / Of splendour in the grass, of glory in the flower"; they are essential to all my doings. Kathleen Mills, Sandra Fitzpatrick, and Mary Schweickert sustained me through long, dry hours of isolation. My greatest debt is to Patrick L. Courts, who can never know how much this book belongs to him. These people taught me the meaning of Wordsworth's lines in the last book of *The Prelude:* "By love subsists / All lasting grandeur, by pervading love; / That gone, we are as dust."

ABBREVIATIONS

AWK John Ashbery, *As We Know*

  BI Paul de Man, *Blindness and Insight*

  CP William Packard, ed., *The Craft of Poetry: Interviews from the "New York Quarterly"*

CWS Charles Peck and Roger Ingpen, eds., *The Complete Works of Shelley*

"DA" Roland Barthes, "The Death of the Author"

  DD John Ashbery, *The Double Dream of Spring*

  DN Jacques Derrida, *Dissemination*

  HD John Ashbery, *Houseboat Days*

 "LI" Jacques Derrida, "Limited Inc a b c . . ."

  MP Jacques Derrida, *Margins of Philosophy*

  OG Jacques Derrida, *Of Grammatology*

 PLT Martin Heidegger, *Poetry, Language and Thought*

  PT Roland Barthes, *The Pleasure of the Text*

  RM John Ashbery, *Rivers and Mountains*

"SD" Paul de Man, "Shelley Disfigured"

"SEC" Jacques Derrida, "Signature, Event, Context"

  SM John Ashbery, *Self Portrait in a Convex Mirror*

  SP Jacques Derrida, *Speech and Phenomena*

  ST John Ashbery, *Some Trees*

  TP John Ashbery, *Three Poems*

  WD Jacques Derrida, *Writing and Difference*

POETRY as EPITAPH

INTRODUCTION

The essential relation between death and language flashes up before us, but remains still unthought. It can, however, beckon us toward the way *in which the nature of language draws us into its concern and so relates us to itself, in case death belongs together with what reaches out for us, touches us.*
— Martin Heidegger, *On the Way to Language*

> *No marble, no conventional phrase;*
> *On limestone quarried near the spot*
> *By his command these words are cut:*
> > *Cast a cold eye*
> > *On life, on death.*
> > *Horseman, pass by!*
> > — W. B. Yeats, "Under Ben Bulben"

For we have omitted the master name of the supplementary series: death. Or rather, for death is nothing, the relationship to death, the anguished anticipation of death. All the possibilities of the supplementary series, which have relationships of metonymic substitutions among themselves, indirectly name the danger itself, the horizon and source of all determined dangers, the abyss from which all menaces announce themselves.
— Jacques Derrida, *Of Grammatology*

The order of the epigraphs at the head of this introduction is intended to visually suggest the structure of this book: a poem, which is also an epitaph, is situated between two philosophical texts. Throughout their work, both philosophers speculate on the relationship between death, understood as the limit of language play, and the operations of language as such. There is an unerasable difference between them, however, which determines the method and content of their thought: while Heidegger thinks of language as presentational or 'incarnative', Derrida thinks of language as ungrounded 'representation'. Caught between them, the poet creates a poem that is overtly intended to work as "unconcealment," as the incarnation of a presence, the embodiment of a voice in words. Yet, he displays that voice as an inscription carved on a tombstone. In

other words, he covertly acknowledges that the poem is representational, that it substitutes itself for a presence that has been absolutely silenced. For the very words that seem to give life simultaneously announce the death of the speaker. Though it seems so lively
that it can halt its readers and admonish them, it is as if the voice
can be heard only because it has been lost, has been erased by death
itself.

This paradoxical contradiction cannot be resolved, not even by
attempting to explain or contain it in the (now familiar) idea that
language evokes "the presence of an absence / the absence of a presence." Clearly, presence and absence are interwoven, and the weaving is as intricate as Heidegger and Derrida, in very different ways,
have shown it to be. And, in the case of poetry, that weaving is not
merely a surface effect that can be unstrung to examine warp and
woof or to determine the priority of one over the other. Poetry, in
fact, may be defined as that which *must function between* the presentational and representational workings of language. This is a point
suggested by Paul de Man in a late essay on the work of Michael
Riffaterre and Hans Robert Jauss. There he writes that "the principle
of intelligibility, in lyric poetry, depends on the phenomenalization
of the poetic voice. Our claim to understand a lyric text coincides
with the actualization of a speaking voice, be it (monologically)
that of the poet or (dialogically) that of the exchange that takes
place between author and reader in the process of comprehension."[1] De Man goes on to expose the fictive, figural strategies
readers and writers use to secure this illusion of voice, but only
after he notes that "no matter what approach is taken it is essential
that the status of the voice not be reduced to a mere figure of speech
or play of the letter, for this would deprive it of the attribute of aes-
thetic presence that determines the hermeneutics of the lyric" (56).
De Man is interested not in a hermeneutics of the lyric but in a deconstruction of the rhetoric that grounds the possibility of hermeneutics. And, with the brilliance that we have come to expect
from all of his work, he proceeds, in this essay, to dismantle the
process involved in the "repression of the figural and literal powers
of the signifier," a repression absolutely necessary to the maintenance of presence in the poem. Yet, despite the energy, the power,
one might even say the mastery, of his deconstruction of the val-

1. Paul de Man, "Lyrical Voice in Contemporary Theory: Riffaterre and Jauss,"
in *Lyric Poetry: Beyond New Criticism,* ed. Chaviva Hosek and Patricia Parker (Ithaca,
1985), 55–72.

orization of presence by Riffaterre and Jauss, his own essay remains haunted by exactly the principle of intelligibility he identifies in the lyric as "the phenomenalization of voice." For this principle sustains criticism as well as poetry, and critics cannot do without it, even in their deconstructive mode.

The present book explores this interweaving of presence, meaning, and representation. It does so by focusing on poetry, the most powerful attempt to incarnate voice, meaning, intelligibility, even 'Truth', in language. Poets, more than any other writers, need to secure presence in their work, but this desire is always threatened by the densely figurative powers that poetry must employ more consciously than any other writing.

Harold Bloom once said that "whether one accepts a theory of language that teaches the dearth of meaning, as in Derrida and de Man, or that teaches its plenitude, as in Barfield and Ong, does not seem to me to matter. All I ask is that the theory of language be extreme and uncompromising enough."[2] Though I disagree that Derrida teaches the "dearth" of meaning, I deeply sympathize with Bloom's desire and passion. But the issue is not quite so simple, as Bloom well knows, and as uncomfortable as compromise always is, it may be the only position finally available to users of language. Situating the poem "in between" two opposed systems of analysis is a precarious enterprise; it seems to defy (or at least evade) logic, and it clearly displays a resistance to making a choice. Part of my intent in this study, however, is to suggest that no choice between representational and incarnative language is genuinely possible. At least it is not possible as long as we use language to 'present' and 'describe' our own concepts. I am alert to the ghostly voices of several excellent critics whose words have been my teachers, and those voices have, on occasion, bridled at the refusal of others to choose between theories of language that appear contradictory. In fact, this issue created one of the most important encounters in contemporary critical thinking. The exchange is fascinating in several respects but, for my purposes, it is most interesting for the light it casts on the issue of using Derrida and Heidegger, in J. Hillis Miller's phrase, "at once."[3]

2. Harold Bloom, "The Breaking of Form," in *Deconstruction and Criticism,* ed. Harold Bloom, Paul de Man, Jacques Derrida, Geoffrey Hartman, and J. Hillis Miller (New York, 1979), 4.
3. Vincent B. Leitch discusses this encounter in *Deconstructive Criticism: An Advanced Introduction* (New York, 1983), 88–97.

In reviewing Joseph Riddel's *The Inverted Bell: Modernism and the Counterpoetics of William Carlos Williams,* Miller cuts cleanly into the heart of the matter by questioning Riddel's use of three distinct discourses: Heidegger's, Derrida's, and Williams's.[4] He worries about a murky collapsing of all three into a sameness that disguises their obvious differences. "Riddel tends to assume that Heidegger, Derrida, Williams, and he himself are each more or less self-consistent and that all four are saying roughly 'the same thing.' This means that one can follow Heidegger and Derrida at once" (25). And he worries about Riddel's seeming inconsistency: "At one moment Riddel sounds something like Derrida. . . . the next moment, on the same page he falls back into Heidegger" (27). Miller's reading of Riddel evokes the specter of an attempted deconstruction that, in the very process of its own activity, ends up confirming the phenomenology it had intended to question. The contradiction he perceives here is analogous to the contradiction displayed by the speaking monument: the maintenance of presence and its undermining occur in the same gesture.

Riddel's response clearly shows his understanding of the differences between the thinkers.[5] He points out that his use of Heideggerean metaphors was not an innocent confirmation of those figures, but an attempt to "display" Williams's "undermining of Heidegger's site." At the same time he acknowledges that he did not "attempt to simulate Derrida's kind of analysis" (57). "I was not presuming to deconstruct Williams' texts," he writes, "but to present his deconstructions. . . . Thus I proceeded to describe what I recognized as Williams' efforts to 'begin again' by turning the 'inside out' (his metaphors), to begin literature again just when it seemed at an end—a project not without its self-conscious contradictions" (58). This last phrase proves to be a key one in Riddel's rejoinder, for it is partly through the figure of "contradiction" that he argues his case. He notes that Miller's own work on Williams found the poetry "entrapped in the very web of privileged metaphors it attacks"; he cites an older Miller essay on Georges Poulet as "an attempt to bridge the irreconcilable distance between Geneva and Paris with the common space of 'literature'" and says, finally, that in Miller's reading of *Middlemarch,* "he does not follow his own advice to conduct a

4. J. Hillis Miller, "Deconstructing the Deconstructors," *Diacritics,* V (Summer, 1975), 24–31.
5. Joseph N. Riddel, "A Miller's Tale," *Diacritics,* V (Fall, 1975), 56–65.

rhetorical analysis of the novel, but offers us a thematic reading of the novel's systematic displacement of all referentiality" (62–65). Riddel's point is that Miller has himself fallen from deconstruction into the presentational mode of phenomenology—a mode that can be understood as "a fall back into Heidegger." This should not be read as an accusation, for Riddel would certainly be aware that such an attack would be self-contradictory in light of his own endeavor to "present" and "describe."

This encounter between two masterful deconstructors offers all the richness that good critical dialogue should, illuminating not just their own methodologies and differences but issues crucial to the critical enterprise itself. Miller is certainly correct to point out that there are irreconcilable differences between a Heideggerean hermeneutics (the unconcealment of meaning) and a Derridean deconstruction (the dismantling of meaning). But Riddel's response is equally compelling, and extremely suggestive, hinting that presentation and description, two strikingly phenomenological methods, do not necessarily exclude deconstructive activity, any more than deconstruction necessarily exorcises the phenomenological. In fact, most essays enact this contradictory combination in a way that may be unavoidable.

It seems to me that at least what one might call a limited phenomenology is inescapable, part of the definition of criticism as such—even the extraordinary deconstructive criticism of J. Hillis Miller himself. Miller's superb essay "The Critic as Host" is as lucid an explication of deconstruction as one could hope for.[6] But, *as* explication, it functions within the very system of metaphysical meaning that deconstruction questions. It may be that one cannot "follow" Derrida and Heidegger "at once," but Miller's essay suggests that we must read them at once. The essay "describes" and "presents" the kind of doubleness on which deconstruction always performs its operations. This method creates the sense that a certain 'phenomenology' of deconstruction is under way, that the essay functions through the unconcealment of meaning. This may seem contradictory, but it is hardly surprising, for if criticism is to function at all, it must always carry this Heideggerean ghost within its workings. Description and presentation, both incarnative gestures, are brought into play at every moment one wishes to produce intel-

6. J. Hillis Miller, "The Critic as Host," in *Deconstruction and Criticism*, ed. Bloom et al., 217–53.

ligibility; they are summoned and commanded by the very system
we identify as language—a system that is, as Derrida has pointed
out all along, classically metaphysical in its dependence upon presence as the ground of meaning. Miller's account of doubleness is
haunted by Heidegger in another, more self-conscious, way: he begins his description of deconstruction with a startling paraphrase of
Heidegger's dictum that "language speaks," a speaking which establishes "world." The critic then spins that "echo" out into the triangular structure that is basic to deconstruction:

> Language . . . thinks man and his 'world', if he will allow it to do so.
> The system of figurative thought (but what thought is not figurative?)
> inscribed within the word parasite and its associates, host and guest, in-
> vites us to recognize that the 'obvious or univocal reading' of a poem is
> not identical to the poem itself. Both readings, the 'univocal' one and
> the 'deconstructive' one, are fellow guests 'beside the grain', host and
> guest, host and host, host and parasite, parasite and parasite. The relation
> is a triangle, not a polar opposition. There is always a third to whom the
> two are related, something before them or between them, which they
> divide, consume, or exchange, across which they meet.   (224)

The "univocal" reading here is understood as the reading that assumes contained or incarnated meaning, while the "deconstructive" reading is the exposition of the play of representation that
produces undecidable meanings. The "third" to whom they are related is a sort of "ghost" rather than "host," since it is that "trace of
a trace" which can never be found *in* the text. But, from Miller's
point of view, both the deconstructive and the univocal readings are
parasitical upon that unpresentable force, which they also "host"
secretly and invisibly. The notion that this force remains beyond
revelation, beyond incarnation, is what distances Miller from Heidegger and moves him toward Derrida. And yet, Miller's sense that
this force allows the univocal and the deconstructive to "meet" remains haunted by the Heideggerean notion of 'gathering' rather
than by the Derridean notion of 'dissemination.'

It seems to me that the "contradiction" here is right on the mark.
A meeting must occur if either deconstruction or hermeneutics is to
function, and that meeting occurs in language that behaves epitaphically. This possibility is suggested figuratively in a moment of
Miller's essay that long ago seeded my interest in the epitaphic gesture. Given the triangular structure of what he calls "interpretation
as such," Miller thinks that "metaphysics might then be redefined
from the point of view of this trivium, as an inevitable rhetorical or
tropological effect. It would not be a cause but a phantom generated

within the house of language by the play of language. Deconstruction is one current name for this reversal" (229). I will argue that the "phantom . . . in the house of language" is meaning itself and that this "phantom" enables the operations of language that contradict its existence.

The "self-contradiction" involved in Miller's descriptive, presentational discussion of the inability of language to 'present' is no accident. Criticism of necessity operates through and within "self-conscious contradictions." If one extends Paul de Man's description of the requirement for voice in lyric poetry, one sees that the principle of intelligibility operates as thoroughly in commentary as it does in the texts it considers. Criticism can contain meaning, can be intelligible, exactly to the extent that it "describes" and "presents" (Riddel's words) its own activity. Such presentational description is one way of achieving a sense of voice and may be the only way of achieving meaning, even in the work of Jacques Derrida—work that so often seems to be activity rather than a description of activity. At the moment deconstruction is written it becomes self-presentational, self-descriptive, and hence, in this respect, 'phenomenological'. And, paradoxically, at that same moment the principle of intelligibility becomes vulnerable, as it does in all writing, and begins to shake apart under the force of representational play, a play that opens up the possibility that meaning can never be contained or incarnated in the text but can only be formulated as a sort of straying from representation to representation in an interminable undecidability.

This movement opens up a text to the abyss that Derrida calls, in the opening epigraph, "the danger itself." This danger is death: the death of presence and the death of meaning that must accompany the death of voice. In this situation the critic is, like Eugenio Donato's Baudelaire, "constituted by an accumulation of memories, an archeological museum of fragments of the past, haphazardly juxtaposed, each a synecdochal textual representation ordered by the accidental metonymic accident of proximity." And, as Donato points out, "the collection of memories . . . count less than their emblem, the pyramid, which we are now in a position to read as the symbol of linguistic representation itself. . . . [The critic] then, being nothing more than a set of representations, is reduced to a cemetery containing nothing but funerary monuments."[7] Criticism

7. Eugenio Donato, "The Ruins of Memory: Archaeological Fragments and Textual Artifacts," *Modern Language Notes,* XCIII (1978), 595.

becomes the epitaph of epitaphs. Nonetheless, we can experience the "death" of voice, of the "principle of intelligibility," the loss of this kind of significance, only by conjuring its "afterlife" as an echo that inhabits the inscription that points to its loss. We understand the death of presence by virtue of a marker that "presents" and "describes" its loss through a peculiar reincarnation of presence in the form of the voice of meaning. This too is epitaphic.

This situation lies at the bottom of the exchange between Miller and Riddel, and I believe it is unavoidable. Riddel turns to an early statement made by Derrida in "The Ends of Man" where he seems to suggest that one must choose between two modes of deconstruction, both bearing certain dangers within themselves, the greatest being that either mode can ultimately end by confirming that which it intended to deconstruct. Riddel believes that Miller's comments suggest that he has chosen the second option: to deconstruct the metaphysics of presence by "stepping abruptly outside and by affirming absolute rupture." He then suggests that Miller's essay suffers a "curious contradiction" since it, too, remains 'inside' metaphysics.[8] But this "curious contradiction" exists at the heart of all postmodern criticism, produced, as Miller himself has said, by the fact that "the 'deconstructive' reading can by no means free itself from the metaphysical reading it means to contest." Both of these critics understand that Derrida's two alternatives are vulnerable to metaphysics. And Derrida has consistently said that neither form can entirely escape the metaphysical system that enables language to bear meaning, no matter how severely it shakes that system. The "curious contradiction" does not just disturb Riddel's and Miller's criticism or Derrida's deconstruction and Heidegger's hermeneutics. It is a disturbance that operates at the core of language, created by the conflict between our need for language to be incarnative and our understanding that it behaves, instead, as representation. The study of representation is always caught within the incarnative net, and vice versa. We may wish to choose and may even elect a choice for heuristic purposes in our critical endeavors, but whichever choice we make is bound to be infiltrated by its opposite.

This paradox is both the focus of this study and that which determines the curious contradiction of my own approch to the texts I explore. My approach is overtly 'descriptive' and 'presentational' at the same time that it deploys several of the insights that deconstruc-

8. Riddel, "A Miller's Tale," 61.

tion has generated. My exploration of texts is frankly in search of
meaning, a motivation that inherently excludes deconstructive reading and aligns me more closely with Heidegger than with Derrida.
For it is exactly here, in the problem of whether or not meaning can
be revealed, that Derrida and Heidegger most certainly part company. Heideggerean hermeneutics is the seeking of meaning, the attempt to lift it out of concealment, though the lifting can never be
complete and the seeking can never culminate in a totalized revelation; it must, as William Spanos has taught us, be endlessly repeated.[9] Deconstruction, however, insists that meaning as such is
only an effect of an illusory system that defines being as presence in
the first place; it is not the revelation of truth but the repetition of
the system itself. In Derrida's words,

> *sense* (in whatever sense it is understood: as essence, as the meaning of
> discourse, as the orientation of the movement between *arche* and *telos*)
> has never been conceivable, within the history of metaphysics, other-
> wise than on the basis of presence and as presence. The concept of sense,
> of meaning, is governed by the entire system of determinations that we
> are pointing out here, and every time that a question of *meaning* is
> posed, it must be posed within the closure of metaphysics. To put it
> quite summarily, one seeks in vain to extract the question of meaning . . .
> as such, from metaphysics, or from the system of so called 'vulgar'
> concepts.[10]

The question of meaning *is* the question of Being, for Derrida as
well as for Heidegger. But in Derrida's case, the question is unaskable; it is, instead, the expression of the very system he wishes to
dismantle. His critique of Heidegger is grounded in the fact that
Heidegger's thought plays out, in the form of a great question, the
same assumptions he wishes to interrogate. When Heidegger asks,
"What is the Meaning of Being?" the question conceals within itself
the presumption that being is presence and that meaning can be determined as presence. The question assumes that meaning can be
brought to light, can be incarnated. In Derrida's thought, to ask the
question of meaning is to remain caught within a metaphysics of
presence that should instead be interrogated from the 'outside'. To

9. For two excellent examples of William Spanos's "temporal hermeneutics" see
"Hermeneutics and Memory: Destroying T. S. Eliot's *Four Quartets*," *Genre*, II
(Winter, 1978), 523–73, and "Heidegger, Kierkegaard, and the Hermeneutic Circle,"
in *Martin Heidegger and the Question of Literature,* ed. William Spanos (Bloomington,
Ind., 1979).

10. Jacques Derrida, "Ousia and Gramme," in *MP,* 51.

ask the question is to be trapped by a system that does not generate 'truth' but only produces the *idea* of truth as an effect of its own operations. In order to step 'outside', Derrida employs the notion of an uncontainable force that seems to escape metaphysics, a force that he calls "differance."

If one considers Derrida's "differance" and Heidegger's "dif-ference" side by side, it becomes clear why Miller finds the thinkers incommensurate. A brief glance will suffice, for now, as prepara-tion for what follows in later chapters. Heidegger begins a medita-tion on "dif-ference" by reiterating the phrase that echoes through-out his later work: "Language *speaks*. This means at the same time and before all else: *Language* speaks." [11] The speaking of language is a "naming" that is also a "calling" which summons Being by estab-lishing a "world." That world is a "gathering" in which "mortals" and "things" come together in a "middle" that is named "inti-macy." But "intimacy" is not "fusion"; when language speaks, it generates an existence that "divides itself cleanly and remains sepa-rated. In the midst of the two, in the between of world and thing, in their *inter*, division prevails: a *dif-ference*" (202). In Heidegger's articulation of "dif-ference," this irreducible division becomes the site of a unity that is both produced by language and necessary to the disclosure of meaning that language enacts:

> The intimacy of world and thing is present in the separation of the be-tween; it is present in the difference. The word difference is now re-moved from its usual and customary usage. What it now names is not a generic concept for various kinds of differences. It exists only as this single difference. It is unique. Of itself, it holds apart the middle in and through which world and things are at one with each other. The inti-macy of the difference is the unifying element of the *diaphora*, the carry-ing out that carries through. The dif-ference carries out world in its worlding, carries out things in their thinging. Thus carrying them out, it carries them toward one another. The dif-ference does not mediate after the fact by connecting world and things through a middle added on to them. Being the middle, it first determines world and things in their presence, i. e., in their being toward one another, whose unity it carries out. . . . The dif-ference for world and thing *disclosingly appro-priates* things into bearing a world; it *disclosingly appropriates* world into the granting of things. The dif-ference is neither distinction nor rela-tion. The dif-ference is, at most, dimension for world and thing. . . . In the bidding that calls thing and world, what is really called is: the dif-ference.   (*PLT,* 202–203)

---

11. Martin Heidegger, "Language," in *PLT,* 198.

Language "calls" "dif-ference" as a "dimension," a time/place of disclosure and appropriation that "determines world and things in their *presence*." As such, appropriative disclosure is an incarnative activity; it allows the appearance of Being, the containment of meaning in a veiled body. But that presence can only be known because it is protected, "sheltered" by absence. Through "dif-ference," which is activated by language, presence "arrives" out of an absence which is part of its essence and which is required as a necessary horizon for its appearance. Language generates "dif-ference" as a place of arrival: "The place of arrival which is also called in the calling is a presence sheltered in absence" (199). That presence is not just brute being but the meaning of Being. Hence, through "dif-ference," "Language speaks" meaning-fully.

Derrida's "differance" is another story.[12] It, too, is a kind of "dimension" rather than an entity, a "middle" that does not "come after the fact" of language, but its operations are quite different from those of "dif-ference." Derrida unfolds the neologism as "neither a word nor a concept." Neither active nor passive, "it, rather, indicates the middle voice, it precedes and sets up the opposition between passivity and activity." This "undecidable" no-thing is the structuring force *and* space that allows the play of language: "it expresses the interposition of delay; the interval of spacing and temporalizing that puts off until 'later' what is presently denied, the possible that is impossible" (*SP*, 136). The "possible" that "differance" defers, that is "impossible," is Being as presence and, hence, the meaning or truth of Being. "Differance," according to Derrida, erases Heidegger's ontico-ontological "dif-ference," turning it into an effect rather than a cause:

> Since Being has never had a "meaning," has never been thought or said as such except by dissimulating itself in beings, then *differance*, in a certain way (is) 'older' than the ontological difference or than the truth of Being. When it has this age it can be called the play of the trace. The play of a trace which no longer belongs to the horizon of Being, but whose play transports and encloses the meaning of Being: the play of the trace, or the *differance*, which has no meaning and is not. Which does not belong. There is no maintaining, and no depth to, this bottomless chessboard on which Being is put into play.   (*MP*, 22)

"Differance" is a "carrying out" but it can never be one that "carries through." Instead of gathering, "differance" institutes "dissemination"; instead of permitting arrival, it produces a "detour, a delay";

12. Jacques Derrida, "Differance," in *MP*, 1–27; "Differance," in *SP*, 129–60.

instead of granting appropriation, it generates "dispossession"; and, instead of confirming the play of presence and absence, it "puts into question the authority of presence, or of its simple symmetrical opposite, absence or lack" (*MP*, 10). And, importantly, "differance" is not "called" by language, is not enabled by speech or, for that matter, by writing. Rather, it is both the force that enables language to operate at all and the force that defers and delays presence interminably, instituting what only appears to be presence as the "trace of a trace," as a bottomless series of representations. If one is to operate from 'outside' metaphysics, then, "as rigorously as possible we must permit to appear/disappear the trace of what exceeds the truth of Being. The trace (of that) which can never be presented, the trace which itself can never be presented: that is appear and manifest itself, as such, in its phenomenon. The trace beyond that which profoundly links fundamental ontology and phenomenology. Always differing and deferring, the trace is never as it is in the presentation of itself. It erases itself in presenting itself, muffles itself in resonating, like the *a* writing itself, inscribing its pyramid in *differance*" (*MP*, 23).

"Dif-ference," as a "gathering" and "presentation" promises a disclosable meaning even though that meaning must be endlessly rediscovered through constant reinterpretation—a process that may be "life-itself" in Heidegger's thought.[13] "Differance," on the other hand, guarantees the endless wandering of meaning from representation to representation; even the trace of that wandering conceals itself and can never be recovered as 'a meaning'. As Riddel has said in a fine study of the relationship between Heidegger and Derrida, for Heidegger, poetic language "introduces us to a 'history' that holds out the hope for some full recovery of presence." But Derrida's "language of *differance* under*writes* the concept difference and renders it a 'simulacrum' of 'undecidable'" and such underwriting means that "the production of meanings turns upon a meaning-lessness, an absence of the commanding, originating word, and the play of the *supplement* which stands for that word in the text."[14]

When language "turns upon a meaning-lessness" it turns upon death, but we should be careful to note the double implications of

13. Harriet Davidson argues this point lucidly in *T. S. Eliot and Hermeneutics: Absence and Interpretation in The Waste Land* (Baton Rouge, 1985), 42–50.

14. Joseph Riddel, "From Heidegger to Derrida to Chance: Doubling and Poetic Language," in *Martin Heidegger and the Question of Literature,* ed. Spanos, 241, 246–47.

"turns upon": it functions on the basis of meaning-lessness and it *attacks* meaning-lessness. Despite the death it announces, the "turning" of representation, of figurative language, is the "life," the production, of meaning which can be stopped only at death, the limit life imposes. Jacques Derrida has noted the resemblance of the sign to the cenotaph in several instances. In *Writing and Difference* he employs one metaphor that is very much to my point. A careful deconstruction of the sign, or of any created structure, "neutralizes" the apparent fullness of meaning, he writes, and the work is, thus, seen to be "somewhat like the architecture of an uninhabited or deserted city, reduced to its skeleton by some catastrophe of nature or art. A city no longer inhabited, not simply left behind, but haunted by meaning and culture. This state of being haunted, which keeps the city from returning to nature, is perhaps, the general mode of presence or absence of the thing itself in pure language."[15] The death of presence leaves a ghost-like trace that is not quite nothingness. The act of representation bears the doubleness of an epitaphic gesture. Like an inscription on a cenotaph, it proclaims death and an empty core, but that emptiness is of a peculiar sort: the emptiness of a nothing that seems, somehow, to signify something. It is the nothingness of a haunting. The sign as a crypt marks the burial place of the dead, but like a crypt, it can serve also as a place for occult and secret meetings. The inscribed stone can never fully incarnate presence but it can bestow a significant, if uncanny, form of 'being'—that form which Shelley calls "vanishing apparitions" or which Ashbery says 'is' *because* it is "cloaked with the shrill / Savage drapery of non-being." That form has the ghost-like ambiguity of being both dead and alive, and it is lodged deeply within the consciousness of most good poets. Poets are motivated by a passion for presence, and a certain uneasiness concerning the loss of presence in writing plays itself out in their poems. That anxiety has by no means vanished from twentieth-century poetry, even in the work of the postmodernists who appear to surrender to "writing without voice." Even Ashbery's cool understanding of language as necessarily representational is accompanied by a sense of loss that casts much of his work into the elegiac mode, and even he is haunted by the ghost of presence, by "whispers out of time."

To free themselves from the apparent death of presence which occurs in the act of representation, to free themselves from Shelley's

15. Jacques Derrida, "Force and Signification," in *WD,* 5.

cry that "when composition begins, inspiration is already on the decline," poets attempt to develop strategies that can accommodate both representational and presentational notions of language. Just as they seem to be crucial to the claims of critical commentary, those strategies are crucial to the maintenance of poetry's claim to privilege—a claim that depends on de Man's principle of intelligibility, with all it implies about voice. More often than not, each strategy involves one version or another of the epitaphic gesture. Poets, using the fact that representation carries death within, attempt to secure presence by triggering the same energies, the "privileges," one grants a gravestone. It is as if they subscribe to Heidegger's notion that "truth, as the lighting and concealing of beings, *happens in being composed.*"[16] They attempt to wrest presence and truth from within the play of absence and presence that happens 'in' composition.

For Heidegger, as surely as for Derrida, this play is intimately related to death. In his thought, human beings experience two "proper" modes of being: they dwell within the "House" of language and they dwell as *mortals,* within the ownership of their own deaths. As Heidegger writes in *Being and Time,* "death is a possibility of Being which Dasein itself has to take over in every case. With death Dasein stands before itself in its *ownmost* potentiality-for-Being."[17] Richardson suggests that in the later Heidegger thought itself is grounded in death as "the negativity of Being."[18] More precisely, he notes that it is "the *comprehending* of Being in its negativity that constitutes the foundational thinking of things" (576). Comprehension (in the sense of both understanding and presentation) of Being can occur only through language, and language must bear death along with Being in order for either to appear. Hence, very often in Heidegger talk of language immediately calls forth talk of death. His provocative work *On the Way to Language* begins, significantly, with a discussion of the death and burial place of a former student and ends with a discussion of the language of Trakl's elegies. This is not, I think, an accident. The "way" to language

---

16. Martin Heidegger, "The Origin of the Work of Art," in *Martin Heidegger: Basic Writings,* ed. David F. Krell (New York, 1977), 184. Hereafter cited in text as "Origin."

17. Martin Heidegger, *Being and Time,* trans. John Macquarrie and Edward Robinson (New York, 1962), 294.

18. William J. Richardson, *Heidegger: Through Phenomenology to Thought* (The Hague, 1967), 572–76.

may be generated by the fact that humankind is always on the way to death, and when language must carry absence in order to unconceal presence, the arrival at meaning is also an arrival at death. "Mortals are they who can experience death as death. Animals cannot do so," Heidegger writes, "but animals cannot speak."[19]

One of the most important purposes of poetry for Heidegger is that it reveals to Dasein its relationship to its own death. In "What Are Poets For?" he says that "to be a poet in a destitute time means: to attend, singing, to the trace of the fugitive gods. This is why the poet in the time of the world's night utters the holy."[20] The poet sings of the "haunting" of the gods, of that "trace" which clearly announces a death that is not quite total absence, though it must be emphasized that neither is it presence. The singing, if adequate, unconceals the "trace of the trace" of their being. The unconcealing of poetry can happen only in relation to death, and Heidegger suggests that any evasion of this creates a dearth of meaning: "The time remains desolate not only because God is dead, but because mortals have not yet come into ownership of their own nature. Death withdraws into the enigmatic."[21]

Poetry, then, by unconcealing absence, brings death "into the open." Yet the recognition that language reveals death is no more negative for Heidegger than it is for Derrida. Absence is never "nothingness" to either thinker. For Derrida it is the space in which humankind creates itself as the representation of representation, as the possibility of writing:

Representation is death. Which may immediately be transformed into the following proposition: death is (only) representation. But it is bound to life and to the living present itself which it repeats originarily. A pure representation, a machine, never runs by itself. . . . Writing, here, is *techne* as the relation between life and death, between present and representation, between the two apparatuses . . . in this sense writing is the stage of history and the play of the world. (*WD*, 227–28)

For Heidegger, absence is inherent in and necessary to Being itself:

But absence is not nothing; rather it is precisely the presence, which must first be appropriated, of the hidden fullness and wealth of what has

19. Martin Heidegger, *On the Way to Language*, trans. Peter D. Hertz (New York, 1971), 107.
20. Martin Heidegger, "What Are Poets For?," in *PLT*, 74.
21. *Ibid.*, 96.

been and what, thus gathered, is presencing, of the divine. . . . This no-
longer is, in itself, a not-yet of the veiled arrival of its inexhaustible
nature.[22]

Despite the radical differences in their thinking, Derrida's focus on
representation and Heidegger's "step back from the representational
thinking of metaphysics" (*PLT*, 185), both focus on language in
such a way as to remind us that we cannot think about language
unless we also think absence, loss, death. They remind us, as Derrida has written, that writing is a defense against the threat it embodies within itself: "There is no writing which does not devise
some means of protection, *to protect against itself*, against the writing
by which the 'subject' is himself threatened as he lets himself be
written: *as he exposes himself*" (*WD*, 224). The desire to make language incarnative and the notion that voice is presence are both part
of an intricate system of self-defense. "Nature is a haunted house—
but Art—a house that tries to be haunted," Emily Dickinson says.[23]
The "house of language" always tries to be haunted by the presence
we call meaning.

Each of the poets I have chosen to study is profoundly, perhaps
obsessively, concerned with the problems I have been merely sketch-
ing out here. Each explores, in the most overt ways, the encounter
between the "presencing" power of language and the absence announced by representation. In all of them the pressures on poetic
language to be 'incarnative' rather than 'representative' are extremely intense. At the same time, these poets clearly understand
language as monumental, the marker of an essential absence. They
seem to be haunted by T. S. Eliot's remarkable moment of insight
in *Four Quartets:*

> And to make an end is to make a beginning.
> The end is where we start from. And every phrase
> And sentence that is right (where every word is at home
> Taking its place to support the others,
> The word neither diffident nor ostentatious,
> An easy commerce of the old and new,
> The common word exact without vulgarity,
> The formal word precise but not pedantic,
> The complete consort dancing together)

22. *PLT*, 184.
23. Emily Dickinson, *The Letters of Emily Dickinson*, ed. Thomas H. Johnson
(Cambridge, Mass., 1965), II, 330.

Every phrase and every sentence is an end and a beginning,
Every poem an epitaph.[24]

If every word is at home, that home becomes Dickinson's "haunted house." Poets write, as John Ashbery says in the words that close this book, "As though all were elegy and toccata / (Which happens to be the case), / The guidelines."

---

24. T. S. Eliot, "Little Gidding," in *Collected Poems, 1909–1962* (New York, 1963), 207–208.

❦ 1 ❧

REPRESENTATION, INCARNATION: WRITING AND SPEECH

But this appearing of the Ideal as an infinite differance can only be produced within a relationship with death in general. Only a relation to my-death could make the infinite differing of presence appear. . . . A voice without differance, a voice without writing is at once absolutely alive and absolutely dead. . . .
We therefore no longer know whether what has always been reduced and abased as an accident, modification and re-turn, under the old names of "sign" and "re-presentation" has not repressed that which related truth to its own death as it related it to its origin.
—Jacques Derrida, *Speech and Phenomena*

Truth, as the lighting and concealing of beings, happens in being composed. All art, *as the letting happen of the advent of the truth of beings, is as such,* in essence, poetry. *The essence of art, on which both the art work and the artist depend, is the setting-itself-into-work of truth. . . . But poesy is only one mode of the lighting projection of truth, i. e., of poetic composition in this wider sense. Nevertheless, the linguistic work, poetry in the narrower sense, has a privileged position in the domain of the arts.*
—Martin Heidegger, "The Origin of the Work of Art"

The epigraphs that open this chapter reveal the key issues of this study. The words of both philosophers contain rich suggestions and complexities which will be explored from various perspectives. For now, my focus is on their radically different ideas about the relationship between language and truth, the central concern for an exploration of poetics. Poets must believe that their work offers, in one way or another, "the lighting projection of truth." This possibility motivates writing. Yet, most good poets have always understood that, as representation, poetry is always threatened by the possibility that words betray truth. As a result, poetry exists in an "in between" state, located on a fine-honed edge between the desire to present the 'thing-itself' and the knowledge that language can only stand in place of that thing.

For Jacques Derrida, writing reveals desire: not truth but a need for truth. Furthermore, he thinks that the active desire for truth is, at bottom, the expression of the human need to confirm one's own existence as a unified whole, an "absolute self-presence," an 'I'. For this reason, language as speech, words that seem to be in proximity with a self, is seen as the primary language, while written words seem secondary, mere signs of a voice. However, he shows that even speech cannot contain truth as presence. It, too, is a signifying system from which the 'thing-itself' is exiled; in fact, the 'thing-itself' is not prior to the system but is, rather, a product of the system, an illusion produced by representation, not the ground of representation. The self is différance in action; the full presence of truth, or a unified consciousness, would be the end of différance, of the activity which is life-itself. Hence, the seeking after truth, which has been the central activity of philosophy from the time of Plato, is in some way the seeking after an absolute that can best be understood as death-in-life: "Since absolute self-presence in consciousness is the infinite *vocation* of full presence, the achievement of absolute knowledge is the end of the infinite, which could only be the unity of concept, logos, and consciousness in a voice without *différance. The history of metaphysics therefore can be expressed as the unfolding of the structure or schema of an absolute will-to-hear-oneself-speak.* This history is closed when this infinite absolute appears to itself as its own death" (*SP*, 103).

Vocalization, language as speech, seems to promise the living presence of truth, of a unified speaking subject. But, as Derrida unfolds the speech-act he discovers only a series of self-representations, of displacements, that suggest a fragmented and fugitive subject running from its own intuition of "my-death," of its own nonbeing. The nonbeing of truth as presence is concealed by a self-created 'Ideal' of full-presence which one deeply desires, even though it is only in relation to "my-death" that the Ideal, the truth, can appear at all. Truth appears as the ground of representation, which is to say as the ground of language, when in fact it is an "infinite differing" from language, constructed as the object of desire. Once it is understood that truth is an effect of language, not a cause, and that even speech is a form of "writing," then "we no longer know whether what was always presented as derived and modified representation of simple presentation, as 'supplement', 'sign', 'writing', or 'trace', 'is' not in a necessarily, but newly, ahistorical sense, 'older' than presence and the system of truth, older than 'history'" (*SP*, 103)

For Derrida, then, the "absolute will-to-hear-oneself-speak" is a yearning for totality, for meaning, for a full self-presence that seems

to guarantee one's being. An Ideal, or an "infinite absolute"—
whether it is conceived as a Platonic 'Form' or as a 'God', whether
it is Heidegger's notion of 'Being' or Shelley's 'Power'—is an illusion that consciousness creates as it plays out its radical desire for its
own coherence, its own integrity, its own 'truth'. The mind *is* the
play of differance, a play that begins in division, in the deferral of
presence that accompanies the processes of differing. The nature of
consciousness forbids the existence of an absolute, determinable
truth.

   This process is "writing" in Derrida's thinking, and writing in
its conventional sense is an activity that displays differance, exposes
all that speech conceals: the impossibility of ever attaining the sort
of full presence, the totality and coherence, that abides in our understanding of the word "truth." Writing, even if it is disguised as voice,
can never contain or present truth; it is always "re-presentation,"
and it is not representation of a presence that "once was." It is the
representation of representation; the "original" which language
seems to represent is produced only by the process of the representational activity. Writing, as inscription, exposes this situation; it
demonstrates that truth cannot be contained, found, or presented in
words. From Derrida's perspective, words only seem to stand in
truth's place and, thereby, to behave as substitutions for an absolute. In fact, that Ideal never existed. By showing that truth is only
an effect of language and not its source, that it is not something language "re-presents" but something that is instead a fiction born out
of desire, writing has "related truth to its own death as it related it
to its origin."

   Heidegger, on the other hand, insists that truth "is," and that it
"happens in being composed." For him, it is precisely through language that the "advent" of truth occurs. As I argue in Chapter 3,
this "happening" of truth in language is not a matter of representation for Heidegger. Truth is not an 'absolute' that exists outside of
language or that can be presented in language as a content perfectly
imitated and thereby contained. It is, rather, an activity, an event, a
"setting-itself-into-work" that language, better than any other medium, enables. In Heidegger's thought, it is the purpose of poetry
to initiate this penetration of truth into being, and for that reason
poetry "has a privileged position." Language, as poetry, is presentational; it incarnates truth as an active presence in the world.

   These two contrasting ideas—the first suggesting that language
is always the mark of an absence, the representation of a representa-

tion which operates as the empty tomb of a "dead" truth, and the second suggesting that poetic language "embodies," gives worldly life to an otherwise invisible but existent truth—point to a problem with which poets have struggled at least since the time of Plato. Poetry's claim to privilege resides primarily in an age-old concept of poetic language as presentation rather than representation; it rests in the claim a poet makes to have embodied a truth, to have given it a voice. Nonetheless, poets have always been deeply disturbed by the representational aspect of words as 'signs', as potential displacements and even erasures of truth.

Even the most cursory glance at the history of poetic theory illustrates the problem. Plato, that most suspicious poet, vacillated between a view of poetic language as incarnative, as "voicing" the presence of the god, and a view of language as flawed mimesis, a representation tainted by the fact that it *cannot* present the god immediately as 'truth'. In the *Ion,* for instance, he claims that "the poet is a light and winged thing and there is no invention in him until he has been inspired and is out of his senses and reason is no longer in him. . . . God himself is the speaker and through them he is addressing us."[1] The notion of inspiration is always one of presence, of the incarnation of the truth in the Word; the "soul" is made present and revealed by the "body." Yet, in the same work, Plato treats poetry as a mere mimetic chain of interpretation: the energy of the god is transmitted like that of a lodestone, but it is not directly presented, it is represented· "The poets are only the interpreters of the gods by whom they are severally possessed. . . . Do you know that the spectator is the last of the rings which, as I am saying, receive the power of the original magnet from one another? The rhapsode like yourself and the actor are intermediated links, and the poet himself is the first of them. . . . Thus there is a vast chain of dancers and masters and undermasters of choruses, who are suspended, as if from the stone, at the side of the rings which hang down from the Muse" (*Ion,* 15). Here, the poet is not "embodying" the god, is not filled with his presence. Rather, he is at his "side." There is an unerasable, if minimal, space between them, one that demands interpretation. And interpretation is immediately transformed into representation, a "performance" of the poet's understanding. Book X of *The Republic* makes it clear that mimesis

1. Plato, *Ion,* in *Critical Theory Since Plato,* ed. Hazard Adams (New York, 1971), 13–19.

as representation is a degradation of the 'truth': "the imitator is a long way off the truth, and can reproduce all things because he lightly touches on a small part of them, and that part an image."[2] In a situation where truth is perceived as a transcendent Absolute, it can be known only insofar as its "fullness" is comprehended. Such comprehension involves an internalization of the whole. Imitation inevitably fragments totality into images that can never correspond to the whole exactly or completely enough. As close as Plato's poet is to the god, then, he is still a "long way off." Mimesis, the representation of a representation, the copy of an "image," is at least three removes from the Ideal. The spatial metaphor is important; it is in that space that language becomes vulnerable. If poetry is from the first derivative, it is vulnerable to error, even to Derrida's "errance," the movement which he defines as "the indefinite drift of signs . . . linking representations to one another without beginning or end . . . a representation of the representation that yearns for itself therein as for its own birth or its death" (SP, 103).

It is only by holding on to the paradox that the god is both present and represented that Plato can prevent this endless drift. If the god is "voiced" by the poet, both beginning and end seem present in the act of incarnation; the yearning, the desire for what is lost, is erased in the moment of fullness. Even though he insists on the Ideal as both outside of, and within, language, the *Ion,* because it presents poetry as speech and performance rather than writing, can obscure its own contradictions. However, when Plato openly encounters the issue of writing in the *Phaedrus,* it is "writing without a voice" and it is precisely the potential for errance that causes him to reject it:

> The painter's products stand before us as though they were alive, but if you question them, they maintain a most majestic silence. It is the same with written words; they seem to talk to you as though they were intelligent, but if you ask them anything about what they say, from a desire to be instructed, they go on telling you just the same thing forever. And once a thing is put in writing, the composition, whatever it may be, drifts all over the place, getting into the hands not only of those who understand it, but equally of those who have no business with it. . . . And when it is ill-treated and unfairly abused it always needs its parent to come to its help, being unable to defend or help itself.[3]

2. Plato, *The Republic,* trans. B. Jowett (Garden City, N.Y., 1953), 291.
3. Plato, *Phaedrus,* in *The Collected Dialogues,* ed. Edith Hamilton and Huntington Cairns, trans. Lane Cooper (Princeton, 1953), 521.

Representation, then, behaves "as though it were alive," but Plato's phrasing suggests an equivalent between silence and death. If the representation is empty of speech, it is empty of life. That "majestic silence" is the silence of the sign, which can be animated only by interpretation—and interpretation is vulnerable to drift and error. Writing exposes, for Plato, the danger that is potential, but repressed, in his metaphor of the representational chain. It is the mimetic nature of writing that makes it fallible. Writing, mimetic language, is not mediatory by his definition; it does not *conduct* the truth but rather substitutes itself for the voice. Writing, "dead" discourse, is contrasted to a "living speech" that is "the original of which the written discourse may fairly be called a kind of image (*Phaedrus,* 521). As image, it is vulnerable to misprision; it can be "filled up" with error.

In the *Phaedrus,* speech is seen to be "original" in a way it cannot be in those sections of the *Ion* where "poets are only the interpreters." There, the notion of interpretation inevitably implies a rift between the Word of the god and the words of the poet. It is in this rift that language as representation must occur. Within the space of loss, which is also a temporal gap, within the brief lacuna between being "filled with" the god and uttering the word of the god, an act of interpretation springs into being and translates itself into representation. Speech is "living" for Plato only as long as he can obscure its representational function in favor of its incarnative function. As incarnation, it brings truth "into" the world, offers it a site in which to act; language serves as the "container," the conductor of its presence. As representation, however, it can only stand-in-place-of and, thereby, imply the distance of the origin. One of the things that written words "go on telling you . . . forever" is that, as Derrida says, "all signifiers . . . are derivative with regard to what would wed the voice indissolubly to the mind or to the thought of the signified sense, indeed to the thing-itself."[4]

The purpose of all this is not to indulge in a superficial reading of Plato. Derrida has already thoroughly explored that philosopher relative to these issues.[5] Rather, my intent is to point toward the unresolved conflict between an understanding of language as incarnative and a view of it as representational that moves through poetics from Plato's time to the present. This conflict is often unbal-

---

4. Jacques Derrida, *OG,* 11.
5. See "Writing Before the Letter," in *OG;* "Plato's Pharmacy," in *DN,* and "White Mythology," in *MP.*

anced by the overwhelming appeal of the concept of incarnative language, an appeal reinforced by its apparent ability to guarantee the appearance of truth in words. Poetry, seen as an act of fully "capable imagination" which "bodies forth / The forms of things unknown," in Shakespeare's apt phrasing, can be seen as a language of revelation, as "inspired" by, and in direct contact with, the truth. If poets can make present "things known," they can, indeed, make claims to "voicing" God and, further, to a God-like activity; they can, in Sidney's words, "grow in effect another nature."[6]

But if (fie of such a but) you be born so near the dull-making cataract of Nilus that you cannot hear the planetlike music of poetry . . . thus much curse I must send you, in the behalf of all poets, that while you live, you live in love, and never get favor for lacking skill of a sonnet, and, when you die, your memory die from the earth for want of an epitaph.

—Sidney, "An Apology for Poetry"

Sir Philip Sidney, writing in 1583 in response to a Puritan attack on poetry, must, of course, avoid any overt suggestion that the poet speaks with the "voice" of the Christian God. Circumspect and wary of the theological implications of the word "inspiration," he cautiously begins his "Apology for Poetry" by noting that the Romans called the poet *vates* merely as a sign of their admiration. Nonetheless, unwilling to surrender entirely the relationship between poetry and the divine, he continues his argument by asserting that the name is "altogether not without ground, since the Oracles of Delphos and Sibylla's prophecies were wholly delivered in verses" and "the high flying liberty of conceit proper to the poet, did seem to have some divine force in it" ("Apology," 153). He becomes even less discreet when he argues in support of "the reasonableness of this word vates." Dropping the careful phrasing of "*seem to have some* divine force," Sidney openly declares that "the holy David's Psalms are a divine poem." And he grounds the notion of "divine" poetry in David's ability to incarnate the Absolute, to grant divinity voice and visibility through his "notable prosopopeias":

For what else is the awaking his musical instrument, the often and free changing of persons, his notable prosopopeias, when he *maketh you, as it were, see God coming* in his majesty, his telling of the beasts' joyfulness,

6. Sir Philip Sidney, "An Apology for Poetry," in *Critical Theory,* ed. Adams, 157.

and hills leaping, but a heavenly poesy, wherein almost he showeth himself a passionate lover of that unspeakable and everlasting beauty *to be seen by the eyes of the mind, only cleared by faith.*   ("Apology," 157, my emphasis)

Certainly Sidney is not consciously expressing a Platonic notion of 'possession' here. Yet, the idea still hovers behind the disclaimers "as it were" and "almost." If one can "see God coming" in the words of the poet and if that poet is further characterized as God's "passionate lover," the aura of possession is not far from the surface of his language. If poetry is perceived as capable of embodying, giving visible form to "the unspeakable and everlasting," it is difficult to suppress the idea that the poet has achieved some kind of immediate contact with the Absolute, a contact that implies that *through* the poet, "he is addressing us." Despite the fact that the notion in its pagan form would be quite unacceptable to Sidney, Platonic 'inspiration' leaves its trace in his thought.

This trace, however, undergoes an important transformation. Sidney is very close, at this moment in the "Apology," to articulating 'inspiration' as 'insight', a translation that is indicative of his desire to retain presence without suggesting that "God himself is the speaker." God does not speak here; David does. But the kind of vision that enables the poet to *present* God is a divine gift made available when "the eyes of the mind" are "cleared by faith," a clearing that both writer and reader must experience to "see God coming." In Christian terminology, such a direct contact with the transcendent 'Truth' would be called an experience of grace, and one has only to read Milton to see how tenuous the lines between inspiration, insight, and grace can be. Those lines may be distinct in Christian theology, but from a poetic perspective the three concepts are so intimately related that despite differences in their surface colorings, they are frequently interchangeable in the most radical depths of their meanings. The intimacy between 'inspiration' and poetic 'insight' is a result of the fact that both depend upon an understanding of Truth as an external reality, superior to the world of time, change, and death. All poetry that makes claims to either concept (and this may include, as the following chapters suggest, *all* lyric poetry) assumes that this "other," immutable world of Absolutes can be experienced *as present,* at least momentarily, by the poet. It further assumes that this presence can be incarnated in the poet's words; and, for the Christian poet, such incarnation can occur only by means of 'grace'. The insight of the poet, the cleared

"eye of the mind," achieves immediate contact with the full presence of a transcendent, eternal world of Truth, but that contact is an
entirely internal experience. In Sidney's phrasing, poetry "delivers"
that world embodied. The poet's vision is not a matter of imagining
"castles in the air," he writes. Rather, this "delivering forth" gives
birth to a presence that "substantially . . . worketh" ("Apology,"
157). That which is beyond sensual apprehension is endowed with
substance by the words of the poem. This is what David is able to
accomplish, and "what else" is such an achievement but "a heavenly poesy"?

As Sidney expands his defense of poetry, he continues to equate
the incarnative potential of poetic language with the divine. The divinity of poets lies in their ability to "make": not just to "imagine"
a Cyrus, but to create one so substantial that the created image can
itself procreate and "bestow a Cyrus upon the world" ("Apology,"
157). There are times when the rhetoric of his essay becomes so un-
reserved that Sidney seems to claim incarnative powers for the words
of the poet that very nearly emulate the Word of God. If God's
Word engendered the natural world, what force lies in language
that "doth grow in effect another nature"? Whatever restraint the
phrase "in effect" might exert on this statement, it is subverted
when the writer goes on to assert not only that language creates,
but that its creation is superior to nature itself: "Her world is brazen, the poets only deliver a golden" ("Apology," 157).

Though Sidney skirts the edges of profanity here, he ultimately
avoids it, for his claim is not, finally, that the poet's words challenge
the Word. Nor is it that God speaks through the poet. Rather, he
articulates poetic creativity as an internal process similar to the
"cleared" vision that enables David's divinity. The poet's "golden"
world is not a truth delivered by the voice of God, but the expression of the 'truth' that God has already created and that already resides within. The poet is not possessed by God, but through God's
grace he is in possession of an "erected wit," which clears the mud-
diness of the "infected will" and "invents" images superior to the
world humankind has wrecked with its Fall. Since the erected wit
and the images it "invents" are both internalized, held together
within the mind's eye, Sidney is able to obscure the gap between
"wit" and its inventions, to disguise the possibility that the invented world may be only a representation, rather than an incarnation, of the Truth one "sees" within. "Invention," however, is a
deeply ambivalent term. Sidney is consistent throughout the "Apol-

ogy" in characterizing invention as both creative and mimetic—that is, as both incarnative and imitative, presentational and representational. Unlike Plato, however, Sidney does not so much vacillate between contradictory concepts of poetic language as attempt to carry both in a single thought.[7]

Poetry, he insists, is "an art of imitation": it is "a representing, counterfeiting, or figuring forth" ("Apology," 158). At the same time, he asserts with equal fervor that those poets who "most properly do imitate . . . borrow nothing of what is, hath been, or shall be; but range, only reined with learned discretion, into the divine consideration of what may be, and should be. These be they that, as the first and most noble sort may justly be termed *vates*" ("Apology," 158). Sidney is echoing the language of Aristotle here, but his thought swerves away from the philosopher's at a crucial juncture. His rhetoric may be Aristotle's but his changes and omissions are significant. The Renaissance writer's coupling of invention with imitation is undoubtedly influenced by two key statements in the *Poetics*. According to Aristotle, "it is not the function of the poet to relate what has happened, but what may happen—what is possible according to the law of probability or necessity."[8] Because Sidney disregards the inherent restrictions implied by "the law of probability or necessity," he is able to shift away from the Aristotelian notion of art as a simulation of nature's development toward completion. Sidney sidesteps nature altogether, reading Aristotle's rejection of "what has happened" as a rejection of natural fact and freeing invention to operate as prophetic revelation, which "borrows nothing of what is." Sidney's Christian vision of nature as a "fallen," "brazen" world cannot accommodate the Aristotelian convictions that "art imitates nature" and that the proper mode of inquiry into art is to proceed by "following the order of nature" (*Poetics*, 7).

Reacting against Platonic dualism, Aristotle suggests that Ideal Forms inhabit nature as unrealized potentials, always in the process of becoming. Nature is a perfecting activity, and art is valued precisely because it can demonstrate that process as it "may *happen*" in its fruition. Sidney's world does not invite imitation of its flawed

7. I am indebted, in this discussion of Sidney, to Murray Krieger's essay "Renaissance Theory and the Duplicity of Metaphor," in *Poetic Presence and Illusion* (Baltimore, 1979).

8. Aristotle, *The Poetics,* trans. S. H. Butcher, in S. H. Butcher, *Aristotle's Theory of Poetry and Fine Art* (New York, 1951), 35.

processes. It is not nature's "workings" that poetry imitates but its "works." And, in taking "the works of nature for his principle object," Sidney's poet is intent upon reparation, a corrective imitation that transforms the flawed world, with which "he goeth hand and hand," into a prelapsarian perfection. Sidney rejects Aristotle's organic, changing nature, then, in favor of a "*divine* consideration" of "what may *be,* and should *be.*" This divergence from Aristotle weights Sidney's thought with Platonic undertones which suggest that the poet is obliged to imitate perfected forms, to incarnate a 'truth' that exists "elsewhere."

In Chapter XXV, 1, Aristotle speaks again of imitation: "The poet being an imitator, like a painter or any other artist, must, of necessity imitate one of three objects—things as they were or are, things as they are said or thought to be, or things as they ought to be" (*Poetics,* 97). However, this assertion makes no appeal to a transcendental reality external to the natural world. Art can be seen as presenting an Ideal only to the extent that it simulates the completed perfection toward which nature strives. Aristotle's one brief reference to "higher reality" is explicitly made "with respect to the requirements of art," not to those of the divine, and the reference seems to have no more status or claim to "truth" than the "received opinion" with which he couples it (*Poetics,* 106–107).[9]

Sidney, then, pays lip service to Aristotle: "There is no art delivered to mankind that hath not the works of nature for his principle object" ("Apology," 157). Noting that thought in general is tied to nature, he concedes that poet and nature "go hand in hand." He immediately overturns the Aristotelian underpinnings of this, however, by characterizing the tie to nature as servile and by elevating the poet above all other thinkers because "only the poet, disdaining to be tied to any such subjection, lifted up with the vigor of his own invention, doth grow in effect another nature, in making things either better than nature bringeth forth, or quite anew" ("Apology," 157). Sidney's poet can overleap nature entirely. While Aristotelian thought is clearly at play in his notion of imitation, it is filtered through a Christian idealism that restores a covert Platonism to the poet's thought and with it, the burden of incarnating truth as *content* rather than representing it as it "happens." Aristotle's influence is undermined by a theology that cannot admit the unfolding of per-

9. See *Aristotle's Theory of Poetry and Fine Art,* 168, for Butcher's convincing argument that this section of *The Poetics* is central to Aristotle's notion of truth.

fection in a natural world that fell, with Adam, into a corruption so gross that "our erected wit maketh us know what perfection is, and yet our infected will keepeth us from reaching unto it" ("Apology," 158). Poetry is obligated to present the Ideal itself, "perfection," and Sidney must turn inward to an internalized vision of truth that is available only in the "cleared" mind. Such truth can be known only through our "erected wit" as a kind of intuition. This abdication of nature permits the concept of imitation to slide into the oracular voicing that readmits Plato into the "Apology." For instance, Sidney writes that the greatest poetry "did imitate the inconceivable excellencies of God" and that it is just "the meaner sort of painters who counterfeit only such faces as are set before them" (158). Aristotle's basic tenet, that "the objects of imitation are men in action," is displaced by the suggestion that the proper objects of imitation are "nothing of what is."

Statements such as these certainly describe poetry as performative, prophetic, and presentational. They imply at least a strong similarity between Sidney's poet and the poet of the *Ion*. If the poet's project is to "imitate the *inconceivable* excellencies of God," to "range into the *divine* consideration of what may be," to "borrow nothing of what *is*," then, logically, "there is no invention in him until he has been inspired." But, as his discussion of David's "divine" work shows, Sidney stops short of Plato's next step: he cannot affirm that "God himself is the speaker." He is constrained not just by theological considerations but by his own commitment to defining poetry as imitative. At the same time, his desire to retain presence is so powerful that he resists identification with the poet of *The Republic,* that "imitator who is a long way off the truth." The incorporation of inspiration into a "cleared" vision guaranteed by faith not only avoids the problem of blasphemy, it accommodates the linguistic paradox that allows imitation to appear as truth, as "the outward beauty of such a virtue" ("Apology," 158).

The complete internalization of the poetic activity idealizes it in the extreme. Vision, invention, image are purely intelligible entities, released from the sensible taint, the imperfect dross of the "second nature." Sidney's rejection of the aristotelian link between art and nature is entirely consistent with—in fact, necessary to—an interior activity that secures poetry's embodiment of truth. If the poet "invents" those images "seen by the eyes of the mind" and if the images are sanctified by the fact that the inner eye has been "cleared by faith," then the "invention" can be seen as freed from any exchange with the "outside," whether that exchange be with God as inspiration or with nature as imitation. Circumscribing invention, vision, and image within the "same" interior site negates the space between Ideal and image, between poet and God, in a way that Plato, with his exterior "gods" and "nature," could never achieve. The unity of the mental site suggests the concurrence of counterfeit and original; it obscures the divorce between image and Ideal. The temporal and spatial proximity implied by "in-sight" promises a co-presence of counterfeit and original that signals their interpenetration, an interpenetration that may be defined as incarnation.

For Sidney, the act of imitation, understood in this way, is sanctioned by God Himself. In one important section of the essay, he suggests that imitation is less a matter of copying the "excellencies of God" as if they were visible aspects of His face than of imitating God's own creative act. To invent images of the "inconceivable" is to mimic God's own invention of nature through the Word. God's creation justifies, indeed enables, the poet's: "Neither let it be deemed too saucy a comparison to balance the highest point of man's wit with the efficacy of nature; but rather give right honor to the heavenly Maker of that maker, who, *having made man to his own likeness,* set him beyond and over all the works of that second nature: *which in nothing he showeth so much as in poetry, when with the force of a divine breath he bringeth things forth* far surpassing her doings" ("Apology," 158, my emphasis). "The high flying liberty of conceit" no longer just "seems" to have "some divine force in it" at this point in the "Apology." Sidney dispenses with all caution, not only affirming the presence of a divine force, but specifying that force as "breath."

"The force of a divine breath" is, of course, crucial to Sidney's sense of language as incarnative; the breath bestows life upon the body of the invented image. It is the voice that Plato finds dangerously absent in writing and present in the moment of the *Ion* when "God himself is the speaker." Nevertheless, Sidney's "maker," even when "with the force of divine breath he bringeth things forth," cannot evade language as representation. Ultimately, the "space" between language and the Ideal surfaces in his thought. The rift exposes itself at the moment when the internal coherence of image and truth must be expressed, delivered to the "outside"—the moment when image becomes writing. "Any understanding knoweth the skill of the artificer standeth in that idea or foreconceit of the work, and not in the work itself. And that the poet hath that idea is manifest by delivering them forth in such excellency as he hath imagined them" ("Apology," 157). Sidney represses the distance between Ideal and its "outside" representation and writing. The lacuna between the "foreconceit" and its manifestation is obscured by his own characterization of poetry as brought forth by "divine breath." "Divine breath" gives birth to the poem as a voicing of the Ideal; Sidney reconstitutes a Christian version of the voicing of the god at the moment when "the force of a divine breath" permeates his poetics. The incarnative nature of voicing is indicated by his use of the metaphors "delivering" and "bringing *things* forth," and the potency of the idea that language incarnates divine breath obscures any hiatus between conception and expression.

Nonetheless, a disturbing difference is evidenced by the very notion of "foreconceit." Even in Sidney's phrasing, the "invention," the "idea" is peculiarly separate from the work itself. Despite the incarnative metaphors, the statement that "skill . . . standeth in that idea . . . and not in the work itself" locates the "foreconceit" somewhere before-behind-above it and further implies that something escapes incarnation; something is lost in the process. The "work" appears to be mimetic of the figure, here named "foreconceit," in which Sidney has managed to coalesce invention, image, and truth as one presence. But if the distance between poet and God can be veiled by the internal ideality of that construct, the rift between "inside" and "outside," between "invention" and "work," remains.

That Sidney "forgets" the space between inside and outside is an indication of the hypnotic strength that resides in the portrayal of poetry as vocal—as speech and not writing. This erasure of spatial and temporal distance between idea and work in his poetics is similar to the movement Derrida describes in Hegel's thought: "this phonic relationship between the sensory and the intelligible, the real and the ideal, etc., is determined here as an expressive relationship between an inside and an outside. The language of sound, speech, which carries the inside to the outside, does not simply abandon it there, as does writing. Conserving the inside in itself as it is in the act of emitting it to the outside, speech is par excellence that which confers existence, presence (*Dasein*) upon the interior representation making the concept exist" (*MP*, 90). Clearly, for Sidney the manifestation, in its "excellency," conserves "the inside in itself." In fact, "that the poet *hath* that idea" at all is *proven* by the work; that is, the work, as long as it can be perceived as an incarnative "delivery" of "divine breath," "confers existence, presence upon the interior representation." If poetry is incarnative imitation, then imitation must be vocal: "Poesy therefore is an art of imitation . . . that is to say a figuring forth—to speak metaphorically, *a speaking picture;* with this end, to teach and delight" ("Apology," 158, my emphasis). The metaphor of the "speaking picture" stabilizes the entire web of Sidney's strategies for interweaving the contradictory notions of poetry as both incarnative and imitative. "It is not rhyming and versing that maketh a poet," he writes, "it is that feigning of notable images of virtue" ("Apology," 159). For Sidney, those feigned images, idealized to such an extent that they appear as the thing-itself, are never silent. His belief that poets are superior to philosophers because they create "a perfect picture" that can "possess the sight of the soul" (160) can be sustained because that "perfect picture" is the painting of voice: the vocalizing and vocalized image. And that image "speaks" the light of truth: "the grounds of wisdom . . . lie dark before the imaginative and judging power if they be not illuminated or figured forth by the speaking picture of poesy" (161). Unlike Plato's, Sidney's poem/painting never maintains the "majestic silence" that might force him closer to Plato's oscillation between representation and incarnation. Speech intervenes, rescuing language from the death-like silence of the sign which would transform poetry into a memorial marking the loss of the Ideal. Nothing is more emblematic of his desire to retain presence through voice than his metaphor of the "speaking picture," and the presence the voice promises exerts its hegemony over the entire "Apology."

This hegemony is inadvertently revealed in Sidney's tongue-in-cheek ending. "I conjure you all," he writes, "to believe, with me, that there are mysteries contained in poetry, which of purpose were written darkly, lest by profane wits it should be abused; to believe, with Landino, that [poets] are so beloved of the gods that whatsoever they write proceeds of a divine fury; lastly to believe themselves, when they tell you they will make you immortal by their verses" ("Apology," 177). In spite of the ironic touch of self-parody here, Sidney's words suggest the complexity of his situation. The "mystery" in poetry resides in its incarnative power, its ability to "deliver forth" the "truth" despite its mimetic nature, despite the fact that, as sheer representation, poetry is blatantly fictional. "The poet never maketh any circles about your imagination to conjure you to believe for true what he writes," Sidney has said earlier (168). Yet in the end every poet says, "I conjure you all," and this one completes his "Apology" with a moment of intuitive insight that sets the stage for all that follows in the present book. If you refuse to believe that poetry can incarnate—can present, through its mimesis, a truth that "proceeds of divine fury"—then, Sidney says, "thus much curse I must send you, in the behalf of all poets, that while you live, you live in love, and never get favor for lacking skill of a sonnet, and, when you die, your memory die from the earth for want of an epitaph" ("Apology," 177). To reject the presencing power of poetry, to reject the ability of language to embody a 'truth', is to lose the power of one's own name, that primary representation of self-presence. Writers who surrender incarnative language surrender the power of the speaking monument, of the inscribed stone. They lose the benefits of the epitaphic gesture, the sort of inscription that marks presence if only by pointing to its absence. Sidney's curse threatens skeptics with endless desire and the complete annihilation of being, even the sort of "nonbeing" that an epitaph bestows. His curse is a comic reminder that without the "body" of the word, even the word that marks its death, the "soul" of truth quite simply, "is not," Presence cannot even be known as lost, "for want of an epitaph."

> These words are ineffectual and metaphorical.
> Most words are so—No help!
>   —Percy Bysshe Shelley, "On Love"

Sidney evades the contradictions in his double vision of poetic language by internalizing (and thereby idealizing) invention and imitation, a move that permits the seductive potency of his own metaphors for "voice." But a later poet, a close reader of both the "Apology" and of Plato, is unable to rest quite so happily in the paradox.[10] Shelley's "A Defence of Poetry" is permeated by the rhetorical commonplaces of both his predecessors; his language is saturated with Platonic and theological metaphors, and his desire for presence is so passionate and unremitting that it motivates much of his best writing, poetry and prose. His desire, however, takes the form of an unsatisfied quest for an adequate language, and the cry that "these words are ineffectual" echoes throughout his work. It

10. Shelley nearly quotes Sidney in several places in the "Defence," and he translated works by Plato including *Ion*. See *CWS*, VII, 233–51. All references to Shelley's prose are drawn from this edition, which is also the source (VI, 202) of the epigraph that opens this section.

thoroughly erodes the idealist tendencies in his thought, which are the effects of his desire. If the "Defence" sometimes appears to be an exemplary culmination of the kinds of double vision evident in Plato and Sidney, its genuine importance lies in the fact that Shelley is essentially a skeptical revisionist responding to their thought, not simply synthesizing it.[11] His case demands extensive attention here since it exposes problems that appear repeatedly in the works of the poets to whom the rest of this study is devoted. Like Herbert, Shelley is committed to capturing the evanescent visitations of an Absolute into the mutable world. Though the agnostic Shelley would never conceive of these visitations as the appearances of Herbert's God, they are, nonetheless, structurally similar. Both poets wish to capture in words the moments in which the truth of an infinite Ideal appears in the world. Shelley's need to incarnate "Power" is as intense as Herbert's to build his altar. One has only to compare Shelley's "Hymn to Intellectual Beauty" with Herbert's "The Flower" to be struck by the startling similarity of their situations— and the stark differences in the "objects" of their desires.

Like Wordsworth, Shelley sees the mind as "self-haunted," writing that thought can only "with difficulty visit the intricate and winding chambers which it inhabits" and explaining with a near-paraphrase of Wordsworth's lines 65 to 80 in "Tintern Abbey": "It is like a river whose rapid and perpetual stream flows outwards;— like one in dread who speeds through the recesses of some haunted pile, and dares not look behind" (*CWS*, VII, 64). And, in this same moment of "Speculations on Metaphysics," Shelley delineates a problem that motives much of John Ashbery's work, particularly *Three Poems:* "If it were possible to be where we have been, vitally and indeed—if, at the moment of our presence there, we could define the results of our experience,—if the passage from sensation to reflection—from a state of passive perception to voluntary contemplation, were not so dizzying and so tumultuous, this attempt would be less difficult" (*CWS*, VII, 64).

While all of these poets are vastly different in terms of their styles, themes, and special concerns, they share at least one great problem: the representational aspects of language are in direct conflict with their desire to present 'truth' as either the meaning of being or the being of meaning. Their "will-to-speak" is a will-to-

11. See Earl Wasserman, *Shelley: A Critical Reading* (Baltimore, 1971), 204–21, for an excellent discussion of Shelley's relationship with Platonism.

incarnate that seems inherently defeated by the very "bodies" of the words that they must use. All of them develop strategies for using language in such a way that its tendency to "bury" truth, to announce its "death," is transformed into a force that generates the presence that seems lost. They all write poetry as epitaph.

Shelley's "Defence" might seem, at first glance, to be an extraordinarily confident assertion of the incarnative power of poetry. He writes, for instance, that "poets are the hierophants of an unapprehended inspiration" and that a "spirit" speaks through them, though they are "sincerely astonished at its manifestations." They are "possessed" by a "Power" that they are "compelled to serve" whether they wish to or not (*CWS*, VII, 140). Most importantly, for him the *raison d'être* of poetry is to embody: "it arrests the vanishing apparitions which haunt the interlunations of life, and veiling them, or in language or in form, sends them forth among mankind. . . . Poetry redeems from decay the visitations of the divinity in man . . . every form moving within the radience of its presence is changed by a wondrous sympathy to an incarnation of the spirit which it breathes" (*CWS*, VII, 137). Nonetheless, Shelley is a poet whose conflict with representational language is so overt and consciously explored that it is the subject of much of his prose and the theme of some of his finest poems. Consequently, despite the fact that, with the exception of Ashbery, he is not historically precedent to any of the poets with whom this work is concerned, he serves as its illustrative point of departure. And he serves well precisely because the same mind that writes "poets are the unacknowledged legislators of the world" (*CWS*, VII, 140) also writes, "These words are ineffectual and metaphorical. Most words are so—No help!"

Shelley's is a strikingly "modern" mind, engaged in a self-conscious struggle to satisfy an intense longing for unmediated contact with an Ideal, a yearning that is at odds with his demystified understanding of language as representational, as a displacement of the same presence he seeks to incarnate. Yet, despite his linguistic skepticism, he never wavers in his conviction that poetic language is privileged because of its ability to incarnate the truth of being, because it "arrests the vanishing apparitions which haunt the interlunations of life, and veiling them, or in language or in form, sends them forth among mankind." It is for this reason that poetry is "indeed something divine," that it is "at once the center and circumference of knowledge" (*CWS*, VII, 137). As his use of this ancient metaphor for God indicates, poetry is not, for Shelley, merely in-

spired by the "divine," it occupies the very place of divinity. Such
an extravagant claim is not made lightly even by an agnostic, and
for Shelley it is made at great cost.[12] But this understanding of
poetry as necessarily incarnative, set against his understanding of
language as a 'sign' that displays distance and difference, generates
his cry that words are ineffectual and that there is "no help!" Few
poets have desired a transparent, truth-bearing language more than
Shelley, and few have been more deeply skeptical about the ability
of language to suffice.

Like so many poets before and after him, Shelley resorts to a
conception of language as a haunting, as the sort of speech suggested long before his time by the Book of Job, when Elihu hears
the voice of God in his "wondrous works" (37:14), and as the kind
of presentation that Ashbery will call, 160 years after Shelley, "active memorials."[13] When Shelley attempts to explain *how* language
incarnates, he turns to a notion of words as living (which is to say as
breathing/speaking) monuments: "Poetry lifts the veil from the
hidden beauty of the world and makes familiar objects be as if they
were not familiar: it reproduces all that it represents, and the impersonations clothed in its Elysian light stand thence-forward in the
minds of those who have once contemplated them as memorials of
that gentle and exalted content which extends itself over all thoughts
and actions with which it coexists" (*CWS*, VII, 117).

In superficial ways, the structure of Shelley's thought here resembles Sidney's. Like the Renaissance poet's, his is a poetry of revelation that makes visible the hidden truth by making the natural
world appear, as he later says, "quite anew."[14] Representation as reproduction is not meant as a simple copy, but intended in a more
incarnative sense, closer to Sidney's insistence that a poet must not
just imagine but "make" a Cyrus. Still, just as Sidney saw his invented image, even though it is filled with "the force of divine
breath," to be nonetheless an "imitation," so Shelley understands

12. For the most thorough discussions of Shelley's religious skepticism, see the
extensive studies by two of his best readers: Wasserman, *Shelley: A Critical Reading*,
and Harold Bloom, *Shelley's Mythmaking* (Ithaca, 1969).

13. The phrase "active memorials" comes from John Ashbery's "Fragment," in
The Double Dream of Spring (New York, 1976), 81.

14. "It creates anew the Universe," Shelley says, echoing Sidney. But he goes on
in a manner of his own: "after it has been annihilated in our minds by the recurrence
of impression, blunted by re-iteration" (*CWS*, VII, 137). The blunting effect of language is the focus of his concern in the essay "On Life," which I investigate later in
this section.

his reproduction as something other than direct presentation. It is, he says, an "impersonation," and in that word he complicates and deepens the paradox so evident in Sidney's "Apology." Poetry as impersonation rather than imitation is both more alive and more closely related to death than Sidney would have conceded. Impersonation—a gesture that attempts to both erase and announce difference—must incorporate the "thing-itself" so effectively that it can *act* in its place, not just stand in its place. Impersonation, which must be understood as both allusion and illusion, is still not strictly representational. It operates as a double gesture which suggests the incarnation of representation and, thereby, a kind of living force that imitation does not allow.

Nonetheless, the apparent liveliness of Shelley's impersonations is duplicitous; they are "clothed in Elysian light," light from the world of the happy dead. "All high poetry is infinite" (*CWS*, VII, 131), Shelley insists, and certainly he intended the "light" to suggest its immortality. However, light from the Elysian fields, from the land of the dead, cannot evade a certain implication of loss, of life diminished even as it attains immortality. Such a presence is ghost-like, wavering, and ephemeral. "Impersonations" clothed in "Elysian light" perform 'living' in a way that a copy never can, but their vitality is wrapped in the aura of death. The figures that "stand thence-forward in the mind" evoke a sense of the dead forever alive that is ambivalent and undeterminable. Such ghostly impersonation is neither dead nor alive but both. It is in between; it crosses over forbidden borders, transgresses the most basic distinction established by the human psyche. Shelley's "immortal" presence depends upon this "in-betweenness," upon its escape from the confinements of both this world and the nether world. For Shelley, this ghostly quality of inhabiting two opposed worlds saves poetry from the divisiveness of signification and sanctions poetic language as truth.

The metaphor remains, nonetheless, very disturbing, and Shelly complicates it further by defining the impersonations as "memorials." If he were linguistically nihilistic enough to present the memorials as simple signs of absence and the impersonations as only artful fictions, the problem would be much less complex. The memorial would function as an empty sign open to a subjective and interpretive "filling" by any reader. It would not, however, be able to make any claims to truth. Consequently, Shelley's final line denies both the subjectivity and the irrevocable loss that this sense of

memorial would suggest. He insists that the reproduction represents an "exalted content" that is not only present but co-present,
in and with its own representation. The reproduction, then, must
contain that within which *it* is contained. Not for nothing has
Shelley said, contradicting Plato, that "it reproduces *all* that it represents." Reproduction without loss is protected from being understood as a substitute, an imitation, or a displacement of its origin; it
can only be understood as procreation, that is, as a projection of the
original *into* its own reproduction—a projection that does not debilitate either the quality or integrity of the place of origin. This, a
typical gesture for Shelley, is an attempt to guarantee the objective
'reality' of the "exalted content," to prevent poetry from appearing
as a purely personal, interpretive experience. It is an attempt to secure the content as having an independent, ontological status.

The ghostly nature of poetry, then, does not, in Shelley's mind,
behave as substitution. His metaphors come into play because he
needs a notion that can encompass language as both representation
and incarnation. The middle ground of a "haunting" offers the ideal
site for such ambiguous interplay. It seems to suggest a nearly unthinkable proximity between the represented and its representation,
which Derrida would certainly see as "at once absolutely alive and
absolutely dead." Shelley does attempt to repress "death" in favor
of his belief that "a poet participates in the eternal, the infinite, the
one" (*CWS*, VII, 112). The idea of participation is entirely consistent with his description of a poetry that operates as a container for
an "exalted content" which also "extends itself *over* all thought and
actions with which it coexists."

Yet, when he must describe how the poet participates, how the
poem incarnates, Shelley's metaphors threaten the cohesion he asserts. The proximity he attempts to establish between the Absolute
and poetry is not, finally, a guaranteed proximity. Death intervenes
from the very beginning of the poetic process. The ambiguity of
the Elysian figures is disturbing enough, but it deepens when Shelley
declares that even the unmediated appearances of the Absolute itself
are "vanishing apparitions." And, since the "apparitions . . . haunt
the interlunations of life," since they require the period of invisibility between the old moon and the new, their status as representations of absence seems doubly confirmed. But, ever careful in his
defense of presence, Shelley is being extremely precise here—after
all, in the interlunar period, the moon only *seems* to have vanished.
The apparitions "haunt" and "veil" that which is only an apparent

void. They appear as affirmations of presence in dark periods of illusory absence. In a sense their purpose is to correct the illusion that
invisibility *is* absence. As always, Shelley questions not presence itself but the limits of human perception. However, if perception of
the Absolute is limited to a haunting in the dark, and language can
incarnate the haunting only as the ghost of a ghost, then the ability
of poetry to present, rather than represent, is tentative indeed. The
poet's metaphors betray the conflict between his desire and his
understanding that language can never be adequate to the full presence for which he yearns.

Behind Shelley's statement that "poetry reproduces all that it
represents" are the lines from Plato with which we began: "the imitator is a long way off the truth, and can reproduce all things because he lightly touches on a small part of them, and that part
an image." Shelley's revision of Plato is instructive. It is as if he
chooses to forget the intent of Plato's words, an intention that
reduced poetry to a third-rate mimesis because of its distance from
and fragmentation of "the truth." He focuses on the notion "can
reproduce all things," ignores the phrase "because he lightly touches
on a small part of them," and then shifts the idea of "image" away
from copy toward incarnation. The reworking of Plato is neither
wishful thinking nor casual self-justification; it is entirely consistent
with Shelley's idiosyncratic and eclectic metaphysics. So, also, is his
notion of incarnative language as a ghostly image of that which it
contains and by which it is contained. The relationship between this
oddly qualified idealism and language that emerges in the "Defence" is clarified elsewhere in his prose, where the gap between his
belief, his desire, and his skeptical stance toward language is repeatedly evidenced. In the long run language remains, for Shelley, a
medium he deeply distrusts. This distrust generates the skepticism
that Shelley's finest readers have found in his work.[15]

From a psychological perspective, Harold Bloom is exact when
he asserts that Shelley's thought is best described as an "apocalyptic
humanism." Shelley certainly holds to the idea that humankind
can, at any moment, move beyond the divisions and distortions of
daily living into a perfected state of being and that this happens in
the absence of any 'God'. Bloom, however, presses Shelley's humanism toward a stronger rejection of Idealism than seems quite

---

15. The most powerful reading of Shelley's skepticism remains, for me, Harold
Bloom's in *Shelley's Mythmaking*.

appropriate. He believes that Shelley posits a transcendental "one" and then maintains a "skeptical opening toward the possibility of such a power."[16] If one thinks of that power as an anthropomorphic deity, or as a Platonic Ideal, Bloom is certainly correct. In terms of Shelley's poetics, however, I would modify Bloom's statement to this extent: Shelley's skepticism is focused not on "the possibility of such a power" but on the possibility of language ever obtaining an immediate contact with that power. The question for Shelley is not whether the power exists, or even whether it can be experienced. It is, rather, whether or not poetry can incarnate the presence, whether it can be "known" through language. Shelley's skepticism about the Absolute is expressed most often as a questioning of whether his certainty of that felt presence can be articulated, or grasped, by language. As he writes in "Mont Blanc," "the wise, and great and good" hear the "mysterious tongue," the "voice" of presence, but the best they can do is to "interpret, or make felt, or deeply feel."[17] *Felt* presence is not questioned, but our ability to formulate that presence in the words of rational certainty is always questioned.

Shelley's Power is more closely analogous to a pure life force, a generative and unifying energy, than it is to either a deified "one" or a static Platonic Ideal.[18] He himself names it "being" or "life" in the "Defence" and two closely related essays, "On Life" and "On Love." In the latter he makes it clear that the words "love," "life," "power," and even "God" are only fragmenting and inadequate signs for the modifications of this single force. In "A Refutation of Deism," Shelley overtly identifies power as Being, writing that "the word power expresses the capability of anything to be or act. The human mind never hesitates to annex the idea of power to any object of its experience. To deny that power is the attribute of being, is to deny that being can be" (*CWS*, VI, 55). Whatever we choose to call this force (and Shelley's own word "unity" may come closest to his deepest understanding of its nature), it remains an immutable Absolute which expresses itself in the mutable world. Though he continually interrogates humankind's relationship to

16. Harold Bloom, Introduction to *Selected Poetry and Prose of Shelley,* ed. Harold Bloom (New York, 1966), xxiv.

17. Shelley, "Mont Blanc," in *Selected Poetry and Prose,* ll. 76–83. All references to Shelley's poetry are from this edition.

18. For contrasting and informative views on Shelley's Platonism, see both Bloom, *Shelley's Mythmaking,* and Wasserman, *Shelley: A Critical Reading.*

"Power," Shelley does not question its existence. To the extent that Shelley grounds human being in unity—a concept strikingly similar to Heidegger's Being—he remains more an idealist than a skeptic. He is, perhaps, most precisely described by Derrida's term *onto-theological*, which expresses a commitment to Being as presence whether or not that presence is conceived in the form of a deity.

The poet obviously rejected deism, but he sustained the kind of powerful, if highly personalized and eclectic, idealism that would capitalize the word *Being*. And he clearly understood the connections between religion and his own "godless" philosophy. His reading of Christianity, for instance, does as much to instruct us about his systems of belief as it does to explore what he saw to be the perversions of theistic faith. Most importantly, in this "skeptical" attack on religion, much of Shelley's antipathy is directed toward the illusions created by language in its inability to embody the 'truth'. He insists that the word *God*, like so many others, is a reductive and deceptive misnomer that creates a dangerous dualism in the mind. It is one of the kinds of 'signs' that he labels "frail spells" and "poisonous names" in the "Hymn to Intellectual Beauty."[19] In "The Essay on Christianity" (*CWS*, VI, 227–54), Shelley argues that Christ Himself understood "this name to have been profanely perverted" (*CWS*, VI, 229). He explains that Christ rejected the vulgar notion of a God as the distant Creator of a material world and understood God as "the interfused and overwhelming Spirit of all the energy and wisdom included within the circle of existing things . . . as something mysteriously and illimitably pervading the frame of things" (*CWS*, VI, 229–30). This "Spirit" is not a being, it is "Universal Being." And it is available to language only to the extent that words can say what it is not: "The universal Being can only be described or defined by negatives. . . . Where indefiniteness ends, idolatry and anthropomorphism begin" (*CWS*, VI, 232). This is a typical move in Shelley's thought: the positive assertion of a felt presence is immediately followed by a skeptical assertion that language fails in its encounter with that presence. If the purpose of poetry is to "arrest" the flow of Being in the world, to embody it "in language or in form," and if words can only operate negatively, then the poet writes under terrible constraints.

The ambivalent figure of impersonations clothed in Elysian light has, obviously, the "indefiniteness" necessary to prevent idolatry.

19. *Selected Poetry and Prose*, ed. Bloom, 82.

For Shelley, idolatry is generated by a pure representative activity in which the solidity, the clarity, of the sign displaces the represented utterly. One worships the sign rather than the Being it represents. Impersonations that dwell "in between" the mortal and the eternal, that elicit the qualities of both worlds, would seem to avoid the profanity of displacement that makes Shelley so apprehensive. In this sense, the "negativity" that death injects into Shelley's metaphor is a necessary quality of incarnative language, a quality that prevents the "veiling" action of language from producing "idolatry."

When Shelley asserts in the "Defence" that "poetry redeems from decay the visitations of the divinity in man" (*CWS*, VI, 137), "divinity" must be read as the "Universal Being," as the life force in which humankind participates. And the word *in* should be emphasized. Humans are not visited by the divine in the way that Plato's poets are visited, as inspiration from "outside." The divine is already projected into humanity's mutable being. *Visitation*, as Shelley uses the term, does not imply that the divine comes and goes, in and out of temporal existence—a misunderstanding that has prevented readers from seeing that the "Hymn to Intellectual Beauty" is in part about the poet's discovery that his own blindness and inability to articulate make Beauty *appear* to withdraw. The opening lines are reasonably clear about its presence: "The awful shadow of some unseen Power / Floats though unseen amongst us." The long strings of analogies that follow his opening all refer to things that exist as modifications of the "one," which are only momentarily perceived. The heart of the poem lies in Shelley's question: "—where art thou gone? / Why dost thou pass away and leave our state / This dim vast vale of tears, vacant and desolate?" (ll. 15–17). And the poem answers that question, reminding us that the power is "amongst us," even "though unseen," by exposing the ways in which the mind can obscure Beauty from itself. "All we hear and all we see" may be "doubt, chance and mutability," but, like the moon that exists despite its invisibility in the interlunar stage, the unseen Intellectual Beauty exists, as the poet says in his final lines, in "every form containing thee," including "himself" and "all human kind." Shelley is careful to remind us that the "harmony in Autumn" only seems "as if it could not be, as if it had not been!" It is, then, as if human perception moves in and out of its own awareness of the eternal presence of "Universal Being," rather than as if the power could be permanently lost. But the deep grief in the poem, the awful anxiety, occurs because Beauty seems lost when the mind is self-deceived. It appears to be lost if one forgets that the "inconstant wing" of "summer winds" has its own eternal constancy, that "moonbeams" are not erased, but only covered by "some piny mountain shower." The ambiguous simile, "like memory of music fled," with its refusal to clarify whether it is the music or the memory which is lost, reveals the poem's basic problem. The "inconstant glance" of which the speaker accuses "Intellectual Beauty" is, at least in part, produced by the "inconstant glance" of the mind into the 'truth'.

The "spirit of Beauty," Shelley writes, "consecrates *all* human thought" (ll. 13–15). The desperation in the series of questions that follows this assertion is grounded in the conflict between that understanding and the apparent disappearance of the sacred source of speculation itself. The questions, asked in the seeming absence of the Ideal, are a kind of profanity. And when the question "where art thou gone?" is explored in the next three stanzas of the poem, it evokes a discussion of the inadequacy and perverting power of language. At no point does the poet question the presence of Beauty except in this context of the infirmity of his own perceptions and language. At every point he articulates the inability of human beings to consistently perceive that force because of their own failure to respond to the "messenger of sympathies." The great poignancy of the poem resides in the delicacy of the poet's balance as he speaks from within a moment of apparent loss, from within the moment when Intellectual Beauty seems to have withdrawn its consecration from his words. He continues to write despite his understanding that such loss has to do with his own failure to articulate the Ideal, that withdrawal occurs because the "awful Loveliness" escapes as "whate'er these words cannot express."

The poem strongly suggests that there is a causal relationship between the apparent withdrawal of the Spirit and the failure of language:

> No voice from some sublimer world hath ever
>   To sage or poet these responses given—
>   Therefore the name of God and ghosts and Heaven,
> Remain the records of their vain endeavour
> Frail spells—whose uttered charm might not avail to sever
>   From all we hear and all we see,
>   Doubt, chance, and mutability.
>
>   (ll. 25–31)

The implication here is that if the poet could discover the proper language, the Power could be made permanently present as being-in-the-world, that such language would "sever . . . doubt, chance, and mutability" from sensual impressions, "all we hear and all we see." "I vowed that I would dedicate my powers / To thee and thine," he writes—a vow that is made after he explains how he has erred in his naming, strayed through words into "poisonous names" (l. 53) that obscure, utterly, the thing he seeks. It is only in silent "musing" that he experiences the presence of the Unseen Power, and at that moment language abandons him, reducing words to a "nameless" cry. "I shrieked and clasped my hands in extacy!" That wordless moment has generated the poet's dedication of his language to the Spirit, but dedication alone will not suffice; he also needs words that can "arrest" the "vanishing" of the "apparition," that can light its presence even though its very form is "like darkness" (l. 45). And, in the time of this poem's writing, he feels deprived of those words.

"Have I not kept the vow?" the poet asks, and calls upon "the phantoms of a thousand hours / Each from his voiceless grave" (ll. 164–65) to witness to his undying hope for the full emergence of the Power from its "unseen" condition. But the grave is voiceless, the phantoms remain silent, and this moment of the poem ends in a supplication that is also a confession: "That thou—O awful LOVELINESS, / Wouldst give whate'er these words cannot express." The last stanza, quiet and resolved, suggests that the surrender of language inherent in his confession that "these words cannot express" initiates the perception of the Power that had been unseen. It is as if the turn away from words to the "awful Loveliness" bestows the presence he seeks. The autumnal serenity of his ending echoes his opening lines, both in its tone and in its clarification of where one properly looks for the unseen spirit, that is, in "every form containing thee." It is, paradoxically, as if the poet's examination of the failure of words has confirmed the being of the unseen Power. Certainly the poem never unveils that Power, but it behaves as a "memorial," as an "impersonation clothed in Elysian light." It presents the Power as an "apparition" haunting the words that declare its absence. Shelley's poem operates within the form of a "negativity" that prevents "idolatry" through "indefiniteness."

Since presence is beyond language, even profaned by it, poetry can only reveal by concealing in a "veil." Those who utter the word *God,* Shelley writes, speak from a desire for that which they already possess; such a one "only aspires to that which the divinity of his own nature shall consider and approve." (*CWS,* VI, 231). It is, however, important to note that divinity does not *just* exist within human beings; they, like the impersonating poem, contain and are contained by Universal Being:

> We live and move and think, but we are not the creators of our own origin and existence, we are not the arbiters of every motion of our own imaginations and moods of mental being. There is a Power by which we are surrounded, like the atmosphere in which some motionless lyre is suspended, which visits with its breath our silent chords, at will. Our most imperial and stupendous qualities—those on which the majesty and power of humanity is erected—are, relatively to the inferiour portion of its mechanism, indeed active and imperial; but they are the passive slaves of some higher and more omnipotent Power. This Power is God. And those who have seen God, have, in the period of their purer and more perfect nature, been harmonized by their own will to so exquisite a consentaneity of powers as to give forth divinest melody when the breath of universal being sweeps over their frame. (*CWS*, VI, 231–32)

There are several ideas here to which I will return, but the point now is that the divine is everywhere and always present, "like the atmosphere." It is not perceived, however, unless one is "harmonized" by one's "own will." The vision of God is described by Shelley in temporal terms, as a "period" of heightened awareness, of "purer and more perfect nature" in which the mind responds with an "exquisite" consent to the equally exquisite consent of Power. That awkward word, *consentaneity,* seems to be Shelley's attempt to convey this double play as a single gesture. Consentaneity is an intense, momentary willingness to be harmonized that emerges simultaneously from the Power and "the divinity of our own nature." More accurately, it is the momentary experiencing of the harmony that always exists between Universal Being and the individual human being whom it permeates. This privileged moment, this stirring of Being against our "silent chords," produces a single "divinest melody," but this is not the music of words. This inexpressible moment of perception is the "haunting" visitation that can only be articulated through "negatives" and "indefiniteness." It is this that poetry must "redeem from decay."

This moment of absolute presence, of prelinguistic, perceptual perfection, in which we "have seen God," or the Power that "is God," is exactly what poetry must recover in language if it is to "purge from our inward sight the film of familiarity which obscures from us the wonder of our being" (*CWS*, VII, 137). But, at best, poetry can only veil the haunting *apparition* of its appearance;

it can behave as a memorial that reminds the "divinity within" of its former perception of unity. Great poetry can, Shelley believes, "reanimate, in those who have ever experienced these emotions, the sleeping, the cold, the buried image of the past" (*CWS*, VII, 137). The incarnative limits here are rigorous. Poetry may "reanimate" but it does not breathe life into presence itself; it warms and awakens an "image" of a "past" experience of presence that is already lost at the moment language is brought into play. Again Shelley resorts to an epitaphic metaphor for incarnation. Motivated by an impulse to resurrect presence, to bring the buried image forth like a Lazarus from the grave, the metaphor nonetheless admits death and loss. For, in Shelley's case, poetry can never resurrect Lazarus himself but only his ghost. The reanimation is also an "impersonation" and, though it bears Elysian light, it cannot recover the full presence of the Power or even the full moment, the "period," in which unity with that Power is experienced. As he writes in the "Defence," poetry is initiated by the experience of unity, by the emergence of "the divinity" within the poet's "own nature," but "the most glorious poetry that has ever been communicated to the world is probably a feeble shadow of the original conceptions of the poet" (*CWS*, VII, 135). The feeble shadow, like the *ka* of the mummified dead in ancient Egyptian religion, may be the immortal double of the vanished presence, but something of the power of the original is lost. The buried image is reanimated in a radically weakened condition, given life *by* an apparition and *as* an apparition.

Harold Bloom has said that "Shelley's agnosticism was more fundamental than either his troubled materialism or his desperate idealism." He is right to remind us that this is, indeed, a *desperate* idealism, because it is utterly deprived of the traditional ground of either a Christian or platonic dualism. It is, in fact, Shelley's radical rejection of dualism as a valid mode of thought that produces the "troubled materialism" Bloom notes. The problem is neither that Shelley is an inconsistent idealist whose thought is flawed by materialist tendencies, nor the reverse. It is not that he holds two positions that disrupt each other. Rather, the difficulty for Shelley is that *language* operates in terms of dualisms; it creates thought as a perversion of "truer" perceptions which are corrupted by words that divide the "one" into the "many." His essay "On Life" shows his reluctance to locate himself in either the materialist or the idealist camps. Instead, he attempted to break down the boundaries altogether, convinced that they were merely illusions created by the frailties of the language in which he was forced to think. At the core of Shelley's thought is a highly individualized monism that he knows escapes the givens of ordinary language. Bloom characterizes Shelley as "a tough-minded Humean poet . . . plagued by an idealistic and pseudo-Platonic heart." In Bloom's psychological terms, this division between heart and head may generate a monistic system that attempts to accommodate both.[20]

The essay "On Life" suggests that, after passing through a youthful commitment to materialism, Shelley attempted to erase the ground upon which the terms *idealism* and *materialism* depend. In doing so, however, the poet never surrenders the kind of idealism he expresses in his "Essays on Christianity." In that respect, perhaps Bloom's hierarchy might be reversed: Shelley's idealism is more fundamental than either his "troubled materialism" or his "intellectual agnosticism." His skepticism is with him at all times, but it emerges as an effect, not a cause. His rejection of dualism does not produce the surrender either of his commitment to an Absolute Power or of his belief in the empirical validation of knowledge. It does produce an encounter with language that inevitably results in the kind of skepticism that is most threatening to him as a poet. Language cannot be adequate even to his nonplatonic idealism unless it can incarnate an untainted, unmediated presence, and it cannot accommodate Humean empiricism unless it is accepted as entirely representational. In the face of a monism that denies this basic opposition, language can never satisfy the poet's needs. This failure does not cause Shelley to reject the Ideal, but to locate it outside of language altogether. Whether it is named "Power," "Life," "Love," or "Unity," Being remains present. As he says in the "Defence," it "abides," but it abides beyond any "portal of expression" (*CWS*, VII, 137). Presence is absolutely extralinguistic and, while he is driven as a poet to "arrest" that force in words, the difficulty of his enterprise is evident to him from the beginning. In some ways Shelley's stance is similar to that of the finest postmodern poet of our own time, with this important difference: Ashbery surrenders the presence of the Absolute and thus is able to write about, and from within, the inability of poetry to arrest Being. Shelley yields nothing. Rather, he initiates in his work a great struggle

20. Bloom, Introduction to *Selected Poetry and Prose,* xiv, xix. For an extensive discussion of the complexities of Shelley's monism, see Wasserman, *Shelley: A Critical Reading,* chap. 4, "The Intellectual Philosophy."

against language itself, refusing either to surrender his conviction
that "the power is there," as he writes in "Mont Blanc," or to succumb to a naïve incarnationist view that can ground language in the
'truth'.

This struggle is displayed in "On Life." Shelley begins the piece
by distinguishing life from its traditional meanings as nature, as
sociopolitical existence, or even as the universe of birth and death.
These are merely familiar and "transient modifications" of a "mi-
raculous" force. Then, in a line directly repeated in the "Defence,"
he asserts that the "mist of familiarity obscures from us the wonder
of our being" (*CWS*, VI, 193). He goes on to renounce dualism,
"the shocking absurdities of the popular philosophy of mind and
matter" which had created his youthful attraction to materialism.
"This materialism is a seducing system to young and superficial
minds," he writes. "It allows disciples to talk and dispenses them
from thinking" (*CWS*, VI, 194). The essay develops not as a treatise
on life, but as a treatise on language; the distinction made here between talk and thought only hints at the depths of Shelley's linguistic skepticism.

With some reluctance he identifies himself as a kind of idealist: "I
confess that I am one of those who am unable to refuse assent to the
conclusions of those philosophers who assert that nothing exists
but as it is perceived" (*CWS*, VI, 194). The resistance implied by
the phrasing is rooted in his desire to eradicate the dualism imbedded in the "philosophy of mind and matter" that this "confession" might seem to confirm. The rest of the essay is an attempt to
clarify his position as a monist operating within the confines of a
language that habitually constitutes thought in terms of polar opposites. He writes that "the difference is merely nominal between
those two classes of thought, which are vulgarly distinguished by
the names of ideas and external objects" (*CWS*, VI, 196). The
phrase "merely nominal" centers the entire essay. It is clear that
Shelley understands both materialism and idealism to be expressions of the 'same' which language has fragmented. Both systems
are seen as delusions created by the tendency of language to substitute words for thought rather than to provide words that incarnate thought. Throughout the essay, "systems" are simply words,
"marks employed to denote the different modifications of the one
mind" (*CWS*, VI, 196). Reality is entirely outside the play of language, "the relations of *things* remain unchanged, by whatever system" (*CWS*, VI, 196). Furthermore, he writes, "how vain it is to

think that words can penetrate the mystery of our being! Rightly used they make evident our ignorance to ourselves and this is much" (*CWS,* VI, 194).

Language that can expose ignorance "is much," but such language can create a dangerous void. Even philosophy, whose "object" is to reveal "new truth," can slip into the emptiness of signification: "It makes one step toward this object; it destroys error, and the roots of error. It leaves . . . a vacancy. It reduces the mind to that freedom of words and signs, the instruments of its own creation. By signs, I would be understood in a wide sense . . . almost all familiar objects are signs, standing, not for themselves, but for others, in their capacity of suggesting one thought which shall lead to a train of thoughts. Our whole life is thus an education of error" (*CWS,* VI, 195). Shelley's intolerance of "vacancy" is intrinsic to both his psychology and his philosophy. It implies an empty space, a fracture in being that denies presence, the absolute "oneness" which, for him, defines existence itself. Man is, he writes, "incapable of imagining to himself annihilation . . . there is a spirit within him at enmity with nothingness and dissolution. This is the character of all life and being" (*CWS,* VI, 194). For Shelley, there is no guarantee that, in its compulsion to fill space, the mind will not misuse "its own creation" and give itself, not the "new truth," but an "education of error."

For the space of freedom created by philosophy is as vulnerable as it is necessary, and the spirit that is "at enmity with nothingness and dissolution" may resort, in a kind of habitual desperation, to filling the void with a distorting shadow play of signs. The immaterial, arbitrary, and self-referential qualities of language, which offer freedom and create the proximity of "conception and expression" in the "Defence," are poetry's greatest assets, but they are also its greatest danger. The danger resides in "errance," the "indefinite drift of signs . . . linking representations one to another without end." Shelley calls this tendency of signs to refer only to other signs an "education of error." Words that behave as the representation of a representation initiate a process that he clearly identifies as a threat to truth, or to presence as Being. The "train of thoughts" consists of signs that are self-generating and substitutive, "standing not for themselves, but for others," and the freedom of mind that "would have acted" is enslaved by a series of representations that wander into each other, straying away from the reality of Being in their progress. Signification can create the space it is intended to fill.

Such an activity announces its own fracture from reality and initiates the perception of difference that the essay "On Life" insists is pure delusion.

For Shelley, life is absolute unity, a unity so complete that thoughts themselves are "things," intrinsically joined with the material world which they present (*CWS*, VI, 196). But language interrupts the oneness Shelley perceives: thought must be embodied to be expressed, and the body of the sign presents a threat to genuine presence. "Thoughts and feelings arise with or without our will and we employ words to express them," he writes, but continues, "How vain it is to think that words can penetrate the mystery of our being!" (*CWS*, VI, 193). Thought may sustain such a close interchange with the material world that it can appear as the thing-itself, but as soon as the need for expression enters the structure, the division between inside and outside reasserts its dominance over unity. The space of freedom becomes a potential abyss. The mind can misperceive the instrument it has created to express thought as the thing-itself. Language is the poet's only hope, but he cannot admit language into his vision of perfect unity without cracking that vision severely. No wonder he cries out, "No help!"

To eradicate the difference between thought and the material world, then, the poet must free thought entirely from the workings of signification, from representation. Thus, when Shelley asserts that "nothing exists but as it is perceived"—a phrase he repeats so often that it is a touchstone in his work—he is not idealizing the outside, as Sidney does, by transforming it into a language that appears to have absolute proximity with thought. Instead, he defines thought as something much closer to perception or apprehension: the intuitive and immediate understanding of reality. Separating language from perception entirely, he suggests that in its "best and happiest"[21] moments, thought stands in perfect coincidence with the thing upon which it is employed. This is not an expressive, nor even a linguistic, state. Rather, it is "reverie": "Those who are subject to the state called reverie feel as if their nature were dissolved into the surrounding universe or as if the surrounding universe were absorbed into their being. They are conscious of no distinction. And these are states which precede, or accompany, or follow an unusually intense or vivid apprehension of life" (*CWS*, VI, 195–96).

The connections between "reverie" and the period of "purer and

21. This famous and much misunderstood phrase from "The Defence" does not bear any relation to poetry as a record of sweetness and light. Rather, it records the privileged moment of unity.

more perfect nature" in "On Christianity" are so close that Shelley seems to be describing the same experience through different metaphoric structures. In both, this brief moment of "intense or vivid apprehension" offers an immediate experience of reality, of the truth of existence, which words like *subject, object, material,* or *ideal* can only belie. "Reverie" is certainly analogous to the "exquisite . . . consentaneity of powers" that Shelley compares to having "seen God." It is important to note that the mind is "subject to the state called reverie"; it does not create it. Subjective creation by the individual mind would grant the state a purely imaginary status that would be an anathema to Shelley's thought. In both essays, the poet is careful to guarantee the particular kind of objectivity that is necessary if one wishes to make truth claims for any mental experience. And, even for Shelley, objectivity must be validated by locating it "outside" purely mental activity. Though he attempts to dissolve the separation between inside and outside as part of his effort to erase dualisms, he is forced to use the division in the service of 'truth'. For instance, in the essay "On Christianity," he introduces the idea of a periodic perception of Universal Being only after first insisting that "we are not the arbiters of every motion of our own imaginations and moods of mental being." Those mental qualities are "active and imperial" relative only to other more limited aspects of the human mind. Relative to "the Power by which we are surrounded" they are "passive slaves."

As uncharacteristic as it is of Shelley to approve the loss of freedom, this sort of submission is required by his metaphysics in order to protect his notion of consentaneity from falling into a state of chimeric fantasy. It is even more important to establish a certain objectivity in "On Life," since his metaphors intensify consentaneity to an extreme. "Dissolution" and "absorption" imply an even more radical unity than the "harmony" in "On Christianity" which still suggests two distinct entities, though in such perfect accord that they appear as a melody. Here, in keeping with the general intent of the entire essay, all distinction is erased: boundaries disintegrate so thoroughly that one cannot even be sure whether one absorbs, or is absorbed by, the "surrounding universe." So it is necessary to reiterate that this is not simply a hallucinatory experience of pure subjectivity. Thus his immediate and direct assertion that the "mind, as far as we have any experience of its properties, and beyond that experience how vain is argument! cannot create, it can only perceive" (*CWS*, VI, 197). Shelley's curious sanction of passivity, which seems so out of keeping with the rest of his humanist ideology and with Romanticism in general, is disturbing only if we substitute our own understanding of the word for Shelley's.

Passivity, for this poet, is a willed opening to the flow of being; it is both active and passive, a voluntary acquiescence. Consentaneity clarifies the concept: those who yield are "harmonized by their own will" as well as by the willingness of Power to reveal its presence. The activity on both parts is interdependent and benign. It is not, however, a kind of inertia. As in many other places in Shelley, Heideggerean terminology is useful here. Being calls out to human perception in order to reveal itself, and human perception actively responds to that call. Shelley should not be understood, then, as suggesting that the mind is only a passive recorder. Mind's active perception of the universe confirms its unity with the universe, and in the same moment it unveils material existence. Mind does not, then, create the substantial world, but does actively enable its appearance. In so doing, mind constitutes itself as thought and the world as thought in a oneness that does not deny material existence but validates it. As he does with all other dualisms, Shelley attempts to erase the distinctions between perception and creation. For Shelley, the mind, at least "as far as we have any experience of its properties," offers evidence for his monism rather than for the subject–object dualism more typical of Romantic vision. From his point of view, the flash of unity that he calls perception disproves the *language* that opposes a material (outside) world to an ideal (inside) representation of that world. Nonetheless, he cannot discard the language of dualism if he wishes to substantiate the objective truth of his belief. Consequently, he is extremely careful in his phrasing, using an assertion like "nothing exists but as it is perceived" to master division and to convey the interdependence of mind and world. The use of *as* in Shelley's phrasing is purposely ambiguous. It suggests both that the world exists in the manner in which it is perceived and that the world exists in the moment in which it is perceived. Spatial and temporal differences are hidden by the double play in the meaning of *as,* a necessary concealment that enables the appearance of unity.

As children, we have an "intense apprehension" of this oneness, Shelley writes, but in the maturing process, we become habituated to "familiar objects as signs standing not for themselves but for others." As a result, "in living we lose the apprehension of life" (*CWS,* VI, 194) to the "vanity" of representation. This "mist of familiarity obscures from us the wonder of our beings" (*CWS,* VI,

193). The slippage of sign into sign creates a mist so dense that we even lose sight of the nature of our own minds:

> Nothing exists but as it is perceived. The difference is merely nominal between those two classes of thought, which are vulgarly distinguished by the names of ideas and of external objects. Pursuing the same thread of reasoning, the existence of distinct individual minds, similar to that which is employed in now questioning its own nature, is likewise found to be a delusion. The words *I, you, they,* are not signs of any actual difference subsisting between the assemblage of thought thus indicated, but are merely marks employed to denote the different modifications of the one mind.   (*CWS*, VI, 196)

Shelley goes on to insist that not only are the words that distinguish between minds delusive but the discrete 'I' is itself an illusion, "devoid of the intense and exclusive sense usually attached to it." Every mind is "but a portion of the 'one mind'" (*CWS*, VI, 196). If we fail to perceive this, the blame again falls on our tendency to misperceive signs as the things themselves; it is the fault of the human tendency to become so habituated to the "familiar" that the "mist" appears as the reality.

Shelley's strategy for internalizing the outside is even more powerful than Sidney's and certainly more consciously constructed against the forces of division. Nonetheless, it fails at the same moment that Sidney's does—when the internal must be expressed to the outside, that is, in the encounter between thought and language. When one faces the problem of expressing the true apprehension of unity, "it is difficult to find terms adequate. . . . We are on the verge where words abandon us, and what wonder if we grow dizzy to look down the dark abyss of how little we know" (*CWS*, VI, 196).

The causal relationship here is important. Ignorance, "the dark abyss," results from the fact that on the "verge" of truth, "words abandon us," and Shelley does not just mean that appropriate language cannot be found. Representative language always initiates abandonment. Because it inevitably drifts into a self-referential state that excludes Being as such, it misleads the mind with "merely nominal" differences which, in turn, create the chimeric "train of thoughts" that is nothing more than an "education of error."

Shelley metaphorizes his abandonment by language as the cliff-edge of nonbeing. Facing the dark abyss, human beings face "annihilation," the "nothingness and dissolution" with which they *must* be "at enmity" since that enmity is "the character of life and being."

The abandonment by language leaves humans on the "verge" of death. Yet, this abandonment is required to sustain a oneness that is never "any actual difference," that manifests itself as "modifications" of the same. Only silence can sustain Shelley's version of truth, but only an intrinsically representational language can express it. The paradox is unbreakable, and as a result, Shelley's finest work is always written "on that verge where words abandon us" and is always balanced on the very edge between being and nonbeing. "What wonder if we grow dizzy," and what wonder that Shelley should characterize poetry as an epitaphic haunting. For Shelley, haunting evokes truth precisely insofar as it remains in a state of being that exists on the "verge." On the verge, it evades the "seductive" dualisms that allow the mind to deceive itself with "the instruments of its own creation." The poem must exist somewhere between the enmity with nothingness that is life and the dark abyss of death and ignorance. The "deep truth is imageless," Demorgorgon says in *Prometheus Unbound* (II, iv, l. 115), and to appear at all it must, like Demorgorgon himself, be veiled. Without the veil of language, we are faced with "a mighty darkness / Filling the seat of power" (II, iv, ll. 3–4). But the veil does not bestow full presence, full being; it is an Elysian light that marks the interpenetration of the Absolute into two worlds, united by virtue of poetry's status as "in between," as apparition and memorial.

This writing on the verge is a dangerous activity, and Shelley is fully cognizant of the delicacy of his balance. In a dazzling essay on "The Triumph of Life," Paul de Man has suggested that the fragment is concerned with "the discrepancy between the power of words as acts and their power to produce other words" ("SD," 47). The "violence and grief" he notes in the poem are certainly in keeping with Shelley's anxieties about the fracture between self-referential language and the truth of Being. Shelley's Rousseau, according to de Man, discovers that words "themselves, literally, are actions. Their power to act exists independently of their power to know" ("SD," 49). In the face of this self-generating power without knowledge, writers cannot secure their own meanings: "The power that arms their words also makes them lose their power over them. Rousseau gains shape, face or figure only to lose it as he acquires it" ("SD," 49). This description of Rousseau's predicament seems to me to be applicable to Shelley's general understanding of both the situation of the poet and the dynamics of veiling in poetry. And de Man's identification of the "shape all light" as the "model of figuration in general . . . beyond the traditional conceptions of figuration as modes of representing, as polarities of subject and object, of part and whole" ("SD," 61) is certainly consistent with Shelley's own desire to remove language from the play of dualistic thought.

De Man's description is also striking in its similarity to the workings of the Elysian figures in "The Defence." He has not located just the center of the "Triumph" in his essay, but the center of Shelley's entire project as a poet. "Shelley Disfigured" shows that it is impossible to locate the "shape all light," this "figure of figuration," on either side of any logical polarity. She dwells in neither light nor dark, waking nor sleeping, life nor death. In fact, as de Man argues, the structure of Rousseau's encounter with the "shape all light" displays a total "confusion" of opposites. It erases the possibility of polarizing itself, and therefore, like the meaning of the poem as a whole, the figure's "meaning glimmers, hovers and wavers, but refuses to yield the clarity it keeps announcing" ("SD," 53). It is this announcing and refusing of clarity in the same gesture that Shelley's "Defence" claims to be the proper, even "divine," activity of poetry. It is that "divine" activity which lifts "the veil from the hidden beauty." Yet it can do so only through "impersonations clothed in its Elysian light"; it unveils by veiling. Viewed from within Shelley's own thought, this double gesture is entirely appropriate, concordant with the appearing of truth itself, an appearing which occurs as the visitation of an apparition.

De Man argues that the "shape all light" figures, or better, prefigures, a certain structure of forgetting that is also displayed in the thematic movements of the fragment: "The birth of what an earlier Shelley poem such as 'Mont Blanc' would still have called the mind occurs as the distortion which allows one to make the random regular by 'forgetting' differences" ("SD," 54). Shelley might have disputed the word *distortion* here, but not, I think, the rest. In Shelley's thought (though certainly not in de Man's) the forgetting of differences is the recollection of unity, of the poet's sense of truth. And it is precisely this forgetting of differences that the figures of Elysian light should generate. In order for them to operate "as memorials of that gentle and exalted content which extends itself over all thoughts and actions with which it coexists," the recollecting operation must first be enabled by a process of erasure: "Poetry lifts the veil from the hidden beauty of the world, and makes familiar objects be as if they were not familiar." The erasure of familiarity, this "lifting away" of the known to reveal the unknown, is for Shelley the erasure of signification. "Familiar objects," he wrote, "are signs standing, not for themselves but for others," signs which create "an education of error."

In the "Defence," Shelley presses the idea even further, describing the corruption of language as a process in which metaphor degenerates into sign. Metaphor cannot incarnate the Ideal itself, but it remains "vital," alive, as long as it remains a language of similarity. As such, it is an "approximation to the beautiful" and reveals the "hidden beauty" of things by revealing the "hidden" relationships poets perceive: "Their language is vitally metaphorical; that is, it marks the before unapprehended relations of things and perpetuates their apprehension, until the words which represent them become, through time, signs for portions or classes of thoughts instead of pictures of integral thoughts; and then if no new poets should arise to create afresh the associations which have been thus disorganized, language will be dead to all the nobler purposes of human intercourse" (*CWS*, VII, 111). "Vitally" functional language pictures, gives body to, "integral thoughts," that is, to the relationships that exist *between* the various modifications of the one mind. Signification, on the other hand, disorganizes—it displays difference, it classifies and fragments integrity into "portions or classes," dismembering the whole until it is "dead." This murder of language by language is enacted by a passage through time, which makes the unfamiliar "familiar" and erodes the incarnative "picture" into the representative "sign." It is up to the poet to reverse this process, to "forget" the familiar sign in order to perceive and present "the hidden beauty" it covers. Forgetting the familiar entails the forgetting of difference, of the delusions created by signs in the play of representation, as he describes it in "On Life."

In this sense the violent forgetting initiated by the "shape all light" in "The Triumph," is not necessarily a negative event. If one recalls that Shelley has insisted that the maturing process is one in which people forget those "reveries" of their childhood wherein they experienced truth "as if their nature were dissolved into the surrounding universe or as if the surrounding universe were absorbed into their being," then Rousseau's forgetting of his "history," his forgetting of the past, is potentially the beginning of a period of "purer and more perfect nature." Nonetheless, Rousseau, in a state analogous to the "freedom" offered by philosophy in "On Life," is sadly vulnerable to the icy clarity of "a new Vision, and its cold bright car" ("The Triumph," l. 434); the vacancy created by his contact with the shimmering and ungraspable "shape all light" is immediately filled by the "severe excess" of the triumph of life, an excess that proves to be an excess of signification. The figures are depleted, exhausted, deprived of life by the "signs" of their existence, by the "mask after mask" that erupts from each form as symbols of depravity. All the figures, caught in the wild danse macabre that surrounds the chariot of life, stand "not for themselves but for others, in their capacity of suggesting one thought which shall lead to a train of thoughts." In this sense the triumph can be read as a picture of a mind in which signs generate other signs, creating a train in which "life is thus an education of error."

To avoid "error," however, Shelley must repress the representational aspects of language in favor of an incarnative "veiling" that can never *fully* disclose the truth. Consequently, his effort to reveal is directed not toward the truth–itself, but toward its "visitations." He consciously substitutes the "privileged moment" for the presence of the Absolute within the poem. It is the moment of "consentaneity" that he portrays, in which consciousness and the Absolute join "in the middle." For the Ideal and her "sisters" remain irrevocably outside language; they "abide" beyond even the poetic idiom. His use of *abide* is a careful one, drawing upon all its connotations of dwelling, continuance, enduring, and awaiting. Power and its modifications continue to dwell beyond language, enduring its nonarrival even as they endlessly await it. Finally, "there is *no portal of expression* from the caverns of the spirit which they inhabit into the universe of things" (*CWS*, VII, 137) The veiling of the apparitions can never reveal the whole truth of *what* they are, but only *that* they are. Poetry presents not the Absolute, but its "radience." Veiling, then, is a gesture of both concealing and unconcealing. It is a dynamic process that allows the appearing of "Power," "Beauty," or the "One" in its "working," yet hides the nature of its Being. It should be remembered that for Shelley (as for Heidegger) veiling always misrepresents.

"Adonais" demonstrates the ambivalence of the notion of veiling. In this poem the "universe of things" is itself a veil. The world does not image the Absolute in any genuinely Platonic sense. For the Ideal penetrates its own creations: it projects itself, of necessity, into that world which then both reveals and conceals it:

> the one Spirit's plastic stress
> Sweeps through the dull dense world, compelling there
> All new successions to the forms they wear;
> Torturing th'unwilling dross that checks its flight

To its own likeness, as each mass may bear
And bursting in its beauty and its might
From trees and beasts and men into the Heaven's light.
("Adonais," 43, ll. 381–87)

Even as the Spirit compels the world into "forms," it is captured
within the form that "checks its flight." But the world expresses the
Ideal only through analogy. Things are formed by Spirit "to its
own likeness" as it "sweeps through" them. If representation is the
embodiment of truth, the truth is concealed, buried within the image it constructs of itself, by the very nature of the mimetic/creative
act. Shelley's statement in the "Defence" that images "directly participate in the life of truth" must be understood in this context;
"Adonais" operates as a kind of extensive footnote to the phrase.
The dynamics of revealing are clear in stanza 43; the concealing activity, and particularly the ability of the image to misrepresent, are
explicated by the poem as a whole. Finally, the Ideal can be fully
revealed only in death, when the "mourning veil" of air is stripped
away and the veiling of the "dome of many-coloured glass" is shattered. Shelley's plainest statement that death and truth are interlaced
and as double as veiling itself occurs in his sonnet, "Lift not the
painted veil which those who live call Life." The unveiled truth
means the loss of life in both poems.

Life is both incarnative and representational, a masking which
makes presence visible, but hides its true face. To "make visible" is
not to stand-in-place-of or to substitute for an original. In Shelley's
phrase "the images of Truth participate in the life of Truth" the
emphasis must fall on *participate* and *life*. Presence is never questioned, but in life it can show itself only as its own distortion and as
a fragment of a dynamic whole which "sweeps through" the world
of things. As soon as it is "arrested," made still, in its image, when
it is prevented from "vanishing," it loses what Shelley calls its
"original force and purity." We are left with an immobilized fragment of the Ideal which is not "untrue" but is not the whole truth.
For Shelley, truth made visible is, by definition, truth veiled.

Yet the visible image, the representation, is essential to the lighting, or at least coloring, of truth. In this idea rests Shelley's justi-
fication of metaphor, and herein resides the last turn of thought determined to reappropriate presence in a language that is openly
representational. For the veiled apparition "transmutes all that it
touches and every form moving within the radience of its presence
is changed by wondrous sympathy to an incarnation of the spirit
which it breathes: its secret alchemy turns to potable gold the poi-

sonous waters which flow from death through life; it strips bare the naked and sleeping beauty which is the spirit of its forms" (*CWS*, VII, 137). "Wondrous sympathy" is the ground of his whole strategy. Poetry offers "news of a kindred joy" to those who already carry the Ideal within, who are already "possessed" by the Spirit. It is the "sympathy" of kindred spirits, a sympathy mediated by poetry, which allows the expression of the incarnative moment into the world. The Ideal remains "unspoken" even as the moment of its *appearance* is transmitted by poetic language in order to illuminate the spirit within. Poetry functions as "the lighting projection of truth" in this way for Shelley. Though this projection of truth bears some resemblance to Plato's representational chain, the differences are important. Shelley recognizes that the full presence of the divine is displaced by the fragmentary re-presenting of its effect in the world and that the effect is made visible only by the duplicitous activity of the "impersonating" image. Only his insistence on the presence of the privileged moment and on the idea that the analogy participates in the thing-itself restrict the potential for errance that disturbed Plato. The possibility of endless drift is closed by the ability of the poem to bring to light the Ideal within the kindred spirit that already "hides" it. There representation is restored to presentation, and reparation is made: the "radience" transforms an unfulfilled incarnation into a full "incarnation of the Spirit." The poem stimulates the reader beyond the fragmentary and (now) visible moment into an experience of "insight" that seems to Shelley, as it did to Sidney, to promise the fullness of absolute presence.

But Shelley is far from secure; the chain of representations disturbs the closure proffered by sympathy and, aware of the dangers of the representational image, of veiling as inevitable misrepresentation, he cannot eliminate the sense of loss that accompanies the transference of the Ideal into the world. His whole sense of representation is one in which presence "yearns for itself therein as for its own birth or death." The prophetic assurance of earlier statements in the "Defence" is deeply shaken by his description of the act of composition; at the end of the work the description of the poetic process is one of representational inadequacy:

> the mind in creation is as a fading coal which some invisible influence, like an inconstant wind, awakens to transitory brightness. This power arises from within, like the color of a flower which fades and changes as it is developed . . . could this influence be durable in its original purity and force, it is impossible to predict the greatness of the results; but when composition begins, inspiration is already on the decline, and the most

glorious poetry that has ever been communicated to the world is probably a feeble shadow of the original conceptions of the poet.   (*CWS,*
VII, 135)

Poetic language, even at its "incarnative" best, in all its Elysian ra-
diance, cannot bring the "origin" fully to light. The doubleness of
veiling is fully operative behind his words. Poetry may "arrest the
vanishing apparitions" but it is, finally, itself ghost-like, a dark image, a "feeble shadow" of the "transitory brightness" that fades in
the bodies of words. The statement that "when composition begins, inspiration is already on the decline" is burdened by the sense
that the poet loses "voice" as he finds language. Such loss of presence is related to the fact that poetry is rarely speech for Shelley.

Yet the poet does not feel this absence of voice that Plato de-
plored as only deprivation. He accepts it as inevitable and, in one
moment, suggests that it is an asset. For him the possibility of reinterpretation is guaranteed by "sympathy" and is of inestimable
value; age after age "fills" the voiceless work with new meaning:
"and after one person and one age has exhausted all its divine
effluence which their peculiar relations enable them to share, another and yet another succeeds, and new relations are developed,
the source of an unforeseen and an unconceived delight" (*CWS,*
VII, 131). This is perfectly consistent with a theory that depends on
kinship and sympathy, and that suggests the Ideal is carried within
each human being. But poetry as interpretable writing is also the
crux of his troubled sense of loss. For when he overtly faces poetry
as writing, he faces signification, representation, "composition,"
the drifting away from the source that bespeaks absence. Though
the "will to hear oneself speak" is everywhere evident in Shelley's
work, poetry is, finally, portrayed as "writing," as an act of memory and textual weaving: "a careful observation of the inspired
moments, and an artificial connection of the spaces between their
suggestions, by the intertexture of conventional expressions; a necessity only imposed by the limitedness of the poetic faculty itself"
(*CWS,* VII, 136).

Perhaps the most famous lines of the essay depict poetry as writing, not speech: "Poetry is the record of the best and happiest moments of the happiest and best minds."   Poetry as the "record" of
moments is the remembering and writing down of the moment
that was privileged by presence, but was so transient that it can only
be represented as a ghostly image.

The terrible nostalgia for presence, which for Derrida is seen as
"the will to hear oneself speak," is motivated in Shelley (as it is in

all cases, according to Derrida) by the desire for "absolute self-presence." Because Shelley seeks voice as inspiration, even as he loses it in poetry as "record," his notion of self-presence is also an ambivalent concept. It is the desired end of all poetry, but the nature of its appearance is a combination of self-revelation and self-loss: "self appears as what it is, an atom to a universe" (*CWS*, VII, 136). Self "appears" in much the same way that an image "appears"; that is, it is visible only as a fragment, complete in itself, perhaps, but as an infinitesimal representation of the infinitely irrecoverable whole that has given it form. To image oneself as "an atom to a universe" is to find "my-death" even as one finds absolute knowledge of "my-self." It is to find, simultaneously, one's origin and one's end. Here, as so often in Shelley, "that which related truth to its own death as it related it to its origin" is *not* repressed. And the surfacing of this relationship is allowed by the poet's recognition of poetry as writing-without-voice, as memory, as a futile attempt to recover presence. Note the paragraph that leads up to Shelley's revelation of the "truth" of self-presence:

> We are aware of evanescent visitations . . . always arising unforeseen and departing unbidden, but elevating and delightful beyond all expression, so that even in the desire and regret they leave, there cannot but be pleasure, participating as it does in the nature of its object. It is as it were the interpenetration of a diviner nature through our own; but its footsteps are like those of a wind over the sea, which the morning calm erases, and whose traces remain only, as on the wrinkled sand which paves it. (*CWS*, VII, 136)

The Ideal writes itself into visible existence, but it brings itself to light only as its own sign, and the sign can be read only after the fact; it is inscribed on the sands of memory. It leaves behind "pleasure" but the elegiac tone of the paragraph throws the emphasis on desire and regret.

The writing on the sand reads like an epitaph and, like the Elysian figures, it has "related truth to its own death as it related it to its origin." This interpositioning of truth is Shelley's defense against his regret, a way of satisfying his desire. Truth, defined as that which dies in the moment of its appearance and appears only in the moment of its dying, seems to escape from the conventional movement of signification. For Shelley, such an existent cannot be displaced by its own sign, it is simply confirmed as that which must always be veiled. The figures clothed in Elysian light, Shelley's "figure of figuration," in de Man's phrase, and his linking of the figures to a poetry defined as "memorial," is clearly a double gesture: it acknowledges the loss of presence in language as sign and, at the same time, seems to authenticate presence in the form of an immortal haunting—the haunting of truth in the form of meaning, removed from the domain of the sign and located between the life of silence and the death of representation.

The poet understands that it is impossible to evade the "intertexture of conventional expressions," but this "artificial connection" is not, he believes, inherent in poetry. Rather, it is "imposed by the limitedness of the poetic faculty itself"—imposed, that is, by a failure of human language in its encounter with the truth of Being, a truth that can be known only through its concealment, which points to presence by noting its loss. There remains in Shelley, then, the conviction that "original conception" exists as a silent, pure presence untainted by the signifying play of language which produces only "feeble shadows." This birthplace, this origin, abides both within and without the mind, shadowed forth from within by language and shadowed outside the mind by that "everlasting universe of things" so deeply considered in "Mont Blanc." The "messenger of sympathies" reveals the singularity of the origin, but language always "intervenes." That is, it stands between truth and mind, both traversing the gap and reinforcing it. Words, at their best, enable the interpenetration of shadows. At their worst, they behave as "poisonous names" which distance humankind from the silent Power and murder as they represent. Always, for Shelley, "the voices of the desert fail"; language can only echo "a loud, lone sound no other sound can tame." Yet, without the desert voices, this undomesticated sound remains apart. Hence, poets must seek, in the "still cave of the witch Poesy," the shadows of its presence. They must search "among the shadows that pass by / Ghosts of all things that are, some shade of thee, / Some phantom, some faint image" ("Mont Blanc," II, ll. 45–47).

This passionate seeking for "some faint image" of the truth, of the power "that *is*," motivates the work of every poet we are about to explore. And Shelley's intuition that the power dwells in "voiceless lightning"—always "Silently there . . . but silently!"—strikes directly to the core of each writer's project. For the poets' words, while they must break this great silence, must not shatter its "light" into fragments that can only dispossess poets of the whole they wish to embody. The words must not become the mere noise of representation. Hence, poets are compelled to seek exactly the right words, words which seem to 'belong' to truth, and which are unique and pure enough to master presence, to incarnate it and bring it into the world as meaning. Derrida has called this quest for the right word a "nostalgia," a longing for the "master-name" that never existed in the first place. He identifies "the other side" of this nostalgia as a seeking for "the name of Being," as "Heideggerean Hope" (*MP,* 27). On the shoulders of "Heideggerean Hope" rests the possibility that language can express, contain, or present truth or meaning as such. A heavy burden, indeed.

The rest of this study is concerned with the various ways in which this hope plays itself out in the works of George Herbert, William Wordsworth, and John Ashbery, and in the thought of Derrida himself. All of the writers sustain their hope for meaning against an understanding that language substitutes itself for, even corrupts, the truth/meaning structure in the moment of its articulation. All of them fall back, in very different ways, on Heidegger's belief that truth "happens" in being composed, despite the fact that none of them escape the problems explored so passionately by Shelley. Like Plato, all understand that the image is " a long way off from the truth." Like Sidney, Herbert and Wordsworth turn to a radical internalization of the image to guarantee its proximity to the truth. But Derrida and Ashbery, disabused intellects who believe that union with truth is death itself, must avoid that strategy. They turn, instead, to an articulation of the sheer drive of desire through a language that cannot, must not, satisfy desire by allowing it to culminate in fulfilled meaning. In their cases, the search for the right words purposely defers the arrival of truth; and both point to the differing of their own language from the meaning it posits. For both, this deferral and differing are life itself.

What unites all these writers is that they use language in a fundamentally epitaphic manner, in such a way that it evokes presence by inscribing its *loss.* This is what Derrida would call a classically "metaphysical" gesture, one that, as both he and Heidegger have pointed out, is loaded with theological implications. The next chapter explores the "onto-theological" crux by examining one of its oldest formulations. This ancient form (parable) is always played out as a highly conscious attempt to use language as a veil that 'unveils' the familiar by covering it. Read as parable and poem, the Book of Job provides a beginning point for the study of the search for the "right word" that motivates every writer's work.

2

JOB AND THE DILEMMA OF LANGUAGE

> *Oh that my words were now written! oh that*
> *they were printed in a book!*
> *That they were graven with an iron pen*
> *and lead in the rock forever!*
> *For I know that my redeemer liveth, and that*
> *he shall stand at the latter day upon the earth.*
>
> —Job 19:23–25

> *Why have You forsaken me? Why have hidden Your face?*
> *How can You say without me? For*
> *it's not enough with worm and tree and dust. I become*
> *entangled among my words, become diminished*
> *in a vale with no man by me among the shadows*
> *I fear the silence I am entangled in words*
> *without You I see only my hands*
> *and they are too heavy to bear my fallen face*
> *without Your eyes*
> *as a candle the flame I seek your face.*
>
> —Tuvia Rubner, Untitled

The Bible, as Northrop Frye has said, "is more than a work of literature, whatever 'more' means."[1] As a theological and, in certain respects, a cultural center of European and American thought, it occupies a unique position among texts, coming as near to serving as an "origin" as any text can and exerting all the mastery that the notion of origin summons. Despite the singularity of its status, it has nonetheless been treated from the beginning as a text open to interpretation, and as both a revelatory and a literary text at least since the Middle Ages. The "literariness" of the Book of Job is the subject of this chapter. In fact, the focus here is even more constrained: the text under consideration is the King James translation. This is to say that the text is a work created through the power-

---

1. Northrop Frye, *The Great Code: The Bible and Literature* (New York, 1982), xvi.

ful filter of seventeenth-century Christian thought—thought that
made, perhaps unconsciously, certain writerly choices that would
have been unthinkable to the first Job poet (or poets—the Hebrew
text is itself complicated by the possibility that it is the work of several hands).

A startling example of the force exerted by that distinctly 'logocentric' vision occurs in Job 19:25–26 of the King James Version.
There, a misreading displays the incarnative desire for presence and
the rejection of a language that evokes absence, which are inherent
in Christian thought.[2] Marvin Pope's much admired translation of
the Hebrew is this:

> I know my vindicator lives
> A guarantor upon the dust will stand;
> Even after my skin is flayed
> Without my flesh I shall see God.[3]

The King James Version, controlled by the Christian concepts of
the Incarnation and the resurrection of the body, erases the Hebraic
acknowledgment of disincarnated presence entirely:

> For I know that my redeemer liveth, and that
> he shall stand at the latter day upon the earth:
> And though after . . . worms destroy this body,
> yet in my flesh shall I see God.
> (Job 19:25–26)

The history of the translation and dissemination of biblical texts
demands theoretical study for its own sake, but that is not my concern here. Rather, I have chosen to approach the King James Version's Job as a single seventeenth-century English poem that metaphorizes the struggle between incarnative desire and language as a
representational act that always haunts poetry—Christian or not.
One radical thematic structure unites the Hebrew Job and the English, despite their obvious discrepancies. Job's cry, "Oh that my
words were written . . . graven . . . in the rock forever," is the culmination of this theme, which renders the great struggle between
human words and God's word. Perhaps this is because, as Robert
Alter has said, "the nexus of speech that binds man and God" is the
"quintessential biblical notion—the concept that binds the Bible it-

2. I am indebted to Nahum and Minda Rae Amiran for pointing out the oddity
of this translation and discussing its implications with me.
3. *The Anchor Bible Job,* trans. Marvin H. Pope (Garden City, N.Y., 1973).

self into a comprehensible volume."[4] This "nexus" is considered here, and it relates the Book of Job to the other poems this book will explore.

In discussing the continuing application of this millennia-old notion, Alter presents the contemporary Hebrew poem that serves as an epigraph to this chapter, and he goes on to note that "this is not merely an abstract doctrine but, as the framer of these lines knows with a penetration of artistic intuition, an informing poetic principle. . . . God speaks the world and man into being and man answers by speaking songs unto the Lord."[5] Alter is concerned only with biblical poetry, but this ontotheological perception of language, this balancing of 'being' between Word and words, generates the necessity of finding the "right words" that every poet experiences. It is the theological expression of the poet's search for a language that can incarnate truth. In Rubner's phrasing, the great question is this: "How can You say without me?" And the great problem is always that "I fear the silence I am entangled in words."

The Book of Job begins in silence. Four friends sit hunched together in the dust, grieving. For seven days and seven nights not a word is spoken. One has lost all that can be lost, has suffered beyond human limit, has only the shreds of his own life, breath enclosed in a sick, a dying, body. His friends come to mourn with him and to comfort him. There are no words adequate, there is only silence: seven days and nights of silence. "After this opened Job his mouth, and cursed his day." The curse explodes the silence, and words now break in great waves from all four men. None of them is able to stop speaking. They are compelled, obsessed, driven to find, through "saying," the Truth. Possessed and passionate, they quest, through and with language, for God, the Word. Each tries again and again to utter "the right word," one that can incarnate, can reveal His ways and words. Instead, speaking of Him and for Him, all four err. Human, tempted by death and iniquity, they sin; they fall into language. Three fall so far that they will receive God's condemnation. Job, who understands the paradox of speaking of, or even to, the Word *with* words, will fall less radically, finally securing salvation for himself and his friends by sacrificing

---

4. Robert Alter, *The Art of Biblical Poetry* (New York, 1985), 211.
5. *Ibid.*, 212. The untitled poem by Tuvia Rubner is translated by Alter, *ibid.*, 211.

language itself to the Logos.[6] Job will transform language into an altar as well as a sacrifice, offering himself, in and through his words, to the Word. But Job, too, will err. Never losing sight of the danger he places himself in, he too will misuse words. Attempting to make language fully presentational, he will try to erase the gap between sign and signified; thinking to guarantee his own presence through words, he will, instead, become only another sign to be interpreted.

Though Job longs for silence, he persists in speaking and listening. If one of them could only find the *right* words, he could return to silence: "Teach me, and I will hold my tongue. . . . How forcible are right words!" (Job 6:24–25). But the voices are impotent; words die as soon as they are spoken; nothing changes, no truth is found. There are no right words; words only create misprision, defensiveness, anger, pain. And they evaporate; words are mere sound fading with each breath, shattering against the incomprehensible Logos which remains ominously silent, locked into reticence and concealed in His great distance. The Word does not dwell with human beings. All each can do is repeat the already spoken and create a dangerous chain of repetition that is not broken until the accusatory voice of the Logos intervenes: "My wrath is kindled against thee, and against thy two friends: for ye have not spoken of me the thing that is right" (Job 42:7).

The Book of Job metaphorizes the failure of human language to reveal and embody the Truth. It dramatizes the contest between words and the all-encompassing Word: the Logos, the God who ventures His own creature, who gambles Job's very existence on the chance that the "upright man" will not fall so completely into the death of representation that he will "curse God, and die." Being, act, virtue are irrelevant; God's bet with Satan is entirely a wager over words: "Touch his bone and his flesh and he will curse thee to thy face," challenges Satan, and *his* words begin a drama entirely of words, about words that refer to the Word. The playing-out of the drama is a passionate attempt to destroy the representative nature of language, to transform mediation into immediacy, to incarnate

6. My use of *Logos* and *the Word* should not be seen as anachronistic here, since I am treating the King James translation as a Christianized English poem and since the notion depends upon an ontotheological absolute, an Ideal that "grounds" the ancient Hebrew text. Given Alter's linguistic "nexus," we are operating, even in the ancient text, within a logocentric concept of Being which makes the terms quite usable.

Truth. The words spin around four enigmatic themes: sin, death, language itself, and the Logos. Each is inseparably interlocked with the others. There is enormous tension, created by Job's desperate desire to restore God to presence by speaking the right words. This desire conflicts with his ironic knowledge that he can only use words that are precariously balanced on the edge of the linguistic abyss, the edge of the curse.

Job is a poet; he alone knows and lives on the fine line between prayer and self-condemnation. His friends retreat into representation and repetition, repeating the language of the fathers: "Inquire . . . of the former age," Bildad suggests. "Shall not they teach thee, and tell thee, and utter words out of their heart?" (Job 8:8, 10). But the received language is not enough; it is tainted with presumption, with the hubris of presuming know the unknowable and to speak the unspeakable. And it is pure sign, declaring God's absence by virtue of its claim to stand-in-place-of the Logos itself. Even as it displaces the Word, human language presumes to represent God in yet another sense: to speak in His behalf. Thus, even as it repeats, their language drifts further and further from Logos: wandering from silence to counsel, to accusation, to presumption, to self-condemnation. Each text generates another text situated one step further from the origin. Job understands the implications of this wayward drift from counseling to accusing: "Ye are forgers of lies, ye are all physicians of no value . . . Will ye speak wickedly for God? . . . Will ye accept his person? will ye contend for God?" (Job 13:4–8). The language of the fathers cannot incarnate the truth of God's Being; it can only displace it, and this is *because* it represents it. In Job, as in Plato, the representational chain may be suspended from God's side, but it suffers from the gap that is both created by interpretation and makes interpretation possible. Job's friends make themselves God's representatives (in both senses of that word) by virtue of presuming, always, to correct interpretations of His Word. They fail to allow for the possibility of misinterpretation inherent in the space between God and themselves.

Job, on the other hand, is so highly conscious of the possibility of error that he is incapable even of directing his voice toward God. The distance between them cannot be spanned by mere words; the gap can only be filled by God's presence. For Job, human words are both erroneous and futile unless they carry the very breath of God, incarnate Logos in language, participate in the Word rather than substitute for it. It is only Job's periodic reminders of this—reminders directed as much to himself as to his friends—that prevent his complete fall into misspeaking. He understands that "all the while my breath is in me, and the spirit of God is in my nostrils; my lips shall not speak wickedness, nor my tongue utter deceit" (Job 27:3–4). He avoids wickedness and deceit but is not able to avoid the representational play of language, the differential activity of the sign, the catastrophic activity which produces the gap that allows interpretation and annihilates full presence. As he desperately attempts to vocalize the truth of his being, he discovers the chaos and the violence that such an attempt at self-presentation creates. The more Job exercises the will to speak, the less authentically he is perceived by his friends. Finally, he becomes a mere text, open to each man's misinterpretation. Job learns that the sin of language, its representational function, its tendency to stand-in-place-of, not only distorts and displaces the adamantly silent Logos but also displaces, even erases, the self. The will to speak, to achieve self-presence, backlashes into self-destruction.

The situation has added complexities. It is not just that when human beings speak *of* God they risk the error of hubris, but also that when they speak *to* God they cannot be certain that they are heard: "If I had called, and he had answered me; yet would I not believe that he had hearkened unto my voice" (Job 9:16). The distance between Job and his God, the space between language and Logos, is so great at this moment that he cannot be sure even of his own perceptions; he is, unlike his friends, too aware of the dangers of interpretation. And this awareness intensifies as he experiences the misreadings and misspeakings of his friends. Doubt becomes conviction: "I cry out of wrong, but I am not heard: I cry aloud, but there is no judgment" (Job 19:7). Therefore, even against the urgings of his friends, Job steadfastly refuses to pray. "I would seek unto God, and unto God would I commit my cause," Eliphaz counsels. But Job is immobilized by his afflictions, concrete representations of God's absence. He can only reply, "My words are swallowed up. For the arrows of the Almighty are within me, the poison whereof drinketh up my spirit" (Job 6:3–4). And later Eliphaz, having drifted from counsel to accusation, retaliates, "Thou . . . restrainest prayer before God. For thy mouth uttereth thine iniquity" (Job 15:4–5).

Job's explanation for his refusal to pray and Eliphaz's accusation present the most difficult dilemma of human language in a logocentric universe. Because he has lost the *ruah* (the "spirit" or "breath" of God), because he is without "inspiration," Job cannot be sure that all language is *not* self-condemnation. With the

"spirit of God in his nostrils" displaced by the "poison" of his afflictions, he cannot be sure that he can speak "the thing that is right."
There is no question of his desire to speak with God, the question is
how to *secure* language, how to make it genuine prayer, how to
keep it from spinning away from its origin into the sin of representation. God's immediate presence is necessary to the integrity of
language, and Job feels he has been denied that. "Surely I would
speak to the Almighty, and I desire to reason with God," he insists.
"O that one might plead for a man with God, as a man pleadeth for
his neighbor" (Job 13:3, 16:21). But Job has seen language fail
even with his neighbor and has felt the denial of even the self-
proximity that speech promises. How can he expect to share the
site of "wisdom" and "understanding" with the far-distant God?
The awful paradox is that human beings can come into God's presence only through language in which God is already present, only
through inspiration and incarnation. Job projects imagined conver-
sations with God (Job 23:1–7, 10:2), but he dares not use ordinary
language to traverse the distance between them. Having lost the
breath of God, he cannot use "poisoned" speech to seek His presence. "Oh that I knew where I might find him!" Job cries. "I would
order my cause before him, and fill my mouth with arguments. I
would know the words which he would answer me, and understand what he would say unto me" (Job 23:3–5). But if words do
not carry the breath of God, "whence then cometh wisdom? and
where is the place of understanding?" (Job 28:20). In order to find
the Logos, he must already contain the Logos. Conversation is not
possible in a language that creates space rather than proximity, that
declares the absence of the Word because it is merely a sign of the
Word. There is no way to secure the passage of Truth across the
abyss between the thing–itself and that which represents it. The
"place of understanding" is the site where humanity and God are in
proximity, where there is no gap to produce the need for interpretation, a place of silence.

Also crucial to Job's refusal to pray is his realization of a further
paradox: though language does not necessarily contain the Logos,
it is always/already contained *in* the Creative Word. To speak to the
Word is a kind of logical absurdity, a tautology. Human language is
both part of the Logos and other than the Logos. Such an ambiguous situation can give rise to enormous anxiety. Speaking with
or of God may, inevitably, be to contest with Him. Given this,
"who will say unto him, What doest thou? . . . How . . . shall
I answer him and choose out my words to reason with him?"

(Job 9:12–14). How can one "choose out words to reason" with a God who already knows all reasons, envelops all words? Job has known the danger all along: "If I justify myself, mine own mouth shall condemn me. . . . I know it is so of a truth: but how should man be just with God? If he will contend with him he cannot answer him one of a thousand" (Job 9:20, 2–3). How can one risk colloquy if to speak with the Word is to contend with Him? Unless one can discover the right words, prayer lies perilously close to curse. Job knows his actions have been "upright," but because God has withdrawn, he can no longer be sure that his tongue is free of iniquity. As a result, Job "holdeth fast his integrity" by avoiding prayer altogether; he evades fulfillment of Satan's prophecy that he will curse God to His face by avoiding the conversation he so deeply desires.

The irony here, of course, is that Job has initiated this entire drama precisely *by* cursing. However, it is important to note that he curses not God but his own existence. Even more significantly, he perceives his existence in overtly linguistic terms. Until the moment of his affliction, Job's identity has been defined primarily by his ability to speak the "right words." He has been the "wise counselor" who "hast instructed many" and "strengthened the feeble" with his speech (Job 4:3, 4). Life for Job has been a matter of the exchange of voices and, understandably, death is figured by him as the absence of speech. The figurative structure of his opening "curse" is revealing. He breaks silence only to speak of his longing *for* silence: the absolute silence of death. He yearns for release not from his trials, but from the *voices* of this world. He pleads for the "solitary" night that lets "no joyful voice come therein" and for the grave where "now should I have lain still and been quiet," among the other "kings and counsellors" who "hear not the voice of the oppressor" (Job 3:1–18). Job's metaphors—his frequent references to existence as the unquenchable noise of speech and to death as freedom from that noise—turn his curse, at least in this sense, into a curse against language itself.

The key problem, then, is why Job breaks silence at all. Why speak only to plead for silence? Why initiate a dialogue he knows must fail? Job's own explanation suffices:

> As the cloud is consumed and vanisheth away:
> so he that goeth down to the grave shall
> come up no more. . . .
>   Therefore I will not refrain
> my mouth; I will speak in the anguish of my

spirit; I will complain in the bitterness of
my soul.

(Job 7:9–11)

Though he longs for death because it is the absence of language, for
Job the *fact* of death generates language. It is because human beings
"vanish" that they must utter their "anguish." Human beings risk
words because they are mortal. At this moment in the text, "the
essential relation between death and language flashes up before us,
but remains still unthought."[7] Job will think through that relationship from several perspectives as the dialogue continues. As the discussion spins itself out, as the words begin to circle and recircle each
other, as it becomes clear that their language only interprets, represents, and condemns, all four of the men begin to long for silence.
The futility of words does not relieve anguish but creates it, and the
cry becomes "How long!" How long must words burst forth and
die away with no effect except to generate more words? "How long
wilt thou speak these things?" Bildad cries. "How long shall the
words of thy mouth be like a strong wind?" (Job 8:2). "How long
will it be ere ye make an end of words?" (Job 18:2). And, against
the web of words that can neither present truth nor reveal God, Job
strikes back: "How long will ye vex my soul and break me in pieces
with words?" (Job 19:2). Speech has become a terrifyingly divisive
weapon, a violence by which one man dismembers another. Job's
metaphor is apt: language now fractures utterly, separates self from
word as well as other. He has cursed language, and now language
has become a curse against the speaker himself. Job's cry surges up
out of a new understanding that death is not just a refuge from
words but can occur *within* language as well. One speaks because
one dies and, ironically, dies within one's own speech.

This dark paradox wrings from Job the impassioned "How
long . . . !" In a negative paraphrase of Job's first speech, with its
moving plea for the solitary night and the silent grave, Bildad reminds Job that such solitary silence is the final horror for the one
who misspeaks: "his own counsel shall cast him down. . . . The
snare is laid for him in the ground. . . . His remembrance shall
perish from earth, and he shall have no name in the street" (Job
18:7–17). Death, the snare laid in the ground, can erase even the
one word that seems to fully present the self: the proper name. The
silence that offers refuge is also the silence that annihilates abso-

7. Heidegger, *On the Way to Language,* 108.

lutely. Spoken language leaves no traces. Piling metaphor upon metaphor, Bildad constructs an image of death that denies existence so utterly that it is as if the name has never been. And the notion of such total nonbeing evokes from Job his only plea for pity: "Have pity upon me, have pity upon me, O ye my friends. . . . Oh that my words were now written . . . that they were graven . . . in the rock forever!" (Job 19:21–24). From the abyss of his agon with spoken language, Job cries out for writing, for the inscription of himself into the very rock of the world: for an epitaph.

Job's outburst is motivated by a need to restore permanence to words, to defeat the evanescence of a language that evaporates with the breath of the speaker. Words "graven . . . in the rock forever" unite with God's own creation, exist as long as His work exists. But the notion of engraving words in rock is far more complex than this. Such an inscription transforms world into tomb, a "tomb" that mediates between the mortal living and the immortal dead. It proclaims both the death in this world and the life beyond. Thus inscription, for Job, is an affirmation of absence in the Heideggerean sense; as a "no-longer" that is also a "not-yet." It affirms the absence that is "not nothing," but is, rather "precisely the presence, which must first be appropriated, of the hidden fulness and wealth of what has been and what, thus gathered, is presencing of the divine. . . . This no-longer is, in itself, a not-yet of the veiled arrival of its inexhaustible nature" (*PLT,* 184). "Oh that my words were written!" cries Job.

> For I know that my redeemer liveth, and that
> he shall stand at the latter day upon the earth:
> And though after my skin worms destroy this body,
> yet in my flesh shall I see God.
>
> (Job 19:25–26)

The "for I know" is particularly important here. Job's belief in the imminent "presencing of the divine," in the "not-yet of the veiled arrival of its inexhaustible nature," is the generating force behind his outcry. His phrasing, the ambiguity of "for," implies both a causal and a complementary relationship between his desire to write and the promise of return, *parousia,* the reappropriation of presence. He would write to secure his words until the "latter day" when the return of the Logos can secure them. Writing supplements, compensates for the failure of speech. At the same time, he would write because the act itself complements the radical structure, the 'truth', of his existential situation: his experiencing of the

absence which is both a "no-longer" and a "not-yet" of presence
(both his own and that of the Logos). The epitaphic gesture Job
wants to make is grounded in the idea that the Logos haunts His
own "writing," this Book of the World, that God's presence is reappropriated by His creation in the same manner that writing appears to reappropriate the presence of its author. Logos haunts the
world much as the voice of the dead haunts a speaking monument.
In other words, the act of writing is analogous to God's inscription
of Himself into the world and is, therefore, indirectly validated by
Him. The *act* of inscription is of utmost significance; it represents
God's own gesture in a way that seems forbidden to speech. It acknowledges absence and appropriates presence in a single gesture.
Writing, in this situation, seems not to be dependent on the "right
word" in the same manner that speech is. It is not so much a matter
of right words as of "right act." Indeed, it does not seem important
to Job which of his words should be inscribed. Whatever the words,
the gesture itself proclaims the haunting truth: the truth of an absence from "here," a presence "there," and the promise of return.

It is clear that, for Job, inscription promises a proximity with
truth that speech cannot give. Not only would Job's writing be validated by the promised return of the Logos, but also it would literally be grounded in the Word of the World. Job is suggesting an
epitaph and also a palimpsest: his words written over the surface of
God's. This "double writing" would secure the 'truth' of his own
presence as congruent with God's, in a shared space and time. Such
writing would seem to erase the interpretive gap. His language
would not displace the Word but rather be revealed in and by it.
Writing in the rock would, at last, provide Job with a silent site for
language, a "place of wisdom and understanding." The engraving
would seem a visual symbol of the possibility that human language
can be contained within and sustained by the Creative Word rather
than be imprisoned by and in contention with it.

Yet the promise of inscription demands a price, the highest imag-
inable. The implication that Job's death is integrated with, even necessary to, the inscription is entirely appropriate—no inscription can
be free of such suffering. In a world with Logos at the center, Derrida has said, "Writing is the anguish of the Hebraic *ruah* [wind,
spirit, breath] experienced in solitude by human responsibility." It
is "anguish" because, unlike God, humans must decide "whether
engraving preserves or betrays speech" (*WD,* 9). Job's choice of
preservation is enabled by his belief in the impending return of

Logos; but it is important that the choice occurs only as a result of his experience: the agonizing revelation that speech itself is always betrayal, that speech exiles both truth and self. The exile seems more radical than that imposed by inscription since it denies even the tenuous possibilities that "haunting" provides.

But the inevitable "anguish" of writing cannot be completely mitigated by the absence-that-is-not-nothing. The act of writing inherently exiles the full presence of the author from his or her own creation, much as the Logos is exiled from *His* inscription, the Book of the World. To write is both to suffer the pain of withdrawal and to create an overwhelming desire to take one's words back into oneself. In his desire to repeat God's act, Job risks the anguish God must have experienced in His withdrawal from His world:

> the anguish of a breath that cuts itself off in order to re-enter itself, to aspirate itself and to return to its original source. Because to speak is to know that thought *must* become alien to itself in order to be pronounced and to appear. It wishes then to take itself back by offering itself. This is why one senses the gesture of withdrawal, of retaking possession of the exhaled word, beneath the language of the authentic writer, the writer who wishes to maintain the greatest proximity to the origin of his act. This too is inspiration. (*WD*, 303)

Denied God's breath as inspiration, Job turns to his own. This turn to writing also occurs because his failed attempt to 'voice' truth, to 'voice himself', has made it clear that "thought must become alien to itself in order to be pronounced" and that this happens in a manner which erases the self even as it speaks. Having lost the *ruah*, lost self-presence in speech, he intuitively cries out for a gesture that is essentially sacrificial. Job is willing to exchange life for an epitaph because his thought "wishes to take itself back by offering itself." In this case, "dying" into language seems to offer the reintegration of truth and word. In addition, there is surely some implication, in Job 19:23–27, that the inscription of his words into God's Book promises restoration, promises that his thought will be returned to him at "the latter day" as certainly as that the "skin worms destroy" will once again be flesh. In this moment, Job is willing to risk exile from his own words, to risk exile through death from God's world, to sacrifice himself completely to language as pure sign. The risk is possible only because he perceives that sign, ultimately, as God's own; his inscription would be merely one more in God's Book, awaiting the affirmation of God's full presence. He can surrender to sign only because he perceives it as achieving proximity, perhaps even unity, with its source, God's Word as World, and especially because at the latter day that sign will be "full," that is, beyond interpretation.

Such a 'sign' is no longer a matter of representation but of incarnation. Writing in the rock seems to incarnate human language in and through the incarnated Word we perceive as World and to secure the reincarnation of truth at the latter day. The notion is oxymoronic, of course: the incarnation of truth cannot be a sign at all, but is rather the transparent embodiment of the "thing-itself." "This too is inspiration," Derrida has said in an apt metaphoric pun on "inhalation," which implies the desire to reembody one's thought in oneself. But inspiration, whether it be Judeo-Christian, classical-platonic, or this intricate inhaling of one's own breath, requires a logocentric universe, a belief that one can achieve proximity with words and the Word, that language can embody truth just as the world embodies the Word of God: "And God *said,* Let there be light: and there *was* light." Even so, the notion is always/already threatened. As Elihu will teach Job and his friends, even the haunting penetration of God into His world will not erase the need for interpretation. The notion of incarnation never completely escapes the shadow of representation.

Job's longing to write remains an unfulfilled desire. He is immediately thrust back into the world of inadequate speech, and the voices cointinue to reverberate off, and against, one another until they cease in futility and exhaustion. Unexpectedly, out of the darkness, emerges the voice of a stranger: Elihu, the son of Barachel. Elihu condemns the speech of all four men—Job's because "he justified himself rather than God" and the friends' "because they had found no answer" (Job 3:2–3). It is Job who is most violently condemned, and self-justification (self-representation) is the least of his crimes. The fact that he has chosen to break silence, to speak at all, is his real offense. "He multiplieth words without knowledge," Elihu accuses, and repeats the accusation "he *multiplieth* words" (Job 34:37; 35:16). Job "breeds" language; words generate words. He is accused of a kind of linguistic parthenogenesis in which his words are merely a perverted source of yet more words. His language has not been properly "fertilized," or penetrated by inspiration. Elihu identifies the "inhalation/inspiration" complex underlying Job's call for writing as already inherent in his speech and labels it "sin." Multiplying words without the "paternity" of the Logos calls for total condemnation. Job's sin is identified: it is the sin of speech, empty representation and interpretation:

> Job hath spoken without knowledge
> and his words were without wisdom.
>   My desire is that Job may be tried unto
> the end because of his answers for wicked men.
>   (Job 34:35–36)

The issue here is overtly the question of representation versus inspiration. In contrast to the others, Elihu justifies his own speech by asserting that he exhales the very breath of God, that he incarnates the Logos. With complete confidence, he proclaims that "there is a spirit in man: and the inspiration of the Almighty giveth them understanding" (Job 32:8). This "spirit" is not available to all— "great men are not always wise" (Job 32:9)—but, Elihu asserts,

> My words shall be of the uprightness of my
> heart: and my lips shall utter knowledge clearly.
>   The spirit of God hath made me, and the
> breath of the Almighty hath given me life. . . .
>   Behold, I am according to thy
> wish in God's stead.
>   (Job 33:3–6)

Elihu's words would seem to be an act of unforgivable hubris. Indeed, he openly states what has remained a hidden assumption in the speech of Job's three friends: he speaks "in God's stead." But there is a crucial difference. Elihu does not present himself as God's representative; he presents himself as the *vehicle* of the Logos, as pure medium. His words are neither simple interpretation nor a displacement of the Word. He clearly understands himself to be chosen, to be the "one among a thousand" who is *both* "interpreter" and "messenger." These are those who "ransom" humanity from the hell of misinterpretation, who "shew unto man his uprightness" (Job 33:23–24). The doubleness of their function is significant; as interpreter/messenger ("angel" in some translations), such a figure inevitably speaks "the right word." He utters God's own "interpretation." The gap between language and Logos is closed. The figure is, of course, that of the poet/priest, and as such, Elihu *translates* the Word into words. In a certain sense, he also translates the Word into flesh. For these who incarnate the breath of God also enable incarnation. If a man be ransomed by the Word through His messenger/interpreter, then "his flesh shall be fresher than a child's: he shall return to the days of his youth" (Job 33:25).

Elihu instructs Job in the way to God, and his instructions validate Job's intuitive desire to inscribe himself into the rock of God's world. For Elihu insists that only by reading the Creation can human beings find the place of wisdom and understanding. "Hearken unto this, O Job: stand still and consider the wondrous works of God" (Job 37:14). Such attention will reveal God's own voice:

> Hear attentively the noise of his voice,
> and the sound that goeth out of his mouth.
> He directeth it under the whole heaven,
> and his lightning unto the ends of the earth.
> After it a voice roareth: he thundereth
> with the voice of his excellency; and he will
> not stay them when his voice is heard.
>   (Job 37:2–4)

Yet even according to Elihu, there is little chance of escaping the dangers of representation and interpretation. Only the "one among a thousand" does so. For most, "God speaketh once, yea twice, yet man perceiveth it not" (Job 33:14). Most "may be tried unto the end" for speaking misinterpretations to other "wicked men" who inevitably misinterpret. More importantly, the figure of Elihu in no way alleviates Job's predicament; there is no escape from the paradoxes of logocentrism. Job's inability to span the distance between himself and God, his understanding that one cannot speak to the Logos unless one is already inspired, already contains the Word, is clear. Elihu makes it equally clear that neither can one *understand* the Word unless it is already "understood" within. "Man perceiveth it not" unless he is already "full" of God's breath, His wisdom. One must be a messenger to be an interpreter; one must be a poet/priest.

It is difficult, in reading the Book of Job, not to wonder what might have happened if God had not immediately validated both Elihu's words and his function. Only God's appearance prevents the words falling into the very drift of language Elihu has condemned. The figure remains unproblematic only because of the "presencing of the divine," because of the "veiled arrival of its inexhaustible nature." The figure is justified much as Job would have had his inscription secured: by the unmediated presence of the Logos, a presence that is revealed, as Elihu had promised, in the Book of the World. "We cannot order our speech by reason of darkness," Elihu says (Job 37:19). "Consider the wondrous works of God" (Job 37:14).

> Then the Lord answered Job out of
> the whirlwind, and said,
>   Who is this that darkeneth counsel
> by words without knowledge?
>   (Job 38:1–2)

The voice of God, repeating Elihu's words and rising, literally, out of one of His wondrous works, brings the erratic wandering of words to rest. Elihu has spoken the "right words," as interpreter/ messenger, poet/priest. And the accusatory voice unveils, completely, Job's predicament. Accusing Job of "words without knowledge" in one breath, God demands speech with the next: "Gird up now thy loins like a man; for I will demand of thee, and answer thou me" (Job 38:3). "Answer thou me": God demands the impossible. Man must answer the unanswerable, speak the unspeakable, must "utter words without knowledge"—and must *not*. The Word demands words which must contain the Word. Thus God inhales; this too is inspiration.

The Theophany consists of question after question, all rhetorical. The tautological structure of the rhetorical question is the culminating symbol of Job's dilemma with language. The answer is contained within the question itself; the question is the assertion. In other words, the answers are congruent with the questions, absolute proximity is achieved, and all possible response is silenced by the voice of the Questioner. The Word envelops all words. In spite of this, God demands an answer. Job's response seems profoundly appropriate: "Behold, I am vile; what shall I answer thee? I will lay mine hand upon my mouth" (Job 40:4). Once again, Job seeks silence. Having longed for the presence of Logos, cried out for colloquy with God, he learns that full presence evokes only one possible response—"I will lay mine hand upon my mouth." In the presence of the Logos, one sacrifices language completely. But God will not accept such a sacrifice. He repeats His command: "Gird up thy loins now like a man: I will demand of thee, and declare thou unto me" (Job 40:7). Under this enormous pressure, Job at last stumbles upon the right words: "I uttered that I understood not; things too wonderful for me, which I knew not. . . . Wherefore I abhor myself, and repent in dust and ashes" (Job 42:3–6). Confession is the sacrifice of self through language, here particularly moving since the sacrifice through language is of the self *as* language. Silence is not enough; words must be sacrificed through words. And God accepts, turning His wrath now against the others: "For ye have not

spoken of me the thing that is right, as my servant Job hath" (Job
42:7). Certainly the reference is to Job's final statement, to his confession of failed utterance. The sacrifice of language to Logos transforms Job into the poet/priest who must intercede for his friends.
Job's speech is, at last, prayer. The entire book has affirmed that the
metamorphosis of discourse into prayer cannot occur through any
merely human will-to-speak. The transformation occurs only if
language is first surrendered to God, inhaled by Him along with
the smoke of burnt offerings, before it can be restored to man as
God's own breath. The paradox continues to hold: one must be inspired, must voice the presence of God, if one is to span the distance
between man and the absent God. In the Book of Job, God closes
the gap between Logos and language by presenting *Himself*. Without the benefit of such self-presencing, what is to ensure the transformation of representation into presentation, the transformation
of speech into prayer? How is one to know if one is, indeed, poet/
priest? How is one to build an altar of words if one cannot be sure
of inspiration?

THE VOICE THAT KEEPS SILENCE AND THE
PEAL OF STILLNESS

That oneness, as the integral globe of being encircles all pure forces of what is, by circling through all beings, infinitely unbounding them. All this be-comes present when the balance passes over. . . . If such a passing comes to pass at all, it occurs in the precinct of the balance. The element of the bal-ance is the venture, the Being of beings. We have thought of language spe-cifically as its precinct.

—Martin Heidegger, "What Are Poets For?"

Language, and a finite language, excludes totalization. This field is in fact that of freeplay, *that is to say, a field permits these infinite substitu-tions. . . . This field permits these infinite substitutions only because it is finite, that is to say, because instead of being an inexhaustible field, as in the classical hypothesis, instead of being too large, there is something miss-ing from it: a center which arrests and founds the freeplay of substitutions.*

—Jacques Derrida, "Structure, Sign and Play"

The questions raised by Shelley's work or by the Book of Job are both metaphysical and theological. It is, perhaps, more appropriate to refer to them in Heidegger's phrasing, as "ontotheological." Be-neath the problems introduced by the notions of "inspiration" and "representation" is the necessity of establishing a link between sepa-rate orders of being—orders that are always/already interdependent by virtue of the fact that they delineate and explicate each other. These orders, nevertheless, appear as irrevocably divorced. The rift between Logos and language is analogous to the lacuna between transcendence and immanence, divine and human, the eternal and the mutable, the immortal and the mortal, even between the soul and the body. For the Western mind, no single term in these cou-plings can be fully understood or "known" in the absence of the other. Furthermore, the distinction between modes of being *must* be maintained if either mode is to appear at all. There must be a borderline, a threshold, which marks their difference. At the same time the wound between Being and beings often appears as a ter-rifying void, an abyss of nothingness which threatens absolute an-nihilation unless it can be spanned. Facing this awful void can create a vertigo as fearful as Milton's Satan must have felt, when he leaped from Heaven into that "spacious Gap disclosed / Into the wasteful Deep." A doubleness operates within this "double" notion of existence, then: the boundary must be sustained; and though it cannot heal the wound, the mind must "bridge" the gap.

I have said that Job's deepest desire is to create that "bridge" out of language. He wishes, as Herbert does, to transform words into "reversed thunder," an "Engine against th' Almighty, sinners towre" ("Prayer I").[1] Such a gesture is to throw language toward, into, and against a most awesome silence. The transcendent, the Ideal, the All, the Almighty are (is) always, in *essence,* silent. Totality implies that which cannot be articulated, and articulation implies a "something more" that makes utterance seem to be a fragmentation. Iteration leaves a hidden residue, which Derrida would call "excess" and Heidegger would call the "unconcealed."

Derrida has examined at length the relation between the idea of totality and language as the desire for speech without differance and as "the silence of self-relationship."[2] Such silence, for Derrida, must be seen as a fictive notion, as the illusion of full presence which voice pretends to and Logocentric speech always assumes. From his perspective, this fiction evokes a "unity" which is also the nothingness of death: "The infinite vocation of full presence . . . which could only be the unity of the concept logos and consciousness in a voice without *differance.* . . . *A voice without differance, a voice without writing, is at once absolutely alive and absolutely dead.*" This "voice without *differance*" is meant to evoke the traditional concepts of God and Logos, and it is, for Derrida, the "voice that keeps silence" within the "tomb" of the sign. Silence as full presence, as center or totality, is seen as being the silence of radical absence, of a "nothingness." According to Derrida, the "play" of language as "differance," "trace," "supplementarity," reveals *in itself* the fictive nature of presence, the All, the silent center *which never was* until brought into 'being' by the 'structuring' of the linguistic activity. Language cannot incarnate an origin except as a "pyramidal silence" from which it always "differs" and with which it "defers"

1. *The Works of George Herbert,* ed. F. E. Hutchinson (Oxford, 1945). I have omitted page references since Hutchinson's edition has an efficient alphabetical table of contents. All subsequent references to Herbert are to this edition.

2. The concept is implicit throughout *WD* and is assumed in *OG,* but Derrida's most thorough analysis is to be found in *SP,* chap. 6, "The Voice That Keeps Silence."

contact. This idea of sign as pyramid, which Derrida derives from Hegel, determines language as purely representational, as displacement and substitution, as "a detour, a respite, a delay, a reserve, a representation . . . a detour that suspends the accomplishment or fulfillment of 'desire' or 'will', or carries desire or will out in a way that annuls or tempers their effect" (*SP*, 102, 133, 136). The sign which speech pretends is presentational is, rather, like the *a* in *differance*: "it remains silent, secret and discreet, like a tomb. It is a tomb that (provided one knows how to decipher its legend) is not far from signaling the death of the king" (*SP*, 132). The king whose death is signaled is "the authority of presence" which may be variously read as "center," "God," "transcendentality," even as "man," or "consciousness." The center, Derrida has noted, is "interdicted." It is both "forbidden" and "speechless" and it does not originate language but is created *by* language; it is merely a "function." The silent center is the product of desire, it is "contradictorily coherent. And, as always, coherence in contradiction expresses the force of a desire." Logos is silent for Derrida not because it is folded into itself but because it is a linguistically constituted "central presence which *was never itself*, which has always/already been transported outside itself in its surrogate. The surrogate does not substitute itself for anything which has pre-existed it."[3] Derrida's metaphor of sign as pyramid might more properly be "sign as cenotaph," since even a pyramid assumes the body of the king at its center. Nevertheless, his point is that the sign always announces the silence of a radical absence, a silence which is "not anything."

The All, under these circumstances, is unthinkable, "totalization no longer has any meaning," language always/already "supplements."[4] And the supplementarity of the sign evokes the lack that bespeaks death and the grave. The path of signification "leads from this night pit, silent as death and resonating with all the powers of the voice which it holds in reserve, to a pyramid. . . . there composing the stature and status of the sign. And there, the natural source and the historical construction both, though differently, remain silent."[5]

3. For Derrida's most specific explication of presence in these terms, see Jacques Derrida, "Structure, Sign, and Play in the Discourse of the Human Sciences," in *The Structuralist Controversy: The Languages of Criticism and the Sciences of Man,* ed. Richard Macksey and Eugenio Donato (Baltimore, 1970), 248–49.
4. Derrida, "Structure, Sign and Play," 260.
5. Derrida, "The Pit and The Pyramid," in *MP*, 77.

In his deconstruction of the pyramid as the most appropriate figure for representation, sign, and art itself, Derrida reads Hegel's notion of 'soul' as the 'desire' which he, himself, sees as ultimately the
hunger for self-presence. This unfulfilled "wish-to-say" is the absence at the heart of the pyramid Hegel constructs as a body full of
the soul of meaning. The pyramid as representation can never be
grounded in the 'soul' it supposedly contains since that "content" is
itself an infinitely regressive "representation of a representation."
The pyramid can never be opened to a core. Rather, one will forever
unfold pyramid within pyramid. One circles back from pyramid to
bottomless pit, to the grave which always/already announced both
the pyramid it generated and the nature of the nothingness at its
"center." Hegel, according to Derrida, understands the tomb as a
double figure:

> The tomb is the life of the body as the sign of death, the body as the
> other of the soul the other of the animate psyche, of the living breath.
> But the tomb also shelters, maintains in reserve, capitalizes on life by
> marking that life continues elsewhere. . . . Thus the tomb also shelters
> life from death. It *warns* the soul of possible death, warns (of) death of
> the soul, turns away (from) death. This double warning function be-
> longs to the funerary monument.
>
> The sign—the monument-of-life-in-death, the monument-of-death-in-
> life, the sepulchre of a soul or of an embalmed proper body, the height
> conserving in its depth the hegemony of the soul, resisting time, the
> hard text of stones covered with inscription—is the pyramid (*MP*, 82).

For Derrida, the dialectic, the conservation, the double announcement of the tomb, in the sense that it bespeaks presence, is literally
the wish fulfillment of the pure desire for self-presence that generates the will-to-speak. The illusion inevitably succumbs to the representation it actually is—that is "the detour that suspends the accomplishment or fulfillment of 'desire' or 'will'." The will-to-speak
generates its Logos as an act of self-deception; it promises self-
presence in an act that *evades* death within a notion that can only be
understood as *containing* death. The modern mind has translated
this wish-to-say as "God": "God is the name and the element of
that which makes possible an absolutely pure and absolutely self-
present self-knowledge. From Descartes to Hegel . . . God's infinite understanding is the other name for Logos as self-presence
(*OG*, 98). The will-to-speak, which Derrida here names "God,"
can also be named "silence." It is the paradoxical silence of the All,
of "the infinite vocation of full-presence . . . which could only be

the unity of the concept logos, and consciousness in a voice without *differance*. . . . *A voice without differance is at once absolutely alive and absolutely dead.*" It is, then, the "voice that *keeps* silence" (in the double sense of "keeps"). Underneath all the 'noise' in the Derridean 'play' of trace, differance, errance, and representations of representations, lies the silence of the empty pit, which generates the pyramid of the sign. Representation can be seen as an avoidance of this silence, a detour around the grave, but it always implicates that pit within itself and thereby remains threatened by the death it would evade.

As long as we remain within the space of Derridean thought, the sign must be seen as substitution, as "standing-in-place-of"; substitution is always of one sign for another, the echo of an echo, in a sort of infinite regression. If we move from the Derridean 'field' to the Heideggerean 'open', however, the concept of sign changes and silence is not perceived as the *hollow* echo of the desire for self-presence. For Heidegger, poetic language does not attempt to displace absence but rather exposes presence *because* it exposes absence. It echoes the "fulness" of the silence which it breaks and marks.

Derrida's accusation that Heidegger "valorizes" presence is, I think, indisputable. However, it's important to remember that there is no such thing as simple or full presence in Heidegger's thought; presence is always coupled with absence. He understands absence as "concealment," as the "unrevealed," and it always permeates presence, the "unconcealed." It is, in fact, part of the "essence" of presence as unconcealment, *aletheia,* or truth: "Concealment preserves what is most proper to *aletheia* as its own. Considered with respect to disclosedness, concealment is then undisclosedness and accordingly the untruth that is most proper to the essence of truth. . . . [This nonessence of truth] remains always in its own way essential to the essence and never becomes inessential in the sense of irrelevant."[6] In his discussion of poetry as truth, the philosopher reiterates this basic structure, insisting that the "lighting" of presence "keeps to this curious opposition of presencing in that it always withholds itself at the same time in a concealedness. The lighting in which beings stand is in itself at the same time concealment" ("Origin," 175).

Clearly, the signifying activity of language is not a matter of representation for Heidegger except in the mundane, inauthentic

6. Heidegger, "On the Essence of Truth," in *Basic Writings,* 132–33.

"fallen" language which he names "idle talk." [7] The language to which the rest of this discussion refers is not this everyday language of "utilization" but that of "saying," or "poetizing"—that language which he insists is not a matter of speech or utterance. [8] When Heidegger says that Language is the House of Being, that house should also be named the House of Silence. For Language is the great silence out of which "saying" comes and wherein they dwell together. In other words, it links two modes of being. Heidegger conceives silence as the "all" out of which human language is "given"; it grounds the possibility of utterance. "Silence" is absolute, unfractured "sound"; it is full potential. It is Language, a kind of 'logos'. Fully aware of the analogies between his notion of silence and the traditional 'Logos', Heidegger employs a vocabulary specifically *not* referential to a deity, yet consciously ontotheological:

> *Language speaks as the peal of stillness.* . . . The peal of stillness is not anything human. But on the contrary, the human is indeed in its nature *given to* speech. . . . What has thus taken place, human being, has been brought into its own by language, the peal of stillness . . . language *needs and uses* the speaking of mortals in order to sound as the peal of stillness for the hearing of mortals. Only as men belong within the peal of stillness are mortals able to speak in *their own* way in sounds. . . . Any uttering, whether in speech or writing, breaks the stillness. How does the broken stillness come to sound in words? How does the broken stillness shape the mortal speech that sounds in verses and sentences? (*PLT*, 207–208).

The questions that Heidegger asks and the repetition of "sound in" imply that language does not represent but incarnates bits and pieces of the shattered whole. Utterance is a violent rending of the "peal of stillness," but it is a necessary violence; stillness can be understood as a peal only because it does "come to sound in words." (For the reader unfamiliar with Heidegger, I would like to point out that he puns as habitually as Derrida does, and a phrase like "come to sound" should be understood as to approach, come *toward* sound, as well as to happen in sound.) Silence is not the absence of sound, as his carefully chosen metaphors insist, but the undisturbed source of sound. The peal of stillness inhabits utterance, makes it possible, and is revealed through and in it. It is revealed only because it has

---

7. Heidegger, *Being and Time,* 211–14.
8. Heidegger, "Language," in *PLT,* 189–210. See also the "Letter on Humanism" in *Basic Writings,* where he says, "Language is *not* the utterance of an organism; nor is it the expression of a living thing" (206).

been violated, and it is never revealed in its wholeness. Yet, Language "needs and uses the speaking of mortals," and the violence here is to be understood within the context of a sacramental gesture. The breaking of stillness is coupled with a benign openness established by a sacrifice that involves the surrender of silence by the Word and the surrender of self to silent Language, by humans *in* their "languaging." Recognizing the silence that is pure sound and the nothingness that is pure Being means that human beings must sacrifice themselves to "dread" and death. They must recognize their own finitude in terms of the infinite. Nevertheless,

> in sacrifice there is expressed that hidden *thanking* which alone does homage to the grace wherewith Being has endowed the nature of man. . . . Original thanking is the echo of Being's favour wherein it clears a space for itself and causes the unique occurrence: that what is—is. This echo is man's answer to the Word of the soundless voice of Being. The speechless answer of his thanking through sacrifice is the source of the human word, which is the prime cause of language as the enunciation of the Word in words. Were there not an occasional thanking in the heart of historical man he could never attain the thinking . . . which originally thinks the thought of Being. . . . Obedient to the voice of Being, thought seeks the Word through which the truth of Being may be expressed.[9]

It is important to note that "echo" here is metaphorized as the echo of Being, a Word so full that it *appears* as "Silence" and "Nothing," but this is not the hollow resonance of the tomb of representation. For Heidegger, "Silence" and "Nothing" signify the absolute fullness of the All.[10]

Significantly, we are still in a situation that requires language as

9. Heidegger, "What Is Metaphysics?," in *Existence and Being,* ed. Werner Brock (London, 1949), 389–90.

10. For Heidegger's own defense of "Nothing" as a rejection of nihilism and as a grounding of human being, see "What Is Metaphysics?" This essay was often read as nihilistic, despite such direct statements as: "Pure Being and pure Nothing are thus one and the same. This proposition of Hegel's is correct." Heidegger added a postscript in 1943: "It would be premature . . . to adopt the facile explanation that Nothing is merely the nugatory, equating it with the nonexistent. . . . We should, rather, equip ourselves and make ready for one thing only: to experience in Nothing the vastness of that which *gives every being the warrant to be*" (384). The similarity between this sense of 'nothing' as 'totality' and silence as "the peal of stillness" is striking. The postscript makes the comparison overt, since the analysis of "Nothing" moves directly into a discussion of Word as "the soundless voice of Being" and of Language as the "enunciation of the Word in word" (389).

the crucial link between separate orders of being, which it delineates by the very act of joining them. That Heidegger should turn
to sacrifice as the primary metaphor is perfectly appropriate, for
sacrifice is a universal gesture for opening the path between infinite
and finite.[11] Sacrifice localizes and energizes the pathway between
worlds, even as it validates the differences that allow both to appear.
Furthermore, in the moment of sacrifice it is impossible to determine whether divinity, consecrated site, or human gesture occurs
"first." Does altar "represent" human or divine? Is the god present
before the altar, or does the altar bring the god to presence? Neither
the direction nor temporal sequence of the energy involved in sacrifice can be located precisely in terms of "before" or "after." Note
that the path is cut by "thanking"—*i.e.,* human language—but that
it is always/already an "echo" of Being, *i.e.,* Word. The Word
would, therefore, seem to be prior to language. But priority is not
so easily established in Heidegger's thought: it is only *in* language
that the Word "clears a space for itself," comes into being. Without
thanking, the Word cannot be known as "the soundless voice of
being." Without this sacrifice, which is also the dread of knowing
death, neither Logos nor language 'are'. At the same time, without
the Word and words, the thanking cannot happen, cannot open the
clearing necessary for the being of Logos and language. Temporal
cause and effect are undecidable at this juncture, and the question of
whether language *is* 'representation' is, as a result, unaskable. The
sign, the act of signification, is a "gathering" for Heidegger; it cannot be seen as displacement or substitution.

Nevertheless, Heidegger's thought, like Derrida's, depends on a
structure of difference. The metaphorical "differences" between
them reveal the differences between a mind that conceives of language as potentially incarnative and one that sees it as representational. And, though those lacunae which *must* exist in order for difference to occur remain disturbing, threatening Heidegger with
'representation', they allow him to think of the sign, art, and language in terms of the temple rather than of the tomb. "The peal of
stillness" is revealed by and in its dif-ference. Without dif-ference,
stillness would remain for Heidegger, as for Derrida, "the voice
that *keeps* silence." At stake here is the distinction between dif-

---

11. In this discussion of the sacrificial gesture, I am indebted to Mircea Eliade,
The Sacred and the Profane: The Nature of Religion, trans. Willard R. Trask (New
York, 1959), 20–65.

ference and differance. Dif-ference is not a matter of endless deferral in the sense of delay, detour, or nonarrival as it is for Derrida. Rather, it carries the sense of deferring *to,* of submitting to arrival, to being revealed and concealed in the same gesture. Dif-ference implies the arrival of two "others" at the same moment within the same site. It is, indeed, a "gathering." And it is a dynamic, not a thing: "The dif-ference does not mediate after the fact by connecting world and things through a middle added on to them. Being the middle, it first determines world and things in their presence, i.e., in their being toward one another, whose unity it carries out" (*PLT,* 202). Again we see Heidegger being careful not to establish priority in a conscious effort not to admit representation. This is crucial in his discussion of the temple in "The Origin of the Work of Art"—a discussion that should be read as an exploration of the essence of 'sign'. He specifically chooses the temple because, to his mind, it cannot be misconstrued as "representational art." Like authentic language—*i.e.,* poetic saying—art is always a thinking and an echo of the Word, which opens a "clearing" in which Being and being appear and interpenetrate. The temple, like the echo of the Word in words, "causes the unique occurrence: that what is—*is.*" This 'sign' also "gathers" modes of being, admitting their absence as well as presence, into an existential experience that cannot capture the All but rather hints at it by both revealing and concealing. As in Shelley, the double nature of veiling should always be kept in mind when reading Heidegger: to veil the invisible is to grant it visibility, though never in its totality:

> A building, a Greek temple, portrays nothing. . . . The building encloses the figure of the god and in this concealment lets it stand out into the holy precinct through the open portico. By means of the temple, the god is present in the temple. The presence of the god is in itself the extension and delimitation of the precinct as a holy precinct. . . . Standing there, the building holds its ground against the storm raging above it and so first makes the storm itself manifest in its violence. . . . The temple's firm towering makes visible the invisible space of air. . . . The temple, in its standing there, first gives to things their look and to men their outlook on themselves. This view remains open as long as the work is a work, as long as the god has not fled from it.   ("Origin," 41–42)

We are thinking here in terms of a happening in which no element can be understood as substitution or displacement since it cannot be determined which element is primary or secondary. In other words, representation is "outside," is an "unthinkable" within this site.

The temple remains art, genuine poetic sign, only as long as it is *not* experienced as representation.[12] This is not to say that it does not reveal absence. Full or simple presence, the erasure of the demarcation between Being and beings, would render the temple superfluous. The temple would never be constructed if full presence were not accompanied by an "abyss." "Mortals remain closer to that absence because they are touched by presence, the ancient name of Being." But because presence conceals itself at the same time, it is itself already absence. "Thus the abyss holds and remarks everything." The demarcation must hold as the abyss it is, but the thinker, the poet, "comes to know the marks that the abyss remarks. For the poet these are the traces of the fugitive gods."[13] If one thinks through the distinction between dif-ference and differance, it will become clear that this is not the bottomless abyss of Derrida's pit or pyramid. Nonetheless, observe how fine the line is between temple and tomb. According to Heidegger, modern man, because he has fragmented being into the subject/object distinction, because he has not moved beyond representational thinking, is prone to mistake temple for tomb over and over again. Since "modern" thought "begins" with Plato, the history of Western thought has implicated itself irrevocably in this "erring."

Evoking presence and absence in the same moment, Heidegger's temple bears a strong resemblance to Hegel's tomb, but it cannot be deconstructed in quite the same way because of his refusal to grant temporal priority. The temple ('sign') is more event than object, and one cannot unlayer it as strata of representations or unweave its textuality into warp and woof. In this parable of the sign, it is crucial that neither temple nor "the figure of the god" be understood as representational. Such a notion will make it appear that the "god has fled," that the work is not a work—*i.e.,* is not a work *working,* is not a *happening* of the truth of being. In no sense is the temple to be seen as standing outside the mortal experience of it, but neither is its being subjective. It *is there,* as the repetition of "standing there" is intended to point out. However, its mode of existence is dependent upon human comportment *toward* it as it gives itself to the human.

12. Heidegger's rejection of 'representation' as inauthentic thought is ubiquitous in his work. See especially a late essay, "The Age of the World View," in *Martin Heidegger and the Question of Literature,* ed. Spanos.
13. Heidegger, "What Are Poets For?" in *PLT,* 93.

We are, once again, in the midst of a sacrificial gesture intended to release the Silence of Being, a gesture intended both to unveil the absence of the Whole, of All, of that which remains concealed, and to unveil presence, that fragment which, veiling itself in its sign, presents itself as being-in-the-world. "The peal of stillness" calls on mortal language to violate its unity so it can be seen as unity, and it calls through and across the threshold of dif-ference. "Language needs and uses the speaking of mortals," and "obedient to the voice of Being, thought seeks the Word through which the truth of Being may be expressed." This too is a structure of desire, but unlike Derrida's it promises fulfillment. Fulfillment is not, however, to be mistaken for satiation; the concealed abides and haunts the un-concealed with its absence. Silence rings out through utterance that can never encompass it. That silence which is also Language desires its own rending apart by human words, though words are always inadequate to its fullness, so that it may appear through its dif-ference. And so God said to Job: "Gird up thy loins now like a man: I will *demand* of thee, and *declare thou* unto me" (Job 40:7).

This long detour into twentieth-century rhetoric seems far re-moved from the concerns of George Herbert only if we ignore its metaphorical and structural similarities to phrasing with which Herbert would have been most familiar:

> Have we spoken or announced anything worthy of God? Rather I feel that I have done nothing but wish to speak: if I have spoken, I have not said what I wished to say. Whence do I know this, except because God is ineffable? If what I said were ineffable it would not be said. And for this reason God should not be said. And a contradiction in terms is created, since if that is ineffable which cannot be spoken, then that is not in-effable which can be called ineffable. This contradiction is to be passed over in silence rather than resolved verbally.[14]

14. Augustine, *On Christian Doctrine*, trans. D. W. Robertson, Jr. (New York, 1958), 10–11. All of Herbert's best readers note the influence of Augustine on his thought. Perhaps the most helpful commentaries are Arnold Stein's in *George Herbert's Lyrics* (Baltimore, 1968), xviii–xxix, and Joseph Summers's in *George Herbert* (London, 1954), 76–79. For an interesting discussion of Augustine's influence in terms of the doctrine of grace, see William H. Halewood, *The Poetry of Grace* (New Haven, 1970). An older, but still useful, exposition of Augustine's influence on theo-ries of poetic language can be found in chap. 2 of Ruth Wallerstein's *Studies in Seven-teenth Century Poetics* (Madison, Wis., 1950). Augustine's thought was important enough to Herbert to be singled out as a specific legacy in his will: "then I bequeath to Mr. Bockstocke St. Augustine's workes and halfe yeares wages aforehand" (*The Works of George Herbert*, ed. Hutchinson, 382).

Augustine speaks of the inadequacy of language to the Logos and of language as the progeny of desire. He speaks of a situation which is *in essence* longing, a "wish to speak" rather than a full speaking. A certain amount of anxiety always resides within such a wish to speak, and we would do well to consider it both in Derridean terms as the desire for the presence that carries death with it and in Heideggerean terms as the desire to unconceal that which always remains beyond unveiling. Such anxiety can be terrifying and immobilizing, as in Job, or it can be the gentle, underlying pressure toward correctness found in Augustine. Nonetheless, it is there. For Augustine, this contradiction is to be "passed over in silence" because the nature of the Logos, the desire of God to be revealed in His world, justifies the fragmentation language inevitably enacts. Like Heidegger's "Language," Augustine's "Logos" needs words, has "accepted" and "wished" words, in order to appear as His own dif-ference from them: "For God although nothing worthy may be spoken of Him, has accepted the tribute of the human voice and wished us to take joy in praising him with our words. In this way he is called *Deus*. Although he is not recognized in the noise of these two syllables, all those who know the Latin language when this sound reaches their ears, are moved to think of a certain most excellent immortal nature."[15] The "noise" hints at the silence that is "ineffable," but it does not incarnate that silence as fully as Heidegger would suggest: we are already dealing with "modern thought." This is a kind of representation, and there is in Augustine's thought profound concern with the abyss that is the space of interpretation. He spans the abyss with sacrifice, a "tribute accepted," but the rift remains, and though God, too, desires language, the phrases "nothing worthy may be spoken" and "I have done nothing but wish to speak," haunt the Christian consciousness. The dread of "saying" God is the dread of *sparagmos,* of dismemberment, of fragmenting an order of being the *essence* of which is unity. And accompanying this anxiety is the knowledge that speaking is always a misspeaking, that it happens because of the great distance between the ineffable and the human, and that this distance is the space of interpretation with all its attendant threats.

And yet, the threshold between the human and the divine must be crossed, and it must be crossed from both directions. The human is compelled to the sacrificial gesture; it must inject its own

15. Augustine, *On Christian Doctrine,* 11.

mode of being (the "profane") into the presence of its opposite (the "sacred") in hopes of sanctification. Language must penetrate silence, but the bridge it creates on its way must not be tainted. For the desire to penetrate what Herbert calls "silent eares" ("Deniall"), is coupled with an equally forceful need to draw the silent Logos back into the world of language. Language prepares the way for Logos to enter, to move from Being into being. To speak to God is to initiate a sacrament, and one cannot perform a sacrament unless the ritual instruments have already been sanctified.

Thus we return to Job's predicament: the awful paradox is that man can come into God's presence only through language in which God is already present. If the Word is to be made flesh and dwell among us, that flesh must already be full of grace and truth. It must, in other words, be sacramental as well as representational, must present as well as represent. Without sanctification, words will tumble endlessly away from their silent origin—through a space more bottomless than Satan's, for they cannot have even the small grace of being grounded in Hell.

In attempting to converse with God, then, one must always attempt to be both poet and priest: to converse with God *is* to construct an altar. Herbert's opening poem in "The Church" of *The Temple* is no mere exercise in wit. It is the carving out of a sacred space, a space of desire and sacrifice, of the "wish-to-speak" that will call on, and be called by, Logos in order to allow His eruption into the finite world—a precarious undertaking at best.

❦ 4 ❧

TEMPLE AND TOMB:
THE WORK OF GEORGE HERBERT

And let them make me a sanctuary;
that I may dwell among them.
According to all that I shew thee,
after the pattern of the tabernacle,
and the pattern of all the instruments
thereof, even so shall ye make it.

—Exodus 25:8–9

And if thou wilt make me an altar of
stone, thou shalt not build it of
hewnstone: for if thou lift up thy
tool upon it, thou hast polluted it.

—Exodus 20:25

There is therefore a good and a bad writing: the good and natural is the
divine inscription in the heart and in the soul; the perverse and artful is
technique, exiled in the exteriority of the body.

—Jacques Derrida, *Of Grammatology*

Certainly Herbert is no Job. But if we think in terms of the ineffable
God, of language as breaking the silence of Logos, of the potential
for representation to "pollute" that silence rather than to create a
passageway to and from it, then Herbert's dilemma *is* Job's. The absence of God, the great distance between the human and the divine,
haunts this poet/priest, yet he flings his poetry across that void,
often joyfully and always valiantly. And he does so acutely conscious of the paradox of addressing human words to the Word.[1]

Herbert knows very well the potential for errance, for language
to stray from Logos to sin, from prayer to self-condemnation:

Lovely enchanting language, sugar cane
Hony of roses, whither wilt thou flie?

1. I am indebted to Rosalie Colie's elegant book *Paradoxia Epidemica: The Ren-*
aissance Tradition of Paradox (Princeton, 1966), though we differ radically in the ways
we read Herbert's work and his response to the paradoxes of the doctrine of the
Logos.

Hath some fond lover tic'd thee to thy bane?
And wilt thou leave the Church, and love a stie?
                    Fie thou wilt soil thy broidered coat,
And hurt thy self, and him that sings the note.
                                        ("The Forerunners")

Like Job, Herbert is passionately in search of the "right words."
"Jordan I" and "Jordan II" are only the most famous examples of
this theme, which traverses all of *The Temple*.[2] Unlike Job, this
poet understands from the beginning that the Ineffable desires
human words and that those words are part of the dynamic of the
sacrificial gesture. Yet, he is denied the kind of self-presencing
that finally validates Job's language, and he is, at least by virtue of
his own understanding, at a greater distance from God than Job
could have imagined. Herbert also experiences God's absence in
the Heideggerean sense of a "no-longer" that is also a "not-yet."
For him, however, *parousia,* the longed-for return, is not the kind
of "full presence" Job projects (and receives) with all its promise of
a fully incarnative language. Instead, in *this* world, presence for
Herbert is more like Shelley's "evanescent visitations" or his "Intel
lectual beauty," which, as "the awful shadow of some unseen
Power Floats / though unseen amongst us,—visiting / This various world with as inconstant wing / As summer winds that creep
from flower to flower." And like Shelley, Herbert will try to make
his signs Heideggerean "veils" rather than representations. Herbert
experiences such visitation as "grace" and expresses it as "return".

How fresh, O Lord, how sweet and clean
    Are thy returns! even as the flowers in spring;
To which, besides their own demean,
The late past frosts tributes of pleasure bring.
                    Grief melts away
                    Like snow in May,
    As if there were no such cold thing.
                                        ("The Flower")

The "tributes" of God's absences, "the late past frosts," surrender
themselves to images of His presence, adding to the store of joy.
But, the "as if there were" floats disturbingly behind the poem,

2. A list of the poems concerned with poetry and language would be very long
indeed. In addition to those I consider here, poems such as "The Forerunners," "A
True Hymn," "Prayer I," "The Thanksgiving," "The Holy Scriptures," "Joseph's
Coat," and "The Sonne" all offer access to the issues of inspiration and representation in interesting and even profound ways.

threatening the peace it proclaims. Even as it adds "tributes of pleasure" to our own reading of it, it creates an unresolved tension
in which presence announces absence. Frosts return as surely as
flowers; each evokes the absence of the other.

The visitation of full presence is in no way to be seen as a poetic
fiction in Herbert's work, but the question is whether or not it can
be captured in his work. Certainly it directly affects the capacity of
poetic language. In the felt presence of God, Herbert asserts, language would be fully adequate:

> How should I praise thee Lord, how should my rymes
>   Gladly engrave thy love in steel,
>   If what my soul doth feel sometimes,
>   My soul might ever feel!
>
>   ("The Temper I")

The "should" is important here, for Herbert writes not during the
moment of full presence, but always in recollection of that presence, in an attempt to recover it. The echo of Job is not accidental.
To "engrave . . . in steel" would seem to make the presence permanent, but the nature of writing, of the Logos itself, prevents such
presencing. At best, writing fragments the totality of God's love
into signs that *echo* it as a presence which can only haunt the sign
that marks its absence. In the full presence of Logos only silence is
possible.

Herbert does not, however, write in a moment of total absence.
Such intense and chaotic despair does not allow the production of
language: those moments are also "silent"; they are the seven days
and seven nights when Job and his friends do not speak. The experience of grace leaves behind a kind of orderly residue, a fragment of
the whole through which the All echoes and enables the poem.
Nevertheless, the more distant God is felt to be, the more language
splits into bits and pieces, wandering across the page:

> When my devotions could not pierce
>   Thy silent ears;
> Then was my heart broken, as was my verse
>   My breast was full of fears
>   And disorder:
>   ("Deniall")

The artifice we see here is certainly conscious; the moment of withdrawal is not *present* in the poem, but a skilled representation of it
is. These lines are nearly a visual parody of errance—language

adrift in the absence of a center. The center is "found" in the last
stanza, as nearly all of Herbert's readers note. It was, in fact, probably "found" before the poem's writing, as the consistent use of the
past tense in all stanzas except the last implies. The final stanza is
written in the present of a reordered "now" which seems to blanket
the writing of the entire poem.[3] We should not dismiss the painful
uneasiness or the problem Herbert so carefully delineates merely
because he seems to solve (or resolve) it. When God does not dwell
in words, they are merely empty representations, "broken" and in
"disorder," which "flie asunder." The issue is there; we are pointed
toward the dismemberment of Logos, and much of Herbert's work
deals with the anxiety such a notion causes and with the failure of
language that God does not inhabit. Herbert's project is precisely to
inscribe God into being *within* the world of words, to capture His
"return" in such a way as to allow it to persist within *human* being,
his own as well as others'—a point he makes clear in his poem
"Perseverance."

Despite his affirmation of the felt presence of grace, his insistence that his Lord "didst . . . hold my hand while I did write"
("Assurance"), despite the gem-like balance and serenity of so many
poems manifesting the belief that language is ultimately "something understood," there are tensions in Herbert's work which are
not resolved by the depth and spaciousness of his faith. For Herbert's poems, meditative in structure as they are, are not the ecstatic
outpourings of a mystic who has confidently achieved full colloquy
with God.[4] One has only to compare their tone and content with
Saint Teresa of Avila's *Interior Castle* or *Autobiography* to understand
the difference between Herbert's quiet, intense desire for full presence and that mystical overflow of presence which would, finally,
be representable only by the white silence of the blank page. It is a
mistake to succumb entirely to the crystalline surfaces of even Herbert's most serene poems; there are usually disturbing currents in

    3. This point concerning verb tense is made by Helen Vendler in an interesting
discussion of Herbert's "mastery of the self." See *The Poetry of George Herbert* (Cambridge, Mass., 1975), 258–65. On Herbert's genius for using form as a "hieroglyph," see Summers, *George Herbert,* 123–46.
    4. Though many years and many critics have passed, I still find Louis Martz's
reading of Herbert and most satisfying insofar as it unveils the *structure* of *The
Temple.* See *The Poetry of Meditation* (New Haven, 1954), 288–320. An interesting
complement to Martz is Stanley Fish's *The Living Temple: George Herbert and Catechizing* (Berkeley, 1978).

the depths. Even "Love III" has its exquisite balance shaken, ever so slightly, by the play of welcome and withdrawal and by its past tense. The perfection of its quiet tone can lull one into feeling that one is overhearing a conversation "in the moment." But, as always in Herbert, once presence has occurred, that is, once he "did sit and eat," words cease. Silence, by implication, rings out that presence, but words are not adequate to it. The poem "is" after the fact.

Poetry as a sort of "afterword" seems unavoidable. As we shall see later, Wordsworth explores that condition in depth. Because of the very nature of language, it is extremely unlikely that Herbert could have felt the sort of presence implied by "grace" during the actual act of writing. In ecstatic moments, those in which the Lord could "hold my hand," in the presence of the all-encompassing Word, words are disruptive, even impossible. Whether we think of language as incarnative or as representative, unadulterated presence forbids its operations. As we have already seen, in Derridean thought such an (impossible) event would actualize the totalization inherently excluded by a language which requires both difference (separation) and deferral (nonarrival). Language as such—that is, as an infinite play of substitution—requires the absence of the center, of God. Its purpose is, in fact, to supplement the absence of Logos. The "voice that keeps silence" keeps it as an evasion, as a refusal of the radical absence that Derrida has said is *named* God or Logos.

Even Heidegger, despite his insistence that Logos inhabits language, must admit a certain logocentric absence in order to bring human language into existence. Logos is never totalized in the manner suggested by the experience of grace. It always remains primarily in reserve, as the concealed "silence" he names the "peal of stillness." Logos may penetrate language, but it penetrates as much in the form of the shadow of absence as in that of the light of presence. For Heidegger, Logos as silence cannot be articulated, and "any uttering, whether in speech or writing, breaks the stillness" (*PLT,* 207). Language, even as a temple, is brought into play specifically to call *toward* Being, and words are summoned by Being precisely because it can *never* be unambiguously present. The full presence of God would render the temple superfluous.

To move closer to Herbert, let us look again at Augustine's words: "If what I said were ineffable it would not be said."[5] The presence of the ineffable requires silence, and though language may

---

5. Augustine, *On Christian Doctrine,* 10–11.

conduct *toward* that ecstatic union, words fall away at the moment
of contact. Augustine describes the experience:

> Our talk had reached this point: that the greatest possible delights of our
> bodily senses, radiant as they might be with the brightest of corporeal
> light, could not be compared with the joys of that eternal life. . . . And
> still we went upward, meditating and speaking and looking with won-
> der at your works, and we came to our own souls and we went beyond
> our souls to reach that region of never-failing plenty where *Thou feedest
> Israel* forever with the food of truth and where life is that Wisdom by
> whom all these things are made, both what is past and what is to come;
> but Wisdom herself is not made; she is as she has been and will be for-
> ever; or rather there is no place in her for "to have been" or "to be going
> to be"; one can only say "to be" since she is eternal and "have been" and
> "going to be" are not eternal. And as we talked, yearning toward this
> Wisdom, we did, with the whole strength of our hearts' impulse, just
> lightly come into touch with her, and we sighed and we left bound there
> *the first fruits of the spirit,* and we returned to the sounds made by our
> mouth, where a word has a beginning and an ending. And how unlike is
> this to your Word, our Lord, you who abide in yourself forever, with-
> out becoming old, making all things new [6]

Language here functions adequately as long as it serves as a conduit toward self-knowledge. It can move us toward God until we
"come to our own souls," and it enables us to move "beyond our
souls." Once that beyond has been entered, however, once proximity becomes union, language fails. And it fails precisely because
it is unnecessary and interruptive. It does not need to incarnate the
eternal into the temporal, and even if it just lightly touches "the
never failing plenty" of absolute presence, human language evaporates into the timeless: "there is no place in her for 'to have been' or
'to be going to be'; one can only say 'to be'." The no-longer and the
not yet, the past and the future within which language moves, are
forbidden, absorbed within the overwhelming stasis of "to be"—
the verb of absolute presence which transforms language into pure
breath. Words become an exhalation of self into Logos, a sigh. "We
sighed and we left," writes Augustine, and a poignant sense of loss
murmurs in his words. The loss initiates his return to language
"where a word has a beginning and an ending." His phrasing suggests the problem: human language "comes before" and it "follows

6. Augustine, *The Confessions of St. Augustine,* trans. Rex Warner (New York,
1963), 201.

after"; it is always caught between the "to have been" and the "to be going to be." And the predicament suggests death, the return evokes mortality as a direct contrast to the Word which abides "forever, without becoming old."

Most important, the loss incurred by a return to language generates in Augustine a passionate desire for silence, expressed as a return to presence. He continues immediately with this:

> So we said: if to any man the tumult of the flesh were to grow silent, silent the images of earth and water and air, and the poles of heaven silent also; if the soul herself were to be silent, and every tongue, every sign; if there was utter silence . . . and He himself alone were to speak not by their voice but in His own, and we were to hear His word, not through any tongue of flesh or voice of an angel or sound of thunder or difficult allegory, but that we might hear Him whom in all these things we love, might hear Him in Himself without them, just as a moment ago we two had, as it were, gone beyond ourselves and in a flash of thought had made contact . . . life might be forever like that moment of understanding which we had had and for which we now sighed.[7]

The desire for presence then, is the desire for absolute silence, a point Derrida and Heidegger both make many centuries later. It is also a desire to be rid of the obstructions and fragmentations of *all* language: the language of men, the language of God's own images in His created world, even the "voice of an angel." At bottom, it is a desire to be freed from mediation and from interpretation, to restore the perfect Oneness that language always disrupts.

Only the "peal of stillness" evokes such presence but, even for Augustine, the sounds of language are needed in order to move toward that ecstatic silence, to recover the presence of God. The "silence" that surrounds Herbert's poems should be understood in this context. His poetry does not imply that grace is unattainable, but it also does not suggest the presence of grace—a presence deeply desired by Herbert—during the act of writing.

There are few poems in which Herbert does not "recover" his God, but the fact that the work seems always to be a gesture of recovery implies that, for even this most Christian of poets, writing is generated by the experience of distance and loss. This is not to deny the resolution of tension that Herbert's best readers find in his poems. But I would point to the fact that such resolution inevitably occurs in the final lines; the moment of resolution, as should be ex-

7. *Ibid.*, 202.

pected, results in silence, the end of utterance. A poem such as "The Collar" is clearly an utterance written "after" the resolution of tension, and the resolution occurs as the felt presence of grace.[8] But the poem is not written *during* that experience, and its words do not incarnate *ousia,* presence untainted by absence. Rather, it is a memorial to the experience, a monument with voice, an epitaph. Such poems illustrate Herbert's own awareness that in God's presence the only appropriate response is the sacrifice of language to the Word and an immediate lapse into silence. They are, from one point of view, illustrations of this idea.

Consider briefly "The Collar." This is a poem in which language is shown to *open* a rift between the human and the divine. The poet is "speaking" himself further and further away from Logos; each word seems to widen the gap. But irony is at work here. We should, I believe, take literally Herbert's assertion that "at *every word* / Me thoughts I heard one calling." The images are loaded with double meaning; they are sacred language being used in a profane way. "Every word" echoes the divine, but as the speaker misspeaks, he remains deaf to the words' hidden significance. He fails to read the truth they "incarnate." He fails, for instance, to see that his "lines and life are free" precisely because he has "no harvest but a thorn / To let me bloud." He does not hear the echoing Word that names "harvest," "bloud," "fruit," and "wine" sacred by virtue of the fact that all are images of the ineffable. The speaker's perception of "every word" as "difference," as a sign with merely human reference, results in misrepresentation. The calling, however, finally spans the abyss that language has seemed only to widen and, in the clear sounding of the Word, all that was misspoken is revealed as the errance of misrepresentation.

Herbert's phrasing, "At every word, / Me thoughts I heard one calling, Child!" suggests the transfer of energy along the double lane of sacrifice. The moment of exchange is a culmination of the oscillation between Logos and language, which has been silently occurring throughout the poem. This calling erupts in the word "Child" and evokes a proper response, yet it is the deeply flawed misrepresentation that has *already* occurred that clears the way for the emergence of the call. The call, abiding far within the images the speaker misspeaks, could never have sounded at all without the

8. On this point, see Summers, *George Herbert,* 90–92 and Vendler, *The Poetry of George Herbert,* 131–33.

misspeaking. On the other hand, such words could never have been voiced except that Logos "abides," *i.e.,* awaits their arrival. We are in the midst of the Heideggerean problem of priority which is inherent in the exchange between Language and language. The way has already been cleared by the "every word" at which "I heard one calling." At the same time, "every word" already contained the (unheard) calling within its own fragmented sounding. "Language needs and uses the speaking of mortals in order to sound as the peal of stillness for the hearing of mortals," Heidegger says (*PLT,* 207–208). Even misspeaking enables the echo of God's voice. The Logos is made present as the echoing ambiguity of the misrepresentations in spite of their profanity. It's impossible to determine which "came first," but it is clear that language is not adequate to full presence until it sacrifices itself to the Word: "Child!" And at the moment when that exchange occurs, the moment when language is confessed as wayward error, at the moment of the cry, "My Lord," *silence* breaks through. The peal of stillness sounds out, and the unsaid rings through the words preceding it. The misrepresentations that have threatened to widen the rift, to toss the speaker into the abyss, despite the fact that they conceal God's voice, are suddenly revealed as error, and their wandering is brought to an abrupt halt. They are grounded in the "ineffable."

One of the reasons that the quiet, simple "My Lord" is so deeply moving is that the words, given the structure of the poem, are a confession of the sins of language, of the poet's misreading and misspeaking of the images he himself had used to initiate the break with God. They are a recognition that the "fierce and wilde" ravings always contained the sacramental call, but that he has "polluted" them by misusing them. Like Job, he has "uttered that I understood not, things too wonderful for me which I knew not." The phrase "My Lord" surrenders all that was misrepresented before, and it also surrenders *to* pure silence in the presence of God. If it is a resolution, it is also an offering—the offering of human language to Silence, a sacrifice of speech to the ineffable. Full presence cannot be felt at the calling "Child!" which still seems to come from a great distance; it requires exchange, response, the surrender inherent in the words "My Lord." It is felt in the resolution, the closure, the peal of stillness that follows the final period of the poem. The poem may have been written as a remembering, a recollection of the movement away from Logos in language and toward God in silence, and it may have been enabled by the experience of grace, but it does not incarnate that experience except inasmuch as grace "abides" in the empty spaces following the final words. The poem exists because, at the moment of its writing, the full presence of Logos does not.

"The Collar" is the recovery of a moment of recovery. It is doubly epitaphic: it announces God's absence in the "now" by virtue of the fact that it speaks of the "then," of the moment when grace *was,* and it announces, in the silence that follows the words "My Lord," that full presence is not possible within its own language. The breaking of such silence evokes the presence which is "no-longer and not-yet," which may haunt the poem but "is" elsewhere. The question is whether, for Herbert, such signification is Derrida's tomb-like resonance or Heidegger's "open portico" where "by means of the temple the god is present in the temple." In a poem like "The Collar" the answer seems clear. Language does not fully incarnate presence, but even at its most wayward, it can veil presence, can reveal in the same gesture whereby it seems to conceal. Here, Logos is present in language in the same manner as Heidegger's god is present in his "figure." In "this concealment" he is also revealed ("Origin," 41–42). But the work warns us that if we fall into representational thinking, as the speaker does early in the poem, the god will flee the temple and we will be left with an infinitely regressive series of representations.

To break silence is always to run the risk of misrepresentation. Herbert would have phrased the concern as Augustine did: "Have we spoken or announced anything worthy of God?" Let his own words suffice: "Lord, how can man preach thy eternall word? / He is a brittle crazie glasse. . . . Speech alone doth vanish like a flaring thing, / And in the eare, not conscience ring." What I have "left out" with my use of ellipses here is crucial to the understanding of Herbert's strategy of incarnation, but we must approach it carefully, by way of detour, and return to "The Windows" later.

Herbert's writing is epitaphic in that it is always an effort to inscribe God into presence (though not into existence) and that the nature of this presence is markedly similar to the "haunting" voice that issues forth from the tombstone. In Herbert's work, however, the epitaphic gesture is complex. It is not just the result of the double movement epitaph always performs in a single stroke: the simultaneous enunciation of presence and absence. It is complicated by the fact that, for Herbert, God too is a "writer"; He is first and foremost the great "author" of the Book of the World.

It is easy, after the work of such thinkers as Rosemond Tuve,

E. M. W. Tillyard, and Ernst R. Curtius, for us to treat the medieval and renaissance idea of the Book of the World as a commonplace.[9] The idea is a radical one and should not be clouded in language that has by now become nearly cliché. Foucault revives the genuine complexity of this understanding of nature as a system of signs, as a writing to be interpreted, in his beautiful meditation, "The Prose of the World": "The universe was folded in upon itself; the earth echoing the sky, faces seeing themselves reflected in the stars, and plants holding within their stems the secrets that were of use to man. . . . And representation—whether in the service of pleasure or of knowledge—was posited as a form of repetition: the theatre of life or the mirror of nature, that was the claim made by all language, its manner of declaring its existence and of formulating its right of speech."[10] In such a context, the Book of the World can be seen as God's "repeating" of Himself in visible, "readable," form—almost as visible speech. Humans live within the exfoliation of the Word, a complete and self-sufficient totality where no rift between thing and sign can be admitted.

However, it is doubtful that such perfect self-enclosure, "representation . . . posited as a form of repetition," was ever so impenetrable as Foucault suggests. As we have just seen, even Augustine felt that "images of earth and water and air" and "the sound of thunder" were obstacles intervening between himself and God, despite his insistence that God is "in all things." The problem is that when the world is understood as God's Book, everything begins to function as a "difficult allegory," which demands the most careful reading if God's presence is to be revealed. Like all signs, the world is intermediary; it stands between self and Logos, it points toward separation even as it serves as a necessary link. This flaw in the mirror always existed within the concept of 'mirroring'. Furthermore, if the mirror is also seen as a sign written by God into existence, then His Being is posited within a delicately balanced paradox, one that insists on both the need for representation because God has

9. Rosemond Tuve, *Elizabethan and Metaphysical Imagery: Renaissance Poetic and Twentieth Century Critics* (Chicago, 1947); E. M. W. Tillyard, *The Elizabethan World Picture* (London, 1943); Ernst Curtius, *European Literature and the Latin Middle Ages,* trans. Willard R. Trask (New York, 1963). In this context I should also like to point to another classic particularly important for reading Herbert: Basil Willey, *The Seventeenth Century Background* (New York, 1953).

10. Michel Foucault, *The Order of Things: An Archaeology of the Human Sciences* (New York, 1970), 17.

withdrawn from His creation and on His presence within His own representation. This "doubleness" is an event that occurs "in the begining" of the Word. When God said, "Let there be light," and instantly "there was light," God created world as an utterance of Himself, as a spoken thought. But at the moment that thought is externalized, takes on sensible form, the form becomes a kind of writing. And as inscription, the world is finite, corruptible, and different from God as the self-present Word. In this sense God's withdrawal "happens" in the space between His utterance of Himself and the incarnative moment when that utterance becomes substance as sign. Incarnation and representation are a twin birth. Even if it seems inhabited by the Logos, the written world refers to a Word it cannot contain and thereby points to Logos as an absence that is, at best, a no-longer and a not-yet.

Undermined by its own paradoxes, the notion of the Book of the World as a totality, a unity of God and creation, had to yield. Certainly by Herbert's time the perfect self-reflection of the mirror of being was beginning to warp and crack. The fracture between language, world, and Word was manifest. Thinkers were acutely conscious of the interpretive gap and the occasions it presents for error. Interpretation is part of the scaffolding that sustains the ideas of repetition and reflection. As Foucault suggests, when "the world of similarity can only be a world of signs," then everything is "founded upon the unearthing and decipherment of these signatures. . . . God is recognized by His signature."[11] As soon as interpretation enters the picture, the paradox that supports the picture is once again exposed. An inherent contradiction resides in the vision of the world as a perfect, self-reflective totality instituted and sustained by God's presence, and the vision of the world as "God's signature." The first seems to ensure God's presence, and the second, while it guarantees His authorization, also suggests His exclusion from His Book. To function as the ground of existence, Logos must exist uninscribed, beyond corruptibility and the vagaries of interpretation. God as author can be the unquestioned ground of His world only so long as He is also absolutely "other-than" His world.

The psychic pressures for correct interpretation of God's signs in this context are almost inconceivable to those of us who live in a world of pluralism and subjectivism. The elegance of Renaissance

11. *Ibid.*, 26.

writing should not seduce us into ignoring the tensions that must accompany the interpretive act if it occurs in thought that defines truth in terms of perfect correspondence with an Ideal. It goes without saying that Bacon persistently questioned the "idols" (of tribe, den, theater, and market) that arise from the too easy assumption that reflection, in both its senses, results in correct reading. And even a mind as devout as Sir Thomas Browne's acknowledges anxiety about the dangers of interpretation: "For our endeavors are not only to combat with doubts, but to dispute with the Devil: the villany of that Spirit takes a hint of Infidelity from our Studies, and by demonstrating a naturality in one way, makes us mistrust a miracle in another. . . . Thus the Devil played at Chess with me, and yielding a Pawn, thought to gain a Queen of me, taking advantage of my honest endeavours." [12]

Browne's concern is that interpretation, especially in view of the "new science," will result in the "infidelity" of "mistrust." His sense that there is a "hint of infidelity" in "demonstrating a naturality" is an effect of the recognition that to study "naturality" is no longer to meditate directly on God. The space between God and His works has been felt. And that space is inhabited by the Devil, has satanic possibilities. This was, after all, the epoch of Descartes, in which Derrida locates the "beginning" of the saying of "God" as the desire for *self*-presence (*OG,* 16–17). It is a time when self-questioning is beginning to erode the notion of God's accessibility through His Book, whether it be world or scripture. [13] This is not to imply that the authority of the Book is placed in question but rather that the problems of misreading and miswriting forcefully appear within a heightened awareness of the subjectivity of interpretation. The writing of the Logos remains authoritative; human imitations of that writing are not. From a theological point of view, such writing is vulnerable to the taint of satanic distortion.

This is a concern that inherently arises at the moment when God is first conceived as "author." His writing is thought of as being susceptible to the profane, to the pollution of representation. Plato,

12. Sir Thomas Browne, *Religio Medici,* in *Religious Prose of 17th Century England,* ed. Anne Davidson Ferry (New York, 1966), 78–79.

13. Whenever one "places" a historical "beginning" one is, of course, in error. "Beginning" should always be written in quotation marks. I do not mean to imply here that interpretation had never been problematical before the seventeenth century, but only that the issues involved become defined and expressed within the thought of this moment.

for instance, discusses two kinds of discourse. One is of "unquestioned legitimacy," is "written in the soul of the learner, that can
defend itself . . . the living speech, the original of which the written
discourse may fairly be called a kind of image."[14] The other, written discourse, tainted by human artifice, is the illegitimate off-
spring, the "bastard" and potentially "unnatural" imitation which
defiles its own origin.[15] Nonetheless, as long as God's expression of
Himself is understood as an expression of Word into World, interpretation is a prerequisite to any experience of God's presence *in*
His creation. And that interpretation can only be written as an imitation of God's own "original" act of "writing."

George Herbert wrote under the pressures exerted by all of these
paradoxes. As "The Collar" shows, he certainly felt the fragmenting forces within language and the need to use language in order to
approach the "peal of stillness" that is Logos. Just as certainly, he
understood that his own writing was grounded by the world as an
already written discourse. God's signs were ubiquitous, found in
the creations and creatures of His world and culminating in scripture and His own engravings in the human heart. If one lives in the
Book of the World, then, as Foucault says, "one speaks upon the
basis of a writing," and human discourse is "addressed to that pri-
mal written word whose return it simultaneously promises and
postpones."[16] In this respect the world itself serves as a kind of epitaph, though reading it is no easy task. Existence itself is threatened
by the possibility of interpretive error. But read and write one
must, and Herbert did so in a situation wherein the world has the
ambiguity of being a sarcophagus, inscribed by an Author who is
both present in His text and outside it. Part of the power of Herbert's work resides in his ability to use this paradoxical situation as
both the source and the validation of his poetry. God's writing
offers the potential guarantee of his own incarnative gesture, his
own attempt to transform the tomb into the temple. The rich possibilities of the coupling of tomb and temple with the notion of God's
writing are displayed in his poem "Sepulchre." Here, Herbert identifies both world and human heart with the tomb out of which
Christ burst. The play of the poem is rooted in Herbert's assumption that the "cold hard stone" of earth is both *capable* of "lodg-

14. Plato, *Phaedrus,* in *Collected Dialogues,* ed. Hamilton and Cairns, 521.
15. See Derrida's discussion of "natural" writing as opposed to "artificial" in *OG,* 14–18.
16. Foucault, *The Order of Things,* 41.

ing" and *unable* to imprison his God. The gracious largesse of stones which "in quiet entertain thee, And order" is contrasted to the stony human heart which will not "receive thee." Nevertheless, the reader is reminded, God once "writ in stone," and the saving doubleness of heart as tomb is affirmed in the pun of the final line: "nothing can . . . withold thee." The simultaneous announcement of the opposed meanings in "withold," to hold out and to hold in, points to the paradox of God's Being as both presence and absence which the writing in stone has already implied. The paradox is not resolved and cannot be as long as the Logos "writes" His world. As we will see in the discussion that follows, for Herbert, it is always the inscription on the tomb/heart that saves; without the "letter of the word," humankind is an empty cenotaph—but that letter must also incarnate the spirit.[17] As we investigate Herbert's writing further, we should remember that his poetry, as the imitation of God's own inscriptive act, often roots itself on an unsteady and sometimes dangerous "ground."

It is within this context that we should consider the epigraphs that open this chapter. God commands the establishment of a sacred space, a "sanctuary; that I may dwell among them." But that site is determined as a copy, an imitation of the heavenly tabernacle. It is to be made "after [the] pattern which was shewed thee in the mount" (Exodus 25:40). This human rewriting of the original and eternal divine "writing" must be free of artifice, must be made of God's own untouched 'signs':

> And if thou wilt make me an altar of
> stone, thou shalt not build it of
> hewnstone: for if thou lift up thy
> tool upon it, thou hast polluted it.
> (Exodus 20:25)

The artificial is a kind of image, and image implies a dangerous difference from the original. This difference resides in the "difference" between representation and incarnation. "Hewnstone," because it is

---

17. Herbert is clear about this in his comments on "the offensive places" in *Valdesso's Considerations*: "I much mislike the Comparison of Images, and H. Scripture, as if they were both but Alphabets and after a time to be left. . . . Indeed he that shall so attend to the bark of the letter, as to neglect the consideration of Gods Worke in his heart through the Word, doth amisse; both are to be done, the scriptures still used and Gods Worke within us still observed" (309).

the result of artifice, is "unnatural," an "image" of the original which clarifies its own difference from the natural and suggests the acts of interpretation and representation. The temple must not stand-in-place-of God but must allow Him to dwell *within* in the same manner that He dwells within His own creation. Eliade has suggested that the construction of a temple is always a cosmogony, the repetition of God's act of creating the world.[18] If this activity is viewed as *only* representative of God's act, as displacing it, it must be understood as absolute hubris. Instead, therefore, such "building" must be sanctified by God's presence; God must be "working" within the act itself. As long as God can be perceived *within* the stones of the temple, "the temple continually resanctifies the world, because it at once represents and contains it. In the last analysis, *it is by virtue of the temple that the world is resanctified in every part.*"[19]

If it is to be a "temple," writing must not be seen as the *image* of an original but as its incarnation. The interpretive gap must be effaced, for it is, among other things, the place of artifice, the declaration of the "unnatural." Herbert *must* believe that his "altar" is one "whose parts are as thy hand did frame; / No workmans tool hath touch'd the same." He is always conscious of his writing as imitative of God's acts, and he is fully aware of his imitation as a kind of emulation that borders on contending, Job-like, with God:

> But how then shall I imitate thee, and
>   Copie thy fair, though bloudie hand?
> Surely I will revenge me on thy love
>   And trie who shall victorious prove.
>   ("The Thanksgiving")

It is a contention of love, and one in which Herbert knows that his sacrifice of language can never equal his Lord's sacrifice on the cross. But it is important here that he perceives language *as* a sacrifice and his work *as* "temple." As a result, for him the dangers of representation, of a purely "exterior" language of image, are particularly intense. Blood is the most proper "ink" in which to write, the heart the most "natural" stone available, but we should note the close proximity between "ink" and "sin":

> since bloud is fittest, Lord, to write
> Thy sorrows in, and bloudie fight;

18. Eliade, *The Sacred and the Profane*, 58.
19. *Ibid.*, 59.

> My heart hath store, write there, where
> in One box doth lie both ink and sin.
>   ("Good Friday")

If one can "outer" (utter) God's "natural" writing from within, from the heart, in a language equally incarnative, one can build a temple rather than a tomb. But one can never forget that ink and sin dwell side by side deep within man—the one creation that is *both* temple and tomb.

The sense of human writing as "image" or "imitation" is precisely what threatens Herbert in his own work. It implies a kind of representation that denies incarnation of the "spirit," leaving us with the fragmented chaos of only "the letter." "I much mislike the comparison of Images, and H. Scripture as if they were both but Alphabets. . . . He that shall so attend to the bark of the letter . . . doth amisse," Herbert wrote. It disturbs him that "image" implies only the external, the mere "bark," in contrast to "Gods work within us" (Notes on *Valdesso's Considerations,* 309). Beneath his thought lie Saint Paul's distinctions (2 Cor. 3:4–6), and also Plato's notion of "good" writing, the "divine inscription in the heart and soul," as opposed to "bad" writing. "The perverse and artful is technique, exiled in the exteriority of the body" (*OG,* 14). The image, as representation, is too far removed from the truth:

> May no lines passe, except they do their dutie
>   Not to a true, but painted chair?
>
> .   .   .   .
> Must all be vail'd, while he that reades, divines,
>   Catching the sense at two removes?
>   ("Jordan [I]")

The answer to Herbert's questions may, in the long run, be yes, though the nature of the "vail" of the sign will make all the difference. What's important, however, is that the "good writing" of the Logos remain unquestioned. Human interpretation and imaging of that writing does not; it is always endangered by a notion of sign as a representation vulnerable to misprision.

Still, to acknowledge God as Author is to acknowledge that He can be approached only by virtue of His signs. One can overleap the mediation of 'sign' only through the Christian idea of death, which promises full presence at the price of being-in-the-world, or through grace, a moment of contact that dispenses with human language altogether. There are, then, two pathways to God. First, one may obtain God's grace by discovering (or uncovering) His presence, by correctly interpreting and imitating in one's own utterance and being His divine inscription. Second, one may eliminate the precarious process of mediation through the ministrations of death. For Herbert, therefore, death has "grown fair and full of grace / Much sought for as a good." In this context, it is understandable why his poem "Death" is as much an exploration of misinterpretation as of the thing-itself. It is a traditional meditation not on the death's-head but on our misunderstanding of it as sign:

> Death, thou wast once an uncouth hideous thing,
>> Nothing but bones,
>> The sad effect of sadder grones:
> Thy mouth was open, but thou couldst not sing.
>
> For we consider'd thee as at some six
>> Or ten yeares hence,
>> After the losse of life and sense,
> Flesh being turn'd to dust, and bones to sticks.
>
> We lookt on this side of thee, shooting short;
>> Where we did finde
>> The shells of fledge souls left behinde,
> Dry dust, which sheds no tears, but may extort.
>
> But since our Saviours death did put some bloud
>> Into thy face;
>> Thou art grown fair and full of grace,
> Much in request, much sought for as a good
>
> For we do now behold thee gay and glad,
>> As at dooms-day;
>> When souls shall wear their new aray,
> And all thy bones with beautie shall be clad.
>
> Therefore we can go die as sleep, and trust
>> Half that we have
>> Unto an honest faithfull grave;
> Making our pillows either down, or dust.

In the opening stanza Herbert portrays death as "thing," as object, a mute and empty representation which results from both misprision and misspeaking. It is a skeletal "nothing" which is the "sad *effect* of sadder grones." It is the "bark of the letter" without the spirit: "the *shells* of fledge souls," an "image" and "alphabet" that have been misread. As simply a *memento mori,* death seemed mute only because "we lookt on this side of thee, shooting short." We read it as a representation, a disincarnative sign of absence. But death is transformed when interpreted correctly, in the light of "our Saviours death." Now death is not a mute representation but an action; we do not *have* "a death" but, rather, we actively "go die." Seen correctly, in the "now" of the poem, death is no longer a "dead" representation but a breathing promise of incarnation. The misprision of the first stanza is completely overturned by the rest of the poem.

Herbert carefully turns "uncouth hideous *thing*" into a living activity "fair and full of grace"; he transforms the "nothing but bones" into an experience wherein "thy bones with beautie shall be clad," and the "thing" becomes a "thee" which is "gay and glad." One "correction" is not made, however. The phrase "thou couldst not sing" is left in silence. The poet clearly implies that now death *does* sing, yet the song remains unsung in the poem. And this is an entirely appropriate omission. Of necessity, a Christian death's song is the silent song of full presence, of the ineffable, a song comparable to the peal of stillness that rings out after the gesture of self-surrender embedded in the words "My Lord" at the end of "The Collar." And again, sacrifice is involved: the surrender of "half that we have / Unto an honest faithful grave." What we surrender to death is its own misrepresentation, the flesh "turn'd to dust, and bones to sticks." What we gain at the price of a mere "*Nothing* but bones" is the full "gay and glad" silence of totality, the presence of the All. If Herbert had chosen to incorporate a "death's song" into his poem, he would have fragmented the unity his rewriting of death promises. Human language resides in the "half that we have," which must remain in the grave until "dooms-day" when it is reincarnated as the breath of God. The body, the incarnative 'sign' of the soul, is discarded in favor of the full and voiceless presence of soul itself. It is of utmost importance to Herbert that his poetry not be the empty representation of a death's-head—so important that poem after poem focuses on this issue.

Death and language are intertwined for Herbert, as they are for all writers, but the linkage is never a simple loop. It is an intricate "silk-twist," a Möbius strip, let down by God to secure the relationship of two orders of being. Like Job, Herbert would write to secure his language against his own absence: "That, if I chance to hold my peace, / These stones to praise thee may not cease" ("The Altar"). And, also like Job, he is aware that the presence evoked by inscription is the epitaphic presence of the speaking monument. In fact, the poem immediately following "The Altar" is consciously constructed to read as an inscription on a monument. At one level it is inevitable that "The Altar" should be coupled with "The Sacrifice," which is so tightly connected to it. But Herbert complicates "The Sacrifice" considerably by imaging it in the form of an epitaph. The coupling of epitaphic voice with altar strongly suggests that both serve as sacred openings to the presence of God. "The Sacrifice" makes direct reference to the "halt traveler" motif the poet would have known through *The Greek Anthology*, where such poems are conventionalized as epitaphs. Tuve is unquestionably correct in asserting that the motif also comes to Herbert via medieval monologues in the *O vos omnes qui transitis* tradition.[20] If we take her admonitions seriously, however, we must also consider the facts that the tradition never lost its undertones of monumental "voice" and that Herbert certainly would have recognized the epitaphic nature of the tradition as portrayed by *The Greek Anthology*. My point here is that the locating of altar and "tombstone" side by side, in the first two poems of "The Church," is an important symbolic gesture which allows insight into Herbert's understanding of his writing in relation to the divine. For me his most interesting exploration of the relationship between death and inscription as both sacramental and epitaphic occurs in the remarkable little poem "Church-Monuments":

> While that my soul repairs to her devotion,
> Here I entombe my flesh, that it betimes
> May take acquaintance of this heap of dust;
> To which the blast of deaths incessant motion,
> Fed with the exhalation of our crimes,
> Drives all at last. Therefore I gladly trust
>
> My bodie to his school, that it may learn
> To spell his elements, and finde his birth
> Written in dustie heraldrie and lines;
> Which dissolution sure doth best discern,
> Comparing dust with dust, and earth with earth.
> These laugh at Jeat and Marble put for signs,
>
> To sever the good fellowship of dust,
> And spoil the meeting. What shall point out them
> When they shall bow, and kneel, and fall down flat
> To kisse those heaps, which now they have in trust.
> Deare flesh, while I do pray, learn here thy stemme
> And true descent; that when thou shalt grow fat,

---

20. Rosemond Tuve, *A Reading of George Herbert* (Chicago, 1952), 33.

And wanton in thy cravings, thou mayst know,
That flesh is but glasse, which holds the dust
That measures all our time; which also shall
Be crumbled into dust. Mark here below
How tame these ashes are, how free from lust,
That thou mayst fit thy self against thy fall.

Joseph Summers, in a sensitive and rich reading of this poem, suggests that Herbert "intended the poem itself to be a *memento mori,* to function formally as a hieroglyph. The dissolution of the body and the monuments is paralleled by the dissolution of the sentences and the stanzas."[21] Certainly his perception is correct, but I would suggest further that this poem must be read in light of what "Death" teaches us about reading the *memento mori.* It is Summers's understanding that "the vanity and endurance of our lives and of our ashes provide the sole significance of the flesh and the monuments."[22] If we rest in this, we create the kind of myopic misinterpretation that the poet warns of in "Death." We are "shooting short," looking only on "this side" of a sign that generates energy in *two* directions: toward the temporal and toward the eternal. Such a reading, in the long run, invalidates the poem as a sacred hieroglyph since the purpose of such a sign is to link the human and divine in a single figure. The moral lesson Summers finds in the poem is correct, I think, it is simply not the *whole* lesson. It is true that "the flesh must 'fit' itself 'against' its 'fall' in that, in preparation for its known dissolution, it may oppose its 'fall' into pride and lust."[23] But the monuments (both this particular poem and the stones) teach us a great deal more. This is a poem that moves far beyond the traditional *ubi sunt* or *contemptus mundi.*

Let us begin at the simplest level in the poem, the dramatic situation. The poet is in church where his "soul repairs to her devotion." While he prays, he also meditates on the monuments of the dead buried within the precincts of the church. The temple contains the tomb. Already, the level is no longer simple. Herbert has set in motion several complex relationships, all based on differentiation within unity. He initiates a split in the self that separates soul from flesh, and then he separates "devotion" from thought, locating thought *in* flesh. Two actions, prayer and meditation, happen si-

21. Summers, *George Herbert,* 133.
22. *Ibid.,* 131.
23. *Ibid.,* 132.

multaneously—the soul prays in the openness of the church, while the "thinking" flesh is "entombed" in order to go to death's school, to "learn to spell his elements." For the rest of the poem the soul is left "to her devotion" in a silent spaciousness evoked entirely by way of contrast to the monuments it surrounds—monuments that ultimately are diminished and equated to the fragile flesh which is itself a tomb: the "glasse which holds the dust / That measures all our time." The opening word, "while," sustains the simultaneity of the activities and holds all the divisions together in a coherence that can finally be sustained only by being grounded in the presence of the soul in the temple. The dramatic situation is complicated immediately and purposefully by Herbert with the pun "repair" in the opening line. The soul "goes to" its devotion, leaving the flesh entombed, *and* the soul "mends" itself "while" the flesh faces its dissolution. This sort of doubleness metaphorizes the thematic statements of the poem, and the play with ambiguity operates in nearly every line. Such playfulness complicates the poem immensely and is a powerful hint that the "simple" situation is intended to provoke much deeper speculation.

Without question, we face a reading lesson similar to that which the speaker receives. We are being asked to read from two perspectives, to interpret doubly Herbert's imaging of the church which contains monuments that teach the doubled self a double lesson. We must be sure that we are not "shooting short," then, that we don't forget the "church" when we face the "monuments." The monuments are sanctified by virtue of their location within the church. But they are further privileged by the Christian notion of death as the threshold that offers immediate contact with the divine. In this respect the tomb is a sacred site in the manner of the temple, so that in this poem the flesh "repairs to its [proper] devotion" at the same time that the soul does. But it repairs itself very differently by learning to read signs. When the threshold between the mortal and the divine is perceived as a sign—as it clearly is in a poem that describes monuments as "death's school" for the body which must "learn to spell"—the crossing of the threshold is much less certain, much more tenuous than the immediate crossing offered by grace or death.

To "learn to spell" the "elements" that are "written in dustie heraldrie and lines," interpretation must be brought into play on the site that serves as the threshold between humans and God. In the monuments Herbert creates a threshold that is defined as language and must be transversed by language. In this case, then, the sacred site that differentiates orders of being and is the demarcation between profane and sacred, the "here/now" and the "there/not-yet," is a potential abyss. If one fails to read "doubly" from both sides of the demarcation, if one forgets that the monuments are located in the church, one will fall into the death of representation. In this poem such a death is suggested by the total dissolution of one sign into another, a dissolution that can be halted only if the reader reads the signs as the ambiguous double statements Herbert carefully constructed.

As the space that marks difference, the threshold is a "border-line": a void, uninhabited and, from a certain perspective, nonexistent. It is a mere function, a "no-thing" that allows the transference of energy between orders of being. This "space" between human and divine is functional only as long as it maintains its openness to both worlds. If it is not perceived as a mark between two presences, it generates what Derrida calls an "indefinitely multiplied structure—*en abyme* [in an abyss]" (*OG*, 163). As such, the "abyss" generates the endless series of representations that appear as "dissolution" on the surfaces of "Church Monuments." However, Herbert has, from the first word of the poem, constructed two presences that are consistently at work within it. These presences, soul and flesh, or church and monument, clarify the two orders of being that the inscriptions on the monuments "spell" if we read them "correctly." In this case the abyss brought into play by the assertion of the monument as sign is better understood within the Heideggerean vision that is analogous to Herbert's Christian context. In this sense the abyss, as a sacred demarcation, sustains and motivates the entire complex and establishes the possibility of the distinction between the mortal and the immortal, a distinction which then allows each to call the other into presence. This abyss is not the empty abyss of Derrida but is rather grounded in totality; "it holds and remarks everything." For Heidegger the totality of the abyss is Being or Language as "the peal of stillness"; for Herbert it is God or Logos.

In Herbert's poem we are taught to read signs doubly, as human representations and as incarnations of the Divine Word. We are asked to read as the poet/priest does, to "come to know the marks that the abyss remarks." We are asked, overtly, by "Church-Monuments" to consider the nature of signs: inscription as sign, flesh as sign, even dust as sign. And we must come to know them as they are in a sacred context. If we learn only that it is proper to subjugate the flesh because death demonstrates its absolute subjugation, we have ignored the double movement of sign in a sacred site, the movement which makes the existence of a tombstone possible. And we are likely to slip into a Derridean notion of the tomb as a "representation of a representation" rather than a Christian notion of tomb as threshold.

If we situate our interpretation on "this side" of the monuments, reading only the surface lesson, we are, in fact, forced into such a predicament. From this perspective the monuments are experienced as one stage in a series of dissolving signs which refer only to one another and are all reducible to "this heap of dust." In fact, the sole purpose of the signs seems to be to mark the stages of disintegration, and this marking is itself in the process of disintegration. The "alphabet" of signs from which the body is to "spell" his "elements" seems as undifferentiated as grains of sand. In fact, discerning becomes impossible in the sense of to "distinguish" or "perceive the difference"—a point skillfully made by the ambiguity of the line "Which dissolution sure doth best discern," where it is impossible to decide if "dissolution" is the subject or object of "discern." What the body discerns if it looks only at these "letters without the spirit" is that "monument" represents "bodie" (and vice versa); "bodie" *and* "monument" represent "dust" (and vice versa); and "bodie," "monument," and "dust" *all* represent "glasse" (and vice versa). All signs are so intra-referential that they are ultimately only self-referential. We are, indeed, in the position of "comparing dust with dust, and earth with earth," unable to "discern" or "spell" at all. We balance, in this kind of representational reading, on the dizzying precipice of meaninglessness. Most importantly, if the signs are read only in terms of one another, the all-encompassing sign, dust, finally represents nothing—the "no-thing" of the play in which it participates. Such a reading "forgets" that the "heap of dust," filled with God's breath, is living man. That is, we forget incarnation; forget that body incarnates soul, that the glasse holds the flow of *life;* forget that the monument evokes eternity as well as mortality. In other words, we "forget" that we are in a sacred site where signs "discern" as well as unite.

To "spell" correctly we must remind ourselves of the double meanings in each sign. Without them we are in danger of falling into the abyss because of our inability to "mark" it. If we read carefully, however, we discover that Herbert takes care to prevent such a "fall." We must remember that these are *church* monuments. We are not only at a tomb, but at a tomb *within* a temple. The spatial configuration is important. In one sense this poem focuses on an idea of containment, portraying a series of containers nested within one another. The question of whether the signs are 'empty' or 'full' is immediately evoked. If dust is a "no-thing," then signs are also nothings, for the tomb contains the flesh which is "but glasse, which holds the dust / That measures all our time; which also shall / Be crumbled into dust." The claustrophobia of containment is dissolved by the poem within the same gesture that creates it— not only because of the "dissolution" of each container, but because of the representational play by which each substitutes for, stands-in-place-of, the other. The only thing that prevents claustrophobia from converting to agoraphobia, however, is that the church is re-moved from the representational game. Body, monument, inscrip-tion, and glass dissolve into each other and into dust, but we are not left with nothing. We are left in the openness of the temple whose structure remains untouched. Because it is not inscribed within the words of the poem, "church" does not fall into the slipping and sliding of one sign into another. Instead it resonates in the poem as an echoing silence, openly announced only in the title as a kind of mnemonic device. It exists, in addition, as the entire collection of poems, *The Temple,* which "contains" the particular epitaphic in-scription "Church-Monuments." The temple/church functions as a 'transcendental signified' which grounds the endless drift and dis-solution of one sign into another. It is the "elsewhere" which is also "here" by virtue of a proper reading of inscription. We are, then, within the play of dif-ference rather than differance. The energy of dif-ference allows the gathering in one sacred site of two modes of being. This gathering demands the recognition of the doubleness of all signs, including the monuments. Dif-ference distinguishes and unites; it "first determines world and things in their presence, i.e., in their being toward one another, whose unity it carries out." This is not the unity of dissolution which we have seen a short-sighted reading of the signs produce. It is the unity revealed by marking the difference between human and divine even as they are joined together. Such a unity is determined by both monument and altar *as they reveal* the dif-ference, *as they function* as a site where hu-man and divine "do not subsist alongside one another. They pene-trate each other. Thus the two traverse a middle. In it they are at one" (*PLT,* 202). It is not without purpose that Herbert begins this meditation on the "flesh" of signs with a single but potent reference to the soul.

The entire poem turns on this first moment of difference: "While that my soul repairs to her devotion, / Here I entombe my flesh." The soul is "elsewhere," that is, not in the tomb but in the temple. At the same time the "I" who speaks is both "my soul" and "my body." The "I" exists simultaneously *in* temple and tomb and *as* temple and tomb. In Herbert the human, too, is a sacred site, a temple/tomb enabled by the fact that God writes "in the heart." He overtly plays on this paradox throughout his work. This doubleness allows Herbert to refer to the body as "*deare* flesh" and accounts for the tone of "Church-Monuments," which is light, loving, and free of contempt for the body. The flesh that dissolves always contains the promise of incarnation, that fleshly rebirth so happily portrayed in "Doomsday." Thus, the "I" can "gladly trust" the "school" that only seems to speak of nothingness. Echoing within the inscriptions he will indeed "finde his birth," though only dissolution seems apparent. On the threshold of the monument birth and death are both revealed—as long as all signs are perceived as being grounded by the temple. It is possible to "laugh at Jeat and Marble put for signs" because of the evident vulnerability of human artifice. "Earth" laughs knowingly, however, confident of itself as God's own sign, awaiting His incarnative breath. There is as much optimism as resignation in "Deare flesh, while I do pray, learn here thy stemme / And true descent." The "I" who prays and addresses his flesh at the same time performs a gesture of unification in which all differences are subsumed in the temple/tomb that he is and by the temple/tomb within which he is situated. Thus, to "learn *here* thy stemme / And true descent" implies learning of both human mortality and the reincarnative moment of spiritual rebirth.

The grave is origin as much as end *if* it is read correctly as a sign that incarnates the great "stillness" that penetrates and contains it, the silence of the temple. In this context the words "*gladly* trust" and the statement that "those heaps" are held "*in* trust" emerge from the flow of words with a vehemence that goes unnoticed as long as we are caught within the representational play of signs. Dissolution is only a temporary holding, awaiting the full presence that is "no-longer" and "not-yet," but which is already incarnated in their ambiguity. We are able to "discern" the full significance of to "mark here below" as always/already implicating the "there above" where the "soul repairs to her devotion," if we explore that ambiguity, looking beyond the crumbling surfaces of inscription.

The final lines, then, take on fuller meaning. Indeed, they are

an admonition against pride and lust. But if we have learned our
"stemme and *true* descent," we should also "spell" those lines as a
promise. "Tame" would have implied, for Herbert, not just that
the dust is subjugated but, in usage common in his time, that it is
"domesticated," has been "reclaimed and improved by a process of
cultivation."[24] It has been brought home. Dust can be discerned
in this way only if we perceive the incarnative potential of signs. If
we remember that the tomb is within the external "body" of the
temple, we will also remember that the flesh is the *temple* of the soul
as well as the tomb. And we will recall that God inscribes Himself
within his "dust" as well as His church. Allowing the series of representations to be penetrated by the echo of God's presence in the
temple, we will better understand the double meanings of phrasing
such as "spell his elements, and finde his birth / Written in dustie
heraldrie and lines." Of course this refers to genealogy, to the
names of the forgotten dead whose loins produced this flesh. It also
recalls the fact that man was *originally* "written" in dust; and the
writing on the monuments, as long as it is not read as the "empty
letter," as merely "alphabet" and "image," promises freedom and
reclamation in the last lines. The poem is not without regret, but it
is also not without hope. There is a certain gentle exuberance in the
tone that is simply not accounted for by interpreting the surfaces of
the signs as spelling out only decay and the vanity of life, or as
uttering mere admonishment. There is a quiet reminder at work
behind the surface warning. For it is not just man's dust, his 'sign',
that is reclaimed. In the final line body and soul are united as "thy
self," a gesture that instantly brings the soul which has been "elsewhere" back into full play. It is no longer simply part of the transcendent echo we have been hearing in all Herbert's double meanings. "Fit thy self against thy fall" unites both meanings of "against":
opposition and preparation. The body must oppose sin and sacrifice itself as sign, but such opposition, seen from the perspective of
the soul, is mere preparation, and "fall" can be understood as "for-
tunate" indeed.

The point of this analysis is to suggest both that Herbert is
always aware of language as potentially *only* representative and
that he is equally aware of our predilection for misinterpretation—
so aware that he can afford to play with it. It is also to point out
that in Herbert's writing we must assume that the double gesture
of the epitaph is *itself* doubled by the fact that it is an inscrip-

---

24. This is the definition given in the *Oxford English Dictionary*.

tion carved upon an already inscribed surface. Writing, therefore, involves a complex, dynamic oscillation between the haunting presence/absence of the human in his own language and the equally haunting presence/absence of the divine, as Logos inscribed in this sepulcher of the world. Such is the oscillation that occurs at the moment of sacrifice. The poems are, for Herbert, both site and sacrifice. They are a recognition that God is both "elsewhere" and "here," and they are an attempt to maintain the openness between language and Logos without polluting the pathway with words that widen the rift. As the poet writes in "Love II," if we are kindled with God's fire, "then shall our Brain / All her invention on thine Alter lay, / And there in hymns send back thy fire again." The Word inhales itself in the offering of human language. The idea of poetry as site and sacrifice generates the poem "Perseverance." Consider the opening lines:

> My God, the poore expressions of my Love
> Which warme these lines & serve them up to thee
> Are so, as for the present I did move,
>   Or rather as thou movedst mee.

It's impossible to separate altar from offering here. A careful reading shows that it is not "Love" which warms and serves the lines, but the "poore expressions" themselves. At the same time that they "warme these lines and serve them up," the "poore expressions" *are* the lines being offered. And the ambiguity is intensified with "as . . . I did move, / Or rather as thou movedst mee." The lines are offered to God as both human language and the Word that moves within them. The Word demands words which must contain the Word. Thus God inhales; this too is inspiration.

Despite the sacrificial structure, Herbert's idea of inspiration does not utilize "breath" as a primary metaphor. The focus is on writing, God's writing and human writing. The sacrifice of language is the sacrifice of inscription:

> Of all the creatures both in sea and land
> Onely to Man thou hast made known thy wayes,
> And put the penne alone into his hand,
> And made him Secretarie of thy praise.
>
> Beasts fain would sing; birds dittie to their notes;
> Trees would be tuning on their native lute
> To thy renown: but all their hands and throats
> Are brought to Man, while they are lame and mute.

> Man is the world's high priest: he doth present
> The sacrifice for all; while they below
> Unto the service mutter an assent,
> Such as springs use that fall, and windes that blow.
>
> ("Providence," stanzas 2–4)

It's significant that language is given by God not as 'voice' but as writing: God "put the *penne* alone into his hand." Nature has voice but it is merely an inarticulate "mutter" of "assent." It is writing that elevates man, makes him "Secretarie" and "the world's high priest." The coalition of these titles is important. As "Secretarie" man is privy to God's secrets and writes *for* God. At the same time he writes "for all" *to* God. He conducts a correspondence in two directions, and Herbert clearly equates such an act with sacrificial ritual. Writing is seen as a "service" conveying God's Word, men's words, and nature's inchoate assent across the charged path of the open: "Man is the world's high priest: he doth present / The sacrifice for all." And writing both *conveys* sacrifice and *is* the sacrifice. Herbert continues: "Wherefore, most sacred Spirit, I here present / For me and all my fellows praise to thee."

Herbert's relating of "Secretarie" and "high priest" is a depiction of poet *as* priest. The conception shows him to be analogous to Elihu in the Book of Job. The function of "Secretarie" or "priest" is not so much to 'represent' as to be a vehicle, a "medium," who is also interpreter and messenger. Unlike Elihu's, however, Herbert's words cannot be validated by the unmediated presence of the Logos. As we have seen, such presence is denied by the nature of language as a fragmentation of an ineffable totality. "Church-Monuments" reveals the dangers of writing as "being-in-the-middle," *i.e.,* as sign, and it also demonstrates Herbert's strategy for transforming representation into a kind of incarnation. It does not, however, present a solution to the problem of how the poet can guarantee the 'truth' of his message/interpretation. Therefore, though he performs Elihu's function, Herbert remains in Job's predicament. Because He "put the penne alone into his hand," God has, in effect, demanded of Herbert, as He did of Job: "Answer thou me." The poet must turn to God's own inscriptions in hopes that his writing can veil/unveil the truth. As long as God can be felt as "approaching" within His writing, incarnative language seems possible.

The incarnative gesture is particularly difficult, however, when his God seems to be withdrawing ever further. At these moments, Herbert's anxieties about the adequacy of language surface with high intensity. Withdrawal seems to crack the temple/tomb complex that is essential to incarnative language. And, though it usually promises "return," this return is not always as positively conceived as in poems such as "The Flower," "The Glimpse," or "The Temper." God's retreat inherently transforms His Book of the World into a tomb, but if it does not bear the inscription of His Word, the tomb is not necessarily a temple. In the poem I consider Herbert's darkest, the sacred site of temple/tomb is momentarily fractured, and the Word bodes destruction. Here the "calling" of the Logos is far from being the benign beckoning of the word "Child!":

> Sweet were the days, when thou didst lodge with Lot
> Struggle with Jacob, sit with Gideon,
> Advise with Abraham, when thy power could not
> Encounter Moses strong complaints and mone:
>   Thy words were then, *Let me alone.*
>
> One might have sought and found thee presently
> At some fair oak or bush, or cave, or well:
> Is my God this way? No, they would reply:
> He is to Sinai gone, as we heard tell:
>   List, ye may hear great Aarons bell.
>
> But now thou dost thyself immure and close
> In some one corner of a feeble heart
> Where yet both Sinne and Satan, thy old foes
> Do pinch and straiten thee, and use much art
>   To Gain thy thirds and little part.
>
> I see the world grows old, when as the heat
> Of thy great love, once spread, as in an urn
> Doth closet up it self and still retreat,
> Cold sinne still forcing it, till it return,
>   And calling *Justice,* all things burn.

"Decay" plays on the contrast between "then" and "now," on a past when God was fully present and a present when He seems to have totally withdrawn. It should be noticed, however, that the process of withdrawal has already begun in stanza one, which moves from the intimate, familial "lodge with Lot" to "Thy words were then, *Let me alone.*" God's words fall like cold water after the compelling repetition of "with," which strongly reinforces the idea of easy conversation and cohabitation. The first step away from His creatures seems to be generated by human language. The syntax suggests that "Moses strong complaints and mone" are directly re-

sponsible for God's response. Nonetheless, God remained near
enough "then" to allow unmediated speech, a situation that does
not recur until a projected future when the distance will have become so great that the Word is utterly transformed in its journey
across the void. The spoken Word that originally created the distance, but remained benignly responsive, will become powerfully
operative and carry destruction within itself. The same love that
yielded to Moses and then distanced itself will return as an unyield-
ing, violent explosion.

There is, in this poem, no hint of the regenerative apocalypse
portrayed in "Death" or even the poem "Doomsday." When the
heart is conceived, as it is here, exclusively as "an urn," it continues to maintain the open between human and divine, but the
eruption of God's voice into the world brings a purging rage that
will "all things burn." This, contrary to the "dust" in "Church-
Monuments," is dissolution; nothing remains after the phrase, not
even ashes, to act as signs of God's 'speech-act'. There is only
the white silence of uninscribed space: God's presence as absolute
erasure.

When the heart is temple *and* tomb it can "lodge" desire, death,
and the divine without being threatened with destruction. The
written word seems to delimit the territory of Sin and Satan. Even
The Temple requires an inscription to halt them at the door:

> Avoid Profaneness; come not here:
> Nothing but holy, pure and cleare,
> Or that which groneth to be so,
> May at his perill further go.
>   ("Superliminare")

In the "now" of "Decay," however, there seem to be none who
"groneth to be so." This is a key point in Herbert's thought. The
desire for God, expressed even in a groan, is enough to facilitate the
joining of temple with tomb in the heart. In the second stanza of the
poem, God has withdrawn so far that mediation is needed between
human words and the Word. Yet, He is still within hearing and calling distance, and the nature of the mediation is significant. Aaron's
bell seems both to displace God's voice and to reveal it in a new
manner. One now hears not the Word but the peal of the bell which
defines Aaron as "priest," the figure who becomes necessary at the
moment God retreats. At the same time it identifies the place where
man is in proximity with the (silent) Word. And it "calls" him
there. The speaker's assumption that God might be found any-

where, in "oak or bush, or cave," recalls the casual intimacy of the
first stanza. But the idea is invalidated by the reply to his question
in which "they" identify Sinai as *the* sacred place—an identification
made by virtue of Aaron's bell. "He is to Sinai gone." Nonetheless,
to go to Sinai is still to be available, if only through priestly mediation: "One might have sought and found thee presently."

The withdrawal of God to Sinai is mitigated by the fact that He
still dwells in the spaciousness and light of His world, in the temple
of the mount. The implications of the word *presently* are several.
With his usual facility for compressing optimum significance into
the most casual and ordinary words, Herbert plays on all its meanings at once. In the common usage of his time, "presently" would
have suggested "in person," "on the very spot," "forthwith," "as a
direct result," or "at that time," depending on the context (*OED*).
"At that time" would, of course, convey the contrast between
"then" and "now" which the whole poem iterates. It is important
to see, however, that "presently" also suggests that to seek was inevitably to find, "as a direct result" of the search, the presence of
God "on the very spot." The finding cannot occur, once God is
on the mount, without an active seeking that opens one's ears to
Aaron's bell.

All seeking disappears precisely at the moment "now" enters the
poem. "Decay" splits in half in the resonant gap between "bell" and
"but," formally, temporally, and tonally. The easy conversational
tone of the "then" deepens "now" into a meditative soliloquy, and
the inward turn is entirely appropriate. If one is to seek at all,
"now" it must be within. God's retreat is revealed not as a movement away into the heights of the temple/mountain, but as a movement inward to the depths of the tomb/heart. Ironically, the distance seems even greater, perhaps because the action portrayed is
not that of the seeker examining his own soul, but that of a deadly
battle. Herbert knew as well as Conrad that the heart is full of
darkness. Now God "lodges" with death. "Immure" would have
implied "entombe" to Herbert as well as "to wall in" (*OED*). It is
not death, however, but those ancient harbingers of death, "Sinne"
and "Satan," that press God into further retreat. If the heart is represented only as tomb, it cannot "avoid profaneness." And though
it continues to function as a sacred site, announcing God's presence
and absence, the balance is badly skewed. Rather than allowing a
dynamic oscillation of approach and retreat, the "profaned" tomb
can only hint at a presence growing steadily more distant: "thy
great love, once spread, as in an urn / Doth closet up it self and *still*

retreat." "Decay," then, implies a movement from a time when direct encounter through voice was possible, through one which allowed the mediation of Aaron's bell, to a "now" when God has closeted Himself so far within the tomb of the heart that (in an unusual gesture for Herbert) His trace, His inscription, is not even to be found. The question becomes whether the inscription is not found because it is not sought, or whether the seeking does not occur because the inscription is not there. Either way, the exchange between language and Logos is not operative and, as a result, the heart remains a tomb and God continues to retreat. Such steady closing up, compressing of energy, can only erupt in the explosive return of full presence, voice again, which this time will "calling *Justice,* all things burn."

The heart that grants God only his "third and little part" is always threatened with corruption and annihilation. So, likewise, is writing. God must dwell not in a "little part" but in every word, for "in one box doth lie ink and sinne." Thus Herbert prays with a characteristic condensing of writing and heart into one metaphoric figure:

> Oh, fill the place,
> And keep possession with thy grace;
> Lest sinne take courage and return
> And all the writings blot or burn.
> ("Good Friday")

It is as if the lack of inscription allows the despair and violence of "Decay." I have been emphasizing the importance of the 'spirit' to Herbert, but the 'letter' is also essential. The Word requires the veil of the "body," a letter, in order to be revealed. "Both are to be done," Herbert writes, "the scriptures still used, and Gods worke within us still observed, who workes by his Word and ever in the reading of it" (*Valdesso's Considerations,* 310). God's Word, His writing of His image in the heart, seems to protect that place against profanation, much as the "Superliminaire" engraved above the church door secured the temple. And Herbert deeply desires that protective inscription:

> The spirit and good extract of my heart
> Comes to about the many hundred part.
> Yet Lord restore thine image, heare my call:
> And though my hard heart scarce to thee can grone,
> Remember that thou once didst write in stone.
> ("The Sinner")

The inarticulate "grone" of desire also participates in the sacrificial exchange between language and Logos. It seems to "open" a
pathway through which God's word may emerge as coherent. As
always, however, we cannot assume that the groan happens "first."
The Word makes the groan possible, even as the groan admits
the Word into being. The main point to be made here is that the
"grone" calls out for writing, not voice. It is God's inscription on
the tomb of the heart that unifies that tomb with temple; His Word
spans and links church and grave, altar and monument. This writing shows God to be the supreme artisan; without it His creature
will "vanish into a winde, / Making thy workmanship deceit."
Further, the poet writes, "It is thy highest art / To captivate strong
holds to thee." This particular stronghold can be captured only if
engraved. Herbert goes on to identify the uncarved heart as life-
less tomb:

> O smooth my rugged heart and there
> Engrave thy rev'rend Law and fear;
> Or make a new one, since the old
> > Is sapless grown,
> > And a much fitter stone
> To hide my dust, then thee to hold.
> > > ("Nature")

On the other hand, God's Word, written and properly read,
unites death and life, shows the heart, which appeared "sapless
grown," to be a misperception, only "dead to the *world,*" while in
reality it "keeps house unknown."

> Who would have thought my shrivel'd heart
> Could have recovered greenness? It was gone
> Quite under ground; as flowers depart
> To see their mother-root, when they have blown;
> > Where they together
> > All the hard weather,
> Dead to the world, keep house unknown.
>
> These are thy wonders, Lord of power,
> Killing and quickning, bringing down to hell
> > And up to heaven in an houre;
> Making a chiming of a passing-bell.
> > We say amisse,
> > This or that is:
> > Thy word is all, if we could spell.
> > > ("The Flower")

The Word that is capable of "making a chiming of a passing-bell" is indeed "All." We are reminded that we "may heare great Aarons bell," announcing God's presence and summoning us, even in the death knell; we recall the "harmonious bells below, raising the dead / To lead them unto life and rest" ("Aaron"). But our language can fail, can misrepresent: "We say amisse / This or that is." And that failure is a direct result of misinterpretation: "God's word is all, *if* we could spell." Logos must, he has said, "work by His Word and ever in the reading of it." Misspeaking is almost always a matter of misreading for Herbert. Both imply the fragmentation of Logos into purely representational language: "How hath man parcel'd out thy glorious name / And thrown it on that dust which thou hast made" ("Love I"). In both "Love I" and "Love II" language "sins" inasmuch as it represents rather than incarnates. Such representation is the result of being seduced by the "image" rather than the original. "Wit fancies beautie, beautie raiseth wit," and language drifts so far from its origin that even the beloved "dust," which the lover has substituted for God, is displaced by its own "image," "alphabet," and "bark": "only a skarf or glove / Doth warm our hands and make them write of Love" ("Love I"). Herbert's contemptuous trivializing of the "skarf or glove" that represents the Petrarchan lady (who, by virtue of her "beautie" is, herself, only a representation) is an acknowledgment of the huge distance language has strayed from Logos. This absorption with the image, with the letter rather than the spirit, demonstrated by the poet's artifice, wreaks its own ironic revenge; misprision results in the loss of sight: "Dust blown by wit, till that they both were blind" ("Love II"). The parceling out of God's name is dangerous in the extreme.

It is most dangerous when God's own signs, His stones, are displaced by the hewnstone of artifice, the "unnatural" writing "exiled in the exteriority of the body." If the Word is sculpted by the tool of wit, it may be polluted by technique and become so "unnatural" that it cannot be a sanctuary "that I may dwell among." The risks, of course, are inherent in the command to "make me a sanctuary . . . after the pattern of the tabernacle." Even the best intentions can fall into representation as the mere "exteriority of the body":

> When first my lines of heav'nly joyes made mention,
> Such was their lustre, they did so excell,
> That I sought out quaint words, and trim invention.
> My thoughts began to burnish, sprout and swell,

Curling with metaphors a plain intention,
Decking the sense, as if it were to sell.
                                ("Jordan II," stanza 1)

The "decking" metaphor at work here culminates in the second stanza with "Nothing could seem too rich to clothe the sunne." This is a language exterior even to the body and so corrupt that the inner meaning of "heav'nly joyes" is symbolically prostituted. Those feminine primpings and paintings are "decking the sense, as if . . . to sell." Such language is an act of prideful egotism, a corruption of the self as well as the Word. "Sense" is polluted by representation, which substitutes rather than incarnates image. Ultimately, the "heav'nly joyes" and "sunne" are not veiled by such clothes, they are displaced: "So I did weave my *self* into the sense." "Jordan II" depends on the contrast between an artful, external, "woven" language and a natural, internal one hewn by God. The admonition is to "copie *out*" rather than to cover up. The "bad" writing of technique can only pervert and obscure God's natural writing in the heart. Herbert's "echoing" of Sidney's sonnet in the last stanza is certainly intentional and, in the context of *The Temple,* brilliantly appropriate.[25] We are meant to hear "Look in thy heart and write" when we read, "There is in love a sweetness readie penn'd: / Copie out only that, and save expense." The reference is to "love" both as an activity and as the Word inscribed by God in the heart. And "readie" should be understood as ambiguous, meaning both "easily" written and "already" written.

To Herbert this kind of "copie" would have seemed to be an utterance of the original rather than an "image" hewn by wit. To "utter," in its earlier meaning of "to outer," is to bring forth the already formed, to serve as a vehicle for exteriorizing. It is a word particularly suited to Herbert's notion of adequate language. In this poet's thought, when one "utters" God's inscription, even in fragmented form, reading and writing are grounded in truth—almost in spite of oneself. The parceling out of God's name need not be destructive if it occurs during the uttering of His all-encompassing Word and if it does not wander from Logos during the artificial constructing of an image. If God is felt to be near enough to echo within the meaning, He automatically re-collects His name into the spirit of the letters. "Thy word is all, if we could spell," Herbert writes, and in at least two poems he demonstrates that even the di-

---

25. *The Works of George Herbert,* ed. Hutchinson, 513.

vorcing of its letters cannot prevent a correct spelling of the engraved Word:

> J E S U is in my heart, his sacred name
> Is deeply carved there: but th' other week
> A great affliction broke the little frame,
> Even all to pieces: which I went to seek:
> And first I found the corner, where was J
> After, where E S, and next where U was graved.
> When I had got these parcels, instantly
> I sat down to spell them, and perceived
> That to my broken heart he was *I ease you,*
>   And to my whole is J E S U.
>   ("J E S U")

To fully appreciate Herbert's point in this delicately executed
little poem, we must bring to it most of the ideas we have been exploring. "J E S U" is paradigmatic of the poet's work as an epitaphic gesture initiated in order to recover his God. In the apparent
absence of God, language fragments and writing becomes a way
"to seek" by reinscribing the Word on the monument of the heart.
As always, the attempt to find and rewrite is also an attempt to interpret God's original inscription correctly. And in the process of
reinscribing, the poet discovers the echo of Logos, of spirit, in even
the most erratic letter. The stone of the heart can crumble "even
all to pieces," but the letter of the Word is indelibly carved and
"double" in its meaning. For Herbert, the sign written by God and
properly understood is a "tomb" in the Hegelian manner:

> The tomb is the life of the body as the sign of death, the body as the
> other of the soul, the other of the animate psyche, of the living breath.
> But the tomb also shelters, maintains in reserve, capitalizes on life by
> marking that life continues elsewhere. . . . It consecrates the disap-
> pearance of life by attesting to the perseverance of life. Thus, the tomb
> also shelters life from death. It warns the soul of possible death, warns
> (of) death of the soul, turns away (from) death. This double warning
> function belongs to the funerary monument.   (*MP,* 82)

The stony heart can evoke dissolution of the letter, of "the body as
the sign of death," but it also "shelters, maintains in reserve" the
spirit, "the living breath" of the Word. Each letter of Christ's name,
like the double resonance of the tomb that "consecrates the disappearance of life by attesting to the perseverance of life," is a re-
pository of meaning, a kind of dictionary that enables the correct
spelling of *all* words. The letter as sign is the "body" which reveals

the "soul" of the spirit that perseveres. The spirit of the letter unites the double nature of sign and self as temple and tomb. "Parcels" must be read doubly: as "fragments" and as "packages," small containers that echo the Word, allowing it to sound out as "I ease you." This peal of stillness emerges clearly if we seek hard enough, alert to Aaron's bell. As the poet asserts in "The Search," "thy absence doth excell all distance known: / So doth thy nearness bear the bell making two one." In the process of seeking and spelling, the poet writes the poem, perceives and incorporates the peal of stillness in "every word," and falls into silence once the Word has been restored to the "All"—"to my broken heart he was *I ease you,* / And to my whole is J E S U." Herbert would agree with Augustine: "Although he is not recognized in the *noise* of these two syllables . . . [we] are moved to *think* of a certain most excellent immortal nature." Thus, the poem ends with the restoration of Logos and the sacrifice of language.

"Love-joy" approaches the same issues from a slightly different perspective, focusing on the moment when "I sat me down to spell":

> As on a window late I cast mine eye,
> I saw a vine drop grapes with J and C
> Annealed on every bunch. One standing by
> Ask'd what it meant. I, who am never loth
> To spend my judgement, said, It seemed to me
> To be the bodie and the letters both
> Of Joy and Charitie. Sir, you have not miss'd,
> The man reply'd; It figures JESUS CHRIST.

The reading of this window metaphorizes the correct reading of the Word and, I believe, the reading of Herbert's poems. The vine cannot be properly read unless the letters are "annealed on every bunch," and the letters, in turn, require "the bodie" of the vine as a monument on which to be inscribed. Because the window functions as a monument, the surface meanings of both vine and letters are "doubled," referring to the temporal and the eternal simultaneously. "Love-joy" or "Joy and Charitie" imply each other in their dif-ference and are shown, finally, to be the 'same', a hyphenated inscription of the unifying spirit: "It figures JESUS CHRIST." It's important to note that Herbert writes "*it* figures," not "they figure." For the body and the letters come together as a whole, the annealed window, the translucent monument, which, correctly perceived, reveals even the unwritten Word that shines through. The Word unites the pieces even as it allows us to "discern" them.

Once again, it is impossible to determine which "comes first," the light that shines through or the colors of the window. The veiling of the light in its colors and the unveiling of the colors "happen" in the same moment. The totality of the Logos cannot be written; it is the unseen "white" light. Even the writing of God's name will bring this poem to an end. Nonetheless, if the inscribed monument is perceived as a stained-glass window, the ineffable (the invisible) will tint fragmented human language with its presence, and its light will penetrate the letters with the spirit of truth. This is "A true hymn," one that translates the peal of stillness into the light of truth on a surface where inscription allows us to read in two directions, "Till even his beams sing, and my musick shine" ("Christmas").

Thus, we return to "The Windows," the poem that affirms inscription in Herbert's very special sense: not as representation, but as (translucent) incarnation:

> Lord, how can man preach thy eternall word?
>   He is a brittle crazie glasse:
> Yet in thy temple thou doest him afford
>   This glorious and transcendent place,
>   To be a window, through thy grace.
>
> But when thou doest anneal in glasse thy storie,
>   Making thy life to shine within
> The holy Preachers; then the light and glorie
>   More reverend grows, & more doth win:
>   Which else show watrish, bleak, & thin.
>
> Doctrine and life, colours and light, in one
>   When they combine and mingle, bring
> A strong regard as awe: but speech alone
>   Doth vanish like a flaring thing,
>   And in the eare, not conscience ring.

"The Windows" is grounded in the distinctions made between speech and writing and between "crazie glasse" and windows. At the same time an analogy is established between speech and "crazie glasse," writing and window. We are asked to consider how language is like light and how the engraved surface makes light visible in the same gesture that the light reveals the meaning of the surface. The intricate play of the poem begins with the crucial problem: man, because "he is a brittle crazie glasse," fragments and distorts the "eternall word." Probably we are to understand "crazie glasse" as that fragile glass which "measures all our time" as well as the cracked glass of the distorting mirror. It is as the mirror, however, that man is most deeply flawed. The erratic warps and cracks fragment the Word, reflecting it as "parcelled out" in all directions, tossing back a twisted image of the original. If it is merely reflected by a "crazie glasse," if it is not written *into* that glass, the Word becomes a deeply perverted representation, an entirely external repetition of images corrupted by the surface that "repeats" them. Kept "outside" on the cracked surface, the Word is mere vocalization, and "speech alone / Doth vanish like a flaring thing, / And in the eare, not conscience ring."

But God's "storie" is not spoken, it is written—and not just *on* the window but *in* it. The Word dwells within its "words" as "colours and light." At the same time it exists "without" the window: the great "sunne" in the distance whose shining allows the window to be seen and read clearly. Through His grace, God inscribes in such a way that He fuses Himself and His "glasse" together, fuses "doctrine and life, colours and light, in one." Each exists by virtue of the other. The importance of "combine and mingle" cannot be overestimated in this poem. Here, the Word cannot be exiled to the exterior as representation; it is exterior and interior—"All." The inscription of God's Word, when it is seen as *annealed* in glass, is the *incarnation* of the Word. Man, as the window, gives "body" to "light and glorie," even as the light gives "life" to that body. And the process of annealing also tempers, creates strength and flexibility. No longer a "brittle crazie glasse," the body is re-created.

"But when thou dost anneal in glasse thy storie, / Making thy life to shine within / . . . then the light and glorie / More reverend grows, & more doth win," the poet writes. The phrasing is reminiscent of the closing lines of "The Quiddity," in which Herbert attempts to define the essence of poetry by a process of negation—until the final lines: "But it is that which while I use / I am with thee and *most take all*." The phrases "more doth win" and "most take all" are so deeply ambiguous that it is difficult to fracture them into even double meanings. In both cases the ambiguity is grounded in a notion of language so incarnative that God and man, the Word and words, cannot be separated. "Most take all" can mean that because "I am with thee," *I* most take all, and it can be meant as an offering, an assertion that "while I use" poetry, *God* can "most take all." It is certainly an assertion of language as the force that joins divine and human and as the place where that union occurs: site and sacrifice. In "The Windows" when "the holy Preachers" incarnate the Word, via God's inscription, each "more doth win," and so does God. The annealing process enlivens both spirit and letter, for the final line of stanza two refers to both "thy life" (as light) and "the holy Preachers" (as glass): "then the light and glorie / More reverend grows, & more doth win: / Which else show watrish, bleak, & thin."

This is the ideal. Poetry, like "The Windows," should anneal, within its (translucent) words, the Word. It should serve as a monument within which God's silence peals out and through which His light shines. Such is not always the case; often Logos seems a long way off from language. These are the moments of Herbert's deepest despair, when he will cry out:

> Where are my lines then? my approaches? my views?
> Where are my window-songs?
> Lovers are still pretending, & ev'n wrongs
> Sharpen their Muse:
>
> But I am lost in flesh, whose sugred lyes
> Still mock me, and grow bold:
> Sure thou didst put a minde there, if I could
> Finde where it lies.
>
> ("Dulnesse")

Such awareness of the inadequacy of language, of its fall into the letter without the spirit, that "flesh" of "sugred lyes," can even lead to a moment when poetry is utterly rejected and the poet is left "lame and mute" as nature, able only to "mutter an assent, / Such as springs use that fall." Herbert begins "Grief" with a plea to the natural forces for whom *he* should be "the worlds high Priest":

> O who will give me tears? Come all ye springs
> Dwell in my head and eyes: come clouds & rain:
> My grief hath need of all the watry things,
> That Nature hath produc'd.

His turn to nature occurs because language seems incapable of encompassing the "All." Like his tears, words are only "a narrow cupboard." More to the point, poetry seems inappropriate to the depth of his needs precisely because it is unnatural; it is the "bad" writing of artifice and technique:

> Verses, ye are too fine a thing, too wise
> For my rough sorrows: cease, be dumbe and mute
> Give up your feet and running to my eyes,
> And keep your measures for some lovers lute,

Whose grief allows him musick and a ryme:
For mine excludes both measure, tune, and time.
                    Alas, my God!

The closing cry, so unmeasured, so completely out of tune and
rhyme, is presented as the only language adequate to the scope of
his grief. It is the "natural" cry. It is also, in the context of this
poem, a cry that rises out of the fact that the perfectly executed
rhyme and metrics of the eighteen preceding lines have failed. "Alas,
my God!" expresses that first grief which the poem could not utter
adequately. But the cry also expresses an additional grief, over the
failure of poetry.

When poetry fails, for Herbert, it fails to incarnate. It fails because it does not "utter" God's Word but displaces it, because it behaves like representation. At such moments language points out the
great distance between the human and the divine, exposing the void
rather than closing it. Artifice strips the word of its incarnative potential, "decking" and "curling with metaphors a plain intention"
and allowing "*my* thoughts . . . to burnish, sprout and swell"
rather than God's. When language substitutes itself for Logos, it is
nothing more than a crumbling inscription etched on the surface of
a stone. The stone itself is neither altar nor tombstone, since it
does not 'voice' the haunting echo of Being within being. Such a
surface is simply another empty sign bearing the burden of a self-
referential textuality "written in dustie heraldrie and lines." Artifice
that focuses only on the external image, on the empty letter, cannot transform a surface into a sacrificial site. It can only initiate a
play between signs that hides the "nothing" of dissolution that lies
within. Such poetry will never open a pathway between language
and Logos. When the poet "falls" into its use, he only looks "on
this side . . . shooting short" and finds a deserted husk, "the shells
of fledge souls left behinde." A terrible forgetting occurs; one forgets to seek within for God's own inscription, for the Word God
has "veiled" by annealing it within the heart. When language becomes representation rather than incarnative utterance, the poem
becomes an object rather than a sacramental experience. It can be
looked *on,* but it cannot be looked *through* like a stained-glass window. This kind of poetry is not genuinely epitaphic inasmuch as
epitaph generates an experience of absence as a "no-longer" and a
"not-yet," allowing past and future to haunt the "now." It does not
promise a return; it only announces a leave-taking, a loss without
compensation. For Herbert such an inscription seems radically

"unnatural," a denial of God's act as author of the Book of the
World. Purely representational language denies the possibility that
spirit haunts the letter and forces the reader into an encounter with
signs wherein they seem to be death's-heads rather than monuments. The problem and the solution are made clear in one of the
sonnets from Walton's *Lives:*

> Sure, Lord, there is enough in thee to dry
>   Oceans of *Ink;* for as the Deluge did
>   Cover the Earth, so doth thy Majesty:
> Each Cloud distills thy praise, and doth forbid
> *Poets* to turn it to another use.
>   *Roses* and *Lillies* speak thee; and to make
>   A pair of Cheeks of them is thy abuse.
> Why should I *Womens eyes* for Chrystal take?
> Such poor invention burns in their low mind
>   Whose fire is wild, and doth not upward go
>   To praise, and on thee, Lord, some *Ink* bestow.
> Open the bones, and you shall nothing find
>   In the best *face* but *filth,* when, Lord, in thee
>   The *beauty* lies in the *discovery.*

   The "natural" language in this poem is a "distillation" of the
Word during an act of "discovery." It is utterance, the "outering"
from within of what God has already annealed in clouds, roses, and
lilies—and within human bones. The idea of distillation is complementary to annealing. To condense and purify language until one is
left only with the essence is to discover the Word annealed within
words. It is presumptuously "unnatural" to "make a pair of Cheeks"
of lilies and roses instead of discovering that they "speak thee."
Such an act drives the Word further into the distance; signs become
perverted obstacles to vision rather than windows. They "parcel
out" and obscure the Word rather than distilling it. The path of sacrificial exchange cannot be opened by "poor invention . . . / Whose
fire is wild, and doth not upward go." As a result, such signs are
uninhabited. Even the "best face," if it does not incarnate the Word,
is the empty representation of the death's-head: "Open the bones,
and you shall nothing find / . . . but filth." The proper purpose of
ink is to "naturally" distill the dispersed and translucent cloud of
God's Word into a visible condensation that enables "discovery."
Ink, then, "unveils," reveals Logos even as it "veils" it with a more
concrete "body." If "the *beauty* lies in the *discovery,*" it is because to

discover means both to find and to manifest, to catch sight of and to expose to view.

Writing, then, is a matter of finding and revealing—and, pre-eminently, of seeking and using the right words. They must be always the words already written by God, the natural inscription that must be reinscribed. The project is neither safe nor assured. Rosalie Colie has said that "writing became a sign of grace to the poet," and that to Herbert it seemed "impossible for any poet to be anything but a sacred poet, precisely because all acts of creation were imitations of God's model act."[26] Radical qualifications are needed for these statements. It seems more appropriate to see Herbert's writing as the *seeking* of grace or the re-collection of gestures that approach and admit an experience of grace never found within the poem but rather in the silence that follows it. It is certainly possible that "writing became a sign of grace to the poet," but only if we are referring to *God's* writing, rather than the poet's. For it is "precisely because all acts of creation were *imitations* of God's model act," that Herbert remained anxiously aware that it was dangerously possible to be a "profane" poet—even when writing of God. The rift between God's writing and human imitation must be traversed by interpretation and by an incarnative language that "discovers" the interpretation. There is much room for errance within that space, and the distance can be terrifying. "My grief must be as large / As is thy space / Thy distance from me," the poet writes ("The Search"). And frequently enough language cannot span the distance:

> My throat, my soul is hoarse;
> My heart is wither'd like a ground
>   Which thou dost curse.
>   My thoughts turn round,
> And make me giddie; Lord, I fall
>   Yet call.
>   ("Longing")

Herbert's sometimes anxious, often exuberant, but always consistent project, then, is to bring God "near." He does so by recognizing that inscription is epitaphic, that it allows presence and absence *if* it is constructed as a sacred site that unites temple and tomb, life and death. For writing to be such a site it must be incarnative in the Heideggerean sense, must initiate the sacrificial exchange in

26. Colie, *Paradoxia Epidemica*, 198–200.

which the Word "clears a space for itself" and calls back an echo:
"This echo is man's answer to the Word of the soundless voice of
Being, the speechless voice of Being, the speechless answer of his
thanking through sacrifice is the source of the human word. . . .
Obedient to the voice of Being, thought seeks the Word through
which the truth of Being may be expressed."[27] "Thought *seeks* the
Word," and—as Job knew, as Herbert knew—it is difficult to be
certain if one has found it. Like Job, Herbert contests with his God
and turns to confession, the sacrifice of language to Logos, in order
to secure his words.

> Yet by confession will I come
> Into thy conquest: though I can do nought
> Against thee, in thee I will overcome
> The man, who once against thee fought.
> ("The Reprisall")

Herbert, however, goes a step further than Job. He sacrifices language on an altar constructed from language and offers to God,
within his words, God's own, inscribed on the altar/monument of
the heart. "The Altar" has been seen by some critics as a relatively
superficial exercise in "wit" and as a playful experiment with an ancient tradition.[28] It is an experiment, but one that is genuinely profound. The poem is, I believe, Herbert's response to the command
to "make me a sanctuary . . . after the pattern of the tabernacle."
His response recognizes the difficulties of doing so when one has
also been commanded to build with unhewn stone. Herbert responds by attempting to use artifice to efface artifice. He presents
the "thing-itself." And it is all there: the inscribed monument that
functions as the "tomb" and as the "temple"; the heart that is both
of these; and the sacrificial gesture that seeks God by offering a site
for Him to penetrate and sanctify both words and world. I choose
not to fragment the poem with analysis, and I leave it to the reader
to consider it in view of the preceding pages. As always, Herbert
speaks best for himself:

27. Heidegger, "What Is Metaphysics?" in *Existence and Being,* ed. Brock, 390.
28. For the tradition, see Tuve, *A Reading of George Herbert.* As an example of
criticism that sees the poem as clever but wanting, see Vendler, *The Poetry of George
Herbert,* 61–63.

A broken ALTAR, Lord, thy servant reares,
Made of a heart, and cemented with teares:
  Whose parts are as thy hand did frame;
  No workmans tool hath touch'd the same.
            A   HEART   alone
            Is   such   a   stone
            As   nothing   but
            Thy pow'r doth cut
            Wherefor each part
            Of my hard heart
            Meets in this frame,
            To praise thy Name:
  That if I chance to hold my peace,
  These stones to praise thee may not cease.
O let thy blessed SACRIFICE be mine,
And sanctifie this ALTAR to be thine.

❧5❧

I THINK, THEREFORE I DIE: FROM
AUTOBIOGRAPHY TO AUTO–AFFECTION

All this I do inside me, in the huge court of my memory. . . . I encounter myself; I recall myself—what I have done, when and where I did it, and in what state of mind I was in at the time. . . . From the same store I can take out pictures of things which have either happened to me or are believed on the basis of experience; I can myself weave them into the context of the past . . . and then I can contemplate all these as though they were in the present. . . . It is like a vast and boundless subterranean shrine. Who has ever reached the bottom of it?

—Augustine, *The Confessions*

The memory in some men, 'tis true, is very tenacious, even to a Miracle: But yet there seems to be a constant decay of all our Ideas, even of those which are struck deepest, and in the minds most retentive; so that if they be not sometimes renewed by repeated exercise of the Senses, or Reflection on those kinds of Objects which at first occasioned them, the Print wears out, and at last there remains nothing to be seen. Thus the Ideas as well as Children of our Youth, often die before us: and our Minds represent to us those tombs, to which we are approaching; where though the Brass and Marble remain, yet the inscriptions are effaced by time, and the Imagery moulders away.

—John Locke, *An Essay Concerning Human Understanding*

> The days gone by
> *Return upon me almost from the dawn*
> *Of life; the hiding-places of man's power*
> *Open; I would approach them, but they close.*
> *I see by glimpses now; when age comes on*
> *May scarcely see at all; and I would give*
> *While yet we may, as far as words can give,*
> *Substance and life to what I feel, enshrining,*
> *Such is my hope, the spirit of the Past*
> *For future restoration.*

—William Wordsworth, *The Prelude*, Book XII

Augustine, Herbert, and Wordsworth all wrote, each in his own way, spiritual autobiographies. There are, however, substantial differences between a mind that images self as a "vast and boundless subterranean shrine," one that images self as a "temple/tomb," and one that, in search *for* self, finds "hiding-places" that close when he would "approach them." In his *Confessions,* Augustine suggests that nothing in his past is irretrievable, that his memory, like a huge warehouse, is a "store" of images co-present with each other and potentially present to his writing at all times. And not just images seem wholly available to his call; rather, he says, "I encounter *myself;* I recall *myself.*" When the saint turns to his past, his memory is perceived as a boundless source and as a sacred site which does not represent presence but actually calls presence into being. That is, it is perceived in the manner of a temple—not one that he must construct, but one always available as a "boundless subterranean shrine."[1] Such an understanding of autobiographical recollection is essentially incarnative.

Wordsworth, on the other hand, suggests that the past hides from him, retreats even as he attempts to "approach" it. For him the activity of remembering is an oscillation between openings and closings, "glimpses" and disappearings, presence and absence. The memory is not an already existing shrine awaiting his arrival. Instead, he images autobiography as the process of constructing the shrine itself. It is the attempt to secure presence in words, to create that which Augustine simply discovers. He cannot just turn inward and search the temple within; the poet must build the temple first. He must, "as far as words *can,*" himself "give Substance and life," and establish the shrine which Augustine needs only to enter. And for Wordsworth there is a disturbing possibility that language is not fully adequate to the task. That important qualification, "as far as words can," reveals his great distance from Augustine's temple of the mind and separates him from even Herbert's sense of language as the temple/tomb.

This movement from the *discovery* of presence to the need to *create* presence in words is provisionally called in this chapter the movement from autobiography to auto-affection. I say "provisionally" because it is probable that "autobiography" from a twentieth-century perspective must always be written in quotation marks. The difficulties of defining autobiography as a genre have been discussed by Paul de Man in a fine essay to which we will refer again in considering Wordsworth. He is quite right to suggest that "autobi-

---

1. Augustine, *Confessions,* X, viii, 217–18. All further references are to this edition and are noted by book, chapter, and section.

ography lends itself poorly to generic definition; each specific instance seems to be an exception to the norm."[2] For my purposes
here the term *autobiography* will refer to a writing of "spiritual history" that claims to recuperate that history in full. It is writing that
situates itself as (a paradigmatic) incarnative gesture. The movement
from autobiography to auto-affection is treated here, then, as a shift
from a situation in which it seems possible to recall, to incarnate,
the self as presence to one in which the self must be represented:
'imaged' to itself, by itself, in order to exist at all. Within this
movement the problematics of writing suffer significant changes.

    Autobiography is a relatively "recent" word created out of its
Greek elements, *auto* (self) and *graphus* (written) (*OED*). The inser-
tion of *bio* between these elements suggests that writing determined
as "auto*bio*graphy" is a language that can embody actual life—if
not the living organism, at least the vital force of being. In other
words, it suggests that such writing can incarnate living presence.
Understood in this way the word seems appropriate within Augustine's context. But the incarnative capacity that *autobiography*
implies seems inappropriate to a gesture in which recollection is
characterized as a process of seeing "by glimpses," of seeing the
past "close" even as one approaches it. The distinctions, of course,
are not absolute: as I have already noted, Augustine felt the fragmenting pressures of representational language, and it will become
evident that Wordsworth sought incarnative language as, at least, a
possibility. The differences between the works are to be found not
in the desires of their authors, but in the capacities for language that
seem to be offered by the moments in which they lived. In this context Wordsworth's "autobiography" is better understood as auto-
affection than as the self-written incarnation of presence.

    The term *auto-affection,* coined by Derrida in his work on Rous-
seau in *Of Grammatology,* does not in any way suggest the possibility of incarnating presence. In fact, Derrida uses it to discuss the
processes of thought and writing that forbid presence, the processes that inherently differ from and defer presence when writing
is understood as "supplement," that is, as generated by differance. Auto-affection is directly related to these two "no-things,"
these functions which enable thought and writing in the first place.

---

2. Paul de Man, "Autobiography as De-facement," *Modern Language Notes,*
XCIV (1979), 919–30. De Man's essay suggests the questions that underlie much of
my investigation of Wordsworth.

Like auto-eroticism, Derrida writes, auto-affection is "onanism that permits one to be himself affected by providing himself with presences, by summoning absent beauties. [It is] the restitution of presence by language, restitution at the same time symbolic and immediate" (*OG,* 153). But, Derrida explains, to provide presence by summoning the absent, to restore presence through images or signs in a gesture that is "*at the same time* symbolic and immediate," reveals a radical contradiction. The image seems immediate because it is internal and idealized, but it clearly substitutes for an unattainable presence and undermines immediacy altogether. For Derrida the contradiction is basic to language—perhaps to perception itself—and it further demonstrates for him the ungrounded nature of presence as pure representation. Auto-affection is another name for the play of thought in which presence can never be fully incarnated, but can be evoked only by an endless series of representations which validate it as *always/already* an absence. In its desire for immediacy for full presence, the mind deludes itself: "the presence that it gives itself is the substitutive symbol of another presence, *it has never been possible to desire* that presence 'in person' *before* this play of substitution and this symbolic experience of auto-affection" (*OG,* 153, my emphasis). Within this delusion, desire creates another paradox: as image or "internal" sign, presence is felt to be fully incarnated and fully attained. However, within the logic of auto-affection, "what is no longer deferred is also absolutely deferred. The presence that is thus delivered to us in the present is a chimera. Auto-affection is pure speculation" (*OG,* 153). The pun on "speculation" here is important: because the image gives the illusion of visible presence, it appears to the "eye" which is "immediately" felt as the "I." That illusory presence is also (and only) "speculative" in the sense that it is a conjecture, a supposition that cannot be validated. But a further meaning suggested by "pure speculation" is intended by Derrida— "speculation" as an economic endeavor, a gamble made on the exchange of commodities in the expectation of gaining a profit. What is to be gained from the speculative exchange enacted here is the deferment of absence itself, the putting-off of the recognition that "presence *is* absence" (*OG,* 154). "The sign, the image, the representation, which come to supplement the absent presence are the illusions that sidetrack us," Derrida writes. They sidetrack us from encountering presence as an absolute absence that can be understood only as "death." Auto-affection, presence "delivered to us" as a chimera, defers absence, but within its paradoxical structure,

within the speculative exchange of sign for the thing-itself, it also
reveals "the menace of death" (*OG,* 154). Auto-affection as the
"supplementary" gesture is "maddening because it is neither presence nor absence" (*OG,* 153). It is, rather, that which institutes the
opposition itself, sets up the situation in which each must invoke
the other and the "presence" of the sign must carry within itself the
death of the thing-itself. Because the sign defers absence by being
exchanged for it, it is both "a terrifying menace" and "the first and
surest protection against that very menace" (*OG,* 154).

This "maddening" structure of thought, this "strange economy
of the supplement," substitutes image for presence, sign for the
thing-itself. It denies loss and absence even as it points to that radical absence as the "death" that necessitates substitution in the first
place. "The image," Derrida has written, "is death." He explains:

> the image is *a* death or (the) death is *an* image. Imagination is the power
> that allows life to affect itself with its own representation. The image
> cannot represent and add the representer to the represented, except in
> so far as the presence of the represented is already folded back upon it-
> self in the world, in so far as life refers to itself as to its own lack, to its
> own wish for a supplement. The presence of the represented is consti-
> tuted with the help of the addition to itself of that nothing which is the
> image, announcement of its dispossession within its own representer
> and within its death. The property [le propre] of the subject is merely
> the movement of that representative expropriation. In that sense imagi-
> nation, like death, is representative and supplementary.   (*OG,* 184)

The image as an "announcement of its [presence's] dispossession
within its own representer and within its death" is the image understood as purely "representative and supplementary," that is, as auto-
affection. It is the ungrounded representation of a representation, an
endless process of substitution which forbids representers to capture
even their own self-presence. Derrida comes very close to identifying this activity as thought, as life itself: "the subject *is* merely
the movement of that representative expropriation" (*OG,* 184).

Auto-affection, however, suppresses this situation. The profit to
be gained from its speculative endeavor, from the "strange economy," is the deferral of death and the illusion of a unified self, a self
that can appear to be available to discovery and recuperation in an
incarnative language. Despite this profit, the "dispossession"—the
acknowledgment of a radical absence that the image as substitution
inevitably evokes—remains, according to Derrida, "a terrifying
menace"; it figures forth *a* death and is the figure for, the figuration
of, death in general. The "strange economy" in which the living

mind "sidetracks" itself from death by affecting "itself with its own representation" creates a situation in which "presence *is* absence, the nondeferred is deferred" (*OG,* 154). The imagination fills itself with the "nothing which is the image": the mind experiences that absence as presence and thereby evades the death that the image must convey, since it is a substitution for presence. The economy of auto-affection, then, is one that has "the power of procuring an absent presence through its image; procuring it for us through the proxy of the sign." This procurement is an investment in life against death. Auto-affection protects us against the death exposed in "presence *as* absence," and "it holds it at a distance and masters it. For this presence is at the same time desired and feared." However, "its economy exposes and protects us at the same time *according to the play of forces* and *the differences of forces*" (*OG,* 155, my emphasis). When the mind is seen as self-representing, as imaging itself *to* itself, the desired self-presence must be exposed as illusion: "The presence that is thus delivered to us in the present is a chimera. Auto-affection is pure speculation." The chimera is crucial, for "pure presence, if such a thing were possible, would be only another name for death" (*OG,* 155).

This double movement of exposure and protection absolutely forbids the full recovery of a past self by the "present" writing self, which "autobiography" in the Augustinian sense suggests is possible. Only within a fully logocentric system, an ontotheological notion of being, can the play be stabilized, and presence freed from the taint of absence by being tethered to the transcendental signified: the Word. Within such a system the image offers the possibility of discovery, of revealing the incarnated truth that grounds it and which it incorporates. When language can be brought to rest in the "still center" of truth, it can repress the play of representation, and auto-affection is erased. Augustine can write *The Confessions* as a direct address to his God and validate that address as prayer itself: "When I pray to Him, I call Him into myself," he writes, fully aware of the basic paradox in his thought: "Why then do I ask you to enter into me? For unless you were in me, I could not exist" (I, chap. 2, 18). The paradox allows Augustine's words to be God's Word and his autobiography to be the "utterance" of God's Words. His five-chapter exploration of the paradox culminates in the assertion that secures all his own words: "Everywhere you are present in your entirety, and no single thing can contain you in your entirety" (I, chap. 3, 19).

For Augustine the "I am" is determined by the "I AM THAT I

AM." Existence is certain because the Creator is certain; his being is lived within Being, and that Being penetrates every individual. The self as memory is bountiful and expansive: "Who has ever reached the bottom of it?" Augustine asks. But for him the question is rhetorical and has an answer already embedded within it. His descent into the depths of memory is an ascent to God. The end of his long exploration of himself as memory is the discovery of the God who is both without and within, everywhere and nowhere, who is in "an inner place, which is yet no place" that we call "mind," and who is also the "Truth which is everywhere in session" (X, chap. 9, 220, and chap. 26, 235). God guarantees the unity of the self in spite of its manifold fragmentation. "Great is the power of memory!" the saint writes. "It is something terrifying, my God, a profound and infinite multiplicity; and this thing is the mind and this thing is I myself. What then am I, my God?" (X, chap. 17, 227). He finds his answer in the Presence within: "See what a distance I have covered in searching for you, Lord, in my memory! . . . and there I find you whenever I call you to mind and delight in you" (X, chap. 24, 234). The "I am," the self, is that which remembers God, and that memory marks not a past encounter with an "other" but a living Presence which is also the self and which will surface if one only looks toward it: "Late it was that I loved you, beauty so ancient and so new, late I loved you! And look, you were within me and I was outside and there I sought for you and in my ugliness I plunged into the beauties that you have made. You were with me, and I was not with you" (X, chap. 27, 235). If one seems "outside" the self, it is because one is "outside of God." But this is only a seeming, an appearance which results from misprision, a looking in the wrong direction. Actual divorce from the self or God is impossible, a self-deception resulting from objectification, from treating the Creator as the created. It is a powerful illusion, but one that crumbles before the fact that, always, "you were with me." The most corrupted memory carries within itself an indelible notion of Truth—a Truth that expresses itself as a desire for, and a recollection of, happiness. The "first principle" is not "I think," which carries with it the necessity for an object to be thought, but rather "Truth *is*"—an animating principle prior even to thought. The notion that "Truth is" and is always within me as I am within it binds past and future to the present, weaving the self into a continuous whole. This unity culminates in a moment of pure vitality: "in my whole self I shall cling to you united, I shall find no sorrow anywhere, no labor; wholly alive will my life be all full of you" (X, chap. 28, 236). The "bottom" of memory has been plumbed; its ground is God as Truth, and Augustine's "subterranean shrine" is "full," filled by the radiant unity of self and God dwelling within each other. If the "shrine" is a sacred tomb, it is also a temple within which God and man unite, not in a recollected past but as a single living present.

Augustine's search of the mind as memory is ultimately an exploration of the absolute self-presence (and absolute present) implied in the mystery of God's own "autobiographical" self-definition: I AM THAT I AM. The untranslatable self-proximity here, the denial of time and discontinuity, is shared by the soul that dwells within God and within which God dwells. Augustine's autobiography, then, is not "recollection" as we usually think of it. It is literally self-expression, the externalizing or "utterance" of the dynamic and eternal totality within. Since "God *is,* therefore I *am*" is the "first principle" of his thought, all discontinuities and merely human impositions of sequential time are absorbed by the great integrity of timeless Being. The notions of inside and outside are collapsed into the Being which is everywhere and nowhere, and absolute alienation is unthinkable. Such is the security within which Augustine writes.

This eternal presence enables the circular coherence of his work. *The Confessions* is literally centered by the Word of God. The revelation of the Word as both voice and scripture causes Augustine's conversion in the garden (VIII, chap. 8) midway through the work. His autobiography begins in a recollection of his own birth and ends in a reiteration of the Book of Genesis, the birth of the world. It ends in the beginning. Augustine writes in order to teach through revelation and, appropriately, he closes his work with the word "opened": "What angel will teach an angel? What angel will teach a man? This must be *asked* of you, *sought* in you, *knocked* for at you. So, so shall it be received, so shall it be *found,* so shall it be *opened*" (XIII, chap. 38, 350).

For Wordsworth, "the hiding places of man's power Open," but when he seeks them they immediately "close." And *The Prelude* suggests quite a different order than does Augustine's *Confessions.* The poet begins with a discussion of "escape," "freedom," and false beginnings. His attempts to write are not guaranteed by a transcendent Logos, but rather are "cheered" by "my own voice . . . the mind's / Internal echo of the imperfect sound" (I, ll. 55–

56).[3] In effect he begins the work in the echo of himself, and that echo generates the great question that the poem attempts to answer:

> Was it for this
> That one, the fairest of all rivers, loved
> To blend his murmurs with my nurse's song
> . . . For this, didst thou
> O Derwent! winding among grassy holms
> Where I was looking on, a babe in arms
> Make ceaseless music that composed my thoughts?
>
> (I, ll. 269–77)

The echoing composition of his thoughts is Wordsworth's source and subject in the great poem, but the difficulties of centering such a work in the self prove to be enormous. The center is always in motion. *The Prelude* links together a series of privileged moments similar to Augustine's, but they are by no means the same. They are written as a chain of partial, never total, revelations, which seem unable to center the work and are characterized as "recompense" or "solace" for some unnameable loss. Wordsworth, too, intended to teach in his work, but in the long discussion of its value which ends the poem, the poet's claims are severely limited. When I began, he writes, "I said unto the life which I had lived, / Where art thou?" (XIV, ll. 378–79). He begins in uncertainty and ends there, but in ending he finds no closure; there is no circling back to beginnings here. "Whether to me shall be allotted life, / And, with life, power to accomplish aught of worth / . . . Is all uncertain" (XIV, ll. 388–92). Certainty cannot be gained by grounding his words in the clarity of vision promised by a central truth; rather, Wordsworth, in a gesture perfectly appropriate to the nature of his poem, secures his writing in the understanding of the friend/poet Coleridge to whom the poet is addressed: "To thee," he writes, "the work shall justify itself" (XIV, l. 415). This poem is grounded only in its own words and the mind of its most capable readers.

The Prelude ends, then, not in the beginning, but with the potential loss of world:

> though (too weak to tread the ways of Truth)
> This age fall back to idolatry,
> Though men return to servitude as fast
> As the tide ebbs, to ignominy and shame,

3. William Wordsworth, *The Prelude: Or Growth of a Poet's Mind*, ed. Ernest De Selincourt (Oxford, 1975), XII, 277–86. All subsequent references are to this edition.

By nations, sink together, we shall still
Find solace—knowing what we have learnt to know.
                                        (XIV, ll. 233–38)

In place of certainty, *The Prelude* offers "solace." Its teaching, offered to those "higher minds" (XIV, l. 90) that "have the consciousness of / Whom they are" (XIV, ll. 114–15), is that the recompense
for loss is the mind itself, the power of self-consciousness displaces
the revelation of Truth. The creative mind of man "becomes a
thousand times more beautiful than the earth / On which he dwells"
and is "itself / Of quality and fabric more divine" (XIV, ll. 449–54).

Obviously Wordsworth's "autobiography" is of an entirely different kind than Augustine's, and perhaps the difference is shown
most clearly by the metaphors the two employ in describing their
acts of recollection. When Augustine seeks his "subterranean
shrine," he finds that "so it shall be opened." The opening provides
the clarity of full presence: "I recall myself . . . I can contemplate all
these as though they were in the present." And he can do so because
the opening is into the eternal present of Logos. Wordsworth, experiencing the closing that forces him to build his shrine rather than
simply enter it, describes recollection as a superimposed series of
reflections, reflections as representations:

> As one who hangs down-bending from the side
> Of a slow-moving boat, upon the breast
> Of still water, solacing himself
> With such discoveries as his eye can make
> Beneath him in the bottom of the deep,
> Sees many beauteous sights—weeds, fishes, flowers,
> Grots, pebbles, roots of trees, and fancies more,
> Yet often is perplexed, and cannot part
> The shadow from the substance, rocks and sky,
> Mountains and clouds, reflected in the depth
> Of the clear flood, from things which there abide
> In their true dwelling; now is crossed by gleam
> Of his own image, by sunbeam now,
> And wavering motions sent he knows not whence,
> Impediments that make his task more sweet;
> Such pleasant offices have we long pursued
> Incumbent o'er the surface of past time.
>   (IV, ll. 256–72)

The complex interplay of shadow and substance in this extended
simile deserves its own analysis. But for now it is the reflection of

self, the "gleam of his own image," that demands our attention. At
no point in this moment does the poet clearly "see" the unimpeded
presence of the thing-itself. The reflective medium, the water, interposes itself; it allows image to intrude upon image until presence
becomes so diaphanous that the poet cannot part "the shadow from
the substance." The "nothing" of the image displaces and adds itself to other images until the reflections, the illusions of presence,
cannot be separated from "their true dwelling." To further compli-
cate things, all of this past world is "crossed by gleam / Of his own
image." It is crossed, that is, by his own reflection, in both senses of
the word. A fine, visible portrayal of auto-affection, this scene—
which in a rare pun Wordsworth uses to characterize the process of
recollection as reflection—is a key to the entire poem. "Discoveries" presented as so unstable that they cannot be situated in "their
true dwelling" could never produce a poem that could end with
Augustine's word "opened." Of necessity, *The Prelude* ends with a
paean to the (self-) creating mind, the mind that must reflect upon
and reflect, that is, "image," itself in order to create itself.

  The shift from autobiography to auto-affection that the works
of Augustine and Wordsworth manifest is certainly not to be iso-
lated only within directly autobiographical works. The movement
from language understood as incarnative presencing to language
understood as primarily and dangerously representational is also,
certainly, not something that occurs in a single "catastrophic" moment. The previous discussion of Herbert's enterprise evidences the
erosion of each notion of language by its "other," and, as I have
said, even Augustine must struggle with the fragmentation and
gaps suggested by language as representation. However, the inter-
jection of the self between Being and beings provides a salient point
in which to locate a shift in emphasis from language/thought as a
presencing incarnation to language/thought as representation.
  I have said that the paradox of language for Augustine as well as
for Herbert is that humans can come into the presence of God only
in language in which God is already present. Once the cartesian
moment absorbs European thought, that paradox transforms, becoming: humans can come into their *own* presence only through
language in which the *self* is already present. The effort to keep humans from sliding out of their own representation becomes para-
mount; human breath, human spirit, must be sustained within the
word. And, if a sacrificial gesture is made within the new construct,

it is entirely *of* the self *to* the self, as an image—a representation. If thought had seen itself as balanced between presentation and representation (incorrectly, according to both Heidegger and Derrida), the balance tips entirely toward representation in the seventeenth and eighteenth centuries.[4]

Heidegger understands representational thinking as only one possibility, and a "fallen" one at that, for perceiving Being. Since his sense of "pre-Platonic" thought is analogous to the "Christian ontological experience" of Herbert and Augustine, the contrast Heidegger makes between "the great age of Greece" and "modern thought" is helpful here. For the ancients he thinks that

> the existent does not become existent through the fact that only man faces it in the sense of subjective perception. Rather it is man who is faced by the existent, who is gathered into its presence by the self-disclosing. To be faced by the existent, to be drawn into its disclosure and included and so borne by it, to be harassed by its contradictions and marked by its conflicts—that is the essence of man in the great age of Greece. . . . Quite different is the modern representation, the significance of which is best expressed by the word *representatio*. To re-present here means to bring what is present before one as something confronting oneself, to relate it to oneself, the person representing it, and to force it back into this relation to oneself as the normative area. Where this kind of thing happens, man "gets into the picture" with respect to the existent. But in so far as man thus puts himself in the picture, he puts himself into the setting, that is, into the open horizon of the universally and openly represented. Therefore, man posits himself as the setting, in which the existent must from now on represent itself, that is, be a view or picture. Man becomes the representative of the existent in the sense of the objective.[5]

It is the idea that world exists in a confrontational manner and only in relationship to the self that is important here. Man is no longer contained within the full presence of Being. Rather, Being is *possessed* by man, won by him and only by virtue of his ability to represent it to himself. Further, man is not just "the setting" of world,

4. For a thorough and fascinating discussion of language as part of a total system of representational thought in the late seventeenth and the eighteenth centuries, see Foucault, *The Order of Things*, chaps. 3 and 4. For the (heuristic) positing of the "Cartesian Moment" as a turning point in thought, see *OG*, 16–17, and Martin Heidegger, "The Age of the World View," in *Martin Heidegger and the Question of Literature*, ed. Spanos.

5. Heidegger, "Age of the World View," in *Martin Heidegger and the Question of Literature*, ed. Spanos, 11–12.

but also of his own existence. He exists only within the representational play of his own mind as an image to himself. If Augustine and Herbert could experience the full presence of God as grace, as the unity with silence, it is because their beings are conceived as "happening" within Being, because they are "gathered into its presence," because, finally, they can be "drawn into its disclosure and included and so borne by it"—even if they are "harassed by its contradictions and marked by its conflicts."

Once being becomes *representatio,* however, the self is disrupted—in fact, interrupted—by the space that arises between the representing activity and the representation that is perceived as "being." In this context Herbert's strategies for making language incarnative are simply unavailable to the Romantics. His methods are ultimately dependent on an Augustinian concept of Being and being as distinct but interpenetrating. This is, of course, precisely the existential situation most deeply desired by the thinkers of the Romantic period. The idea is reiterated, rephrased as "unity in multiplicity," or "multeity in unity," or the "universal in the particular." Unity with the transcendental "one" is the dominant theme in all their work. It is not surprising then that Coleridge's definition of "symbol," for instance, should echo a Christian notion of being in a secular context. In fact, it sounds very much as if it described the "statement" made by Herbert's "The Windows." The symbol "is characterized by a translucence of the special in the individual, or of the general in the special, or of the universal in the general; above all by the translucence of the eternal through the temporal. It always partakes of the reality which it renders intelligible; and while it enunciates the whole, abides itself as a living part in that unity of which it is the representative."[6]

Coleridge spent a lifetime trying to validate the ontotheological stance floating behind this definition. His own "autobiography," *Biographia Literaria,* is motivated by his need to do so. But need is not quite belief, and Coleridge is like his own ancient mariner: he has slain his albatross and must tell his story over and over, searching for the something more that can end his terrible isolation and restore his unity with world. The albatross that is his burden is inherited from Descartes. His definitions of 'symbol', or of imagination and spirit, are invalidated by his own understanding of being

6. Samuel Taylor Coleridge, "The Statesman's Manual," in *Critical Theory,* ed. Adams, 468.

itself. The "I am," he asserts, is the "identity" of subject and object and can be expressed "indiscriminately" by the words "spirit, self, and self-consciousness."[7] Here is the crux of the issue. When Coleridge comes to discuss the nature of self or spirit, it *must* be in terms of self-consciousness, and his own discussion radically denies the possibility of identity. Within it the transcendental "third term" is absent, and spirit is understood as an endless play of representation. It is a commonplace that the Romantics replaced God with Nature. This is not, however, quite correct. Nature never becomes the all-powerful transcendent term that can restore unity. Rather, it serves primarily as a mediator, a vehicle through which the self can project and contemplate consciousness. In its journey through nature, the self becomes objectified, traveling in perilously close company with death. The consistent and overt assertion of the early Romantics (with the great exception of Blake) is that unity with nature can be achieved. The revelation that their *poetry* makes, however, is that the separation is final and that the best we can do is to establish a dynamic *relationship* between self and "other"—a dynamic that is life itself, as process and productivity. The still point of transcendent "oneness" is passionately desired and just as passionately avoided within their thought. For buried within the desire is an intuition that such a union occurs only in death.

The self is felt, is lived, as discontinuous and as fragmented, not just from an external nature, but from within. The great project of the period is to restore the integrity of a self that has, by virtue of its own self-consciousness, "fallen" into pieces. The fall is a "satanic" one, originated by the notion of self-engenderment. "We know no time when we were not as now; / know none before us, self-begot, self-raised / by our own quick'ning power," Milton's Satan cries. This is also the cry of the Romantics, who will call that "quick'ning power" the "imagination."

The construction of a unified self grounded in the freedom of imaginative self-creation is the motivation behind the writing of *The Prelude*. Autobiography would seem the foolproof method of guaranteeing self-integrity. Within an Augustinian ontology, it may be that. *The Confessions* are, finally, an "utterance," an "outering" of presence—both the presence of God and of the spirit—in much the same way that *The Temple* is an "utterance" of presence.

7. Samuel Taylor Coleridge, *Biographia Literaria,* ed. George Watson (New York, 1971), 151.

Both works tremble on the brink of representational thought, both struggle with Logos in complex ways, but both authors feel able to incarnate presence in words precisely because being is protected and generated by Logos. Language, for Wordsworth, does not reveal the ineffable silence that haunts words for Augustine, no matter how inadequate the words may be. Instead, it represents a past self that suffers the death of objectification in order to be known at all.

In the fourteen centuries that elapse between the writing of the saint's autobiography and the poet's, Descartes and Locke intervene.[8] A great rupture occurs in Being. The long, slow rumblings of self-conscious rationalism accumulate and erupt in one catastrophic cry: *Cogito, ergo sum!* And the words set in motion a mode of perception that will *allow* Locke to write that "our minds represent . . . tombs" and will *cause* Wordsworth to despair over the possibility that the "hiding-places of man's power" may permanently close. After Descartes, if the mind is a shrine, that shrine marks the threshold between presence and absence, life and death, in a new way: the crossing of this threshold does not bring humans into the presence of God, but brings them to a re-presentation of themselves. The ground of philosophy shifts beneath human feet— shifts toward a platonism of sorts, one that had previously been displaced by Christian ontology.

The cartesian cry which I have called catastrophic does not erase God but, in a significant way, it exiles Him. To say, "I *think,* therefore, I am," is to create subjectivity. It is, in a single gesture, to ground the certainty of Being in self-consciousness and to create God as an *object* of consciousness. In spite of the fact that using inner certitude as a starting point is a most Augustinian method of proceeding, in spite of all his scholastic proofs of the existence of God, his absolute assertion of God as Cause and Creator, Descartes reopened the ancient Pandora's box of dualism. God may be an innate 'idea', but as 'idea' He is denied the kind of presence Augustine experienced and that Herbert still desired and felt possible in moments of grace. A "gap" appears between the "thing-itself" and the thinker of the thing, a gap that must be bridged by representation. The problem of whether the 'idea' is intuitive or learned is second-

8. In *Natural Supernaturalism: Tradition and Revolution in Romantic Literature* (New York, 1971), M. H. Abrams offers a fine discussion of *The Prelude* in terms of the "crisis-autobiography" tradition. I am indebted to his work though we disagree, finally, in our readings of Wordsworth and about the relation between God, Nature, and consciousness.

ary to the notion of 'idea' itself. God is now "outside" along with the existent world, being is an "inside" that extends outward through the senses—and the senses must be interpreted. The room for error is enormous in a system where the basis of thought is doubt.

Furthermore, when "I think" rather than "God is" becomes the ground of certainty, *how* I think becomes of utmost importance. Within this problematic, memory achieves a new significance. It, instead of God, becomes the catalyst of "inside" and "outside," and the continuity of self relative to passing time is determined by its efficacy. In the wake of Lockean materialism, which found its paternity in Descartes by "refuting" Descartes, the memory is no longer an activity of vital presentation guaranteed by presence, but one of re-presentation characterized by fallibility and absence. The memory is second only to perception in the workings of thought, but it is also responsible for the major flaws in the mind. Locke despairs that "it *loses the Idea* quite, and so far it produces perfect ignorance," that "it moves slowly, and retrieves not the Ideas that it has, and are laid up in store, quick enough to serve the Mind." [9] The ground of mind is not an active fullness, but absolute and passive blankness, the nothing of the *tabula rasa* which silently awaits inscription. Furthermore, there are "degrees of lasting wherewith *Ideas* are imprinted on the *Memory*." When ideas fade they "vanish quite out of Understanding, leaving no more footsteps or remaining characters, than shadows do flying over Fields of Corn; and the Mind is void of them, as if they never had been there." [10] If "I am" only by virtue of the fact that "I think," and if thought depends upon a faculty that may allow it to vanish like "shadows do flying," being is terrifyingly precarious.

Under these conditions the *tabula rasa* translates readily into an uninscribed stone hidden in the "tomb" of the mind, and it symbolizes the possibility of *forgotten significance* as much as remembered existence. Locke's version of the mind is analogous to the ruins which so obsessed the thinkers who followed him in the eighteenth century. Jean Starobinski has pointed out that ruins perform a double function. They do not just recall the "remnants of a grand design," but in addition "the ruin *par excellence* indicates an abandoned cult, a forsaken god. It expresses neglect, desertion . . . the initial mem-

9. John Locke, *An Essay Concerning Human Understanding*, ed. P. H. Nidditch (Oxford, 1975), 153.
10. *Ibid.*, 149.

ory has now been lost, to be replaced by a second significance
which resides in the disappearance of the memory that the con-
structor had claimed he was perpetuating in this stone. Its melan-
choly resides in the fact that it has become a monument of lost
significance. . . . It indicates a tendency towards ineffectual remi-
niscence, the same helpless effort of memory, scrutinizing oblivion
without mastering it."[11] The tendency of the mind to behave as a
ruin, which perception creates as "a grand design" but memory
retains in remnants signifying an obliterated totality, is radically
threatening. For life itself, the vital activity of thought, can evoke in
its workings our impending deaths. "And our minds represent to
us those tombs to which we are approaching."

Not only does it represent impending death, then, but the mind
enacts death. If the mind can be "void" of ideas "as if they had never
been there," what is to guarantee the unified persistence of a "self"
through time? "What then am I?" Augustine asks, addressing that
living Presence in his memory. His answer is that he is continuous
with the Presence he questions—one and whole and, in *essence,*
timeless. But we are a long way from the confident spaciousness of
Augustine's "huge court" where "I can take out pictures of things"
almost at will and "I can contemplate all these things as if they were
present." There, presence inhabits the pictures in the way Heidegger's god inhabits his temple. They are not representations, but
evocations. After Locke, Augustine's question can only be asked by
the mutable self to the mortal self, and the response is full of lacunae, shadows, and effaced inscriptions. All represent encounters
with death, the abyss of nonbeing. Such "gaps" suggest the fragmentation of existence into noncoherent "moments" upon which
the unceasing activity of the mind must bestow continuous series of
representations if it is to perceive itself as "one." The self must
create itself by establishing links, by bridging the "gaps."

In other words, the post-Lockean mind experiences alienation
from itself as well as from the "external" world and, just as it does
with world, it attempts to take possession of itself by objectifying,
representing itself to its own subjectivity. Consider the words of
the foremost English "subjectivist" of the Romantic period: "I
am because I affirm myself to be; I affirm myself to be because I
am. . . . It is contradictory to require any other predicate of self

11. Jean Starobinski, *The Invention of Liberty,* trans. Bernard C. Swift (New
York, 1964), 180.

but that of self-consciousness."[12] With this assertion, Coleridge is tossed instantly into the *aporia* he will never resolve:

> It has been shown that a spirit is that which is its own object, yet not originally an object, but an absolute subject for which all, itself included, may become an object. It must therefore be an act; for every object is, as an object, dead, fixed, incapable in itself of any action, and necessarily finite. Again, the spirit (originally the identity of object and subject) must in some sense dissolve this identity in order to be conscious of it. . . . But neither can it be a subject without becoming an object. . . . In the existence, in the reconciling and the recurrence of this contradiction consists the process and mystery of production and life.[13]

By the time he wrote this, Coleridge had completely rejected the materialist psychology that had seemed to deny the unity that was always his deepest desire. Yet the struggle to integrate the mind is nowhere resolved in his passionate idealism. The intensity of thought in this passage, the fall into paradox, and the acceptance of "contradiction," result from a desperate need to establish the unity of self—a desire, a longing, a nostalgia that characterizes the entire period. The inability to escape Descartes' "first principle" remains the gaping hole in the side of Romantic transcendentalism.

Both the subject/object "problem" and the desire to heal the breach are rooted in the concept of consciousness as an act of objectification by a perceiving subject. Therefore, though Coleridge sees the mind as much less passive than Locke does, its basic structure is disturbingly similar. We are still faced with an "inside/outside" phenomenon that requires representation and negates the possibility of self-presence. A mind perceived as "originally the identity of subject and object" may, in the last analysis, be little different from the *tabula rasa,* a kind of static nothingness. And, though the focus has shifted from how the mind *retains* (or fails to retain) inscription to how it enacts it—*i.e.,* from passivity to activity—the shift exacerbates rather than heals the wound within. For it exposes, even more radically than Locke's paradigm, the fragmentation of self and

12. Coleridge, *Biographia,* 152.
13. *Ibid.,* 153. For careful traditional studies of the "subject/object problem" in relation to literature, see Earl Wasserman, "The English Romantics: The Grounds of Knowledge," in *Romanticism: Points of View,* ed. Robert Gleckner and Gerald Enscoe (Detroit, 1957), 331–46, M. H. Abrams, "Structure and Style in the Greater Romantic Lyric," in *Romanticism and Consciousness,* ed. Harold Bloom (New York, 1970), 201–29. For a more "postmodern" approach, see Paul de Man, "Intentional Structure of the Romantic Image," in *Romanticism and Consciousness,* ed. Bloom.

the activity of thought as an encounter with death. These are precisely what Coleridge set out to erase, but they wander obstinately
through the labyrinth of his writing. The movement in this excerpt
from the *Biographia* is revelatory of both the problem and the power
of Coleridge's desire for "multeity in unity," a power that creates a
subtle blindness.

He begins by stating that "a spirit is that which is its own object."
At first glance this appears to express the kind of self-proximity
found in "I AM THAT I AM." A careful reading, however, reveals
an essential rift, one not present in God's tautology. The space of
the possessive always implies difference. Furthermore, here spirit
possesses itself as an object though it is not "originally an object."
Thus, it is "its own" not just by virtue of a difference in kind, but
also by virtue of spatial and temporal difference. As his thought
spins out, the divisions within the self begin to emerge, exposing
more differences than unity. Originally, the spirit is "an absolute
subject . . . an act." But this, too, is not quite adequate, and Coleridge's thought shifts again, sidestepping the implied duality. Now
the spirit is "originally the *identity* of object and subject" while, at
the same time, it is that "act" which "must in some sense dissolve
this identity in order to be conscious of it." The *dissolution* now "is"
consciousness, and we are back at the beginning dualism, wherein
spirit is a "subject" perceiving itself as "object." And at this moment the crucial *aporia* erupts: "But neither can it be a subject without becoming an object." The wound is open and visible, and
Coleridge's final move is the only possible alternative, the move
into paradox and "mystery."

It is pointless and small-minded to accuse Coleridge of being
"unsystematic" and "incoherent" here.[14] His thought exposes a predicament we all share as part of the company of representational
thinkers, though few explore it in such depth. As long as we think
of consciousness as a perceiving subject defined by its ability to image, remember, and speculate upon its own activity as if it were
"other"—that is, as long as we think of consciousness as "representative"—we remain caught in the paradox Coleridge's writing so
clearly demonstrates. Such an understanding of mind inherently
negates the unity it seeks. We "center" subjectivity in a subject that

14. A good example of a study of Coleridge that "analyzes," subtly disparages,
and underestimates his thought, all in the same gesture, is found in Mary Warnock,
Imagination (Berkeley, 1976).

never exists, one which is, to borrow from Derrida, "contradictorily coherent. And, as always, coherence in contradiction expresses the force of a desire. The concept of centered structure is in fact the concept of a freeplay based on a fundamental ground, a freeplay which is constituted upon a fundamental immobility and reassuring certitude which is beyond the reach of freeplay."[15] Coleridge is clearly participating fully in the centering process Derrida describes. He *must* assume the "fundamental ground" and assert the "freeplay" at the same time. But, just as clearly, he intuits the ground as a sign of death and attempts to obscure it even as he asserts it. For him such a move is crucial.

Coleridge is wrestling with a demonic consciousness that must be transformed into angelic unity for him to continue to use the words *self, subject,* or *I am.* For if he rests in any one of the sequence of terms that define his situation, he surrenders to nonbeing. Even if consciousness is "originally the identity of object and subject," that origin is radically unthinkable since subjective consciousness, at that point, does not exist. Thought "must in some sense dissolve this identity in order to be conscious of it." The act of dissolution that "is" self-consciousness is *also* the act of objectification, and it must always/already have occurred for subjectivity to "act" at all, since "neither can it be a subject without becoming an object." Coleridge is refusing priority to either subject or object in order to sustain an identity of self which, nonetheless, cannot escape the play of difference.

The play is also one of differance, and what is being "differed" and "deferred" here is the absolute nonbeing of death. The originary "act" of consciousness (which can never be placed since it has always/already happened) is objectification, and objectification, the birth of consciousness, involves a kind of murder or, better, suicide. To divorce and immobilize the self as object is to make it "dead, fixed . . . and necessarily finite." Coleridge reveals this and then "defers" it by asserting that consciousness is "therefore" an act. But the evasion betrays itself immediately, for as act, spirit fractures its own unity and murders by objectifying. And, since it is always/already an object, the subject carries its own death within. To be self-conscious is both to enact a killing and to view the immobilized memorial of what once lived. It is to split and fix the self as an image/object that is "dead" and *therefore* available to "specula-

15. Derrida, "Structure, Sign and Play," 248.

tion" in the word's double sense of thought and vision. At the heart of "the process and mystery of production and life," then, is the certainty of death: I think, therefore I die. But Coleridge's thought, refusing priority and circling around and around itself, endlessly defers the death it carries within, translating, via "contradiction" and "mystery," objectification into "production" and death into "life."

The fact that God is displaced by Nature in Romanticism has everything to do with a concept of self in which being is defined as self-consciousness and wherein self-consciousness implies an unhealable wound.[16] The struggle for unity is a war against death, and nature is the site where the battle is enacted. Alienation from world, as Blake knew better than any, always indicates self-alienation. For Wordsworth and Coleridge the divorce from nature becomes the visible emblem of the need to reintegrate the self in such a way that the "mystery" of life can be understood as natural "process" and "production." It is an attempt to emulate a nature seen as a perfectly balanced economy where there is no loss without recompense and where all happens as a part of an endless recurrence within a great totality. The compulsive focus on a reunion with nature is an evasion of self-fragmentation by displacement, by "naming" it a separation from nature. At the same time, the displacement generates a metaphorical structure which suggests the possibility that the self can be restored to its original, if always lost, integrity.

It is important to realize this double function in order to see that, at bottom, God is not replaced by nature, but by consciousness, that which projects itself into nature in order to objectifiy itself. Nature mediates between subjectivity and self-consciousness, but it is *thought* that certifies being and thereby replaces God. Coleridge thought of God as "*The* Friend."[17] There is a significant difference

16. Abrams discusses the "replacement" of God by nature in *Natural Supernaturalism*. He has oversimplified the act of displacement that occurs, ignoring the insidious hole in Being that self-consciousness creates. Geoffrey Hartman, on the other hand, never forgets that the "apocalyptic" unity promised by "God" and "Christian history" is unavailable to the Romantics from the moment that existence is perceived as a matter of mind and nature, lacking God as a mediator. See, for example, his "Antiself-consciousness and Romanticism," in *Romanticism and Consciousness,* ed. Bloom, 287–98.

17. The phrase is recorded by Wasserman in "The English Romantics," 34. The entire quote is an interesting example of Coleridge's circularity: "to make the object one with us, we must become one with the object—*ergo* an object. *Ergo,* the object must be itself a subject—partially a favorite dog, principally a friend, wholly God, *The* Friend."

between this notion and an Augustinian experience of God. God's Being as "*The* Friend" suggests an intimate *relationship*. A friend exists "outside" the self, is the "other" in a dichotomy that demands that a relationship must be established in the first place. The interpenetration of being and Being is displaced by the idea of constituting a link between being and Being, and the notion requires a mediating term. In the case of the Romantics that term can be either the objectified self or nature, but both finally reside in the activity of thinking. As Hegel phrased it, "the principle of restoration is found in thought, and thought only: the hand that inflicts the wound is also the hand that heals it."[18]

As Geoffrey Hartman has pointed out, however, the Romantics' inability to ever quite "heal the wound" is evidenced everywhere in their poetry, especially by the Wordsworthian figures of the Solitary and the Wanderer. "It is," Hartman writes, "consciousness that alienates them from life and imposes the burden of a self which . . . a return to the state of nature might dissolve. Yet their heroism, or else their doom, is not to obtain this release."[19] The "burden of self" is hardly a new notion; certainly even Augustine bears that burden. The crucial differences to a poet like Wordsworth are that the burden cannot be shared and that it is borne by a self whose existence as a consciousness announces its isolation, its fragmentation, and its own mortality. "I recall myself," Augustine writes exuberantly. For the Romantics, however, the phrase must be "I *memorialize* myself." One can no longer look within to find simple presence, when the act of "looking" initiates and exposes the subject/object predicament. "Speculation" by a self upon its own existence can, as Lacoue-Labarthe suggests, be the enactment of the great human tragedy.[20]

Lacoue-Labarthe's concern is with the German Romantics, but his thought is equally applicable to the British. He teaches us that Abrams's use of "the spiral" as *the* figure representative of Romantic thought is both brilliantly appropriate and badly misread. The resort to "the spiral" is an attempt to account for the dialectic of mind/nature, which implies the final unity of both on a higher plane. Such unity is more appropriately figured by the "traditional" circle. Furthermore, final unity implies a kind of stasis not possible

18. Quoted by Hartman, "Antiself-consciousness and Romanticism," in *Romanticism and Consciousness,* ed. Bloom, 291.

19. *Ibid.*

20. Philippe Lacoue-Labarthe, "The Caesura of the Speculative," in *Glyph,* IV (1978), 57–84.

in self-consciousness and denied by the figure of the spiral itself. The spiral is intended as a metaphoric expression of *Aufhebung,* of negation and conservation. The process can be understood only if it is grounded in the fullest kind of self-presence and, in that case, the most appropriate figure would be the ancient "closed circle." Our turn to the spiral reveals an intuition that the energy of production cannot be brought to rest in presence, that the circle cannot close without risking collapse. The Hegelian process itself reveals self-presence as a necessary fiction, as the product of desire translated into belief. The self-engendered mind constitutes itself, Lacoue-Labarthe writes, as a kind of theater wherein it plays out, through the "literary operation," its own "auto-conception." In the space of the theater, consciousness enacts the tragedy of the subject/object "contradictions," experiences moments of *peripetia,* and achieves its own *catharsis.* After demonstrating that the "absolute subject" and the "absolute object" can be metaphorized as "liberty" and "natural necessity," respectively, he continues:

> Indeed, the possibility offered by the fable or scenario of tragedy is that of the maintenance (for the benefit and in the sense of liberty) of the contradiction of the subjective and the objective—since the tragic hero is (as Hegel will also say) "at once guilty and innocent" in struggling against the invincible. The hero, in struggling against the destiny which bears responsibility for his thought, *provokes* an inevitable and necessary defeat and *voluntarily* chooses to expiate a crime of which he knows he is innocent and for which, in every sense, he must pay the price. Culpable innocence and the "gratuitous" provocation of chastisement: these would be the solution to the conflict: the subject *manifests* its liberty "by the very loss of its liberty." The negative, here, converts itself into the positive; the struggle (be it ever so vain or futile) is, in itself productive.[21]

This is, I think, an appropriate description of the play exhibited by Coleridge in his attempt to explicate the origin of spirit. Furthermore, that play rests finally on representation, the ability of mind to remember, to memorialize itself. As Lacoue-Labarthe notes, "only mimesis . . . authorizes the tragic pleasure," that pleasure of "converting the negative into being." And representation aids the mind in "preserving itself from its own fear" in its "sojourning with death."[22]

What humans win in the struggle with self-consciousness is an

21. *Ibid.,* 65.
22. *Ibid.,* 63, 67.

undefeatable sense of freedom, of their own *power,* and in Wordsworth and Coleridge that power is characterized as imagination. Coleridge's famous definition of imagination rests entirely within this intricate web of representation as self-creation. The lines between self-consciousness and imagination are fine indeed:

> The primary imagination I hold to be the living power and prime agent of all human perception and as a repetition in the finite mind of the eternal act of creation in the infinite I AM. The secondary I consider as an echo of the former, co-existing with the conscious will, yet still as identical with the primary in the kind of its agency and differing only in degree, and in the mode of its operation. It dissolves, diffuses and dissipates in order to recreate; or where this process is rendered impossible, yet still, at all events, it struggles to idealize and to unify.[23]

The first moment in imagination is already mimetic, a "repetition." Further, whatever else the imagination may create, it is first and foremost *self*-creating; it allows the human mind to repeat the "infinite I AM." The leap Coleridge makes from "primary" to "secondary" should alert us to the similarities between the "imagination" and his definition of consciousness—with all its attendant problems. In spite of his terminology, once again priority is obscured, the "primary" being already "secondary" since it is a "repetition in the finite mind": once again the "act," which "echoes" by fracturing the I AM, is one of acknowledged dissolution and a (desired) recuperation made problematic in his own iteration of it. Imagination is consistently named by Coleridge as that which creates unity, but the longed-for unity always remains problematic, as the final sentence in his definition clearly demonstrates. Even here Coleridge cannot avoid the dangerous rifts always/already imposed by his "first" cartesian principle: "I am because I affirm myself to be." Because of this even the primary imagination is already secondary and can be nothing *except* the "repetition" of something irrevocably other and outside—the "infinite I AM." "It struggles to idealize and to unify," Coleridge writes, as if he is speaking of thought in general. This, then, is the situation within which Wordsworth wrote the great epic. The full title, *The Prelude: Or Growth of a Poet's Mind: An Autobiographical Poem,* takes on added resonance when understood as an act of imagination that is "a repetition in the finite mind of the eternal act of creation in the infinite I AM." When that act "dissolves, diffuses and dissipates in order to recreate" and

23. Coleridge, *Biographia,* 167.

when this dissolution occurs within a struggle to "idealize and to unify," then autobiography is overtly an act of auto-affection. Such writing can operate only "in the middle," in the tension between the requisite act of dissolution and the energizing force of the desire to idealize and unify. The struggle is, at bottom, between the necessity of representation and the passion for incarnation. And it clearly establishes writing as a monumental gesture, in which one's epitaph must be reinscribed continuously and repeatedly to prevent the erasure of 'voice' *as* consciousness. For the inscription is itself the "image" that demonstrates and guarantees the living act of mind, even as it suggests that the full presence of mind is irrevocably lost, displaced by the image it constructs.

"To thee," Wordsworth writes, addressing Coleridge directly, "the unity of all hath been revealed" (*The Prelude,* II, ll. 220–21). But, he continues,

> Hard task, vain hope to analyse the mind
> If each most obvious and particular thought,
> Not in a mystical and idle sense,
> But in the words of Reason deeply weighed,
> Hath no beginning.
>
> (II, ll. 228–32)

Hard task, indeed. If the self cannot be grounded "in the beginning," the poet asks,

> How shall I seek the origin? Where find
> Faith in the marvellous things which then I felt?
> Oft in these moments such a holy calm
> Would overspread my soul, that bodily eyes
> Were utterly forgotten, and what I saw
> Appeared like something in myself, a dream,
> A prospect in the mind.
>
> (II, ll. 346–52)

In *The Prelude* the "prospect in the mind" will ultimately confirm the living activity of the mind. That prospect of the "I" which displaces the prospect of the eye, that auto-affection, will be presented as autobiography, and the "history of the poet's mind" will be the epitaphic inscription that gives voice to the freedom and productivity, the heroism, of a mind that is self-creating and self-sustaining in the face of death and loss. Such is the "solace" offered by writing, of such is Wordsworth's "abundant recompense."

6

AUTOBIOGRAPHY AS "TENDER FICTION"

*He reflects upon the impression that objects make upon him, and only in
that reflection is the emotion grounded which he himself experiences and
which he excites in us. The object here is referred to an idea and his poetic
power is based solely upon this referral. The sentimental poet is thus always involved with two conflicting representations and perceptions—with
actuality as a limit and with his idea as infinitude; and the mixed feelings
that he excites will always testify to this dual source.*
         —Friedrich von Schiller, "Naive and Sentimental Poetry"

> *   lost*
> *Amid the moving pageant, I was smitten*
> *Abruptly, with the view (a sight not rare)*
> *Of a blind Beggar, who, with upright face,*
> *Stood, propped against a wall, upon his chest*
> *Wearing a written paper, to explain*
> *His story, whence he came and who he was.*
> *Caught by the spectacle my mind turned round*
> *As with the might of waters; an apt type*
> *This label seemed of the upmost we can know,*
> *Both of ourselves and of the universe.*
>   —Wordsworth, *The Prelude*

If the Romantics evaded the "death" inherent in the displacement of
God by their use of "I think," they did not do so naïvely. Self-
consciousness, freedom, and death as an interrelated complex are
imbedded within the concept of 'imagination'. It is certainly true
that "death" is avoided, within the structure, but it is not denied.
Rather, the Romantics attempted to think beyond death by going
through death. A careful look at Coleridge's comments shows that
the twentieth-century valorization of imagination as pure, creative
life force is much stronger than theirs—perhaps a result of our own
desires and need to "evade." We must not refuse to understand
Wordsworth when he gives us again and again, especially in "Spots
of Time," the growth of consciousness as a direct result of the
encounter with death. We must listen when he tells us, in the culmination of his long sojourn, that the end of the journey is *not*

reunion with nature but a courageous self-consciousness. The highest minds, he writes, have "the consciousness / Of whome they are, habitually infused / Through every image and through every thought" (*The Prelude*, XIV, ll. 114–16). "This alone is genuine liberty," he insists, and he writes from within a full recognition that his own human pattern has involved the evasion of this liberty as much as the desire for it.[1] When liberty is imagination and imagination is creative self-consciousness, when self-consciousness always reveals death, one does not move easily toward it "in one perpetual progress smooth and bright" (*The Prelude*, XIV, l. 135). The genuine liberty of the mind tells, as Wordsworth says his own work does, "of lapse and hesitating choice, / And backward wanderings along thorny ways" (XIV, ll. 137–38). But, Wordsworth asserts, the "higher minds" *will* finally achieve "the consciousness / Of whome they are"—in all their mortality. At the same time, these minds will refuse to "substitute a universe of death" (XIV, l. 161) for the vital activity of thought which reveals that universe. It is by virtue of this refusal that they make proper claim to the infinite: "Our being's heart and home / Is with infinitude . . . and something evermore about to be" (VI, ll. 605–607).

We should take Wordsworth at his word here and not rest too easily in any sense that "home" is an achieved unity between mind and nature. There is no question about his desire and nostalgia for that unity; the question is whether he ever achieved it. M. H. Abrams, one of Wordsworth's finest readers, offers an excellent discussion of *The Prelude* as part of the literary tradition of the intellectual progress of "The Long Journey Home" in which man ends where he begins, though in a transformed state. Abrams is certainly correct about the dynamics of the journey. He notes, for instance, that "Wordsworth describes the process of his breakdown as the cumulative fragmentation and conflict of once integral elements."[2] But Abrams responds blindly to some of his own insights, culminating his argument by asserting that "the poet's recovery, correspondingly, is represented as a gradual reintegration of all that had been divided . . . his mind and outer nature."[3] It is on this point

1. On this point, see Geoffrey Hartman, *Wordsworth's Poetry, 1787–1814* (New Haven, 1964). It was Hartman who first noticed the resemblances between Wordsworth's poetry and epitaph (or inscription), and it was he who taught me that self-consciousness always implied for Wordsworth an encounter (or, according to Hartman, the avoidance of an encounter) with death.

2. Abrams, *Natural Supernaturalism*, 278–92.

3. *Ibid.*, 284.

that we most strongly disagree. Wordsworth does not, I think, achieve the serene stasis of reintegration with nature, and the journey is not terminated in "a home which is a recovered paradise." Abrams bases his conclusion on the famous Mount Snowden episode, which he believes demonstrates the unification of mind and nature, and on the opening book of *The Recluse*. The fact is that "home" is not the "end" of *The Prelude*. As Abrams himself argues, the "end" of the epic is the *writing* of it.[4] For Wordsworth the activity of writing always displaces the arrival "home"; writing is the seeking of home and the endless deferral of arrival. He was never able to complete *The Recluse*, that major work to which he considered *The Prelude* merely an introduction, and in fact he was never satisfied that *The Prelude* itself was finished. It was published only after his death, forty-five years after the initial writing. Wordsworth remains the solitary wanderer until the end when writing is no longer possible. I would argue that for this poet writing "happens" *because* a final unity is impossible. As Derrida has noted, in his discussion of another great Romantic, Rousseau, "when nature as self-proximity comes to be forbidden or interrupted, when speech fails to protect presence, writing becomes necessary" (*OG,* 144). To the postcartesian consciousness, writing is a primary strategy for guaranteeing self-presence, though it is one that never quite suffices.

The Mount Snowden episode is exactly what Wordsworth tells us it is: "the emblem of a mind." It seems to me, however, that the poet is extremely careful *not* to create it as a symbol of unification. It is, as most readers note, a symbol of exchange, and the nature of "exchange" depends upon a principle of separation—a separation that not only contradicts the notion of unity, but allows the dynamic activity of thought in the first place. This should become clearer when we consider *The Prelude* in detail, later in this chapter. For now let it suffice to say that the one source of "unity" the scene delivers is within a deep and threatening abyss from which the poet is distanced and which, significantly, is hidden from sight. It is certainly a "hiding-place" of "power," but it remains closed to speculation. The moon, separate and opposed to the mist, though involved in a process of reciprocal exchange, shines upon this seeming "ocean" (which displaces the "real" ocean, a point to be recalled later), and the mist lies beneath

> All meek and silent, save that through a rift—
> Not distant from the shore whereon we stood

4. *Ibid.*, 286–89.

A fixed, abysmal, gloomy, breathing place—
Mounted the roar of waters, torrents, streams
Innumerable, roaring with one voice!
(XIV, ll. 55–60)

Wordsworth often refers to mind as an abyss, and it's important to notice that this one is "fixed"—always a hint of death in Romantic thought. It is equally important that this abyss is the source of unity and expresses it through "one voice." Most significant perhaps is the mark of "difference" it displays, the gap in the principle of exchange everywhere else operative. It alone does not reflect the light of the moon; within it the voices seem self-generative. Nonetheless, the voices, *because* they are "one voice," make a meaningless "roaring." Meaning resides in a differentiation, imposed by self-consciousness, which this "natural" unity denies. Mind must "mark" itself, must explore and thereby fragment its own continuity, if it is to produce meaning. The abyss—a metaphor for both mind and grave in Wordsworth—is an image of the necessary and unavoidable chasm in self-consciousness that *enables* thought even though it reveals itself as a "death."

In reference to whether or not "unity" is achieved between the mind and nature at the end of *The Prelude,* allow Wordsworth to speak for himself, in the culmination of his meditation on the Mount Snowden emblem:

Prophets of Nature we to them will speak . . .
Instruct them how the mind of man becomes
A thousand times more beautiful than the earth
On which he dwells . . .
In beauty exalted, as it is itself
Of quality and fabric more divine.
(XIV, ll. 444–54)

These are the closing lines of *The Prelude,* an overt statement of difference. The end to which Wordsworth returns is clearly the mind, not as a unification with nature, but as that which has marked its own separation from nature in order to become a "thousand times more beautiful" than the object of its thought. I am not, of course, suggesting that nature "disappears"; it is always part of a double structure which, for Wordsworth, is life itself. But that structure is irrevocably double, and no matter how deeply he desired the "paradise" of final unification, he never achieved it. What's more, Wordsworth knew that such unification is found only in death, the absolute loss of consciousness. That which is desired, therefore, is also forbidden and feared. The "Lucy Poems" are the embodiment of his knowledge, and for precisely this reason Lucy is both an admonitory and an ideal figure. It is her paucity of self-consciousness that allows the close proximity with nature that enables nature to say, "This child I to myself will take" ("Three Years She Grew") and to completely absorb her into itself:

> No motion has she now, no force;
> She neither hears nor sees;
> Rolled round in earth's diurnal course,
> With rocks, and stones, and trees.
> ("A Slumber Did My Spirit Seal")

On the other hand, to take up residence solely within the mind also implies death, and Wordsworth never recommends such a suicidal solipsism. In fact, the subject/object opposition is consciously reinforced by him as a preventive measure. "Recollection" becomes an "object" upon which a subject "works." It is important that even the idea of immortality is derived from the process of recollecting. In a fascinating note to "Ode: Intimations of Immortality from Recollections of Early Childhood," he recalls the following:

> Nothing was more difficult for me in childhood than to admit the notion of death as a state applicable to my own being. . . . *My* difficulty came as from a sense of the indomitableness of the spirit within me. I used to brood over the stories of Enoch and Elijah, and almost to persuade myself that whatever might become of others, I should be translated in something of the same way, to heaven. With a feeling congenial to this, I was often unable to think of things as having external existence, and I communed with all that I saw as something not apart from, but inherent in my own immaterial nature. Many times while going to school have I grasped at a wall or tree to recall myself from this abyss of idealism to reality. At that time I was afraid of such processes.[5]

In one sense all of *The Prelude* is the reiteration of the process by which the poet learned to "admit the notion of death." What is particularly interesting in this excerpt from the note is the psychological doubleness at play. The persistent sense of the immortality of the spirit ratifies an "immaterial nature," which in turn suggests a translation into heaven that exposes the death of the *material* self

---

5. Wordsworth, "Note to Ode: Intimations of Immortality," in *The Norton Anthology of English Literature,* ed. M. H. Abrams, et al. (New York, 1974), 175.

even as it promises life. The inability to accept death is a "diffi-culty" to be overcome, therefore, because immaterial conscious-ness, a unified subjectivity without an object, invokes a potential loss of self, which is finally a failure to differentiate between subject and object. Once again, the undifferentiated is characterized, in a typical gesture, as an "abyss" that generates fear. At bottom this fear is of the *loss* of self-consciousness, and Wordsworth will con-tinue all of his poetic life to "grasp at a wall or tree to *recall myself* from this abyss."

We return, thus, to the "heroism" that Hartman and Lacoue-Labarthe have noted in the "tragedy" of self-conscious speculation. One must "admit" the notion of death in order to defeat death *if* being is grounded in "Cogito, ergo sum." For Wordsworth the crucial weapons in the war against death are memory and writing. He takes them in hand fully understanding how fragile both are and, more important, understanding that both are mimetic, re-presentations that can never capture the original "present" in which thought operates upon an object, whether that object be the self or nature. Consider, in this context, Wordsworth's most famous defi-nition of poetry: "it takes its origin from emotion recollected in tranquillity: the emotion is contemplated until by a species of reac-tion the tranquillity gradually disappears, and an emotion, kindred to that which was before the subject of contemplation, is gradually produced and does itself actually exist in the mind."[6] In spite of its "tranquillity" the "origin" of poetry is an unstable and always/already mimetic situation, a recollection, a contemplation upon a past moment, and it creates a second representation, an emotion only "kindred" to its represented "original." This copy "does itself actually exist in the mind" and is in turn represented by the poem. A progressive series of representations is set in motion, a series which, in Coleridgean terms, is "productivity" and "life."

We are here encountering what Derrida calls "that dangerous supplement" (*OG*, part II, chap. 2). This is an articulation of auto-affection: that is, a series of representations *of* the self, pro-duced *by* the self, generates a "presence." Within the series, self-representation disguises itself as self-presence and seems to "actually exist in the mind." Derrida refers to auto-affection as "the condition of an experience in general . . . the as-for-itself—subjectivity"

6. William Wordsworth, "1802 Preface to the Lyrical Ballads," in *Literary Criti-cism of William Wordsworth,* ed. Paul M. Zall (Lincoln, Neb., 1970), 57–58.

(*OG*, 165–66). This condition is the discovery the poet makes as he writes his "autobiography." Self-consciousness as auto-affection is the origin of poetry for Wordsworth: *The Prelude* shows it to be the origin of the poet as well. As we have already noted, as soon as "Cogito, ergo sum" is the "first principle," autobiography, of necessity, becomes auto-affection: the creation of a self by a self.

Wordsworth's insistence on the need for an incarnative language must be examined within this play of self-representation.[7] If poetry "takes its origin from emotion recollected in tranquillity," its source is located entirely within an image of self constructed by the self. Within such radical idealization language seems to achieve exactly the kind of proximity that external nature denies.[8] The writer experiences his existence as a *coexistence* with the image within. The absolute internalization of the process Wordsworth describes is prerequisite to the kind of presence that can, within this speculative moment, be achieved. The incarnative power of language resides in the felt presence of the recollected (and recollecting) image. But Wordsworth cannot completely admit such total idealization, even though it constitutes and protects the presence. To do so would be to succumb to the "abyss of idealism," to "my own immaterial nature." Neither can he admit the image as simply representation, as a sliding series of substitutes for presence. Either admission would "admit the notion of death," either in the form of solipsistic madness or in the recognition that self-presence is ultimately unattainable.

Wordsworth's own analysis of the representational structure of poetry places him in the position either of surrendering the meaning of being as unity or of locating that meaning in the poetic act itself. It cannot provide him the more traditional sense of meaning as a transcendent content, as an external Truth which language must incorporate. He is, in the deeper sense of the phrase, caught in a double bind. As Schiller notes, the "poet is thus always involved

7. In "Autobiography as De-facement," Paul de Man made the point that the play of self-representation is at work to some extent in all texts (922). This chapter is my attempt to pursue the questions de Man raises and, while he would almost certainly have rejected my approach, I wish to express my debt to him, a debt that is shared by innumerable other critics who have profited from his thought.

8. There is obviously some similarity between Wordsworth's idealization of the image and Sidney's, with the important difference that Wordsworth is far more conscious of his own motivation. Derrida's analysis of Hegel's internalization of the image is relevant to the discussion that follows—as it is to my exploration of Sidney. See *MP*, 90.

with two conflicting representations and perceptions—with actuality as a limit and with his idea as infinitude."[9] The conflict is expressed by Wordsworth in the opposition between his desire to write autobiography (actuality as a limit) and his clear understanding that being cannot be located in the imaging of a past self, that being is always "something evermore about to be" (his idea as infinitude). For Wordsworth the only escape from the double bind is, indeed, to treat it as a "dual source." And this move generates his absolute insistence on an incarnative language—the very thing his own perceptions of poetry should logically eliminate.

A mind caught within the net of representation can hold onto meaning, presence, even self-presence only by repressing that structure through the power of the *felt* self-proximity that imaging as imagination bestows. Such minds, as Wordsworth says, must have "the consciousness / Of whome they are, habitually infused / Through every image and through every thought." This infusion of self into image is precisely what Wordsworth means by incarnative language. The gesture is directly related to his understanding of the workings of epitaph. We will explore this relationship in detail in the discussion of his "Essays upon Epitaphs," which follows. For now, I focus on only one side of the double epitaphic gesture. Part of the purpose of epitaph is to restore the presence of the dead. Equally important, however, is that it embody the living consciousness of its writer, which must be "habitually infused / Through every image." In this sense the double function of epitaph is, obviously, analogous to the double bind that Wordsworth faces in writing *The Prelude*.

As we have seen, Wordsworth's claim is not that language embodies any external "thing-in-itself." Rather, the mind incarnates by contemplating itself as a "thing," an object. To do so it must image itself. That "kindred" image must be "gradually produced" until it "actually exists in the mind." The actuality of the image is dependent on the ability of words to incarnate *as* the infusion of thought, to grant thought "presence" that is comparable to the body's constitutive presencing of soul. Wordsworth describes the process of infusion in the second "Essay upon Epitaphs." "Every mind must," he writes, "learn the art of bringing words rigorously to the test of thoughts; and these again to a comparison with things,

9. Friedrich von Schiller, *"Naive and Sentimental Poetry" and "On the Sublime,"* trans. Julius A. Elias (New York, 1966), 116.

their archetypes, contemplated first in themselves, and secondly in relation to each other; in all which processes the mind must be skilful otherwise it will be perpetually imposed upon."[10] The imposition Wordsworth warns against has been identified in his previous paragraph. There he has criticized Pope's epitaphs by saying that "the thoughts have their nature changed and moulded by the vicious expression in which they are entangled, to an excess rendering them wholly unfit for the place they occupy." The problem is that the thoughts are not incarnated, not "infused" with the words as soul is with body. Rather, the words behave as containers, as molds, or, as he will later assert, as "dress." This is a "perpetual" threat, inherent in the representational aspect of language wherein word displaces thing. Such language is "vicious" because it produces only "entanglement," not a genuine fusion of thought and word. The mind must be "skilful" to avoid such superficial and wandering relationships, and Wordsworth's procedure for guaranteeing the presence of thought within word demonstrates both his skill and the depths of his need to repress representation in favor of incarnation. He does so by describing the process as self-reflection, in both senses of the term. The process is so intensely idealized that it is utterly protected as presence within the mind.

In the "art" he professes, words must first image thought, embody it so that it may be compared to "things." Note, however, that the "things" are already "word/thoughts"—are, in fact, "their archetypes." Thought, then, compares its own image in the *world* with its own image in the *word*. If "things" are characterized as the prototypical exemplars of incarnative words, then both are, finally, "prospects in the mind" (*The Prelude*, II, ll. 352). The comparison only seems to detour "outside" through the world of "things." Ultimately, the relationship established is between one image of thought and another. Such rigorous testing of words by thought is a testing for congruence between images *of* thought. The congruence is crucial to the structure, for that proximity appears as presence, as incarnation. At the same time, the notion of the detour must be maintained by Wordsworth. "Things," after all, are "the wall or tree" to which one must cling to prevent death and madness. The

10. Wordsworth, "Essays upon Epitaphs," in *Literary Criticism of William Wordsworth*, ed. Zall, Essay II, 116. All further references to the "Essays" are to this edition. The three essays have begun to receive the attention they deserve. In addition to de Man's work, Frances Ferguson has used them as the central statement of Wordsworth's poetic theory in *Wordsworth: Language as Counterspirit* (New Haven, 1977).

detour, then, is both admitted and denied, in a double gesture that Wordsworth will duplicate when he speaks of the "tender fiction" of the speaking monument.

If we read this description of his method for ensuring the proper embodiment of thought in the light of his definition of poetry, it is evident that the creative mind does not break out of its perfect self-enclosure at any point. But Wordsworth's phrase "does itself actually exist" erupts into the middle of all this and must be accounted for. If we remember that what actually exists is the "emotion" brought into play by the process of recollection, that it is not the recollected emotion itself, the poet's notion of incarnative language makes more sense, even within such an obviously representational structure. What is incarnated by "the art of bringing words rigorously to the test of thoughts," is the living presence of that which establishes relationship: not the "things," but the act of comparing them which language permits.

Yet the mind cannot act without objects, and it is only the "felt-presence" of the image as body that guarantees the life and stability of thought. Wordsworth must identify language as incarnative in order to offer his mind an object of thought "in-the-first-place." As such, the incarnative word functions as "a wall or tree," as a ground for thought. Importantly, it can be perceived as "outside" the play of the mind that contemplates it. It can, in other words, be felt as a detour, as an infusion of mind into world that represses thought as dangerously "immaterial." The image can appear, at least momentarily, to delimit thought by virtue of its embodiment; it can be an "actuality as a limit" which stabilizes "idea as infinitude." The mind leaps beyond, outside of, its incarnation; it leaps toward "infinitude" and is thereby lost. However, despite the loss—one to which Wordsworth is very sensitive—the incarnative word remains as essential to thought as the "wall or tree" is to life and sanity.

Incarnative language in Wordsworth's understanding suggests an escape from "the abyss of idealism" wherein one cannot differentiate subject from object. As that which delimits thought by objectifying it as a "body," incarnation affirms that "things have external existence," even as it protects their presence by idealizing it. The idea becomes a "thing" on which the mind speculates; it offers thought a base for its activity, a place of (temporary) repose. Under these conditions what is incarnated, made present, is relationship itself, the play of the mind between thought and the world *as* thought. The self will always escape this play, but it affirms its own existence in the process. The purpose of incarnative language is to institute the relationship between thoughts that are formulated as images that mark the passing of thought; it is to "render them fit for the place they occupy." Their "place" is to separate the abyss of "one voice" into the differences that constitute thought.

The constitutive nature of incarnation is clear in Wordsworth's statements. When he writes that words as "body" provide what the natural body provides, "the habitation of a rational . . . an immortal soul," we must not leap to the notion of the body as Herbert's mere "shell of fledge souls" ("Death"). For Wordsworth the body does not relate to the soul as either its container or its dress. Incarnative language is, he specifically notes, "not what the garb is to the body but what the body is to the soul." And words are themselves, he continues, "a constituent part and power or function in the thought" (Essay II, 125). Soul is actualized by body, and words enable thought to "actually exist." Incarnation is not a "vestment" of thought, then, but constitutes it as "power" and "function."

Given this definition of incarnative language, it makes no sense to think of Wordsworth's poetic endeavor as an attempt to embody some external presence, a transcendent Truth. Within Wordsworth's system—one which both admits and denies language as representational—incarnation can only bestow body as the ghostly sense of presence appropriated by the movement of auto-affection. This self-haunting is extremely powerful in his case, able to produce both the fears expressed in the note to "Ode: Intimations of Immortality" and the kind of metaphoric shifting that occurs in the Mount Snowden episode. If he were unable to assert the "actual" existence of an image, an incarnated existence that is "power" and "function," he could not treat the world as an image of mind. "Things" could not be made to represent thought; thought could only represent things. It is only because image is understood as an incarnated actuality that the world can be read as "the emblem of a mind . . . shadowed *there*" as the "express / Resemblance of that glorious faculty / That higher minds bear with them as their own" (*The Prelude,* XIV, ll. 79–90).

In Herbert's system the Mind shadowed by world is God's own; and the poet reads the Book of the World to uncover the eternal presence of Logos within *His* created images. As we have seen, this creates its own difficulties for a writer, but it at least suggests the possibility of a firm ground. Wordsworth reads world to uncover the workings of his own mind. He attempts to ground his thought in a self-presence that must be continuously created. Further it must be created as those incarnated images held together by an activity that depends on the images appearing to be outside of the mind's own play. In Wordsworth's case the ground is constantly shifting under his thought, and as a result incarnative language is a much more ambiguous and ambivalent notion than a logocentric poet could ever have suspected. If Herbert's attempt to incarnate presence in the form of truth is always pressured and eroded by the representational nature of language, Wordsworth's attempt is even more severely threatened. He is in the position of admitting language as, simultaneously, representative and incarnative. Clearly, many of the distinctions we have previously employed in earlier discussions will not apply to *The Prelude*. Those distinctions are as blurred as the lines Wordsworth draws between "inside" and "outside," as nebulous as those "prospects in the mind" which the poet both desires and fears.

This wavering of language between its incarnative and representative functions can be stabilized by the poet only to the extent that he can depend on memory as a ground that unifies and evidences the process of the mind. In this sense "recollection in tranquillity" is not only the origin of poetry; it is the necessary condition of thought itself. "Home" for this poet can never be a reconciliation with nature. At best he will learn to be at home *with* the notion of death and to feel at home with his being as that which always escapes death by leaping beyond the monuments of himself that he images. As Schiller notes, "the object here is referred to an idea and his poetic power is based solely upon this referral." But referral means that he must "re-member" his past and passing self, reconstruct them as a "body" which fuses the two together in the language of his poetry.

Since the power of referral requires the remembering of the objects to be referred and the establishing of relationships, it is clear why recollection is the crucial activity for Wordsworth—an activity upon which imagination, the epitome of thought, is radically dependent. Memory is the key to self as well as poetry, but the poet asks, "How shall I seek the origin? Where find / Faith in the marvellous things which then I felt?" (*The Prelude*, II, ll. 346–47). How, indeed, when "what I saw / Appeared like something in myself, a dream, / A prospect in the mind" (II, ll. 350–52). The anxiety in speculation can be overwhelming. Wordsworth will alleviate his anxiety by locating the self not in the recollected, but in the act of recollecting, an act that is, finally, imaginative self-recreation. He cannot, however, eliminate anxiety. Memory is the "ground," but memory, in a very post-Lockean way, is fallible: "I cannot say what portion is in truth / The naked recollection of that time, / And what may rather have been called to life / By after-meditation" (III, ll. 613–15). Further, it's possible to be "mis-led . . . by an infirmity of love for days / Disowned by memory" (I, l. 615). The mind, Wordsworth writes in a heavily loaded phrase, is "self-haunting" (VI, l. 158; XIV, l. 280), and nature, because it is represented by memory, is also a "haunting" (I, l. 469). Imagination, as the activity of memorializing and then responding to its own representation, is a "self." It is also the power whose primary function is to establish a link between these two "ghosts," the power that both calls them to life and marks them *as* ghosts. And it arises from an abyss that is both origin and grave. Imagination is characterized by Wordsworth as "that awful power," which "rose from the abyss like an un-fathered vapour" (VI, ll. 563–64).

This self-engendered, ghost-like power, we should remember, is the "theme" of *The Prelude* (XIV, l. 206), and this theme is presented as autobiography, the most explicit kind of self-consciousness. Wordsworth, like Coleridge, treats imagination and self-consciousness as coalescent. Immediately after announcing his "theme," Wordsworth leaps into the discussion of the "higher mind," the imaginative mind, as the wholly self-conscious mind. And it is the purpose of the "higher mind" to exercise the freedom of self-representation that generates life and bespeaks death in the manner that postcartesian consciousness always must. As long as we think self from within the structure of representation, imagination is appropriately perceived as Wordsworth metaphorizes it—as the exercise of freedom in the face of death, an exercise that always carries death within itself. For clarification, consider again Derrida's assertion that

> if one moves along the course of the supplementary series, he sees that imagination belongs to the same chain of significations as the anticipation of death. The image is death . . . *the* image is *a* death or (the) death is *an* image. Imagination is the power that allows life to affect itself with its own re-presentation. The image cannot re-present and add the repre-senter to the represented, except in so far as the presence of the re-presented is already folded back upon itself in the world, in so far as life refers to itself as its own lack, to its own wish for a supplement.
>
> (*OG,* 184).

We have seen that the "supplementary series" in Coleridge's defini-tions of self-consciousness and imagination are, in the long run, identical, and so in a more "poetic" and less "systematic" way are they in Wordsworth. And both "powers" are ones that "allow life to affect itself with its own re-presentation." Even though auto-affection is unavoidable when being is grounded in the statement, "I am because I affirm myself to be; I affirm myself to be because I am," presence is lost within an infinitely regressive series of representations whereby "life refers to itself as its own lack, to its own wish for a supplement." Nonetheless, this loss and this "production" are the "mystery" of life.

Autobiography is, in this context, *the* supplement explicitly initiated "as the anticipation of death." It can no longer be a "confession" to God, the eternal presence, it can no longer "utter" that presence from within. Instead, it must behave representationally and stand-in-place-of a past self that must suffer the death of objectification in order to be known at all. It is an inscription which marks the "no-longer" of a self always projected toward the "not-yet" of a presence which never arrives. "Visionary power," the poet writes, derives from both memory and its failure:

> The soul
> Remembering how she felt, but what she felt
> Remembering not, retains an obscure sense
> Of possible sublimity, whereto
> With growing faculties she doth aspire
> With faculties still growing, feeling still
> That whatsoever point they gain, they yet
> Have something to pursue.
>   (II, ll. 316–22)

Surveying the "prospects in the mind," speculating upon "recollected hours that have the charm of visionary things . . . / That throw back our lives . . . / A visible scene" (I, ll. 631–35)—this is the enactment of Lacoue-Labarthe's "speculative tragedy." The struggle toward self-presence within a "system" that denies presence *means* that there will always be "something to pursue." Writing is one method of taking pursuit, of searching for "home," but it will not erase the fact that man's "home" is always "with something evermore *about* to *be*." For Wordsworth this situation is the "origin" of poetry, and within it poetry is inherently epitaphic.

The Prelude may be the most comprehensive "epitaph" in our language, and it is intended, as Wordsworth said all epitaphs were, to be "a record to preserve the memory of the dead, as a tribute due to his individual worth for a satisfaction to the sorrowing hearts of the Survivors, and for the common benefit of the living" (Essay I,

96). In the case of *The Prelude* the preservation of memory is as much for the "benefit of the living" poet as for that of future generations. It is "solace" and "recompense." He is his own "sorrowing survivor," and the act of inscribing the poem affirms his imaginative life even as it announces the "death" of the writer. The epitaphic gesture is "deduced from the higher feeling, namely the consciousness of immortality," he writes (Essay I, 34). But he speaks of a much different kind of immortality than Augustine or Herbert would have conceived. We should keep in mind that "intimations" of immortality derive from the mind's ability to recollect, to image itself as "past." Further, we should recall that "immortality" implies the death of material being and notice that it resembles the "possible sublimity" of "something evermore about to be." For this poet immortality has everything to do with the mind's potential for generating itself, and self-generation certifies death even as it struggles to defeat it. It is essential, therefore, that one continue writing. Within this context the memorials that one constructs, even if they are "ruins," have a "renovating virtue" because the *act* of writing affirms the life of mind. The affirmation is, nonetheless, an epitaph; thus the poet writes:

> I would give,
> While yet we may, as far as words can give
> Substance and life to what I feel, enshrining
> Such is my hope, the spirit of the Past
> For future restoration
> (*The Prelude,* XII, ll. 282–86)

And full of "hope," Wordsworth continues his poem with "yet another / Of these memorials" (XII, ll. 286–87), another of the "spots of time" which "retain / A renovating virtue" (XII, ll. 209–10).

This conjunction of "spots of time" with "memorials" offers entry into the structure of *The Prelude.* In 1798–1799 Wordsworth wrote the "Two-Part Prelude," and we now know that this poem generated the completed masterpiece.[11] It consists almost entirely of "spots of time" which are later incorporated into the epic as signifi-

11. Hartman, in *Wordsworth's Poetry,* characterizes the "spots of time" as moments in which Wordsworth approached the full freeing of imagination from the external world. He believes that Wordsworth never fully allows himself to engage in such "apocalyptic" freedom. I would suggest that the imagination cannot function at all without the external world in Wordsworth's case and that if he is unable to enter fully into imaginative freedom, it is because he intuits the connections between idealization and death.

cant moments of insight, what we now call "privileged moments."
In one sense the entire *Prelude* is *primarily* the iteration of these iso-
lated moments of intense significance, linked by material that seems
both "less important" and "more autobiographical." These are moments when Wordsworth's poetic voice soars and all the meaning of
his being seems to be revealed. Nonetheless, the question remains:
what precisely *is* revealed? Why do such moments totally engross
both poet and reader? Wherein lies their beauty—and a power so
intense that it seems almost to detach them from the surrounding
text? We can all call up our favorites: the Chartreuse incident, the
boat-stealing scene, Simplon Pass, Mount Snowden, the hanged-
murderer. Yet what is the meaning of the name in the turf, what the
significance of the "naked pool," the "beacon on the summit," or
the "girl who bore a pitcher on her head" (XII, ll. 245–51)? And
why does Wordsworth refer to the spots of time as "memorials," to
language as giving "substance and life" through "enshrining," a
gesture normally reserved for the burial of the sacred dead? The
mere coupling of "substance and life" with "enshrining" should
bring us up short. Why do so many of the spots of time involve
violence, theft, and—either figuratively or literally—being lost?
Why the many encounters with death and the persistent dread of
"low breathings coming after me"? There are no unambiguously
"happy," privileged moments in *The Prelude;* even the exuberant
skating scene is interrupted by "the reflex of a star / That fled"
(I, ll. 450–51). I do not have the answers to all these questions.
The girl "who bore a pitcher on her head," for instance, remains for
me an evocative and disturbing enigma.

    The most provocative puzzle, however, lies in the phrase itself,
"spots of time," and in Wordsworth's reference to these as "memorials." He insists that through these moments that are also monuments "our minds / Are nourished and invisibly repaired." Reparation of the mind implies a healing of a wound. Yet the curative
Wordsworth offers seems always to reveal that most painful gash:
the unavoidable connection between self-consciousness and the
need to "admit the notion of death as a state applicable to my own
being." The metaphorizing of time as space, a "spot," the coalescence of that "spot" with language, and the use of the inscribed
stone as catalyst open up complexities in *The Prelude* that call for a
careful, perhaps circuitous, approach. Let us begin with the poet's
"beginning."

    "Was it for this?" Thus begins the "Two-Part Prelude," and the question erupts several times: "Was it for this?" Yet the poet never clarifies what "this" is. Certainly he is referring to the act of writing itself, but there is something more at stake here. *This:* the pronoun of the nearby. *This:* the pronoun of the *already* or *about to be* mentioned, which suggests something so near in space and time that it pretends to presence even as it announces itself as always a "no-longer" or "not-yet" and being always, ever so slightly "outside" of the referring self. *This:* the pronoun of reappropriation, which attempts to draw the "other" back toward that self who has, in his iteration of *this,* both recognized and refused to surrender to distance. "Was it for this?" Wordsworth asks, and autobiography begins—an autobiography that must be auto-affection. The necessity for self-representation is embedded within the phrase itself, within the acknowledged past of *was* and the pretended presence of *this,* within the spatialization of time, the temporalization of space which these words inscribe.

The next fifty years of Wordsworth's life are spent exploring the implications of his question, and the purposefully unspecified *it* and *this* are packed with all the ambiguities of being itself, of being that refers to itself *in* writing *as* writing. Writing: the spotting of time, erupting out of the desire to know, to discover meaning, the desire to be *this* as a result of the *it was.* Writing: the externalizing of self-representation, the radical operation of a mind that perceives existence as grounded in the "I think." Wordsworth's fall, or perhaps ascent, into the "egotistical sublime" is a leap into *graphesis,* into the inscribing of self as the primary assertion of the freedom of being. And his "autobiography" is the overt expression of the covert assumption that the mind writes and reads world in order to exist at all. The *this* as a 'sign' slides imperceptibly into the "past" and into the "other" even as the writer attempts to appropriate it to the self. The *this* as *writing* marks the *I* as being past as surely as *was* marks *it* as past. Thus, the very moment of writing is an epitaphic gesture.

It's entirely appropriate that "being" and "writing" are collapsed into the intimate yet distant and open-ended space of the word *this.* For regardless of his apparent subject matter, Wordsworth's poetic project is always to incarnate the thinking self, to embody his thought without immobilizing it, to give it visible and spatial form, *and* to keep it moving. It is never sufficient to deposit the self in the fragment of memory that is the "image as death, the death as image." He attempts to embody the moment of meditating on that image. He wants to incarnate the "species of response" as well as the memory to which it responds. In other words, he wants to "present" and stabilize the thinking self as well as the content of thought—but to stabilize it in such a way that it does not occur as "past," as "fixed" memory. If such a "presentation" could be achieved, it would allow the words of his poem to serve the same function as the "wall or tree" in the poet's note to "Ode: Intimations of Immortality": they would offer something "other" to cling to, an "other" that would affirm an incarnated life and prevent a kind of solipsistic madness.

Wordsworth, then, will always strive for incarnative language. We noted earlier in this chapter that his most extensive discussion of language as body, with all the "presencing" that notion implies, occurs in his "Essays upon Epitaphs." The discussion of the poet's "method" of incarnating shows that this is not as surprising as it might seem. The conjunction of incarnative language and epitaphic language bears the weight of certain ironies, but it is not, as Frances Ferguson suggests, "in direct opposition with factual deaths."[12] The kind of incarnation Wordsworth explores is fully in keeping with his existential situation as a writer. It cannot offer simple presence, and the poet is aware of this. For him language "incarnates" in very much the same manner that Starobinski has shown us that a ruin incarnates.[13] It marks a lost significance as well as a residue of meaning, still readable in the crumbling surface. The residue of meaning is best understood as the mark of an intention to mean; not as a meaningful content, but as a sign of a meaning-making activity engendered by the human mind. This imposition of mind upon material is the residue of meaning marked by the ruin; the content may be lost, but the sign of an intent to mean remains.

Wordsworth's lifelong insistence that poetic language must be "natural" is closely related to his sense that the most poetic words, like ruins, must lie somewhere *between* humankind and nature. Like a ruin, they must mark consciousness, yet they must be recognized as always on the verge of reabsorption into the natural word. Words must, therefore, mark a significance that escapes incarnation at the same time that they initiate incarnation. A word, like a crumbling column, stands on the brink of disembodiment; it is the mark of difference trembling on the edge of reunification with the "one" that nature is. Such poetry offers "natural" hope "plucked like

12. Ferguson, *Wordsworth: Language as Counterspirit,* 31.
13. Starobinski, *The Invention of Liberty,* 180.

beautiful wild flowers from the ruined tombs that border the high-ways of antiquity."[14] If it offers immortality, it is the immortality implied in the note to "Ode: Intimations of Immortality" (and in the ode itself) wherein consciousness is "translated" into that something rich and strange, the disembodied soul, leaving behind only the sign of its "having been." Incarnative language, rather like the body in the grave, marks the "it was" as a "this" which is "no-longer," and it hints at the "something evermore about to be."

In the "Essays upon Epitaphs" Wordsworth explicitly identifies the notion of simple presence within inscription as a "tender fic-tion." Furthermore, the "tender fiction" of presence is just as ex-plicitly related to the "intervention of the imagination." Writing and imagination as supplementary structures generated by death could not be more openly exposed than they are here: "Thus death is disarmed of its sting, and affliction unsubstantialized. By this tender fiction the survivors bind themselves to a sedater sorrow, and employ the intervention of the imagination in order that the reason may speak her own language earlier than she would other-wise have been enabled to do. This shadowy interposition also har-moniously unites the two worlds of the Living and the Dead" (Es-say I, 104). The phrase "shadowy interposition" deserves our careful consideration. Clearly it refers to the imaginative "intervention" which permits the tender fiction of presence in the inscription. However, *intervention* itself is provocative. To perceive imagination as "intervening" between humans and death is to place it "in the middle," between those great adversaries, being and nonbeing. Imagination, then, *is* an interposition, and it *occupies* an interposi-tion. The "shadowy interposition" is, thus, not just the imaginative act but the inscription itself, which imagination must "occupy" in order to create the tender fiction. The inscription is like that ghostly ruin that "interposes" between mind and nature.

The workings of epitaph are also strikingly similar to the work-ings of incarnative language in Wordsworth's description of "the art of bringing words to the test of thoughts." In both cases language demands the "interposition" of imagination, seen as the incarnative creation of images that appear to have the felt presence of voice. The crucial difference between incarnative language as "power" and "function" and the power and function of the epitaph resides in the

---

14. Wordsworth, "Reply to Mathetes," *Literary Criticism of William Wordsworth,* ed. Zall, 86.

fact that the epitaph is located "outside" the thinking self in a way
that the incarnative word seems not to be. Without the idealizing
force of internalization, Wordsworth cannot repress representation;
he feels its gaps and distances. The covert double gesture in which
the poet admits and denies the "detour" involved in "properly" incarnative language is repeated here, overtly, in his designation of
epitaphic voice as a "tender fiction." When words are "fit for the
place they occupy," between thought and thinking, the presence
within is unquestioned. When that between-ness is located "outside," is seen as an inscription that both "intervenes" and "interposes," the representative quality of language cannot be suppressed.
Even as fiction, epitaphic voice has some "function" and "power."
It "harmoniously unites," but such an interposition, *as writing,* is
recognized as "shadowy" indeed. That "shadowy interposition" is
the "self-haunting" that *The Prelude* inscribes. Writing's status as
"in between" unites the "dead" self of memory and the thinking
self that meditates on its own image in the same manner that it unites
the "two worlds of the Living and the Dead." The union occurs as
a kind of wavering cohabitation of the "shadowy *inter*position"
which language occupies between the thinker and the thought.

   The inscription on the tombstone, the tender fiction of presence
as "in between" nature and consciousness, should remind us of
Derrida's description of the nature of signs in general. The stone
and its inscription behave "somewhat like the architecture of an uninhabited city, reduced to its skeleton by some catastrophe of nature
or art. A city no longer inhabited, not simply left behind but
haunted by meaning and culture. This state of being haunted,
which keeps the city from returning to nature, is perhaps the general mode of presence or absence of the thing itself in pure language" (*WD*, 5). The Wordsworthian epitaph, as this "ruin" which
is "not simply left behind but haunted," is generated by a death
seen as the catastrophe of both nature and art. For it is haunted by a
'voice' that is only a fictional construct, and that construct has been
created by an imaginative consciousness that is itself only a "shadowy interposition." The epitaph is, therefore, inhabited by two
ghosts: the fictional "presence" and the intervening imagination. It
is "*un*inhabited," though "not simply left behind." Like the detour
that is no detour, this desertion that is no desertion is a crucial notion for Wordsworth in order for self-consciousness to defer the
death of unity, "keep the city from returning to nature." The tender
fiction of presence offers a "sedater sorrow" in two ways, then.

Most obviously, it alleviates grief over the loss of the dead "other" by permitting the dead to pretend to presence. Less obviously, but just as importantly, it allows the poet to behave as his own sorrowing survivor. The word serves as a "skeleton" from which "present" consciousness always escapes, but which marks (*i.e.,* "incarnates") the moment of a prior "habitation." It is this that distinguishes it from a mere natural object. Inscription is the *trace* of the mind always imaged as "past" and always leaping toward the "evermore about to be." Sorrow is "sedater" by virtue of the life-affirming activity of thought, but note that it is not erased; thought that images itself "epitaphically" is always ambivalent.

Wordsworth implicitly understood his poetry as this "tender fiction" and explicitly identified it as "a speaking monument" (Sonnet III, *The River Duddon*). "A grave," he wrote in the "Essays upon Epitaphs," is "a tranquillizing object." Its tranquillity results from its interposition between humans and a nature that may "cover" it with turf or "besprinkle" it with wild flowers. But the tranquillity also springs from the power of the inscribed monument "by which it is defended" *against* nature (Essay I, 104). It's clear that this tranquillity results from submitting to the tender fiction of presence instituted by the "shadowy interposition" which is both imagination and inscription. Such tranquillity is closely related to the "recollection in tranquillity" which generates poetry.

The inscribed stone, then, incarnates presence in a special way for this poet. It represents the privileged, but *evacuated, remains* of a presence. An epitaph, he writes, preserves memory, and it must be "accomplished in *close connection with the bodily remains of the deceased*" (Essay I, 96; Wordsworth's emphasis). Words "accomplished" in this context do not embody a presence. Rather, they "incarnate" as a form of the "left-behind," that which consciousness has vacated; they "incarnate" deincarnation. There is little wonder that ruins and poetry were so closely associated in Wordsworth's imagination. Ruins like Tintern Abbey, the Charteuse, or the Ruined Cottage signify lost meaning as well as the residue of meaning which remains balanced on the edge of natural absorption. They are poetic "words," a kind of "natural" language, bodily remains that depend on the "nothingness" of a haunted space "in between," on a "shadowy interposition." Still, Wordsworth insists that writing must do "what is most needful and most difficult in an epitaph to do; namely, to give to universally received truths a pathos and spirit which shall readmit them into the soul like revelations of the moment" (Essay III, 124). This statement hints at the nature of the connection between the "spots of time" and epitaph. As "revelations of the moment," the spots of time always bespeak a death, not just in content, but precisely because they are "recollected in tranquillity." Functioning epitaphically, they provide the tranquillity of the gravestone, exposing themselves as supplementary structures from which the "present" consciousness flees even as it attempts to use them to center and fill itself.

It is the business of epitaph to "incarnate" spirit as well as to "give . . . spirit." Words should be "not what the garb is to the body, but what the body is to the soul, themselves a constituent part and power or function in the thought" (Essay III, 125). One of the things "the body is to the soul" is its residue, that which soul passes beyond, that which is left behind to mark the passing and, finally, to dissolve. Therefore, the notion of words as body is as dangerous as it is seductive, for the "word/body" is mortal, and as epitaph it points to the "otherness" and "elsewhere" of spirit. Thus, though it is "most needful" to present spirit, it is also "most difficult," and the rest of Wordsworth's statement exposes the difficulty as an *aporia*. If words as body are "constituent part and power" of thought, they are also that from which thought *must* escape if it is to be immortal. On the other hand, if thought is to remain stable and to be protected from an infinite drift through meaninglessness, it must be "incarnated."

In *The Prelude* the precarious situation of thought as incarnated in writing is explored in "The Dream of the Arab," a vision introduced by an impassioned and despairing question:

> Oh! why hath not the mind
> Some element to stamp her image on
> In nature somewhat nearer to her own?
> Why, gifted with such powers to send abroad
> Her spirit, must it lodge in shrines so frail?
>
> (V, ll. 45–49)

The desire for "some element . . . in *nature* to stamp" thought on is the desire both to achieve unity and to proclaim difference—it is the desire to engrave stone. Such an act, however, would transform nature into a tombstone, a speaking monument "voicing" the "tender fiction." What nature offers here is a ruin of only relative permanence. There seems no way out for Wordsworth *except* the tranquil acceptance of the "shadowy inter-position" belonging to a self-conscious language striving toward nature. Yet, one cannot write "on" nature, and books must supplement this lack. But even books, like bodies, are "shrines" of the spirit; a volume, the poet writes, is a "poor earthly casket of immortal verse" (V, l. 164). And, as the dream reveals, the "casket" may be buried, may suffer deincarnation as surely as the body.

Yet, the threat of burial and deincarnation, terrifying as it is, is preferable to "artificial" language, to the infinitely more dangerous *pretense* at incarnation. Because it is suspended between consciousness and nature, incarnative language is always threatened with absorption into the entirely natural, threatened with Lucy's fate. But the "clothing" of thought in artifice utterly destroys the "in between" status of language. And that status is essential for the "haunting" cohabitation of mind and the ghost of lost presence. Inscription instituted as pure artifice can no longer behave as a ruin. Instead, it creates ruin: "Words are too awful an instrument for good and evil to be trifled with; they hold above all external powers a dominion over thoughts. If words be not (recurring to a metaphor before used) an incarnation of thought, but only a clothing for it, then surely they will prove an ill gift, such a one as those possessed vestments, read in the stories of superstitious times, which had power to consume and to alienate from his right mind the victim who put them on" (Essay III, 125–26). Thought, "clothed" but not "incarnated," is transformed from "spirit" into "devil," and words are not inhabited but "possessed." Words that have "power to consume" have the power to inflict utter dissolution, deincarnation of the self. And the disembodied self is absolutely unstable, alienated from "his right mind" and victimized by a "counter-spirit unremittingly and noiselessly at work to subvert, to lay waste, to vitiate, and to dissolve" (Essay III, 126). What surfaces in Wordsworth's thought here is a "demonic" version of the "immaterial nature," the "abyss of idealism," he describes in the note to "Ode: Intimations of Immortality." In this situation one will not be "translated . . . to heaven" but will be sent to the bottomless hell of madness, thrown into an ungrounded movement out of one's right mind, into fragmentation and endless dissolution. Artificial writing, which cannot provide a site for the "tender fiction" of presence, is radically "unnatural." Nonetheless, even when writing is understood as epitaphic and presence revealed as a "tender fiction," the lines between natural writing and demonic writing are very fine. The demon of alienation can appear unexpectedly at any turn.

At such moments Wordsworth clings to the tombstone at least as often as he reaches for wall or tree. Ferguson has puzzled over the fact that "funeral monuments seem, in Wordsworth's discourse, almost to be the first poetry." For her the answer to the puzzle is that Wordsworth grounds his work in human passion, that the death of the *other* initiates "the search for meaning in the visible world" as an effort to restore "content" to the "affections."[15] This is certainly not untrue, but it is incomplete. The epitaph is a "first poetry" for Wordsworth primarily because it offers a site that, even as it reveals the "death" of self, is a visible symbol of the "speculative tragedy" that *is* postcartesian thought.

When he institutes writing as an "enshrining," insists that its separate and significant moments are "memorials," Wordsworth recognizes intuitively that he can never attain the unity of pure self-presence, that something is always lost even if there is "abundant recompense." Loss, recompense, and freedom are the structuring forces of *The Prelude*. They are the "story" it tells, and they are the requisite terms of the "speculative tragedy," the act of mind, the poem represents. When writing reveals the wound, the only possible recompense lies in autobiography as auto-affection. Auto-affection provides the necessary pretense at continuity and presence. Perhaps even more important, it also inscribes "re-cognition," an added comprehension of self that creates apparent meaning and value. The spots of time, as epitaphic gestures presented as autobiography, permit the poet to reinterpret himself, to read his past like a traveler reading a tombstone. In this sense auto-affection is

> the operation that substitutes writing for speech and also replaces presence by value: to the *I am* or to the I am present thus sacrificed, a *what* I am or a *what I am worth* is preferred. . . . I renounce my present life, my present and concrete existence in order to make myself known in the ideality of truth and value. . . . The battle by which I wish to raise myself above my life even while I retain it, in order to enjoy recognition, is in this case within myself and writing is indeed the phenomenon of this battle. Such would be the writing lesson in Jean-Jacques' existence. The act of writing would be essentially—and here in an exemplary fashion—the greatest sacrifice aiming at the greatest symbolic reappropriation of presence. . . . Death by writing also inaugurates life. (*OG*, 143)

We can substitute Wordsworth's name for Rousseau's here, with one added point: Wordsworth knew that if "death by writing also

15. Ferguson, *Wordsworth: Language as Counterspirit*, 132–33.

inaugurates life," writing must be understood as an epitaphic gesture, as an "enshrining" in the hope of "giving substance and life"
by virtue of "these memorials." The "renovating virtue" of the
spots of time, then, lies in the fact that they *can* be written, that the
act of writing affirms the "I am," even if that "I" can never be fully
present in the idealized memorial it constructs. Indeed, the pleasure
of "re-cognition," of knowing the self, is at stake here, both as the
effort and the reward of the writing process. Unity, continuity, self-
proximity are not achieved by the act of reading the past self because the past is constructed by the self and because the act of writing is "a species of *reaction*" to the *recollected*. Yet, that act is also life
itself, the "process and mystery of production." The struggle to
idealize and unify is what counts, and that struggle "is" thought.

Ferguson is surely correct in thinking that Wordsworth considered epitaph the "first poetry." In view of this we should reassess
our ideas about *The Prelude* as presenting any "return" to natural
unity. Most important, we should reconsider whether or not the
spots of time really portray the penetration of transcendence into
the world. There is no question about Wordsworth's desire for
unity with both nature and the self. That desire initiates the writing
of *The Prelude*. Certainly it is true that the work is replete with
overt commitments to a "spirit" that "rolls through all things," to
the "One" which is the definition of transcendental thought. But
the phrase "rolls *through*" is itself disturbing; a stabilized presence is
problematic. Also, the dynamics of the work itself question the
very possibility of transcendent union.[16] We do the poem an in-
justice if we focus only on its most obvious statements. We deny its
"life," its concrete reality as process and production. For *The Prelude* is a poem constantly interrupted, haunted by lacunae and fragmentation. These lacunae force the poet to keep writing, to write
in search of self and as *an affirmation of* living thought. Often enough
Wordsworth faces the rifts in Being (and in his writing) head on.
In one sense the *content* of the spots of time is metaphoric of the
process of their being written. They speak of moments of seeming
continuity, of self-proximity, suddenly fractured by a flash of self-
consciousness that reveals separation and loss.[17] They represent the

16. J. Hillis Miller made this point brilliantly long ago in his study of Wordsworth's sonnet "Composed upon Westminster Bridge." See "The Still Heart: Poetic
Form in Wordsworth," in *New Literary History,* II (Winter, 1971), 297–310.

17. Both de Man and Hartman recognize the fracture in being that occurs in the
spots of time, though they do so from entirely different points of view.

poet's desire to establish continuity of the self throughout time, but the continuity is always "interrupted" by his own "species of re-action" to his recollections—that reaction which *is* writing for Wordsworth.

In his own words, *The Prelude* has not told of "one perpetual progress smooth and bright," but rather "have we retraced, / And told of lapse and hesitating choice, / And backward wanderings along thorny ways" (XIV, ll. 135–38). The poem behaves, as the poet says

> Even as a river,—Partly (it might seem)
> Yielding to old remembrances, and swayed
> In part by fear to shape a way direct,
> That would engulph him soon in the ravenous sea—
> Turns, and will measure back his course, far back,
> Seeking the very regions which he crossed
> In his first outset; so have we, My Friend!
> Turned and returned with intricate delay.
>
> (IX, ll. 1–9)

The turn and return, the "intricate delay" are absolutely character-istic of the poem—and of postcartesian thought. The "fear to shape a way direct" is the fear of the loss of self, the fear of engulfment by the "ravenous sea" of oneness, an engulfment that is the absorption of differance and the end of conscious being. The "ravenous sea" is that ocean which is both origin and end: "Never did a child stand by the side of a running stream, pondering within himself what power was the feeder of the perpetual current, from what never-wearied sources the body of water was supplied, but he must have been inevitably propelled to follow this question by another: to-wards what abyss is it in progress? What receptacle can contain the mighty influx?" (Essay I, 94). The "feeder," the "abyss," and the "receptacle" are all the Ocean, Wordsworth continues, and the Ocean is "nothing less than infinity." It is our inevitable linking of origin and end that generates our sense of immortality. Yet, the fact that the ocean of origin always evokes the abyss of end makes the seeking of home an ambivalent enterprise.

This is the sea of the Great Ode, which "our souls have sight of" even though "inland far we be." And it is because we "hear the mighty waters rolling evermore" that we are "haunted" by the am-bivalence of that "immortal sea." It echoes insistently while we "keep watch over man's *mortality*." The haunting echo of the abyss within the origin must produce "thoughts that do often lie too deep

for tears" ("Ode: Intimations of Immortality"). The origin must
not be "found" because the end must be deferred (and admitted) by
thought.

We must recognize that this is also the sea that waits "beyond /
Far, far beyond" in the Mount Snowden episode, the sea that would
engulf thought and must, therefore, be displaced, must appear to
"dwindle and give up his majesty, / Usurped upon far as the sight
could reach" (*The Prelude,* XIV, ll. 47–50). The "emblem of a
mind" inherently "usurps" the sea which is origin and end, that
unity without consciousness. Memory (the "re-turn") and representation (the "turn . . . with intricate delay") differ and defer the
river of thought from the ocean it will finally empty into. Yet that
ocean will persist in echoing in the space of the "intricate delay,"
the auto-affection that denies self-presence though it asserts the
freedom of self-creation.

It is not just "fear to shape a way direct" that generates the representational structure of *The Prelude.* Wordsworth's understanding
of his own creative activity displays a rift in the "self" that necessitates a kind of writing which can only be reappropriation within an
epitaphic language of the "no-longer" and the "not-yet." In at least
one section of the poem Wordsworth overtly meditates on writing
as auto-affection. In this meditation he exposes the impossibility of
attaining the unity he seeks. Addressing Coleridge, the one reader
whose understanding he was certain of, Wordsworth attempts to
justify his wanderings through memory, his autobiographical "la-
bour." The poet writes that he has "endeavoured to retrace / The
simple ways in which my childhood walked" (II, ll. 2–3), and his
endeavor is "explained" with a rhetorical question: "One is there,
though the wisest and the best / Of all mankind, who covets not at
times / Union that cannot be . . . ?" (II, ll. 22–24). The question
exposes both his desire and its futility. It initiates a meditative pause
in his narrative, which radically disrupts his "story," and explores
the impossibility of a united self. For a brief moment Wordsworth
opens wide the abyss and looks into the rift. Yet he experiences it as
a "tranquillising" moment, referring to it as an expression of "a
warning voice to tame the pride / Of intellect and virtue's self-
esteem" (II, ll. 20–21). Both the admonitory quality and the tranquillity of the experience are analogous to the peculiar kind of
existential "happening" that occurs at the side of the grave. And the
moment itself is clearly an examination of the process of "recollection in tranquillity" that generates poetry. In the midst of this
heightened consciousness of his own activity, Wordsworth recog-

nizes that the "self-esteem" resulting from any presumption of self-*unity* is unwarranted, and his "tranquillity" results from the fact that the covetous pursuit of union is "tamed"—briefly tamed by an insight that, given the poet's project, he must finally disregard:

> A tranquillising spirit presses now
> On my corporeal frame, so wide appear
> The vacancy between me and those days
> Which yet have such self-presence in my mind,
> That, musing on them often do I seem
> Two consciousnesses, conscious of myself
> And of some other Being.
>
> (II, ll. 27–33)

"Self-presence," here, suggests the autonomy, the discrete self-containment, the "otherness" of the past. The self is present *in* the mind, not *as* the mind. The implication is that, called forth from across the "wide vacancy," past selves seem internal but self-sufficient, both inside and outside. Their "self-presence" separates them from the thinker as the *objects* of his thought. Yet since they are experienced as memory, they are internalized. Thus, they are "present" and "absent," self and other. The self is doubled, he writes. However, we should notice that there is another significant, though unnoted, step toward fragmentation inscribed here. The self who considers the activity of "musing," who actively announces the double self that is possessed as "myself," is also a consciousness. There are three operative consciousnesses then: the "my-self" that is the possessed object of recollection, the "myself" who recollects, and the self who steps back and recognizes this doubleness—the self who writes, "often do I seem two." Self-representation spans the "wide vacancy," stitches the edges of the wound, but it does not heal it. Here, within the very genesis of re-union, the rifts in cartesian self-consciousness rise up and must be acknowledged. If this is a "tranquillising" moment, it is not because it is a recuperative one. The temporary understanding of life as a purely representational activity displaces the longing for home and provides a respite from the anxious pursuit of the origin that threatens to kill.

Wordsworth was certainly not ignorant of the fact that the nostalgic consciousness is also the "threatened" consciousness. Long before he wrote this section of *The Prelude* he wrote of that precarious moment when the fracture with nature becomes irrevocable but is, nonetheless, rejected by the mind. Such a nostalgic pursuit of home, he writes in "Tintern Abbey," made him "more like a man / Flying from something that he dreads than one / Who sought the thing he loved" ("Tintern Abbey," ll. 70–72). The "something that he dreads" and "the thing he loved" are "the same": self-proximity, a unity that is "home" and immortality—*and* is death and the loss of self-conscious being. In Book II of *The Prelude*, Wordsworth achieves, briefly, relief from this flight "from" and "toward" the One. The interruption is a moment of insight that the poet will blind himself to, but it is free of "dread," because the self is momentarily redefined as productivity rather than as unity. It is a life-affirming moment, one when self is no longer "flying from something" that must, in the long run, reveal discontinuity or seeking the "something" that is, ultimately, death. Discontinuity is temporarily accepted as thought itself. The "I" is affirmed by its ability to represent itself, not by its representations.

The poet, however, cannot remain "tranquil" if he wishes to *be* a poet. The self that writing attempts to reappropriate is that third consciousness, the "I" who images the double "my-self" into existence. That "I" leaps immediately beyond its own representations. Those representations which become "my-selves" are possessed by, but not one with, thought. In this situation the effort to unite the self can only lead to an infinite series of supplements, representations that add to the given image but always suggest that the given needs more, that it is suffering from loss. That loss is of the consciousness that has always/already escaped from its auto-affection, its representations of itself. If the moment seems tranquil, it is because Wordsworth does not, cannot, follow through on the implications which this "interruption" in his story suggests. To do so would have meant the acceptance of being as utterly groundless and the surrender of the desire for unity that generates his thought in the first place. In order to say "I" the poet must find a ground, bring the supplementary series to rest. He needs to find a "center," and to do so, he simply sidesteps his own insight. He moves to more familiar ground.

With no transition whatsoever, Wordsworth steps out of his own interruption—and presumably out of the momentary "tranquillity" it provides (and threatens)—into the "centre" of his childhood activities. And, as so often in Wordsworth, that center is a stone:

> often do I seem
> Two consciousnesses, conscious of myself
> And of some other being. A rude mass

> Of native rock, left midway in the square
> Of our small market village, was the goal
> Or centre of these sports; and when, returned
> After long absence, thither I repaired.
>
> (II, ll. 33–39)

The move to "the old grey stone" is so characteristic of the poet's work that it is nearly paradigmatic. The stone is, once again, the ground where he attempts to stabilize thought. It serves the same purpose as the "monumental" pile of stones in "Michael," the stony ruin that is Tintern Abbey, or the crumbling stones of "The Ruined Cottage." Ultimately, these markers which must be written and read in order to center the self are all "gravestones": the stones in "The Two April Mornings" or "The Boy of Winander." They are the stones in the wall the poet has grasped at "to recall myself from this abyss of idealism," all those stones that stabilized consciousness by serving as a "midway" site for the "tender fiction" of presence. Furthermore, by virtue of its function, "the old grey stone" is linked to the stone that is a *book*. It is directly related to that book/stone in the dream of the Arab which affirms self-consciousness but is threatened by the apocalyptic "sea" of absolute unity. When we read of "the old grey stone," we should recall that the book is the stone that substitutes itself for nature, that other "speaking monument" (*The Prelude*, VIII, l. 173), and that it is, thus, a site for a multiple "haunting"—by self and nature, by the traces of the dead who have passed through, and by the mind that reads and writes. As Wordsworth tells us, the book/stone is the "sacred catacomb / Where mighty minds lie visibly entombed" (III, ll. 341–42). The "old grey stone," like the ruin, like the book/stone, secures the binding together of "one great society alone on earth; / The Noble living and the Noble Dead" (XI, ll. 394–95).

The book/stone/catacomb is always epitaphic. "The old grey stone . . . *midway* in the square," which is "goal" and "center," is directly related to Wordsworth's definition of the primary function of epitaph: to serve as "a visible center of a community of the living and the dead" and to "introduce" the living "stranger" to the "company of a [dead] friend" (Essay I, 103). The "old grey stone," then, immediately evokes that coalescence of tombstone with book and the situating of self-consciousness at the site of death which are the consistent ground of Wordsworth's writing. Furthermore, this singular site defines him *as* poet. "Daring thought," he writes, "that I might leave / Some monument behind me which pure hearts /

Should reverence" (*The Prelude*, VI, ll. 55–56). The thought is "daring" because the poet speaks of engraving *The Prelude* as his own epitaph. But the thought is also necessary, for the inscribing of an epitaph is the "fixing" of identity. This point is made eminently clear in Book X where, in the moment of his deepest despair, a tombstone allows Wordsworth to know himself *as* poet. The French Revolution has revealed existence to be cataclysmic and volatile, the poet's mind is chaotic and fearful, but the gravestone remains a "tranquillising object," and in proximity with it Wordsworth affirms who he is. "The day deserves / A separate record," he writes, speaking of the fall of Robespierre (X, ll. 13–14). Yet, what he immediately "records" has nothing to do with France's "cruel son." Instead, he writes of a graveyard where "an honored teacher of my youth was laid":

> And on the stone were graven by his desire
> Lines from the churchyard elegy of Gray.
> This faithful guide, speaking from his death-bed,
> Added no farewell to his parting counsel,
> But said to me, "My head will soon lie low;"
> And when I saw the turf that covered him,
> After the lapse of full eight years, those words,
> With the sound of voice and countenance of the Man,
> Came back upon me. . . .
> I thought, still traversing that widespread plain,
> With tender pleasure of the verses grave
> Upon his tombstone, whispering to myself:
> He loved the Poets, and, if now alive,
> Would have loved me, as one not destitute
> Of promise.
>
> (X, ll. 537–50)

This incident, which Wordsworth describes as a "green spot" in a "desert," occurs in the midst of despair so thick that it borders on madness. The poet has been wandering through his days "—with a voice / Labouring, a brain confounded, and a sense, / Death-like, of treacherous desertion" (X, ll. 412–14). The "green spot" of the grave is typical of the spots of time, portraying an encounter with death, the "lost" being "found," and the surrender of the "tender fiction" of presence—the fiction that seems to restore self-presence. The dynamics of the encounter stabilize the wavering mind, and the poet is granted knowledge of who he is. If the poet feels himself "not destitute of promise," it is because he has "found" himself as a writer of epitaphs and experienced the significance of that identity in the same moment. The understanding of the fact that the poet writes epitaphs and the importance of that writing are doubly reinforced by his graveside experience: by the structure of the experience itself, which is clearly a restorative and tranquilizing moment, and by the content of the engraving on the stone, the fact that the epitaph is from Gray's elegy. We should recall at this moment in the epic that Wordsworth had insisted that his purpose in writing *The Prelude* was to "fix the wavering balance of my mind" (I, l. 622) and "to understand myself" (I, l. 627). In one sense, the entire poem is a repetition, expansion, and reenactment of this important "spot of time" in which the self is affirmed as a writer of epitaphs and a "pretender" to presence—an affirmation that means both that one must keep writing in order to *be* and that writing must always be a sign of a past self which has moved beyond its own inscription.

It is, however, only by sustaining the tender fiction of presence that one can "fix the wavering balance" of the mind without immobilizing the self into a "dead" image. One must "forget" that epitaph only marks the past and hints at the future, if one is to stabilize "time" in a "spot" and protect the continuity of self without "murdering" that self. Even if one knows, as Wordsworth clearly did, that great poetry is always a "history in the shape of a prophecy," one must submit to the pretext of a voice operating "here and now." Yet, there is never really a present for Wordsworth. It is not just that the content of his work always focuses on the past or that he knew that poetry is always an intricate inscribing of "recollection." It is also that he understands writing as a kind of "conjuring" and that he distinguishes the poet as one concerned *essentially* with nonpresence. The poet, he writes, is unique in that he is "affected more than other men by absent things as if they were present."[18] The "as if" is important here, for no matter how much Wordsworth's writing, his very being, depend on the "tender fiction," he cannot totally forget that it *is* a fiction. He must, therefore, constantly return to the "stone" which most powerfully activates and animates the fiction by offering a "midway" point for the cohabitation of ghosts.

Let us now return to the "old grey stone," the "rude mass of native rock . . . *midway* in the square." In doing so we return to the moment in which the tender fiction has been usurped by an interruption that focuses on the act of writing itself. The interruption

18. Wordsworth, "Preface," in *Literary Criticism of William Wordsworth*, ed. Zall, 49.

has exposed a purely representational consciousness, which is not present, but always somewhere beyond, in pursuit of itself. The force of that moment of insight—a moment in which writing both allowed and evaded the power of the recognition that "present" consciousness cannot be incarnated *as* present—creates a situation that is an anomaly in Wordsworth's work. The "old grey stone" has disappeared. The supplement has failed:

> when returned
> After long absence, thither I repaired,
> Gone was the old grey stone, and in its place
> A smart Assembly-room usurped the ground
> That had been ours.
>
> (II, ll. 36–40)

The past has been usurped by the "present." The single consciousness, that "Old Dame / For whom the stone was named" (II, l. 43), has been "usurped" by a multiplicity of consciousness, metaphorized by the "Assembly-room." "The ground that had been ours," the "ground" of a unitary consciousness in possession of itself, is now a gathering place of the many who are indisputably "others." The displacement that occurs here is the result of the disruptive moment of insight. That moment has forced from the poet a deeply sublimated, metaphorical acknowledgment that, at this moment in his writing, the "tender fiction," the epitaphic "centre" has been lost. The stone remains only as pure representation, as memory a fact that brings the "tender fiction" so close to the surface of thought as fiction that it is incapacitated, ineffectual as center. The poet is suddenly in the position of having to supplement his own "supplement."

He begins his pursuit again, and the chase leads him immediately to another "stone," this time a more openly monumental structure. He takes an intricate "turn and return" to a place "where *survived the ruins of a shrine* / Once to our Lady dedicate, and *served / Daily with chaunted rites*" (II, ll. 62–65, my emphasis). A supplement that can serve and "be served" substitutes for one that has failed. The supplement, Derrida has written, "if it represents and makes an image," does so because of "the interior default of a presence . . . it produces no relief, its place is assigned in the structure by the mark of an emptiness" (*OG,* 145). Even the ruins of a shrine will not be wholly adequate to presencing the self. The poet must seek and accumulate more and more such epitaphic "spots." And he does so only to discover that the actively thinking consciousness will always escape into "time." He must, therefore, keep writing, and often enough he does so "more like a man flying from something that he dreads than one / Who sought the thing he loved."

Duration, the leaping "away" of consciousness, is the "problem"; spatialization seems, for Wordsworth, to present a solution. "Spacing" time in an epitaphic site is a highly sophisticated gesture, since the peculiarities of such a site suggest a "now" charged with meaning at the same time that they articulate time as always/already a "past" and a possible "future." Frank Kermode has warned us of the dangers of making a "sharp *a priori* distinction between time and space" and has shown how our creation of "fictions" is precisely the coalescence of space and time. Fictionalizing, he writes, is "giving meaning to the interval between *tick* and *tock* because we humanly do not want it to be an indeterminate interval between the *tick* of birth and the *tock* of death." Wordsworth's spatialization of time is an attempt to *fill* that interval with meaning, an attempt to transform *chronos,* simple succession, into *kairos,* a "*point* in time filled with significance" which may also be a "moment of crisis." Certainly this is an adequate description of Wordsworth's "spots of time." But Wordsworth writes from within what Kermode calls the "third stage" of consciousness, a mode of thought that understands its own fictional construct *as* fiction. Time is not, therefore, fully "redeemed" by the "spots of time," for even as the poet attempts to "fill" one interval with the representational image, another interval springs immediately into being, the duration/space between the writer and his inscription. It may be, as Kermode suggests, that in the "third stage" of consciousness "to be really free of time we should have, perhaps, to be totally unconscious."[19] It is certain that self-consciousness, as long as it perceives itself in the postcartesian manner as self-representation, can never be *free* of time nor can it "redeem" time in a "homecoming." Somehow, the thinker will remain perpetually "outside" himself as a thought, perpetually trying to "fill" that interval even though such a replete unity of self implies death. In the third stage the mind remains irrevocably "self-haunting."

We move a bit closer to the import of the "spots of time," both for Wordsworth and his readers, if we consider them in relation to auto-affection and to their function as "memorials." If we remem-

---

19. Frank Kermode, *The Sense of an Ending: Studies in the Theory of Fiction* (London, 1966), 53, 57, 47, 57.

ber that the epitaphic gesture "incarnates" a "self-haunting" rather
than a self, we will see that they do, as Wordsworth insisted, reveal
"substance and life." The "substance" lies in the recollected image
and the "life" lies in the mind that speculates upon that image but
moves always beyond it to the "something evermore about to be."
The *act* of "enshrining" carries at least as much significance as "the
spirit of the past" which is enshrined. From this perspective, we can
at least approach the meaning of "the drowned man," when Wordsworth writes that he could view the "spectre shape / Of terror"
with "no soul debasing fear" because his "inner eye had seen / Such
sights before" (V, ll. 450–54). Or we can begin to understand why
the "monumental letters" of the murderer's name carved in the turf
provide the poet with an insight of "visionary dreariness" *and* "a
spirit of pleasure" (XII, ll. 240–66). If we remember that a tombstone is a "tranquillising object" because it establishes a site for the
speculative play of self-consciousness within the "tender fiction"
of presence, we will begin to understand why Wordsworth creates
his autobiography as an accumulation of memorials, why auto-
affection, for him, must "spot" time in the form of monuments.

Within this context, that "emblem of a mind" which is the
Mount Snowden episode takes on a deepened resonance. Nature is
seen more clearly, not as "home," but exactly as Wordsworth portrayed her: as "a handmaid to a nobler than herself" (XIV, l. 260).
The desire for union yields to the principle of exchange in which
nature "serves" consciousness as a vehicle through which it can reflect upon itself as it moves endlessly toward the "something evermore about to be." Nature becomes an "emblem" which can also
be read as an epitaph. We are called upon to read the Mount Snowden "emblem" in the light of one other "spot of time," located
squarely in the middle of the epic. Wordsworth calls it a "type . . .
of the utmost we can know" (VII, ll. 644–45).

As all of his readers notice, Wordsworth is at this moment in the
midst of the traditional epic "visit to the underworld." London is
portrayed as a Dantesque "hell" through which the poet moves
in an anxious, dreamlike daze. Unseeing and unseen faces swirl in-
distinguishably around him, a "huge, fermenting *mass* of humankind" (VII, l. 621). Conciousness is so minimal that "the shapes
before my eyes became / A second-sight procession, such as glides /
Over still mountains, or appears in dreams" (VII, ll. 632–34). The
undifferentiated unity of the outward spectacle is so forbidding that
it seems internal, like the *projections* of the mind upon nature or

itself. The poet wanders aimlessly through his nightmare, "lost /
Amid the moving pageant," until he is brought to a halt, much as
the traveler is halted by the gravestone along the way:

> I was smitten
> Abruptly with the view (a sight not rare)
> Of a blind Beggar, who, with upright face,
> Stood, propped against a wall, upon his chest
> Wearing a written paper, to explain
> His story, whence he came, and who he was.
> Caught by the spectacle my mind turned round
> As with the might of waters; an apt type
> This label seemed of the utmost we can know
> Both of ourselves and of the universe;
> And, on the shape of that unmoving man,
> His steadfast face and sightless eyes, I gazed
> As if admonished from another world.
>
> (VII, ll. 637–49)

What the poet experiences here, and what we are asked to experience, is the power of the wayside monument and the import of its
epitaph. That "unmoving man" who is "propped against a wall,"
wearing his own epitaphic autobiography, is a "speaking monument" calling admonishment from "another world." In proximity
with the "monument," the poet is suddenly so intensely self-
conscious that the experience is felt as a violent reversal: "my mind
turned round / As with the might of waters." Wordsworth has
been spared from the flood. His mind has "turned round" from the
hellish spectacle of a "mass of human-kind" which appears as a
"natural" and unconscious force. From the nightmarish spectacle
of his own semi-conscious state, it turns to a heightened self-
consciousness produced by his reading of "a written paper." Attached to a figure as immobile as stone and "propped against a
wall," the inscription differentiates, distinguishes the Beggar as
"other" from a dangerous unity, the mass of humanity. It prevents
the Beggar's absorption into this "natural" stream of human generation which is so "huge," so "fermenting," that it seems, finally,
inhuman. And it is the inscription that prevents the monumental
figure from simply disappearing into the stone of the wall itself.
Only the writing reveals any trace of consciousness within the
stony exterior.

In this sense the epitaphic "autobiography" redeems the Beggar's
existence from a kind of nonbeing, announcing his significance

within a "spot of time." But it also offers a kind of redemption to the poet so deeply affected by the monument he reads; it offers an insight into the inwardness of a mind separated, by virtue of blindness, from the spectacle in which the poet is "lost." The *blind* Beggar can "speculate" only upon his own representations, can exist for himself only within auto-affection. And his situation is perfectly expressed by the autobiographical writing which is also his epitaph. He "begs" for a reader of a mind that *must* be "self-haunting." Wordsworth has created a figure highly evocative of his own situation as a poet, a figure deprived of "speculation" upon the external world, terribly vulnerable to solipsism, and in touch with physical nature only by virtue of his written text and by being "propped" by the wall. "Many times," Wordsworth wrote, "have I grasped at a wall or tree to recall myself from this abyss of idealism to reality." In the encounter with the blind Beggar, he again grasps at a wall, this one enriched by the ghostly cohabitation he and the Beggar share within the written word. "A written paper" can be as powerful as a wall if one needs to "recall myself from this abyss." And if the inscription is both autobiography and epitaph, the phrase "recall myself" is at least doubled in meaning. Through writing one can construct oneself at least as a recollection and make good use of the fact that the recalling is always epitaphic. One can escape the nightmarish threat of "mass," of the mindless "moving pageant" of unity, only by admitting "the notion of death as a state applicable to my own being."

"Points have we all of us within our souls / Where all stand single," Wordsworth writes (III, ll. 188–89). "Not of outward things . . . have I been speaking" but of this "genuine prowess." Yet, he acknowledges that "it lies far hidden from the reach of words" and that the most he can do is "make breathings for incommunicable powers" (III, ll. 187, 191). Nevertheless, "I am not heartless," he insists, for "is not each a memory to himself" (III, ll. 187–93). Indeed, this man's work shows that each is a "memory to himself," and if the poem cannot present the "genuine prowess" that is the thinking consciousness of the living, what "saves" is that it *can* "re-present" the memory that each man is to himself. Writing "redeems" man's progress through time not by defeating time but by working epitaphically. Like an inscribed stone, Wordsworth's great poem provides a site that allows the singular kind of haunting suggested by his version of the speaking monument. The "tender fiction" of presence never completely erases the fact that the poet leaves his work behind as "bodily remains." Yet, as long as we can participate in the fiction as readily as we do at the grave, we can "imagine" the ghostly voice, and the mark of the poet's "having been" will reinforce, rather than deplete, that "speculation."

This is the "mystery of words" that Wordworth speaks of in *The Prelude* when he metaphorizes them as darkened graves, capable of "translating" nature into the disembodied divine:

> Visionary power
> Attends the motions of the viewless winds,
> Embodied in the mystery of words:
> There, darkness makes abode, and all the host
> Of shadowy things work endless changes,—there
> As in a mansion like their proper home,
> Even forms and substances are circumfused
> By that transparent veil with light divine,
> And, through the turnings intricate of verse,
> Present themselves as objects recognized,
> In flashes, and with a glory not their own.
>   (V, ll. 595–605)

We must read Wordsworth's statement here through the closing lines of *The Prelude*. If words, as graves, as inscribed stones that "embody," can reveal the "light divine," it is because they offer a site within which the minds of reader and poet *act*. The "act of the mind" is a "self-haunting," is auto-affection *as* life, and that act can "instruct them how the mind of man becomes / A thousand times more beautiful than the earth / . . . as it is itself / Of quality and fabric more divine" (XIV, ll. 448–54). As long as they allow this sort of speculation, which embodies the life of thought, then words can enact a unique kind of incarnation. Thus, buried deeply in the dark "mystery of words," there is hope. Words may be tombs, but as such they are the "proper home" of "objects" and allow them to be "recognized," at least in "flashes." And the "re-cognition" of the mind that speculates on those objects buried in the "intricate turnings of verse" bathes them "with a glory not their own," the "glory" which is the residue of thought itself. This is the "abundant recompense," the "solace" of poetry. Without such hope no poet would ever write.

7

THE OTHER SIDE OF NOSTALGIA AND THE DISINTEGRATED "I"

What we know, or what we would know if it were simply a question here of something to know, is that there has never been, never will be, a unique word, a master-name. . . .

There will be no unique name, even if it were the name of Being. And we must think this without nostalgia, that is, outside of the myth of a purely maternal or paternal language, a lost native country of thought. . . . The other side of nostalgia, what I will call Heideggerian hope, comes into question. I am not unaware how shocking this word might seem here. Nevertheless, I am venturing it, without excluding any of its implications, and I relate it to what still seems to me to be the metaphysical part of "The Anaximander Fragment": the quest for the proper word and the unique name.

—Jacques Derrida, *Margins of Philosophy*

You can neither define
Nor erase it, and seen by torchlight,
Being cloaked with the shrill
Savage drapery of non-being, it
Stands out in firelight.
It is more than anything was meant to be.

—John Ashbery, "Litany"

The last chapter's discussion of *The Prelude* ended with the comment that without "hope" no poet would ever write. Such a bald assertion deserves more consideration, especially since this study concludes by exploring the work of John Ashbery, a poet who would seem to present a serious challenge to my remark. Ashbery is a writer who lightly, ironically, but also violently, breaks many of the traditional forms that we have come to accept as part of the definition of lyric. A quick glance at a line from "Litany" demonstrates immediately some of the more obvious differences between his work and that of the poets we have already explored. "It is more than anything was meant to be" is intended to be read in several different ways at once. It may state that "it" is greater than, and therefore beyond, the being of any *thing;* or it can suggest that the *phrase* "it is" was intended "to be" more than anything else; or it may mean that the "it" now means more than was originally intended. And so on. The context does not stabilize its meanings, except to confirm that the line is an utterance "about" meaning and being. Ashbery writes on the edge of what he has called "the lyric crash" (*TP,* 104). Yet the lines he writes and the edges on which he balances remain just short of the great fall he always anticipates and barely avoids. To call him the most masterful poet "of our times" is not to say that he is a "better" poet than others who remain more closely associated with a Wordsworthian sort of lyricism. I mean the statement quite literally. John Ashbery's central concerns, the "subjects" of his poems, are also the central concerns and "subjects" of the contemporary mode of thought we have come to call postmodernism.

With its focus on difference, the fragmentation of being, the unavailability of truth, and the relativity of meaning, postmodernism is hardly confined to literary studies. One has only to think of the Heisenberg uncertainty principle, for instance, or of Einstein's speculations on time and space, to perceive how generally integrated into late-twentieth-century life the postmodern assertion of the absence of a provable ground, the "absence of a center," really is. Without such a ground, without a final or original point of reference against which human thought can be measured, there is no *logical* possibility of asserting the presence of truth, meaning or even a coherent "speaking subject." Ashbery is the poet of our times in the sense that his work is unfailingly conscious of this postmodern situation, and situating, of thought. In the current terminology of literary criticism he is *the* poet of differance. He is a lyricist who continues to write even though he is fully disabused of the idea that a privileged moment can be embodied in the lyric, of any belief that poetry can embody the thinking self as meaning or truth, and of any hope that the lyric can establish or reveal being as a full presence. He does not, however, lose all hope for the presencing power of language; he sustains it in a new and minimal form. His is an epitaphic poetry even more extreme than Wordsworth's—a poetry in which the "something evermore about to be" is projected as always/already lost. In his work being is always, as the title of a recent poem implies, a movement through a "Haunted Landscape," and that landscape is both the open-ended perspective of a decentered mind and the uncontained perspectives offered by an eccentric world. For Ashbery the mind is not "*self*-haunted," but rather is a pure process of haunting, untethered from any origin.

Ashbery's "hope" for language strongly resembles the silent and convoluted kind that Jacques Derrida displays everywhere in his writing, a writing that erases the hope for presence as nothing more than "nostalgia" but depends in subtle and important ways on the presence of the kind of meaning that it denies. Before we can move comfortably into the work of the poet, we must look in more detail at the work of the philosopher, his intellectual brother. I begin with a summary.

The poets we have considered thus far offer variations on this theme of hope, a theme that is at least as old as the Book of Job. Job's nearly desperate hope is to discover the "right words," which could embody the truth of his being and restore the presence of God. His deepest need is to find words that neither displace God's own nor sin against God, words that can function as prayer, rather than as the curse that carries death within. It's clear that Job needs and wants an incarnative language. His cry, "Oh that my words were now written! oh that they were printed in a book! / That they were graven with an iron pen and lead in the rock forever!" (Job 19.23—24), expresses both that need and an intuition that the language which confirms truth may also bring death. For such writing is epitaphic, a representation that bears within itself the curse that he must avoid, the curse of a language that stands-in-place-of being.

That Herbert's situation is much less "mythic" and more complex than Job's does not change the fact that they share essentially the same hope. His, too, is a search for the "right words," and their rightness is determined by their incarnative powers. The fear of displacement, of representation, never disappears from his work, even though he develops a powerful strategy which seems able to incarnate God's own Word, as the unity of meaning and being, in his poetry. This strategy uses the belief that God Himself has already written incarnatively, has inscribed His truth within humans and within His world. If truth is understood as already within, poetry can become "utterance"—the expressing of this truth to the "outside" called writing. Herbert understands that an immediate presentation of the Word is not possible, that he is deprived of any mythically "Jobean" contact with the Voice in the whirlwind which could ratify full presence. But by seeing poetry as epitaphic, as the double assertion of presence and absence which God's own creation seems to reveal, his work can be justified—if not totally purified. Herbert's hope remains, like Job's, one for a language so untainted by absence that it can be a pure transparency colored only by God's light. He metaphorizes that desire in "The Windows," suggesting that language can present truth through a process of "annealing" in which truth, if it is penetrated by God's "sun," can appear. In a sense he settles for translucency. And he understands that the translucent word can be achieved only if one sacrifices the representing self, sacrifices one's own words on the altar of the Word, which can be located on the sacred sites of either the temple or the tomb.

Wordsworth's incarnative gesture marks a radical shift in the ground of truth and being, a shift from the outside to the inside, from Logos to cartesian consciousness. With that shift, the representative nature of language surfaces with a new force, displaying the "failures" of words which can only stand-in-place-of-truth rather than embody it. The epitaphic qualities of poetry, which have both distressed and enabled poets from the first, are fully exposed in that moment when the ground of truth becomes thought itself. As a result, Wordsworth necessarily uses the epitaphic gesture as the generative *source* of his writing. And, as source, the epitaph must be perceived as incarnative language; it is crucial to his project as a writer and to the existence of a "self" as he understands it. The epitaph, as either an inscribed stone or as poetry, must be perceived by him as a privileged site which offers the possibility of cohabitation to all the "ghosts" of consciousness and world. Without such a site, the mind that is "self-haunting" would be utterly without hope.

In Wordsworth's case that hope is not lodged in the "light" we associate with Logos, but in the dark "mystery of words." For him that mystery lies in the workings of language as epitaph, in which "visionary power" seems to be "embodied" so thoroughly that poetry is able to constitute a privileged site (very like the gravestone)—a site wherein "shadowy things" remain endlessly alive, "work endless changes." The force of that internal activity, which Derrida calls "auto-affection," not only represses his recognition that incarnative language is a "tender fiction" in poetry, but at the same time guarantees a self-presence so complete that he is able to say, "Points have we all of us within our souls / Where all stand single" (*The Prelude,* III, ll. 188–89). This singleness, this unity of self, is understood by him as being "far hidden from the reach of words" (III, l. 187) but it generates the possibility of meaning and the desire for incarnative language in the first place. It is that "point where all stand single" which is the abode of the "visionary power" that "attends the motions of the viewless winds," and attends them with such incorporative intensity that both seem "embodied in the mystery of words" (V, l. 597). His belief in the attending power of self-presence is so strong that it can unite the outside "winds" with the inside "visionary power." It dominates his poetry to such an extent that he is able to feel that "even forms and substances . . . present themselves as objects" in words which, because they incarnate, are an object's "proper home" (V, l. 600). The singleness of self carries such magnetic force that all presence returns to it: the light that exposes objects as present, "in flashes," is "a glory not their own" but the light of the speculative mind, and within this "flash" the mind feels itself *as* "visionary power," as the power to "see into the life of things."[1] The "turnings intricate of verse" are all "returns" to the "point where all stand single," which he calls in "Tintern Abbey" the "living soul."

Despite all the obstacles encountered by the speculative movement which we explored in *The Prelude*, Wordsworth holds fast to this immovable point, a point analogous to T. S. Eliot's more theological vision of "the still point of the turning world."[2] This immovable point offers Wordsworth (as it later will Eliot) a place of repose, a pause in the wild temporal flux of thought, a ground for memory that seems to unite place and time, and seems a "space" in which the visionary "moment" can happen. At the same time, in a necessary reversal, the fact that each one is "a memory to himself" confirms, for Wordsworth, a self-presence that survives even the vagaries of memory. But it survives outside of language, beyond words that are mere "breathings" of "incommunicable powers" (*The Prelude*, III, l. 191). The moment in "Tintern Abbey" when the poet can "see into the life of things" is exemplary of all the "moments" in his work. Even those that evoke violence and disruption reveal their meanings in "that serene and blessed mood," the moment of tranquillity, of rest, that Wordsworth requires for both the writing of poetry and the encounter with an inscribed stone. The visionary moment, the moment at the grave, and the tranquil moment in which poetry is written are all, in this respect, "one," and all depend upon that single point called the "living soul." These in turn are dependent upon the ability of consciousness to recall its (past) self; even after "a long absence . . . the picture of the mind revives again," Wordsworth writes, "And so I dare

---

1. Wordsworth, "Tintern Abbey," l. 46 in *The Norton Anthology of English Literature*, ed. Abrams, *et al.*, 152.
2. Eliot, "Burnt Norton," in *Collected Poems*, 177.

to hope / Though changed, no doubt, from what I was" ("Tintern Abbey," ll. 61–65). The web of interdependence here is unbreakable as long as its center, "the point" where "we all stand single," holds. That point of absolute self-presence weaves into "one" the possibility of incarnative ("proper") language, of the privileged moment ("spots of time") and of privileged sites (poem and stone). Only this glistening and unbroken web allows Wordsworth to "dare to hope," against all the forces of death and change, that his writing can incarnate, can bestow

> as far as words can . . .
> Substance and life to what I feel, enshrining
> Such is my hope, the spirit of the Past
> For future restoration.
> (*The Prelude*, XII, ll. 282–86)

His hope, then, depends upon the coherence of this interwoven and circular system, the system that we have called, after Lacoue-Labarthe, the "speculative tragedy." Certainly the system is contradictorily coherent. And, as always, "coherence in contradiction expresses the force of a desire" (*SP*, 159). Wordsworth felt the pressures of the contradictions, experienced the inevitable anxieties in facing the breaks in coherence, and defeated them, ultimately, by simply asserting the dominance of the mind over dissolution and fragmentation. Though from the perspective of contemporary thought his victory is that of the tragic hero who raises his fist against overpowering odds, who wins by losing, the recompense remains in the "glory" of the struggle, the light that asserts the meaningful being of an individual mind in the face of time, death, violence, and disintegration.

Neither Wordsworth nor Herbert found the pure, transparent, unobstructing Word which they sought. The Word remains a dark mystery. Both suffered the death and loss inherent in language which must behave representationally, and both tried in different ways to find a release from their predicament by turning to the unique kind of haunting presence that epitaph seems to suggest. Their poetry establishes the sort of being that is neither the "nothingness" of absence nor the "thingness" of presence, but is that strange coalescence of presence and absence which is so saliently evoked by our word *ghost*. Despite the disturbances created in their work by the opacity and uncontainable flow of words which cannot be made entirely into the constitutive bodies of souls, each poet held tenaciously to the hope that language can "deliver forth" that presence as truth, as the "meaning of being." To surrender this hope would be to surrender the principles that define lyric. For whatever else the lyric may be or do, it always attempts to claim meaning as presence—and as its own.

This is not to say that the claim to present meaning (or the claim to meaning as presence) is always expressed in the ways we have thus far seen. In Ashbery's work such claims can take on unusual, even barely recognizable, forms. But the claim to a language that can incarnate meaning, whatever form that embodiment may take, unites lyric poetry into one great enterprise: the desire to *be as meaning* and to mean as a presentation of being. This holds even for poetry that appears to reject meaning in its most general sense, as paraphrasable content.[3] This desire for an incarnative, revelatory language binds together works that are radically different in style and intention.

The hunger for the unity of meaning and being within a language of revelation is an essential motivation of lyric poetry and should not be misunderstood as a product of a "naïve" past. It holds for all poetry, including the most sophisticated postmodern works, which purposefully attempt to block the notion that meaning can be presented as content or that the poem presents a meaning that exists outside of its own workings. While such poetry seems to reject the Wordsworthian hope, it does so only at first glance. A poem like Ashbery's "The Tennis Court Oath," which outraged so many of his readers because of its "impenetrability" and "meaninglessness," is exemplary. This sort of writing affirms, first and foremost, its own representational play; it operates as a performance of the premise that language behaves like Shelley's "signs" which lead only to other signs in an "education of error." The poem exposes the ability of words to slide into one another in such a way that meaning is washed under by the unrestrained flow of multiple meanings. At the same time that such poetry demonstrates this sliding effect, its exclusion of outside reference seems to lock the play of meanings within its own boundaries. Because they fore-

---

3. The nature of "meaning" is, of course, an enormously complex issue with a long history of philosophical and literary discussion. In this chapter, I use the word in this most generalized sense unless I explicitly note otherwise. I take my cue from Derrida, who establishes this generalized notion of *meaning* (as that which is "communicated") in order to oppose it to *signification* in his essay "Signature, Event, Context." I'll be exploring that essay in some detail shortly, but for now, I wish only to note that I am using the word *meaning* to suggest the content that a reader "understands" to be conveyed by a piece of language.

front language itself as both the medium and subject of poetry, these poems attempt to be so exclusively self-referential as to resist interpretation altogether. Much of Ashbery's work is of this sort, which Gerald Burns has labeled "hermetic" poetry—poetry that seems to be a "self-contained linguistic structure" that "arrests the function of signification."[4]

But, as Derrida has shown, the apparent immobilization of signification that seems to be promised by "self-contained" linguistic structures is only an illusion. Self-reference *is* self-representation, and as such it is the paradigmatic instance of the attempt to unify word and being as meaningful presence. From this perspective, a work that is self-contained can be seen as an attempt to push the incarnative gesture to its furthest extreme, as an attempt to create its world as "pure" meaning united with "pure" being in words untainted by any contact with an outside. Such work, then, inherently establishes its *own* being as an Ideal which incorporates its total meaning into the bodies of its words. In other words, despite the fact that its surface might suggest a complete withdrawal from any attempt to embody meaning, hermetic poetry tries to *absolutely* contain meaning. It performs the classic logocentric gesture, the necessary first step toward fulfilling the "hope" of all lyric poetry. Postmodern poetry that denies any reference to an external meaning still clings to the possibility of incarnative language. It does not so much give up signification as try to force signification into a perfect unity with itself.

Such unity, as we have seen in Wordsworth's use of the image as an idealized and internalized object, always bespeaks a desire for self-presencing through self-representation. Signification, in this situation, becomes an attempt toward perfect self-representation, one that avoids any detours into the outside world; it is a movement toward pure being and uninterrupted oneness. The more a poem appears to evade meanings, the less it seems to be caught in the play of representation that would deny its presence as a "thing-in-itself." It seems to "presence" itself entirely, to fully incarnate its own totality, to become meaning as being. If such self-containment were possible, the hermetic poem would be the absolute incarnation of itself, as autonomous and free of interpretation, as impenetrable and concrete, as an uninscribed stone. Hermeticism displays the wish to transcend the play of differance, the play that creates the

4. Gerald Burns, *Modern Poetry and the Idea of Language* (New Haven, 1974), 1.

dangerous space of difference and deferral and also creates, within that space, the possibility of interpretation.

If we feel an absence of meaning in a poem like "The Tennis Court Oath," it is because its incarnation of itself has succeeded to such an extent that its presence approaches the inscrutability of a natural object, an inscrutability directly proportionate to its "thingness." The more it "transcends" representation as differance, the more it fills the space required by the interpretive act. From this point of view, Ashbery's poem succeeds precisely insofar as it antagonizes those critics who are so angered by its incomprehensibility. In a certain way, then, poetry that emphasizes its "medium" rather than its "message" tries to present itself as the thing-itself, tries to *be* world as absolute presence. Hence, it makes a literally incorporative gesture that depends upon the hope that language can incarnate meaning as the unity of word and being.

If, for a poet, meaning and being *must* seem to coalesce, it is because language itself institutes the relationship between the two and generates the "hope" which to some extent we all share. In the everyday, unthought, and largely intuitive "happening" of the language in which we live, all of us hold to Wordsworth's "tender fiction." We treat his "hope" as if it were a simple, given reality, assuming that words, by "enshrining," can protect being and effect "future restoration." Every time we speak or write believing that we can be understood, we operate within the assumption that meaning can be restored to presence and clarity. Poets, however, must be alert to language in ways that our everyday living can neither allow nor afford. Poets are poets precisely because of a heightened awareness of the powers and failures of a language that seeks to create meaning and being rather than to repeat them. A poet's hope for a meaningful language must be sustained, in an extraordinarily self-conscious way, against the forces of representation and repetition that ordinary language always blindly employs, even though in order to communicate language presumes transparency and its own ability to "contain" meaning. If everyday language must forget the gap between word and thing in order to function, the poet cannot avoid this gap. Hence, the desire to make words "bear" meaning—in the double sense of "carry meaning" and "give birth to meaning"—is at stake when a poem is written.

At the same time, the desire to eliminate meaning as an effect of representation and repetition always remains an active drive in the poet, since meaning as anything other than presence inevitably suggests the possibility that the poem is nothing more than the mere shadow-play of uncontrollable references. This need to remove poetry from the unlimited flow of representative movements is often expressed, as Sharon Cameron has argued, as an attempt to remove language from the flow of time.[5] A stubborn resistance to time is, as Cameron's superb analysis of Dickinson's work shows, one prevalent characteristic of lyric poetry, but not its most universal or radical characteristic. Rather, the striving toward atemporality operates as the metaphorical expression of a deeper motivation: the desire to make the poem "actual," to bring it into being. It is not just, as Cameron elegantly demonstrates, that the lyric battles death by attempting to defeat time, but also that it attempts to generate life by refusing signification, by escaping from the movement of representation, by denying its status as substitution for the thing-itself. Its desire to give birth is at least as powerful as its refusal to admit death. The move toward atemporality is, at its base, a move toward full presence, toward what Archibald MacLeish calls the "palpable" fullness of the thing itself.

MacLeish's poem "Ars Poetica" serves as an example of both the necessary links and the equally necessary conflicts between meaning and being, presentation and representation:

> A poem should be palpable and mute
> As a globed fruit,
>
> Dumb
> As old medallions to the thumb,
>
> Silent as the sleeve-worn stone
> Of casement ledges where the moss has grown—
>
> A poem should be wordless
> As the flight of birds.
>
> .   .   .   .   .   .
>
> A poem should be motionless in time
> As the moon climbs,
>
> Leaving, as the moon releases
> Twig by twig the night-entangled trees,
>
> Leaving, as the moon behind the winter leaves,
> Memory by memory the mind—
>
> A poem should be motionless in time
> As the moon climbs.
>
> .   .   .   .   .   .

5. Sharon Cameron, *Lyric Time: Dickinson and the Limits of Genre* (Baltimore, 1979).

A poem should be equal to:
Not true.

For all the history of grief
An empty doorway and a maple leaf.

For love
The leaning grasses and two lights above the sea—

A poem should not mean
But be.[6]

What MacLeish longs for here (and the poem is "about" longing, as
the words "*should* be" indicate) is an embodiment so full that it
would, indeed, be inarticulate: "mute," "dumb," "wordless" and
"silent as . . . stone." What the poet achieves, however, is a meaning that can only sound out by virtue of the fact that his overt statements are displaced by the representative activity of the poem. The
meaning resides in a conflict between "what" the poem says and
"how" it says it. As the string of similes demonstrates in open contradiction to the message it carries, the poem can "be" only through
a process of substitution: word represents "thing" (fruit) which, in
turn, represents word (poem) but only, of course, *as* word. The
contradiction between MacLeish's incarnative method, his working
by analogy, and his assertions about what "a poem *should* be" reveals the interdependence of meaning/being he says he wishes to
reject. The statements of the poem are clearly not its meaning;
rather, the meaning resides in this interplay between desire and necessity, in the echoing effect created when a statement against representation can be made only through representation.

A poem "palpable and mute / As a globed fruit" would, indeed,
be "wordless," and that is the deepest irony that MacLeish strikes.
As we have seen in the Book of Job, in the work of Augustine, and
in Herbert's poems, full presence is silent, and such silence denies
the possibility of poetry altogether. It is a luxury that the poet may
long for but can ill afford. Such fullness would certainly be "motionless in time," but it would not be or need poetry. What "Ars
Poetica" expresses in the play and beautiful effects of its similes is
that the poet's desire to translate word into thing, to present meaning with such a powerful immediacy that it can appear as incarnated
being, is trapped by a language that resists the desire. The closing
statement should be recognized, in this respect, as a self-defensive
gesture, an attempt to "englobe," to enclose the poem's meanings

6. Archibald MacLeish, *New and Collected Poems, 1917–1976* (Boston, 1976),
106–107.

as fully as "fruit." But the statement is genuinely ironic in that it cannot come to rest in a single meaning. The fact that it carries meaning is a self-contradiction which corrupts its stability. In addition, its assertion is in direct contradiction to the structure of the poem itself, a structure of comparison that evokes difference, the most obvious sort of representative displacement. As assertion, "A poem should not mean / But be" defends against signification, against the representative movement of substitution that threatens to fracture meaning and being, and against the waywardness of interpretation. As part of the poem, however, it readmits all of these into the sanctuary it protects.

Furthermore, the representative movement has been there all along, as MacLeish clearly understands. He metaphorizes it in the figure of the moon: "A poem should be motionless in time / As the moon climbs." The climbing moon is, of course, an illusion created by the position of the perceiver, fixed on the rotating earth, to whom the moon's orbit remains invisible. This illusion of stasis within movement is more than a fine image of the workings of the poem itself. It is also, in this work, the radical requirement for the emergence of meaning as being. Just as it is the unseen and therefore "motionless" movement of the moon that "releases" the trees from the nothingness of night, that brings them into being "twig by twig," so it is the obscured and denied movement of representation that allows the meaning of the poem to appear as being. The ghostliness of the poet's night/moon/tree image is strikingly appropriate to the sort of presentation that the poem actually achieves, a presentation that depends upon the haunting residue of a meaning felt as something "left behind" when we experience the contradiction between assertion and form. In the figure of the moon as a revelatory force that seems "motionless in time," the poem exposes being as an "elsewhere" which only exists, "memory by memory," because of a "leaving." The twice-repeated word is crucial, pointing to the fact that the climbing of the moon which enlightens is also the "leaving" of the moon. This "leaving," the loss of the thing-itself, "releases" the unseen into being, brings forth the "night-entangled trees." But it also "leaves" them behind in such a way that being occurs as memory, as that most intimate form of representation which exists in such close proximity with the self that it is felt as presence. The poem, then, is "not true." It cannot "be" moon, fruit, bird, or ledge, even if it "should be."

The phrase "equal to: / Not true" is a double assertion perfectly in keeping with the doubleness everywhere else in the poem. If we have paid attention to the poetic functioning of "Ars Poetica," and not just to its statements, the claim to equivalence carries its own kind of "truth." It suggests that the mode of being of poetry is as strong as, and "like," being as such, that being, too, involves a desire to possess the thing-itself which can be fulfilled only through an analogical representation of the thing. In that sense, the poem can "be" as fully and powerfully as the world can "be." Both are released from the obscuring, meaningless, and entangling night by a leave-taking that leaves behind, in the form of memory, the invisible movement of representation. As the central stanzas show, the being of world depends upon the haunting presence of the "no-longer/not-yet," the motionless movement of the moon that allows appearance to occur only "twig by twig . . . memory by memory." "Ars Poetica" is, then, quietly and distinctly Wordsworthian in its portrayal of being as a longing for presence that is, finally, a self-haunting and an invocation of *epitaphic* presence. Importantly, it is also Wordsworthian in that it posits a "single point" of perception wherein meaning and being repose as a unit. The "I/eye" that observes the fruit, gazes from the window, and marks the climb of the moon must be conceived as inhabitable, as a stable point of arrival, before it can be understood as the site of the left-behind. Without the presumption of the "I/eye," the entirely visual metaphors, the figures through which the poem works, would sink back into the meaningless night.

It is important to notice that the "silent . . . sleeveworn stone" is a "casement" ledge. It defines the difference between inside and outside as an *opening* between the two, as a window to the wordless world of being. It is only so long as the "I/eye" is situated firmly at the solid casement—only so long as it can use its framing and distancing, its representing function, without being caught up in that function—that the illusion of motionless movement can hold. In this poem the single point of the situated "I/eye" perceives meaning as being because it remains immobile and coherent. Displace the eye, or shift its position, or allow it to move *with* the moon, and the illusion that "the moon climbs" disintegrates, the fruit will not appear, and the twigs remain concealed forever as "night-entangled trees." The "I/eye" must remain a "still point" in order to secure the incorporation of meaning into being, even if (or especially if) that incorporation occurs through a representation that allows being to *appear* as presence.

MacLeish is as dependent upon "the still point of the turning world" as Eliot is, and like Wordsworth, he too requires the single point of the "living soul." It is in this respect that "Ars Poetica" seems most obviously postromantic. Despite the doubleness of the poem and the paradoxical loopings of its final statement, it attains to a certain ground that stabilizes the interplay between presentation and representation, meaning and being. A postmodern poet, however, surrenders that point. As long as it holds, Ashbery writes, "the soul is a captive, treated humanely, kept / In suspension, unable to advance much farther / Than your look as it intercepts the picture."[7] In this situation, he says, it is true that "life is englobed," but "one would like to stick one's hand / Out of the globe" ("Self-Portrait," 69). Ashbery wants to escape exactly what MacLeish most desires in a poem that "should be" like "a globed fruit." The breaking of the claustrophobic "englobing" of being requires a violence awesome in its simplicity and power; it requires only the recognition that

> The secret is too plain. The pity of it smarts,
> Makes hot tears spurt: that the soul is not a soul,
> Has no secret, is small and it fits
> Its hollow perfectly: its room our moment of attention.
>
> ("Self-Portrait," 69)

This postmodern destruction of the "secret" that "has no secret," this erasure of the stable site to which all returns, this reduction of the single point to a no-thing in a "hollow" that is only a "moment of attention" undermines severely the crucial interpenetration of meaning and being in language. Ashbery's next lines are these:

> That is the tune but there are no words.
> The words are only speculation
> (From the Latin *speculum*, mirror):
> They seek and cannot find the meaning of the music.
>
> ("Self-Portrait," 69)

The irony involved in writing words that "are no words" has its roots in a gesture in which language is employed to convey meaning even as it declares the impossibility of containing meaning. Before all of the implications of Ashbery's lines can be understood, we need to look further at the effects of erasing the "still point" of the

---

7. John Ashbery, "Self-Portrait in a Convex Mirror," in *Self-Portrait in a Convex Mirror* (New York, 1975), 69.

"I" on the desire to incorporate meaning into language. For now it should be understood that Ashbery's description of words as pure representation, as mirroring "speculations" that "seek and cannot find the meaning," is both a return to, and a complicated overturning of, MacLeish's "A poem should not mean / But be."

Words that "seek and cannot find the meaning of the music" are words that continue to hope even as they admit failure. A paradox, certainly, yet Ashbery's situation is no more paradoxical than Mac-Leish's, though it does turn the fabric of the interwoven relationship between meaning and being inside out. What remains common to both poets, to all poets, is the intention to mean, though what they intend, how they construct that meaning, and even what they mean by "meaning" are complex and muddy questions. Nonetheless, the Wordsworthian "hope" that language can embody meaning, at least in the manner of the haunted shrine, continues to drive all writing toward at least that kind of minimal and wavering establishment of being.

> But who is it that is addressing you?
> —Jacques Derrida, *Dissemination*

In the poets we have thus far considered, hope is lodged in at least three assumptions: first, that there is a meaning or truth which exists independently of language; second, that language can, if the right words are found, reveal that meaning; and third, that the self is a unified entity, a "presence" which can initiate and ground the connection between truth and words in the form of a meaning brought into being. The third assumption bears the weight of the other two, and it depends essentially on an understanding of being as presence. The desire to incarnate meaning in language is undeniably one version of what Derrida has called the "Heideggerean hope." This hope, which is also an assertion of presence, displays itself as that "quest for the proper word and the unique name" which Derrida believes transverses all of Heidegger's work. Insofar as Ashbery understands words as a quest "for the meaning of the music," he participates in this Heideggerean hope, and he does so as a search for the "right" word, for a language of revelation rather than representation. Ashbery, however, must perform his quest without the support of the central pillar in the entire structure: the felt presence of "oneself," the self-presence that Wordsworth articulates as "the point where all stand single." Logically, once one

has recognized that "the soul is not a soul," writing as the communication of meaning should evaporate. Yet writing holds, *as* meaning, and in the work of even such "demystified" writers as Ashbery
or Derrida, "the point where all stand single" always reappears as
(and because of) the intention to mean.

   That point, however, remains as Wordsworth said, "far hidden
from the reach of words," and at the moment when we try to reach
it through words—which is to say through thought itself—it appears to disintegrate. The self, as a coherent ground, appears only
as the product of the language that seeks it out. It is not, Derrida
insists, the origin of language but an "effect" of language play. The
problem, as we have seen throughout this work, is that it seems impossible to arrest completely the dynamic movement of the sign.
The movement is always representative, and representation always
disturbs the "presence" of meaning as being. The Derridean reading of cartesian consciousness demonstrates that thought itself can
operate only through the series of supplements and displacements
that Derrida has called "auto-affection," and as such, consciousness
cannot be conceived as a "still point" but only as a representing
force. Perceived in this way, the "I am" that seems to present itself
simultaneously with the "I think" comes "after," not before or
"during," thought itself. "I am," then, becomes "I will have been
represented," and hence "the presence that is thus delivered to us in
the present is a chimera" (*OG*, 154). We are, in Derridean thought,
"self-haunting" to an extreme that Wordsworth could not have acknowledged without erasing the word "self" from his phrase and
remaining content with "hauntings"—in the plural. This production of meaning as a kind of phantasmagoria, a sort of magic lan-
tern show, which can only produce the illusion of presence, undermines the concept of self-presence so severely that the hold which
being as presence has exerted over thought is loosened and language
is shaken. This productivity, which Derrida calls "dissemination,"
forbids the use of the word *I* except as the symbolic representation
of a representation. One cannot even say that "I disseminate therefore I am." Language is deprived of its "first principle"—the present
indicative of the verb *to be*.[8] It is left with the infinite play of a force
that cannot even be designated as an origin. Dissemination dissemi-

---

   8. For two extensive discussions of the function of the copula, see Derrida's
"The Supplement of Copula: Philosophy before Linguistics," in *MP*, 175–207, and
"Form and Meaning," in *MP*, 155–74.

nates, it "effects" the "I"—it is not located in it. The hold of presence is loosened and language is shaken, but as Derrida knows and as we will see shortly, neither is broken. That holding power, even though it trembles on the brink, is what allows Jacques Derrida to write.

Nonetheless, the shaking has had powerful effects, the most potent of which is the erasure of the subject as a "self" that can attain presence. The subject is forbidden as a point of origin, as a consciousness that generates language, as an "author." In its total eradication of the subject, deconstruction has moved beyond even structuralism, one of its predecessors.[9] Structuralism, by treating language as a system of rules and codes—as a structure—was able to discuss the system without calling upon the idea of an individual "speaker," and the meanings produced by the system were not dependent upon, or confined by, authorial intention. Deconstruction, however, has been able to show that the idea of system or code depends ultimately upon the metaphysics of presence as thoroughly as any other structure. It cannot do without the idea of a center, a ground, that serves as simply another name for the "still point" that may be designated as "logos," or, for that matter, as the "I."[10] By questioning the concept of systems, Derrida has exploded the still point of meaning more completely than structuralism could have tolerated. He eliminates the idea of a center that allows a structure to hold. As a system, structuralism admits a ground where the play of meaning can "close," or come to rest. Dissemination, a sheer process, always refuses such closure.

One example of the ways in which structuralism readmits a ground into the play of language occurs in a very influential essay by one of its greatest practitioners, Roland Barthes. Though Barthes, a dynamic and often unclassifiable thinker, did not rest long in this moment of replacement, it is particularly important because it is precisely the moment in which he attempts to destroy the functioning of the "I" ("DA," 143). Barthes announced "The Death of the Author" by asserting that "only language acts, 'performs' and not 'me.'" It is only, Barthes insists, when "the voice loses its

9. For histories of the relationship between Derridean thought and structuralism, see Spivak's introduction to OG, Christopher Norris, Deconstruction: Theory and Practice (London, 1982); Jonathan Culler, On Deconstruction: Theory and Criticism after Structuralism (Ithaca, 1982).
10. See "Structure, Sign and Play" and "Force and Signification" in WD for two good examples of Derrida's exposition of the dependence of structure upon "center."

origin, the author enters into his own death" that "writing begins" ("DA," 143). Barthes's dismantling of the authorial self is so thorough that it would seem total. For him the self becomes a kind of assemblage of linguistic and cultural codes. But within this conglomerate Barthes, unlike Derrida, rescues at least one point that can secure meaning. For him the death of the author will "restore the place of the reader" ("DA," 143). The reader is restored as the writer of the text he or she reads.[11] While Barthes's reader is in no way a "personality," it (one can no longer say he or she) does remain a "subject," and that depersonalized and culturally defined subject serves as a ground for meaning. Barthes phrases this new situation of meaning this way: "Linguistically, the author is never more than the instance writing, just as 'I' is nothing other than the instance of saying 'I': language knows a 'subject', not a 'person', and this subject empty outside of the very enunciation which defines it, suffices to make language 'hold together', suffices, that is to say, to exhaust it" ("DA," 145). Despite the emptiness of the reader and the fact that it can be understood as nothing more than a cultural construct, Barthes sustains a "center" that makes meaning, in all its multiplicity and duplicity, possible. Language can be bottomed-out, "exhausted" by its performance; writing is a "performative" space with no content other than the "act by which it is uttered" ("DA," 146). But this performance reinstitutes a subject, if only as a multileveled formal construct. There is, he writes, using Greek tragedy as his example, "someone who understands each word in its duplicity and who, in addition hears the very deafness of the characters speaking in front of him—this someone being precisely the reader (or here the listener)" ("DA," 148). In this essay, Barthes accomplishes the erasure of the author by establishing an even more powerful final point upon which meaning can balance:

> Thus is revealed the total existence of writing: a text is made of multiple writings, drawn from many cultures and entering into mutual relations of dialogue, parody, contestation, but there is one place where this multiplicity is focused and that place is the reader, not as was hitherto said, the author. The reader is the space on which all the quotations that make up a writing are inscribed without any of them being lost; a text's

11. This notion grounds the work of some of the more interesting critics of our moment, thinkers like Stanley Fish, Wolfgang Iser, and Sandra Gilbert. For a good summary of "reader-response criticism," see Jonathan Culler, "Readers and Reading," in *On Deconstruction*.

unity lies not in its origin but in its destination. Yet this destination cannot any longer be personal: the reader is without history, biography, psychology; he is simply that *someone* who holds together in a single field all the traces by which the written text is constituted. ("DA," 148)

One way of understanding how much more radical Derrida is than even Barthes is to notice Barthes's emphasized word "*someone*." The "instance" that writes "I," that says "I," that reads "I," may be "empty" but it is still some "one," it is an emptiness that "holds together," that serves as a "destination," as a "single field." It remains a performative space of coherence that is utterly depersonalized but is not entirely outside the purview of Wordsworth's attending "point where all stand single." Barthes' "instance" or "subject," which does not exist "outside of the very enunciation which defines it," still "suffices to make language 'hold together'" precisely because *it* holds together. It can function as a site, a place of repose. In *The Pleasure of the Text,* the subject is clearly defined as the "site of a loss" (*PT,* 7). But despite the fact that Barthes has surrendered the idea of plenitude and that the subject is "doubled," it continues to hold together as a coherent enclosure of meaning. Such a holding is necessary if the subject is to be able to write himself into existence, even the displaced kind of existence Barthes discusses. As he says, "such a subject returns, not as illusion, but as *fiction*" (*PT,* 92). The distinction here turns on the ability of readers to situate *themselves* in relation to the text, a power that Derrida will deny. Barthes, however, can say that "I write myself as a subject at present out of place . . . calling for a non-site" (*PT,* 63). Such a gesture may set the subject adrift but it does not destroy it; the fictional subject remains a coherent construct instituted by a coherent "instance of saying 'I.'"[12]

However, Derrida, by pushing Barthes's performative metaphor to its furthest extremes, will break the holding power of even this sort of subjectivity. For him, "destination" becomes "dissemination," and the "someone" can never be located as either an originat-

12. Barthes attempts to distinguish his "subject" from subjectivity by defining it as a "fictive identity." He insists that one imagines oneself as an "individual" and that it is this imagined "individuality" that one encounters when one reads a text. But he goes on to suggest that individuality is also "the given which makes my body separate from other bodies and appropriates its suffering or its pleasure . . . and this body of bliss is also *my historical subject*" (*PT,* 63). His "individual" is richly multiple but it still holds together around the center designated by the word *I,* even if, as he says, it is an "anachronic subject, adrift" (*PT,* 64).

ing or final point of coherence. There is only language, performing as representation and repetition and enabled by a force that cannot be represented at all, a force that is both outside of language and operative within its representative play. There is no *one* to be set "adrift," there is only the drift of language itself. In Derrida's case, the "someone" becomes the "something"—pure textuality, "the machine." He eliminates the possibility of the subject as site, either as the displaced site or as the site that can enclose, or be enclosed by, "all the traces." There is no place where quotations can be "inscribed without any of them being lost." A key statement to be remembered here is Derrida's repeated insistence that "there is nothing outside of the text" (*OG*, 158). As he makes clear in *Dissemination,* there is not even a subject conceived as the conjoining point of a cultural web that can serve as a destination of meaning: "The text is remarkable in that the reader . . . can never choose his own place in it, nor can the spectator . . . no spot, in other words, where he would stand before an already *written* text" (*DN*, 290). For Derrida, there is no "site of loss," no way to "call for a nonsite," no way to "write myself . . . at *present* out of place." It is, in fact, the impossibility of any site outside the text that creates "this impossibility—and this potency, too, of the reader writing himself"—an impossibility that "has from time immemorial been at work in the text in general" (*DN*, 290). *Text* must be read here (and everywhere in Derrida) as existence itself as well as in its more traditional sense. Barthes speaks of "the total existence of writing" as a "multiplicity" focused on the reader, Derrida speaks of writing as an existence focused only on its own operations, operations which can never become "total." Everything falls under the machine-like activity of a self-productive text, one with no beginning and no end.

"Auto-affection," "supplement," "the trace," all the figures of representation, are textual "effects" and, most important for our present concerns, the subject itself is merely the product of a "complicated machine" that constructs it as "the illusion or error of the present." This illusion of the "I" is nothing more than an "attending discourse" that "unites the motif of *presence* . . . with the motif of the *auxiliary*" (*DN*, 324). That is, the subject is nothing more than a "theme" of presence brought into play by the workings of a text that create the "motif" of subjectivity, of "reader" and "writer," in the form of discourse itself. Both positions are inscribed by the machinery of language in order for it to affect, and as effects of, its own processes:

But who is it that is addressing you? Since it is not an "author," a "narrator," or a "deus ex machina," it is an "I" that is both part of the spectacle and part of the audience; an "I" that, a bit like "you," attends (undergoes) its own incessant, violent reinscription within the arithmetical machinery; an "I" that, functioning as a pure passageway for operations of substitution, is not some singular and irreplaceable existence, some subject or "life" but only, moving between life and death, reality and fiction, etc., a mere function or phantom. (*DN,* 325)

As we will see in the next chapter, Ashbery's understanding of the "I" is similar to Derrida's, and his sense of the self as a "passageway" causes stress that, though sometimes comic, is always extremely intense in his writing. Ashbery, however, insists that such an "I" is a question, and it is not "a rhetorical question in the impassive grammar of cosmic unravelings of all kinds, to be proposed but never formulated." Rather, it is "the major question that revolves around you, your being here" (*TP,* 51). For now, we should recall that we have encountered this "I" which "revolves around *you*" before, in our discussion of Derrida's term *auto-affection.* This "pure passageway" is required by the operations of representation and supplementation in order for consciousness to delude itself into presence, but at the same time it will not do to call that passageway a "self" since it is only the product of the play that it conveys. As a product, it is always a "you" or a "he/she." The "I," Derrida writes, "is the name of the full force of writing which, in one blow [*d'un coup*], triggers off the tale and keeps it in progress, but it is above all the simulacrum—and that simulacrum must be understood as a force—of an identity that is ceaselessly dislocated, displaced, thrown outside itself, precisely by this kind of writing by force." It is a "dead surface effect" or a "citational effect" in which what is cited is only another text (*DN,* 326, 328, 334). This "citation" is a bottomless interplay of surface effects that cannot be brought to rest in meaning either as the self-presence of an "I" or as the presence of "truth." The textual machine simply "disseminates" itself, endlessly. It is "an undecidable process of opening/closing that re-forms without letup" and, furthermore, it "has the means, within itself, of complicating itself beyond measure, of its own accord, taking its place, each time, within a set that comprehends it, situates it, and regularly goes beyond its bounds after first being reflected in it. The history of the text's geometries is a history of irrefutable reinscriptions and generalizations" (*DN,* 337). In summary, Derrida's point is that meaning "disseminates itself without

ever having *been* itself and without coming back to itself" (*DN,*
351). Existence, then, can be seen as a pure desire to produce a
meaning that can never be achieved—even in the form of a desiring
subject. Hence, when we speak of the "meaning of being," we do
so only out of hunger and fear, because the "frightening quality of
such a necessity solicits the delusion that 'Being' can be mastered as
'presence'" (*DN,* 352). We are the parts and the products of the
"machine" and

> no one is allowed on these premises if he is afraid of machines and if he
> still believes that literature, and perhaps even thought, ought to exorcise
> the machine, the two having nothing to do with each other. This tech-
> nological "metaphor"—technicity as metaphor that transports life into
> death—is not added as an accident, as an excess, a simple surplus, to the
> living force of writing . . . [the machine] instead of falling outside of life
> or perhaps in the very act of falling, provokes . . . deploys that "living
> force" by dividing it, making room for it, enabling it to speak. Plug-
> ging it in and triggering it off.   (*DN,* 292)

Dissemination is not, according to Derrida, the *loss* of the unity
of meaning, not "the loss of that kind of truth." [13] To see it in this
way is to presume that there is something other than the machine,
something "whole" that exists prior to its operations. It is to presume a "single point," as Wordsworth (and even Roland Barthes, in
the moment of "The Death of the Author") presume a site for the
return of meaning. Dissemination is not a "negative second moment, dissemination affirms the always already divided generation
of meaning" (*DN,* 268). We cannot return to dissemination as an
origin, a first moment, neither is it an end—except insofar as death
is an end. For the "end" of dissemination is also the "end" of auto-
affection, of supplement, of the play of the trace; it is the "end" that
would be required by any concept of self-presence as unity, as a
"present."

All presence, including self-presence, is characterized by Derrida
as precisely this sort of fatality. The "I" exists only in relation to its
representations, to its "tracing" functions in its pursuit of presence.
Thus death is a "relation to the absence of traces," to a full presence
that is "the unnameable" except as "a relation to what is called
my-death" (*DN,* 364). It would not be too extreme to say that, for
Derrida, "life" is the production of meaning. It is, however, a pro-

13. This assertion is part of Derrida's ongoing struggle against a return to the
philosophy of metaphysics that always threatens his work.

duction that can never produce meaning-fullness or be located in an intending subject. There is no respite, no still point wherein meaning can dwell; it cannot achieve "Being." Such a still point can only be conceived as death, as the unplugging of the machine. Thus, there is no "I," no "author," and no "reader"—these are only the surface creations of textuality. There is only performance, an acting out, a pretense that *conceals* itself as pretense and that is, therefore, a *new* kind of theater: "The old theatrical organization has become unjustifiable, is no longer answerable to anyone; the old phantoms called the author, the reader, the director . . . have no single, unique, fixed place (stage, wings, house, etc.) assigned to themselves except in the representation they make of it to themselves, of which an account must be given" (*DN,* 296). In the new theater, the speculative tragedy Wordsworth enacts cannot be performed. That tragedy dies with the notion of a self characterized as a central, if buried, "single point." In addition, the new theater specifically rejects Barthes's notion of the reader/listener as a "someone" who can remain far enough "out of place" or outside of the text to hear "the very deafness of the characters in front of him." Both of these "old phantoms" evaporate when the machinery of language, directed toward searching them out, finds only more language. The new theater, then, would seem to deny any "hope" for meaning, for fulfillment, even for any possibility that one can say "I."

Yet the killing of the old ghosts has produced a stage that is not quite so desolate as it might at first appear. For something remains, which differentiates itself from the performance even though it can only be experienced by virtue of its "acting." One old phantom cannot be dissolved: some compelling power "intends" the game, "attends" to its rules, elects to plug itself in at a *certain point* in the machinations of a language already in operation. *Intention* is the structuring and propelling force that keeps the machine running, and if it cannot be contained by any "unique" performance, neither can the play begin without it. Before we explore this in detail in the next section of this chapter, consider briefly the way Ashbery addresses the intentional act which escapes the game in his own masterful performance *Three Poems.* The poet has been laboring throughout the work to establish the relationship between writing and consciousness, between poetry and the meaning of the "I." The culmination of his speculations is presented as a pure performance, as "The Recital." This final poem opens with the poet's discovery of a kind of "dissemination" as the *provisional* answer to the problem of self-coherence, to "the major question that revolves around you, your being here." He has already intuited that the question cannot be "unravelled" as if it were a stable entity which could be dismantled section by section. The question *of* being *is* being for Ashbery, and the only end (or "answer") to the questioning is death. Thus existence becomes the acting out of the question. He begins his "Recital" in this way:

> All right. The problem is that there is no new
> problem. It must awaken from the sleep of being
> part of some other, old problem, and by that time
> its new problematical existence will have already
> begun, carrying it forward into situations with
> which it cannot cope, since no one recognizes it
> and it does not even recognize itself yet, or know
> what it is.
>
> (*TP*, 107)

Ashbery has, at this point, discovered that the self is so radically temporal, so implicated in its own dissemination, that even in the flash of its sudden awakening to its status as a representation of the meaning-making machine called language, it cannot claim that recognition as its identity. Instead, it will already have lost itself to the future, it "will already have begun." It will already have left behind its own awakening and been thrown "forward into situations with which it cannot cope." To cope with a situation is to contain it temporally and to overcome it as a totality, as a domesticated "whole." It is to master a stabilized, self-identical moment and site of being. But such containment, such a "content," can never be achieved. Hence the always "new" and always "problematical existence," which is also always "*no* new problem," cannot "even recognize itself"; it can only continue to exist as "recital," as a repetitive but always new "performance."

Unlike Derrida, though, Ashbery points directly to a "something" that escapes the performing machine, a "something" that exists both before and after sheer performance. These are the closing lines of *Three Poems:*

> A vast wetness as of sea and air combined,
> a single smooth, anonymous matrix without surface
> or depth was the product of these new changes. It
> no longer mattered very much whether prayers were
> answered with concrete events or the oracle gave a
> convincing reply, for there was no longer anyone to

care in the old sense of caring. There were new
people watching and waiting, conjugating in this
way the distance and emptiness, transforming the
scarcely noticeable bleakness into something both
intimate and noble. The performance had ended,
the audience streamed out; the applause still
echoed in the empty hall. But the idea of the
spectacle as something to be acted out and
absorbed still hung in the air long after the
last spectator had gone home to sleep.

(*TP*, 118)

Ashbery suggests here that writing is similar to Derrida's "new theater." As pure staging, it has no "surface or depth," no "living
force" that can appear as "oracle" or "answer." It does not contain
the author or the reader; it is simply an "anonymous matrix,"
which, like the matrix in a computer, conveys and relays, translating one code into another. In this context, the word *matrix* loses its
archaic sense of origin, of maternal source, and forefronts its more
contemporary meaning of being in-between, being the vacant "passageway" that enables meaning to occur. Since the self cannot appear, even to itself, there is "no longer anyone to care in the *old*
sense of caring," that is, in the old way of mystically seeking answers to prayers. Instead of being conjurors calling forth a given
meaning or calling to a given presence, "new people" become
"conjugators," language-learners, performing or "reciting" (in the
old classroom sense of "deriving") the tenses of the verb "to be" in
the first, second and third persons. Such conjugating is, in itself, a
"performance," a "transforming" of "bleakness into something
both intimate and noble."

Ashbery's characterization of performance, then, resembles, but
is not quite analogous to, Derrida's. For the poet there is "something" outside of the "spectacle," "outside of the text," and that
"something" is "the *idea* of the spectacle *as something to be acted* out
and absorbed." The difference between the poet's and the philosopher's characterizations of writing as theater lies in Ashbery's conviction that poetry is inherently demystified. That is, it never conceals itself as pretense or creates the illusion of the sort of presence
that Derrida calls the "old phantoms." Rather, poetry acknowledges itself as "spectacle," as a "recital" and, in so doing, complicates the notion of authorial presence immeasurably. By asserting
itself as a performance in which the performer *intends* the word *I* to
be understood as a self-reference, "formulated" but always aban-

doned, a sort of "character" or "role," poetry creates a complex situation in which the writer is present but only as an intentional structure which activates the text. The writer is devoid of a personal self; the "I" is certainly not self-present or internalized as a content; it is radically proleptic. But the intentionality of the performer is *constitutive* of the fiction of self, which he or she repeats by reciting the otherwise empty form. It is the *recitation*, the "recital" of an "I" that is inevitably "other than" the reciter, that confirms the presence of the performer—merely as an activating intention to perform. The "I" is irrepressibly a "you" or a "he" in the same breath that it "is" the performer. Hence, the poet cannot be seen as *only* an "attending discourse" or an "effect" of the text but as *both* of those and "something" more. The poet is not just a product of textuality but is also the "player," the intentionality that is acting out textuality.

Recitation is not citation. It separates the reciter from that which is recited; it depends upon a certain distance between actor and action (writer and text) that cannot be perceived unless it is clear to performer and audience alike that the actor *intends* the action to *be* a performance. The actor repeats from memory a "pretext," plugs into a machine, but does not become a "mere function" of that machine. Rather in a recital, the act of repetition is an event that proclaims the performer's acting as intentional—and interpretive.[14] Ashbery's description of poetry as "spectacle" and "recital" suggests that he certainly understands his repetition as "reinscription within . . . the machinery," but as a reinscription that is both different from, and makes a difference in, the textual machine that he has entered. Ashbery's "I," like Derrida's, is "both part of the spectacle and part of the audience," but, unlike Derrida's, it is not subordinate to the machine. Intentionality plays with, and in, the machine, but it ultimately escapes reinscription. And it escapes, indeed, as the "living force" that Derrida believes the machine "deploys." Ashbery would not reject Derrida's point, but he would add that the "living force" also deploys the *machine*. That force is best understood as an intentionality directed toward interpretation.

14. William Spanos has developed a concept he calls a "repetition forward" that is invaluable to an understanding of this aspect of Ashbery's thought. See "Heidegger, Kierkegaard, and the Hermeneutic Circle: Towards a Postmodern Theory of Interpretation as Dis-closure," in *Martin Heidegger and The Question of Literature*, ed. Spanos, 115–48, and his book *Repetitions: The Postmodern Occasion in Literature and Culture* (Baton Rouge, 1987).

A recital always repeats a pretext, but as intentional repetition it is always different from previous performances, and that difference is in the interpretation. And recital, as both repetition and interpretation, cannot allow the performer to be understood as only a "citation" or a "dead surface effect" produced by the machine. Rather, both audience and performer (reader and writer) intentionally enter the new theater in order to be joined in the "anonymous matrix" of the writing, which furnishes no answers but offers the opportunity to perform and, thereby, to "transform." There can be no passivity on behalf of either the performer or the "new people watching and waiting, conjugating . . . transforming." All of them act on and in the textual machine, the already written "intertext," but that acting is an event, and it is an event that displays consciousness, the proleptic "I," as an impersonal, contentless intention to transform the "distance and emptiness" into the "intimate and noble." Writing does not offer meaning as oracular content, as "answers," rather, it creates a site, a "theater" in which intentional consciousness becomes intent on acting out the "Idea" of making meaning-as-such.

In that theater the writer is also his own reader; he interprets the text in the process of producing it. As a displaced (no longer/not yet) "I," he understands that he has evacuated his own words, that he, too, is watching, waiting, and conjugating. He is not the content of his text but the performer who reclaims its "distance and emptiness" and who, by virtue of his performance, makes it "intimate and noble." He activates a representation of himself which denies his being as a content, but announces it as an interpretive activity. A recital, then, asserts the performer's intentional entrance into a pretext (in both meanings of that word), it asserts him or her as a "citational" effect of that pretext and, in the same gesture, it proclaims the performer's difference from the text he or she recites. The recital situates the reciter both inside and outside of the text in this way. *Re*citation is not quotation, though it may perform by quoting; it is not just referential, though it is acted out through reference. It is not, in other words, strictly citational and cannot "produce" the performer as only a "dead surface effect." For Ashbery, a recital is the paradigmatic instance in which the intentional "I" must be perceived as both present and absent: present as an intentional act acting itself out and absent as an oracle, an answer, a content.

The particularity of each spectacle, each unique combination of citation and recitation, ends, reducing the theater to an "empty hall." Yet intentionality abides even when emptied of specific content. It abides: that is, it remains, outside of the spectacle, as an active "waiting," as an anticipation of content. The "idea" sustains itself even in the face of "sleep," awaiting the text "as something to be acted"—an acting which, because it is recitation, is always repetition or, to be more precise, what William Spanos calls a repetition-forward.[15] Intention always abides as something "to be," as a forward thrust toward acting out that which has already been and is still about to be absorbed. For the acting out in a recital always expresses what has already been absorbed but, in the process, "transforms" that "old problem" into something entirely new in the same moment that the actor transforms him or herself by virtue of the acting. The doubleness is important here. It is not just that the actor is absorbed by the text but also that the text is absorbed by the performer "conjugating" it, transforming it into the tenses that display its temporal movement. In this way, "The Recital" confirms the presence of an "I," as an intentional structuring, as emphatically as it confirms the loss of the "I" that must erase itself as a personal history in order to perform. Intentionality will always "already have begun" to disseminate, but it remains something other than dissemination. It is integrated into the machine; it recites the "old problem" but, in so doing, "its new problematical existence will already have begun, carrying it forward." What hangs in the air, then, what cannot be erased, even by the deserted theater, is the idea of performance itself, the idea that poetry is an intentional construct which can be activated only by an intentional consciousness. Ashbery's intentionality is pure activity, a pure haunting which is not tethered to the machine but is required by it in order for it to perform. It has been detached from personality and freed from individual performances of the text. Yet, even disembodied, "it still hung in the air long after the last spectator had gone home to sleep." The empty theater remains haunted.

> You can neither define
> Nor erase it, and seen by torchlight,
> Being cloaked with the shrill

15. Ashbery's understanding of being as a thrust forward, as an interpretive act that cannot reach closure but that recollects the past in every proleptic moment, comes very close to Spanos's understanding of Heidegger's hermeneutic circle as a temporal, rather than a spatial, figure.

Savage drapery of non-being, it
Stands out in the firelight.
It is more than anything was meant to be.
                                        —John Ashbery, *As We Know*

The concept of intentionality is neither physical nor psychological in its na-
ture, but structural, involving the activity of a subject *regardless of its*
empirical concerns, except as far as they relate to the intentionality of the
structure. The structural intentionality determines the relationship between
components of the resulting object in all its parts, but the relationship of the
particular state of mind of the person engaged in the act of structurization to
the structured object is altogether contingent.
                                        —Paul de Man, *Blindness and Insight*

Ashbery, then, sustains "hope" for the presencing power of language in the minimal form of a "re-citation" that displays an intentional consciousness in the act of intending toward meaning. This
act, by repeating the "I" as a "pretext," constitutes a fictional "I,"
but it also reveals a consciousness *in the process* of interpreting—
making a difference in, and proclaiming its difference from, the fictional self it activates. Language as performance displays presence in
the form of a radical temporality which Ashbery understands as the
"non-being" of an existence that is, in *essence,* a "no-longer/not-
yet." This nonbeing is a questioning, a thrust forward: a "seeking
of the meaning of the music." The seeking consciousness can never
be perceived as either an embodied or a lost presence: "You can
neither define / Nor erase it." Neither, however, does non-being
mean "nothingness." Something emerges out of the dark and,
"seen by torchlight," the light of the seeker, it "stands out" as
"cloaked with the shrill / Savage drapery of non-being." Something arises within, and because of, the cloak which both conceals
and reveals its force. If the cloak of non-being is "savage," it is because it grants appearance to the inherently disembodied: it is a
primitive and fearsome revelation of that which "is" not, which
cannot be made fully available to presentation. To uncloak the intending consciousness from the words that cover it, which reveal its
existence as non-being, would be to uncover a ghost, to bare its
haunting as only naked process. The "meaning" of the words in
Ashbery's work resides in their functioning as cloaks, which bestow forms that conceal the disembodied nature of the performing
intentionality. The temporal movement of consciousness demands
concealment *in order to be exposed* as "more than any*thing*"—as

more than an uncloaked presence that could appear, could "be." "It is more than anything" because its mode of being is the "non-being" of a past intentionality always lost on its way to the future: "it is more than anything [because it always] was [and it is always] meant [as a] to be."

Ashbery's hope is not that language can incarnate in the manner of a "body" that englobes meaning but rather as a "savage drapery," which covers the process of thought. Words drape the otherwise invisible "I" with a cloak of "non-being" that will allow its movement to stand out in the darkness of nothingness. Such an incarnative gesture declares that the cloak of words is not, in itself, meaning-full except insofar as it reveals the presence of an intention to mean. It does not reveal the content of a self but, instead, reveals the activity of an intending "I" bent on performing an intentional/meaningful act. In this restricted sense Ashbery participates in that traditional endeavor of all lyric poetry: the attempt to unite meaning and being by discovering the "right words." Since, for him, the meaning of *meaning* and *being* is that they cannot rest, cannot be achieved, then they can only be awaited, sought, and performed. And since waiting, seeking, performing, and questioning are the essential characteristics of Ashbery's "being," there is a certain rigorous logic in his notion that poetry unites the two through the *non*presence of words that both seek and cloak a restless *non*-being. For Ashbery, the "right words" create poetry that exposes itself as evacuated: empty of either a content that can be fully revealed or a self that can be contained. At the same time, the "right words" must allow the "savage drapery of non-being" to appear, must transform the no-longer and the not-yet of being into a visible (readable) emptiness that becomes intimate and noble when it is conjugated by performer and audience. In other words, Ashbery attempts to incarnate the impossibility of incarnating the being of the "I" as a stable presence. But in the process he incarnates the "truth" of Being as he understands it: he gives form to time. His work, then, "contains" a content which "means" (in fact, insists) that language cannot contain. Such a violently paradoxical structure would seem unreadable. Yet Ashbery's poetry does achieve the sort of meaningfulness it disclaims, and it does incarnate that intentional consciousness whose disappearance reveals its nature as that which "is," but is impossible either to "define" or "erase." And, at the same time, his work allows the "I" to escape, "to advance much farther" than Being as presence or non-being as absence. It "allows one to stick one's hand / Out of the globe."

If, as Ashbery says, "the soul is not a soul," if, indeed, "that is the tune but there are no words," then the mirror-words which "are only speculation" reflect a consciousness whose seeking for "the meaning of the music" is such a powerful structuring force that the speculum of language reflects its activity as meaning itself. This seems to me the furthest extreme to which one can press the disintegration of the self and still allow language to remain operative. If MacLeish could not escape the play of signification by writing that "a poem should not mean but be," neither can Ashbery escape an incarnation of meaning by insisting that it is only the mirror play of signification devoid of an "I." Just as representation must always disrupt the effort to capture being as full presence in language, so must intention disrupt the disincarnative movement of representation, which is to say that meaning *appears* as an intended "content." The phrase "there are no words" exists and is readable only because there *are* words whose meanings have been contained. And while the phrase can never achieve the full (silent) presence of "globed fruit," it cannot simply disperse into a pure, uninhabited "dissemination." Unlike the stone, it cannot relegate the subject to an "outside" or reinscribe it completely as a mere "dead surface effect."

There are obvious similarities between Ashbery's retention of the disembodied "I," as an intentional consciousness always in flight, and Barthes's notion of the subject who "returns . . . as fiction," who can say "I write myself as a subject at present out of place." Ashbery's subject, as the play of differance, can never serve as a "destination," but it is not a pure dissemination. The poet would rephrase Derrida by insisting that there is *always* something outside of the text, something which, *because* it differs and defers, institutes the text that "recites," but never totally reinscribes, its activity as an effect.

Ashbery confirms a point that Paul de Man made long ago: language, in every way that we understand it, is an intentional structuring or activity. And, as de Man makes very clear, intentionality cannot be understood without "involving the activity of a subject." De Man was certainly correct to warn us away from the physical or psychological "self" and to direct us into the text as the only appropriate site for discovering the force that "determines the relationship between the components of the resulting object in all its parts." There is, he notes, "a radical discontinuity that no dialectic is able to bridge" between the surface of a text and the intention that motivates its meanings. The danger, of course, is that in attempting to find the intentional act that sustains a text, the reader will drift into a psychological adventurism that leads only to positing a physical or "real" author and, thus, to positing a text that is simply "a transfer of psychic or mental content." It should be abundantly clear by now that no text can either totally contain or transfer such a content and that in fact the "real" author must disappear in order for the text to appear at all. As de Man says, literature "asserts, by its very existence, its separation from empirical reality" (*BI*, 23, 25, 17).

But, he was equally correct to warn us of the dangers of ignoring the "activity of the subject" in order to forefront only the relationship between the components of a text. The fact that the gap between the surface of a text and the intention, "the deeper inward experience that determines the choice and articulation of themes," is unbridgeable does not suggest that we can afford to forget its intentional motivation. To do so, de Man writes, is to reify the text into a natural object, to forget that "the intentional object requires reference to a specific act as constitutive of its mode of being." Focusing on American New Criticism, specifically its emphasis on the autonomous nature of poetry and its detachment from personality and intention, de Man notes that New Critics discovered much of value. Nonetheless, he continues, "the rejection of the principle of intentionality, dismissed as fallacious, prevented the integration of these discoveries within a truly coherent theory of literary form" (*BI*, 23, 24, 32).[16]

Writing in 1971, de Man clearly hopes that contemporary continental criticism will disabuse us of the notion that literature is the "autonomous object" that New Criticism proposed. Such reification, he rightly insists, "changes the literary act into a literary object by the suppression of its intentional character" (*BI*, 25). Such an object, like the natural object it resembles, forbids the play of meaning and interpretation which is the definition of language. Certainly both structuralism and deconstruction remove literature from its self-contained isolation. The question remains, however, whether or not even deconstruction has prevented the reification of literature, the transformation of act into object.

The question is this: how far can theory disintegrate the "I,"

---

16. De Man is, of course, responding to the powerful articulation of the "intentional fallacy" made by Wimsatt and Beardsley in 1946. See "The Intentional Fallacy," in *Critical Theory*, ed. Adams, 1014–31.

relegate it to the status of a function or component in the text, and still claim to be thinking about language? If the text is completely uninhabited, at what point does it cease to be an intentional act and become merely another dynamic part of nature? Dissemination, by forbidding the presence of a subject in any form, by reducing the notion of the "I" to a "theme" or "motif," reduces even the intentional, depersonalized subject that de Man and Ashbery retain to a "pure passageway for operations of substitution." Such a reduction suggests that language operates independently of any "singular" intention to mean, that it is genuinely "free play." Oddly, language as absolute free play can take on the characteristics of a reified object, as Derrida's own machine metaphor demonstrates. The objectification of language as a machine may seem far removed from Mac-Leish's "globed fruit" but, like that "palpable" entity, or like the impenetrable stone, it attains ultimately the same sort of inscrutability. Deconstruction assumes the intentionality of a text every time it directs its powers into that text to examine it. Yet by eliminating the intentional subject and by suggesting that intention can never achieve being in the text, dissemination forbids meaning and its interpretation as thoroughly as rock. In this situation, the text is not only free—that is, autonomous—but it is absolutely masterful: it not only controls its own author and reader, it creates them.

Dissemination is the culmination of a process that has been steadily gaining force at least since the work of Freud, Marx, and Nietzsche. It begins when thought no longer speculates upon the nature of a world perceived as external to its own workings but instead becomes the exclusive object of its own speculations. At the moment that thought is conceived as linguistic, as the operations of language, we are forced to turn the "tool" back upon itself as a way (the only way) of examining how it works. What we have discovered in the midst of this endeavor is closely analogous to Kurt Gödel's discovery of the incompleteness theorem in mathematics. His idea was a simple and elegant one: to "use mathematical reasoning in exploring mathematical reasoning itself."[17] His results shook the foundations of traditional mathematics. In lay terms, Gödel demonstrated that when a system is used self-referentially, when it is focused on its own operations, it produces a paradox: a complete, that is a totalized, proof is forbidden by the "proving" system itself.

---

17. Douglas R. Hofstadter, *Gödel, Escher, Bach: An Eternal Golden Braid* (New York, 1980), 17.

When the system is used to prove its own axioms, there will always be something "left over" that the system can neither account for nor disprove. Or, to borrow Douglas Hofstadter's paraphrase of Gödel's theorem, "all consistent axiomatic formulations of number theory include undecidable propositions." Hofstadter understands Gödel's theorem as evidence that "there are true statements of number theory which its methods of proof are too weak to demonstrate." In other words, Hofstadter believes that Gödel showed that "provability is a weaker notion than truth, no matter what axiomatic system is involved."[18]

Truth may dominate proof in mathematics, but in our studies of language, we have certainly not been able to bring the paradoxes created by self-referentiality to rest in this way. We remain in the position of undecidability that Hofstadter attributes to Epimenides's utterance, in which the Cretan asserts that "all Cretans are liars"; the statement is neither true nor false but absolutely undecidable because there is no external referent to ground the play of meaning. When language becomes its own object of exploration, it is deprived of a transcendental reference point in very much the same way that Epimenides's statement is deprived. Its statements about itself are grounded only in itself. If, therefore, we cannot be certain of the ground, we cannot be certain of the utterances. If, as Derrida insists, language grounds itself in a notion of truth as presence, and that notion is itself a product of the metaphysical system that language creates and displays, then we "are" on very shaky ground, indeed. The ground appears to be an entirely internalized creation of the system under investigation. The system locates meaning in the central "point" we call consciousness and understand as a coherent self-presence. Yet by turning language back upon itself, Derrida has found, as dissemination demonstrates, that it "includes undecidable propositions," and the most vulnerable is its own ground, the intuitive sense of self-presence. If the operations of dissemination "prove" that self-presence is an illusion created by the representative movements of a perpetual motion machine that attempts to "fill" itself with a presence it can never attain, then meaning as being is only an impossible dream.

In effect, this discovery dissolves—almost—the hope upon which lyric poetry depends. "Almost" because, as Gödel could have predicted, something escapes Derrida's own machinations,

18. *Ibid.*, 17, 18, 19.

and it escapes in the form of the kind of embodied meaning that dissemination forbids. The escape can be articulated in the manner of an Epimenidean paradox: if we understand what Derrida "means" by *dissemination* then meaning *has* achieved being, and it has been achieved as a statement incorporated by a text. At the same time, if we understand *dissemination* then we must understand that meaning *cannot* be embodied, presented, by the text; it must be "undecidable." Therefore, we cannot say that we understand *dissemination*.

In this Derridean context, we are in a deeply paradoxical situation: even as I write this line, I must intend it to contain meaning; I intend to mean what I write. This is the situation of every writer, including Derrida. At the same time, I must recognize that my meaning cannot be contained by my writing: everything deconstruction has taught us about the play of language and the vagaries of interpretation disallows that possibility. And as long as we operate within this paradox, we remain within the problem of authorial intention. That problem has not been resolved.

From one point of view, the question of intention cannot be asked when one confronts Derridean thought. Intention, whatever else it may involve, is always inherently linked with meaning as an achieved presence in a text, and as such it has been "put out of play" by the premises of the deconstructive enterprise. Derrida has always recognized the paradoxical nature of his project. And, in the most sophisticated way, he has used that paradox as evidence for his own assertions about the overwhelming power of a metaphysics of presence. He has repeatedly noted that the (erroneous) idea of being as presence can command the operations of language to such an extent that all language must always return to meaning as being in order to be understood. Consider this example from "The Ends of Man," one of his earlier and more significant discussions of the difficulties of speaking about meaning from within a system wherein meaning cannot, in theory, attain to presence. He first notes that the "reduction *of* meaning—that is of the signified—first takes the form of a critique of phenomenology" and that it must be conceived as "a kind of break with a thinking of Being." However, he continues, this break can only operate from an "outside" that exists in relation to the "inside" of a system where we all "are":

> But the logic of every relation to the outside is very complex and surprising. It is precisely the force and the efficiency of the system that regularly change transgressions into "false exits." Taking into account

these effects of the system, one has nothing from the inside where "we are," but the choice between two strategies: a. To attempt an exit and a deconstruction without changing terrain . . . by using against the edifice the instruments or stones available in the house, that is equally, in language. Here, one risks ceaselessly confirming, consolidating . . . that which one allegedly deconstructs. . . . b. To decide to change terrain, in a discontinuous and irruptive fashion, by brutally placing oneself outside, and by affirming an absolute break and difference . . . thereby inhabiting more naively and more strictly than ever the inside one declares one has deserted, *the simple practice of language ceaselessly reinstates* the new terrain on the oldest ground. (*MP,* 134)

Though there are times when Derrida's apocalyptic language suggests that he has chosen the second alternative and placed himself "brutally . . . outside," most often he resolves the problem by asserting that "one must speak several languages and produce several texts at once" (*MP,* 135). This is not, however, so much a solution as a further affirmation of the unbreakable hold that meaning as being exerts over thought as such. And this has been his point from the beginning.

There is, then, a certain absurdity in accusing Derrida of undermining his own thought by writing as if he wished to be understood as meaningful.[19] As an attempt to dismantle his project, the accusation is banal, misplaced, and finally irrelevant. As Christopher Norris points out, Derrida intends "to deconstruct the sovereign rationality of western thought, the 'metaphysics of presence' everywhere secreted by a language ontologically blind to its own constitutive figures and metaphors. Like Nietzsche before him, Derrida perceives both the necessity and the impossible nature of his task, since even the most vigilant critique of language must in the end fall victim to its own best insights."[20] Though deconstruction can (temporarily) fall victim to its own insights—as when dissemination falls victim to the fact that it must itself "contain" a decidable meaning in order to remain operative in proving that meaning is *un*decidable—it cannot be destroyed by those insights. For example, a deconstructionist could respond to the paradox by saying that dissemination is not meaningful and is not a concept at

19. This is a frequent ground of attack. See, for instance, M. H. Abrams, "The Deconstructive Angel," *Critical Inquiry,* III (1977), 425–38; Wayne C. Booth, "'Preserving the Exemplar'—or, How Not to Dig Our Own Graves," *Critical Inquiry,* III (1977), 407–23; and Gerald Graff, *Literature Against Itself* (Chicago, 1979).

20. Christopher Norris, *The Deconstructive Turn* (London, 1984), 147.

all but merely the mark of an unnameable (force) that exists outside
of the play of language but must be provisionally named in order to
be "traced" within that play. Norris has argued convincingly that
Derridean thought can always deconstruct its "common sense"
opponents, even when they direct deconstruction's own weapons
against its own enterprise. Such power is, he believes, typical of any
strong philosophical skepticism. When it is met with an equally
powerful opposing articulation (in Norris's view, Kripke's defense
of "intuitive content"), we simply enter a vicious circle of assertion
and response that leaves us "in-between," in a position of un-
decidability that could only be resolved finally by a subjective expression of preference.[21] In effect, we have in this situation nothing
more nor less than a linguistic version of Gödel's theorem, the paradox that a powerful system will always be powerful enough to dismantle itself. Such force confirms the effectiveness of the system
rather than destroying its premises. This should be kept firmly in
mind as this discussion of Derrida continues. I am interested not in
disproving his work but rather in examining the manner in which
even this "marginal" thinker is forced to return to a "center," to a
"still point," at exactly the moments when his work is most intensely involved in denying the possibility of such a point. All of
Derrida's work is a violent "transgression" of the notion of self-
presence that grounds language, but, as he has always known, those
transgressions are transformed into "false exits" by the language he
must use. What follows, then, is not so much a critique of Derridean thought as an echo of one of his basic tenets.

Despite the fact that deconstruction has put self-presence "out of
play" by showing that it is merely a surface "effect," an illusion created by the workings of language, the nature of the self as a "constitutive consciousness" remains a question that must be asked. It
may no longer be possible to conceive of the self as Wordsworth's
"hidden" point, which abides beyond the reach of words, but Paul
de Man's insistence that language is, by definition, an intentional
structure always "involving the activity of a subject" remains un-
deniable as long as we understand language as that which commu-
nicates a meaning. The paradox of using language to communicate
the idea that language cannot contain meaning is the most important residue of the economy of deconstructive thought, and it is

21. *Ibid.*, 144–62.

evasive and precipitate to label the problems created by that paradox as "off base" or "common sense" banality. There is no "profit"
in ignoring the loose end, the unsolved predicament, especially
when it is the *crucial* problem, directly related to whether or not
one can even begin to write, begin to say "I." The production of
meaning is the archimedean lever, the machine with which Derrida
moves his world, and the "point" upon which that lever rests cannot be ignored—even if it cannot be located. To do so is to leave
unquestioned de Man's "deeper inward experience that determines
the choice and articulation of the themes," that determines the intentional structure of Derrida's own texts. It is to ignore the fact
that Derrida writes on the "margins" of a discourse that should,
given his own description of the language machine, forbid such a
writing-on-the-edge. As the two alternatives Derrida presents in
"The Ends of Man" make clear, his writing involves "choice and
articulation" that depend radically on intention. Intention cannot be
thought in the absence of an intending subject or a meaningful content, and both of these are incorporated in the philosopher's texts,
even though he denies their existence as the origin or end of writing. "But who is it that is addressing you?" Derrida asks and then
answers by saying that it is a function, "a pure passageway for
operations of substitution." The purity of the passageway remains
in question as long as we recognize that the choice to speak at all
and the chosen manner of articulation can only be located in the
subject that appears lost to language.

One might wish to begin by asking what triggers the machine.
This question entails some risk since it could evoke several damning
responses, not the least of which might be that the question itself
betrays a serious misunderstanding of the deconstructive endeavor.
To ask the question is certainly to establish one's position solidly
within the "metaphysics of presence"; it is to seek the origin in the
form of a "still point of the turning world." But to remain silent
about this point is to ignore everything that Derridean thought has
demonstrated so saliently. From one perspective, it is the question
that has motivated the entire body of his work. His problem is precisely that the thinking of meaning has always been the thinking of
being on the basis of "self-presence or original consciousness." His
conclusion, phrased in a variety of ways, is that "it is precisely the
operation of the beginning (*ordiri*) which can no longer be grasped"
(*MP,* 172, 160). The question is, then, addressed but not answered.
It is, instead, brilliantly and literally "explained away." There is no
"point" that can be determined as an origin; there is only an "oblit-

erated origin" (OG, 143). Yet we cannot escape the notion of origin any more than we can escape the "inside where we are." And the question cannot be silenced as long as language breaks silence. At the risk, then, of sounding like the child who asks what "came before" the big bang that brought the universe into being, I proceed.

Derrida has, of course, anticipated the question from his first writings. When one asks what pulls the trigger, one asks about (and seeks) either an absolute presence in the form of a Logos or in the form of self-presence, the "I." From a deconstructive point of view, the question is a "hendiadys," the old problem, as Barbara Johnson has said, of which comes first, the chicken or the egg.[22] Derrida's response to the hendiadys created when one asks what triggers the machine of dissemination is an instructive nonanswer that simply puts the question "out of play." The answer is typical of his responses to the problem of priority everywhere in his work, whether one is considering "supplement," "auto-affection," or that key word "differance." As in the instances of those other "non-concepts," when Derrida directs his formidable energies to "the triggering" of the machine, it is to show that there is *nothing* prior to dissemination.

Metaphysical or "classical" notions of temporality cannot refer to that which institutes the possibility of any temporal experience. The words *before* and *after, cause* and *effect* are improper; they do not apply. Yet they must be applied—by Derrida, as well as by his readers. Dissemination is "outside" of the system, which at the same time incorporates it as cause and effect. It is both cause and effect and neither cause nor effect: without origin, without end. He begins by saying that textuality is "born of repetition," that "the first time is already not from around here, no longer has a here and now." He continues, "Even in its first occurrence, the text mechanically, mortally reproduces, ever '*steadier*', and '*deader*', the process of its own triggering" (DN, 292). The triggering happens at the moment the machine is "plugged in" to a language that it repeats in its "first occurrence." Derrida metaphorizes this process of repetition as the "first moment" in various ways throughout his remarkable essay. Dissemination is already part of a sequence that has already begun and is, even "at first," a strange "mirror-effect that germinates and deforms." It is a mirror "like an echo that would somehow precede the origin it seems to answer . . . the effect be-

22. Barbara Johnson, "Rigorous Unreliability," *Critical Inquiry*, 11 (December, 1984), 281.

comes the cause" (*DN,* 323). His metaphorical chain culminates in a description of the "I" as "the distorted *r*epercussions of its language" (*DN,* 325) and as a textuality that is "already marked by duplication, echoes, mirrors" (*DN,* 329). The machine cannot be conceived as self-generating, since it can operate only as part of an already established machinery. It simply repeats and duplicates that machinery in the endless playing out of its workings. The breathtaking circularity of Derrida's exposition, the circularity of the reinscription of every inscription, conveys the impossibility of circularity itself, and we are caught, once again, in paradox, one similar to that which accompanies any statement that one understands dissemination. The argument is powerful, seductive, unerasable. However, outside of *its* borders, its coherence, one returns again to the position of the child in the face of the universe, asking what "caused" the big bang. What was first mirrored in that deforming mirror; what was echoed in the echo; what intends (itself) to be born as repetition; what germinates itself by inserting itself into the "mortal" reproduction that is life? What plugged the machine into the machinery? What motivates choice?

In a certain sense, the big bang theory is Derrida's only answer. If we consider his most seminal "non-concept," differance, we will see that the problem of priority can be dealt with only in a negative way: by closing it out of the picture. Derrida is perfectly, and repeatedly, clear about the fact that he does not intend differance to be understood as an origin. It is not, itself, the buried "single point" upon which his lever can rest. In fact, it "is" not. Differance "is not itself concealed, as if it were something, a mysterious being in the occult zone of a nonknowing" (*SP,* 134). Still, to understand this no-thing, "we will have to point out everything *that* it *is not,* and consequently, that it has neither existence nor essence. It belongs to no category of being, present or absent. And yet what is denoted as differance is not theological, not even in the most negative order of negative theology" (*SP,* 134). Derrida's careful assertion, "And yet . . . differance is not theological," is a necessary avoidance of any connection to an ontotheological position. But it also betrays an unavoidable problem: it will never quite suffice to declare that differance bears no relation to the "ineffable," as long as one can refer to it only by traveling the negative route, the *via negativa* of the "occult zone." He further asserts that, in a language controlled absolutely by the notion of Being as presence, there can be no word for this nothing, "not even the name '*differance,*' which is not a name, which is not a pure nominal unity, and continually breaks up in a chain of different substitutions" (*SP*, 159). In moments like this, it is not naïve to wonder how far such an assertion really is from Augustine's belief that God "is not recognized in the noise" of the name "Deus" but can only be evoked by "this sound." Augustine's "ineffable" also generates and "breaks up in a chain of different substitutions," which both displays and conserves its activity. In Derrida's case, differance establishes a chain in which auto-affection, supplement, and dissemination are all substitutions. They are other unnameable "no-things" which are neither presence nor absence, neither before consciousness nor after it, and it should be obvious that each term "continually breaks up" into the others. It is also evident, however, that each conserves the others, and all depend, ultimately, upon differance, the wedge that Derrida drives into the apparent unity of self-presence. This wedge brings all the other terms into play and allows their operation. It is, thus, perilously close to being itself an "origin." Although Derrida protects it powerfully against this situation, he can sustain that protection only by continuously asserting its nonbeing, by repeatedly affirming that it is beyond, or other than, the play of presence and absence it enables. It is, he writes, "the movement of play that 'produces' (and not by something that is simply an activity) these differences, these effects of difference" (*SP*, 141). It is only "relatively or provisionally privileged," and it is only "the strategic note or connection" that exposes the free play of a system which disguises its dissemination as presence (*SP*, 131).

With his rejection of the word *origin* as a proper referent for differance, Derrida encounters unavoidable difficulties, but ones he predicted from the first. One, of course, is that his defense by way of assertion is clearly a choice of the second alternative he notes in "The Ends of Man": a way to "break with a thinking of being." It is a change in "terrain," an affirmation of "an absolute break and difference," which inevitably inhabits "more strictly than ever the inside one declares one has deserted." As his discussion of negative language indicates, he can articulate differance only by way of allowing it to inhabit the notion of presence, which he "declares" it "is" not. As long as one must speak negatively, that is, must "point out everything *that* it *is not*," one must also point first to everything that "is."[23]

Other difficulties arise when Derrida does not use the language

23. Richard Rorty's essay "Deconstruction and Circumvention," *Critical Inquiry*, II (September, 1984), 1–23, has been very helpful to me in this discussion.

of negativity, and those moments are plentiful in his work. The most disturbing is, once again, temporality—the question of priority, the hendiadys, the chicken and egg problem. Derrida most often expresses differance as movement: "the movement of play," the "temporalizing detour," even "the movement that structures every dissociation" (*SP*, 145, 130). The demands of language, of any comprehensibility, in an utterance concerning movement seem extremely rigorous. We are unable to conceive of movement without also conceptualizing a point of origin, and this holds even for dissemination, Derrida's perpetual motion machine. Movement as such demands a beginning if not an end: it demands a "still point." Even the movement of "free play" must be set in motion, which is to say that it must be thought in terms of an origin and that any description of it will involve references to a system of priority, of a "before" and "after," a "no-longer" and "not-yet." Derrida, it should be remembered, has characterized differance as both spatial and temporal. It is, he writes, an "interval" that "could be called *spacing;* time's becoming-spatial or space's becoming-temporal (*temporalizing*)" (*SP*, 143). If one rejects a system of priority, however, the metaphor moves away from the temporal toward the spatial and culminates in the ancient notion of time as a completed circle with simultaneity (God) at its center. In that situation, the transcendent center was also a "spacing" and a "temporalizing," and everything returned to its "presence." If differance cannot serve as an origin (and it cannot do so without falling into the position of a "still point" which would assume transcendence as surely as "God" or the "I") then we are left with an explosive sort of "spacing" in which temporal *movement* succumbs to spatial *differentiation.* In order to think of differance as both spatial and temporal, it must be understood as that which initiates a system of priority as well as one of differences. In that case, it becomes an originary function, a "first moment." But this is exactly what Derrida must avoid in order to sustain dissemination and his other "non-concepts." He swerves brilliantly away from the idea of origin—and that swerve is crucial to the maintenance of his entire system—but he cannot do without the notion:

> [Differance] expresses the interposition of delay, the interval of a spacing and temporalizing that puts off until "later" what is presently denied . . . it has the desired advantage of referring to differing, *both* as spacing and temporalizing and as the movement that structures every dissociation . . . differance is not simply active (anymore than it is a

subjective accomplishment); it rather indicates the middle voice, it precedes and sets up the opposition between passivity and activity. With its *a, différance* more properly refers to what in classical language would be called the origin or production of differences and the differences between differences, the *play* [jeu] of differences. (*SP,* 129–30).

The need to free differance from the position of temporal priority is legislated by the system it establishes. If it is perceived as an origin, it must be seen as the point of stability wherein meaning achieves being and *becomes* a determinate entity. Hence, Derrida continues, "*Différance* is neither a *word* nor a *concept.*" It is, rather, a "strategic note or connection—relatively or provisionally privileged—which indicates the closure of presence, together with the closure of the conceptual order and denomination, a closure that is effected in the functioning of traces." As long as it is neither a concept (idea) nor a thing (object or activity), the notion of differance refers to "an order, then, that resists philosophy's founding opposition between the sensible and the intelligible" (*SP,* 130). These two oppositions stand for all the other oppositions that appear to ground "classical" thought: passivity/activity, presence/absence, self/other, inside/outside, and so on. Differance *resists* dualism, certainly, but it also *requires* it in order to *be* thought at all. It requires the "concept of concept," and despite Derrida's resistance, it can only be understood as concept. No matter how much differance shakes the classical oppositions that found thought, it can be articulated only as part of a "new" dualism: concept/nonconcept. At that moment, it *is* conceptualized. And this prerequisite is not to be overlooked: it creates an uneasiness in the coherence of Derrida's thought at least as powerful as the disturbance deconstruction generates in classical thought.

The opposition that seems most unerasable is that of "classical" temporality: the before/after opposition that cannot be surrendered, especially if time is perceived as purely sequential, as a "chain of different substitutions" or displacements, rather than as a full circle. The idea of the "trace" through which differance "is effected" certainly cannot dismiss the notion of priority and, for that matter, "erasure" itself can only be understood within the presumption of a piority that *requires* erasing. When Derrida is forced to say that differance "precedes and sets up the opposition"—a situation that as he admits, "classical language," or language as we know it, would call "the origin or production"—then he is forced to conserve the metaphysics of presence in a way that suggests that it is the necessary ground of his own speculations. Even if that "strategic note" is perceived as the musical note suggested by his use of "interval," it remains caught in the system of priority that must be eliminated to prevent differance from falling into the position of "origin." For the musical note cannot be perceived as a musical note unless it serves as a beginning or as a "middle" preceded and followed by other notes. Derrida's claim that differance is this sort of "middle" does not shake the temporal claim that comprehension exerts. To proceed by writing that the middle "precedes and sets up" complicates, but also reinforces, that claim. That which "precedes and sets up" must be prior to the play it "effects," even though it is exactly this priority that Derrida must put out of play. If we are not on the verge of mysticism here, we are at least on the verge of a kind of spatial simultaneity that Derrida's entire enterprise denies. "Simultaneity," he has said, "is the myth of a total reading or description, promoted to the status of a regulatory ideal" (*WD*, 24). Such an "ideal" can hardly be tolerated in an utterly demystified thought such as his. Yet if differance is forbidden as an origin, if it cannot be seen as generative of dissemination, of textuality, then temporality yields to simultaneity and Derrida has not escaped the "myth" of totality.

This setting up that Derrida calls differance has proven to be enormously useful in furthering our understanding of the relationship between meaning/being and language. However, the question remains as to whether the philosopher either escapes or initiates "the closure" of metaphysics by simply denying differance, the status of "origin" or of "subjective accomplishment." When he is forced to articulate it as a no-thing that "precedes and sets up," when he must assert that "differance—is no longer a concept, but the possibility of conceptuality, of the conceptual system and process in general," he is, despite his disclaimers, not entirely "outside" the ancient notions of "Prime Mover" or transcendental Being (*MP*, 26). The transcendent also *is not* life but the "possibility" of life itself. And when auto-affection, the most radical enactment of differance and trace, is seen as "life itself," differance can take on distinctly ontotheological colorings. Auto-affection is, he writes,

> a universal structure of experience. All living things are capable of auto-affection. And only a being capable of symbolizing, that is to say of auto-affecting, may let itself be affected by the other in general. This possibility—another "name" for "life"—is a general structure articulated by the history of life, and leading to complex and hierarchical

operations. Auto-affection—the as-for-itself or for-itself-subjectivity—gains in power and in its mastery of the other to the extent that its power of repetition *idealizes itself.* Here idealization is the movement by which sensory exteriority, that which affects me or serves me as a signifier, submits itself to my power of repetition, to what thenceforward appears to me as my spontaneity and escapes me less and less.   (*OG*, 165–66)

We have already seen that auto-affection, as subjectivity, cannot serve as a ground, a single point, that confirms the "I" (see Chapter 5). It is rather only the activity of self-representation, of the desire for presence that deludes itself into self-presence. But in this description it is difficult to see how that which is "a universal structure of experience," or "another 'name' for 'life'" can be seen as anything other than an origin. It is all very well to present the "machine" as an infinite regression and progression, but what is prior to "life"? And if auto-affection is not an originating point, then how does it establish "complex and *hierarchical* operations"? As Derrida has frequently argued, a hierarchical system requires a point of origin. If the subject cannot serve as a self-present point of origin, then auto-affection must "originate" elsewhere, and that "obliterated origin" is designated as differance.

Earlier in this discussion, differance is also evoked as "life," by virtue of its contrast with death:

> Differance began by broaching alienation and ends by leaving reappropriation breached. Until death. Death is the movement of differance to the extent that that movement is necessarily finite. This means that differance makes the opposition of presence and absence possible. Without the possibility of differance, the desire for presence as such would not find its breathing-space. That means by the same token that this desire carries in itself the destiny of its non-satisfaction. Differance produces what it forbids, makes possible the very thing that it makes impossible.
>
>   If differance is recognized as the obliterated origin of absence and presence, major forms of the disappearing and the appearing of the entity, it would still remain to be known if being, before its determination into absence or presence, is already implicated in the thought of differance. . . . Differance in its active movement—*what* is comprehended in the concept of differance without exhausting it—is what not only precedes metaphysics but also extends beyond the thought of being.   (*OG*, 143)

Several Derridean "themes" are captured in this dense moment: (*a*) the defending of differance against conceptuality by noting that "*what* is comprehended" as concept is not exhaustive, that is, its meaning escapes its writing and is not determinable; (*b*) the presentation of existence (the "breathing-space") as a desire for presence that cannot be satisfied; and (*c*) the refusal to name differance as a point of origin. Much, however, escapes this example of Derrida's powerful consistency. The "broaching" of alienation, that is, the "approaching" or the "piercing" of alienation, suggests that somehow alienation is "prior to" differance. This suggestion is immediately erased by the assertion that "differance makes the opposition of presence and absence possible." Yet this statement is also overturned immediately by erasing differance as a possible origin; it is, instead, an "obliterated origin." The phrase is one of many in which Derrida pushes language to the limits of its comprehensibility. He intends it to suggest an origin that "never was" but there is no escape from the meaning of "obliterated." Such total destruction, such absolute effacement must evoke a point, a being present, that "was" in order for it to have been eradicated. The phrase, then, does not suggest a nonorigin but rather an origin that has been violently destroyed. And it is this that "precedes" and "extends beyond the thought of being." That which precedes thought, which "makes the opposition of presence and absence possible" is, at least, the origin of auto-affection, of subjectivity. Are we, then, to see differance as prior to "life"? If differance is "other than," prior to, and traced in "the history of life," it implicates itself in a kind of transcendence that resembles Heidegger's "Being"—indeed, it may be another name for that "masterword." It might also serve as another name for that "I" which it apparently disintegrates entirely.

Derrida, of course, forbids this translation of his nonconcept into any kind of originating single point of presence. The problem of temporal priority never disappears, however, and when one reads Derrida's articulations of differance it becomes impossible to avoid the suspicion that it is, in some manner, a movement that transcends its effects even as it is displayed in them. It is, he says in *Positions,* the "movement" that "produces different things, that which differentiates, is the common root of all the oppositional concepts . . . is also the element of the *same* . . . is also the production, if it can still be put this way, of these differences . . . it is not simply a concept."[24] The "common root" may not be an origin but, as this oddly organic metaphor suggests, it is tainted by the

24. Jacques Derrida, *Positions,* trans. Alan Bass (Chicago, 1981), 9.

ontotheological structures it attempts to overturn. It evokes the un-decidability of Augustine's unutterable and unprovable "Logos," that transcendent which can be seen as the doppelgänger that dif-ferance both rejects and establishes in order to constitute itself as the other.

As I have said, we must be careful not to fall into the illusion of thinking that this discussion "disproves" Derrida. He is not, any-where in his work, blind to the situation that I have been describ-ing. The problem here is language itself, the nature of thought. He must use the metaphors at hand in order to express something that is, in his thinking, utterly outside of the metaphysics of presence that produces language. Thus, in order to be understood, he must fall back into that system. A language that could operate "outside" of "where we are" is unthinkable; it quite literally is not. That it does not exist does not invalidate Derrida's speculations, but it does mean that the speculations must be incorporated into a system that can and does articulate "I" as consciousness, as the intentional structure, the "point" that holds—even against all reason. Lan-guage, as the display of intention and the incarnation of meaning, has its own kind of perverse power: it can always be exposed as an "impossible dream," but the exposed dream is also shown to be an indispensable one, a dream that *enables* its own exposure as illusion. It lights up as indispensable exactly at the moment that we intend toward meaning. Hence, that intent to mean which may, indeed, require the play of differance remains the point upon which all lev-ers rest—even the lever that throws dissemination into play. If dif-ferance "broaches alienation," then alienation has been felt as differ-ence and desire, felt at the same moment that differance "happens." Alienation, as this felt longing, this explosion of otherness and loss, this "life-itself," can be understood only as a desire to mean, a de-sire that is enacted as a temporal movement and that demands a lo-cation, at least Barthes's "someone" or Ashbery's "Being cloaked with the shrill / Savage drapery of non-being."

If differance is "the root" of the tree of life, it assumes, despite Derrida's "intention" and because of his own articulations, a central position that can take on all the "grafts" that dissemination ad-mits.[25] When I say that differance "assumes" centrality, I mean that it *presumes* a point of operation and that it thus moves, if only se-

25. For Derrida's use of the term *graft*, see *DN*. Jonathan Culler offers a fine analysis of the term in *On Deconstruction*.

cretly, into the position of a "center": the position held by any radical requirement, the position of being the prerequisite force that
"triggers" dissemination, auto-affection, supplement, and all of the
other nonconcepts that are revealed through the "trace" that differance "effects." This thrust outward or, to use an older Existen-
tialist metaphor, this "glance" or "gaze" that discerns and displays
difference and desire in the form of an intent to mean can, probably
must, still be understood as that Wordsworthian "single point," a
point that throws itself into the play of differance so that it can "begin" to mean. We can no longer argue, with Wordsworth, that
meaning returns to this point, and we certainly cannot "define" it.
Yet neither can we "erase" it—even as an "obliterated origin." It
remains as an undercover agent.

   That which escapes Derrida's dismantling of subjectivity, then,
is this intent to mean which requires differance but is also required
by differance. Yet after Derrida, we do not have a "masterword" for
that point. We can no more "prove" this "common sense" intuition
of a "presumed" (and necessary) "I" than Derrida can disprove the
idea of origin without calling forth that idea as part of his proof.[26]
We can no more "prove" the existence of an intending, centered
consciousness than Derrida can erase intention from his own dismantling of that consciousness. But the fact remains that the intention to mean expresses itself in Derrida's own work as incarnated
meaning, as "content." If this were not so, he would be silenced,
unreadable, and irrelevant. As it stands, that embodied intention in-
sinuates itself into every word he writes—as it must into all writing.

   It does not, however, present itself completely, it is not fully embodied being. That is, it does not achieve the full presence of that
rock against which we can only stub our toes. Meaning, as we have
seen repeatedly, haunts a work; it is the play of presence and absence that Derrida has identified better than anyone. Language
without absence, without dissemination, would be as silent or as
incomprehensible as a language of pure dissemination, that language of utter indeterminacy. What allows language both to disseminate and to contain meaning, to represent and present, is the
single point which can be described as this intent to mean and can
be named the "I." We cannot "arrest the function of signification,"

   26. This is, in part, Rorty's point when he writes that "the dilemma can be
summed up by saying that any new sort of writing which is without *archai* and without a *telos* will also be without *hypokeimenon,* without a subject" ("Deconstruction
and Circumvention," 9).

but we cannot make such a statement without the haunting presence of an arrested meaning. As soon as we ask Derrida what he means, we are making a demand that can only be uttered from within that metaphysics of presence which allows the play of presence and absence to be stabilized in an intending "I." And the question of how "free" the "play" of language really is becomes even more mystifying when we ask ourselves what it means to say that we "understand" his answer that meaning is "undecidable," that there is "nothing outside of the text." Without a single point, without a grounded intentional consciousness, without a place of repose in which meaning can come to rest, that statement can have no content: it can be neither uttered nor understood.

To this Derrida would certainly respond that there is no "meaning" but only the traces of meaning(s) created by textuality: "there has never been anything but writing; there have never been anything but supplements, substitutive significations which could only come forth in a chain of differential references, the "real" supervening, and being added only while taking on meaning from a trace and from an invocation of the supplement, etc. And thus to infinity . . . what opens meaning and language is writing as the disappearance of natural presence" (OG, 158–59). But even this calls forth the ghost of an intending "I" projecting an intentional construct. The phrase *come forth*, with its implications of prior being, and the word *invocation*, with its theological loading of supplication or prayer, suggest the tight binding of even Derridean thought to the metaphysics of presence. But there is an even more important suggestion here if we keep in mind that this "chain" is enabled by differance. If differance is not an origin, and if the "real" is "added only while taking on meaning from a trace," then differance seems to invoke a "deeper" root than itself. What motivates the entire system of free play is the drive toward meaning, even if it can only attain it in the form of the trace. Hence, the "disappearance of natural presence" is an event that happens in conjunction with an intent to mean that appears to *allow* the eruption of differance. It would seem, then, that one possible "trigger" for the machine of language is the desire to insert one's meaning into that unstoppable sequence, that "chain of differential references." Such a desire can only be understood in terms of an intending subject—a subject perhaps permanently "hidden from the reach of words" and infinitely more inaccessible than Wordsworth could have known, but nonetheless powerful for all that. While the intending "I" may serve as only a symbol for such an elusive "subject," it seems evasive to call an intention to mean which takes the form of desire anything *else*.

Intention is at the heart of the marriage of language and meaning, and this marriage is so complex, so involuted and convoluted, so covert, that literary criticism has been forced into the ironic position of muttering that it can neither live with the marriage nor without it. The old problem of how meaning relates to intention has produced a kind of exhaustion caused by the apparent impossibility of either uncovering authorial intention or distinguishing it from reader interpretation. Yet for criticism to operate in any form, including deconstruction, it must presume that the text demonstrates intention in at least a minimal form of achieved meaning. Deconstruction, like any critical approach, posits an embodied and informing intention that motivates the surfaces of the text it explores. Without a posited meaning, an initial "understanding," it cannot begin to deconstruct the play of meaning production in that text.

Efforts to deal overtly with the problem of meaning and intention are as diverse as those of E. D. Hirsch and Stanley Fish.[27] To a certain extent, however, even criticism that refuses direct consideration of the issue by disintegrating the subject is inherently caught in the debate. When the author is erased, as in the case of Barthes, or when both author and reader are seen as illusory "effects" of textual dissemination, as in Derrida, the problem of the intending subject becomes much more complicated than the first great "rejectors" of intentionality, Wimsatt and Beardsley, could have imagined. But it does not conveniently go away. It simply goes underground to emerge with a new force at the moment we ask Barthes or Derrida what they "mean." Because writers want to be understood, they are, despite all detours and all diversions, finally dependent upon a grounded intention to mean and the possibility of incarnating that meaning in a text.

From this perspective Derrida's most significant questions may be these: "Is it by chance that the meaning of meaning (in the general sense of meaning and not in the sense of signalization) is infinite implication, the indefinite referral of signifier to signifier? And that its force is a certain pure and infinite equivocality which gives signified meaning no respite, no rest, but engages it in its own *economy*

27. See, for instance, E. D. Hirsch, *The Aims of Interpretation* (Chicago, 1976); Stanley Fish, *Is There a Text in This Class: The Authority of Interpretive Communities* (Baltimore, 1980).

so that it always signifies again and differs?" (*WD*, 25). His own answer has been that it is, indeed, pure chance, free play, that sets this economy in motion. Yet the questions could not be asked if there were only an "infinite equivocality" that denies meaning "respite" and "rest." They require a point to stabilize Derrida's own intention, to achieve the meaning that he clearly assumes such questions contain. This silent point or stability operates everywhere in Derrida's work, sometimes erupting with a startling clarity. In his discussion of Foucault's work in "Cogito and the History of Madness," he writes that there are "formidable and infinitely difficult problems that haunt Foucault's book more present in his intentions than his words" (*WD*, 42). If it were not for the fact that we read Derrida in terms of his own intention, a statement like this one would corrupt his entire project. It does, after all, blatantly contradict his own thought by asserting an intending subject that exists outside the text.

To dismiss Derrida on the grounds of inconsistency here, or anywhere else that we have encountered paradox in his work, is to be adamantly blind. For another paradox is involved in reading the Derridean text: despite the fact that it succumbs to the language of presence—even, through obversion, confirms that language—we are able to understand his intention. We can comprehend some notion of an ungrounded nonorigin, and we can speculate upon a language that operates outside the confines of the words that express it. The Derridean intention to expose the metaphysics of presence always operates within the language of presence, but it also escapes total confinement. In other words, his intention overrides the limitations we have been examining, even as it is reabsorbed by those limitations. Intention propels his thought beyond the shackles of contradiction; it allows his language to operate on "the margins" of the metaphysics that contain it. And the intending reader allows this operation to consummate in meaning. We encounter in Derrida a phenomenon that Paul de Man called "the discrepancy between meaning and assertion" (*BI*, 110), a phenomenon that plays a part in all texts. If we disintegrate the intending subject entirely, there is no way to account for either that discrepancy or the understanding that we achieve despite its activity. The "still point" of the intending "I" is eliminated by the assertions of deconstruction, but it is only by virtue of its activity that we are able to read the deconstructive text. It allows Derrida to press a language inherently contradictory to his enterprise into an achieved meaning. Intention is the invisible force that haunts us through a text that cannot contain or restrain its power.

Derrida would certainly reject my phrasing here and insist that the "Derrida" carried by his texts is no more than the "effect" of its language and especially of style. This "Derrida," he would insist, is a mere "signature," an "attending" illusion that guides my reading of a text that creates both reader and author as marks of its play. Therefore, we engage in a game of language that only pretends to meaning. He has, in fact, demonstrated the "impossibility" of "tethering to the source" even the most personalized kind of writing: the signing of one's own name ("SEC," 172–97). While he acknowledges the "everyday" happening of this "event," which is one of "singular intention," he argues that such writing "is not the means of transference of meaning, the exchange of intentions . . . the 'communication of consciousness'" ("SEC," 94). "Signature, Event, Context" is as elegantly argued as any of Derrida's writings. But it is, perhaps, his most carefully phrased and heavily qualified text. The problem of intention is inherently disruptive to his enterprise, and his attempts to hold it within the notion of "iteration" (the disseminative repeatability of writing) produce an awkwardness that is not resolved. Just as he must retain the word *writing* as a "classical" concept even though he uses it to expose the forces it has "held in abeyance," so must he silently assume that his own intended meanings have been incorporated by a text that speaks against incorporation. The silent assumption is absolutely necessary: "It is," he admits, "to give to everything at stake in the operations of deconstruction the chance and the force, the power of communication." Hence, despite the text's "assertions," his "meanings" here suggest that "the transference of meaning, the exchange of intentions" *must* "hold in abeyance" the force of "iterability" in order for that notion to achieve the "force of communication." In other words, his writing must be exactly what it "is not." The "impossible" tether must not be broken or language would reduce to noise. Once again, it seems, language demands the ground its workings demonstrate to be a pure illusion. I can neither smile at the tongue-in-cheek cleverness of Derrida's hand-scrawled signature, which appears as a sort of forgery at the end of the essay, nor appreciate the duplicitous significance of that gesture, unless I also predicate an intentional consciousness that haunts the writing—and the joke. That haunting lifts writing out of the machinery of dissemination into the meanings that bring this text into its ironic and uniquely Derridean form of play. Without a point of repose, a "singular intention," the multiple play of irony could not appear at all; language would simply slip over a flat surface of literal referentiality. Irony requires a depth that can only be promised by a "buried" point.

The game, then, is a very serious one, indeed. When one must call upon the "communication of consciousness"—the very thing that is against the rules—in order to begin to play, to "give everything at stake" any "power," then we are in the peculiar position of requiring a "ground" that does not appear to "be" a ground. When it appears that an illusion of a self-present, intending "I" is the necessary prerequisite for language to operate, even for it to dismantle itself, then "illusion" is no longer descriptive of that enabling force. Under these circumstances, the distinctions between illusion and truth, between representation and presentation, oscillate so rapidly and so violently that none of these words is quite adequate. Furthermore, Derrida's "appropriation" of the words *illusion* or *effect* becomes as much an attempt to achieve mastery over meaning as the old, erased "masterword": "I " we are left with the certainty that we cannot do without this no-thing, this "obliterated origin," this ghostly intention, and still continue the game. That which is indispensable and absolutely required by the operations of the game, that "root" which enacts differance, may be nameless, but it cannot be only illusory and still be the surge of "power" that runs the machine.

It is Derrida's attempt to retain the functions of intentionality in the absence of an intending subject and within the notion of dissemination that is so troublesome in "Signature, Event, Context." The concept is, as Derrida notes, "phenomenological in character" ("LI," 193). It is, thus, directly associated with an understanding of being as presence and, importantly, with the question Derrida addresses extensively in *Dissemination:* "Who is it that is addressing you?" If one recalls that his answer in that essay claims that "it is not an author . . . not some singular and irreplaceable existence, some subject or 'life'" but, rather, "a pure passageway," then it is difficult to comprehend a statement like "the intention animating the utterance will never be through and through present to itself and to its content" ("SEC," 92). The lack of total presence here is not the problem, the word *animating* is. It appears that by retaining intentionality Derrida reinstitutes the "singular and irreplaceable" life force that *Dissemination* disintegrates. In defending this essay against

John Searle's charge that it erases intention from writing, Derrida
insists that "I have never opposed this position [the function of in-
tention] head on, and Sec doesn't either" ("LI," 193).[28] It is true that
"Signature, Event, Context" is very careful to conserve intentionality: "The category of intention will not disappear; it will have its
place, but from that place it will no longer be able to govern the
entire scene and system of utterance" ("SEC," 192). But where is
that place? Given that the subject is, in Derrida's thinking, an "obliterated origin," it certainly cannot be located there. And if the text
is, as he insists, the "infinite equivocality of meaning," there is no
room in its disseminative process for the constraints on meaning
that "place" intention and that intention provides. Where then, do
we locate this "animating" force that "will not disappear," that
"will have its place"?

The discussions in this book have circled, from the beginning,
around the possibility that such a "place" is always felt as a ghostly,
privileged, and even "sacred" site—the site of the absent presence,
or the present absence, the site of the "haunting" that Derrida feels
in reading Foucault and that we feel in reading Derrida. Sacred sites
always carry a sense of being off limits, of being somehow "taboo,"
and often the taboo generates the system that then declares it to be
off limits. Such has been the case with language in deconstructive
thinking: the linguistic system, turned back upon its origin, literally "displaces" it, turning it into a "*dis*appearance." The "I" has
been disembodied but it has not, as Derrida agrees in "Signature,
Event, Context," been eliminated. The "power" of language depends on the fact that writing covertly announces the singularity
that dissemination seems to disintegrate. "Signature, Event, Context" clearly demonstrates the potential for language to drift away
from its origin. It reveals the ability of intention to obscure itself, to
operate ironically, to be multifaceted, to play with meaning as sheer
possibility, and still to *hold*. It does not "govern" in the form of an
achieved "singular" meaning, and it does not govern as an intending "I" that can be fully recovered or fully contained in the text.
But its governing force is not diminished for all that. It is, instead,

28. Derrida's refusal of a "head on" encounter is justified by the fact that deconstruction can never indulge in such direct opposition. From its point of view, to
do so is always/already a confirmation of the status quo. But this statement seems
evasive here, for deconstruction has undermined and corroded the possibility of intentionality precisely to the extent that it has dismantled the intending subject and
demonstrated the "infinite equivocality" of meaning.

transformed into an invisible ground. It is not a ground in the Wordsworthian sense—that is, it is not a hidden being far beyond the reach of language. Rather, it functions in Ashbery's sense as a non-being draped by language and revealed by the floating movements of that drapery.

It is this holding power, this dangerous affiliation with origin and center, that Derrida cannot admit into his system. It particularly cannot be admitted as a covert operation that might suggest a still point which exists "outside of the text." Hence, in a typical move to constrain and displace the governing power of such "classical" notions, he proceeds in "Signature, Event, Context" by noting that the intending "I" is authored by differance. Differance, "the irreducible absence of intention or attendance to the performative utterance" is, he continues, what "authorizes me . . . to posit the general graphematic structure of every 'communication'" ("SEC," 192, 193). The authorizing force, then, "the animating utterance," is an "irreducible absence," and intention is not just displaced but erased.

The coupling of differance with intentionality is entirely consistent with Derrida's thought. For if the subject "is" auto-affection, intentionality could be nothing else. But if intention is to be understood as the play of differance, then Derrida's charge that Searle has misread his essay is, at least in this context, off center. Derrida chides Searle for his careless reading by pointing to his own carefully qualified assertions concerning intention: "I must first recall that *at no time* does SEC invoke the *absence,* pure and simple, of intentionality. Nor is there any break, simple or radical, with intentionality. What the text questions is not intention or intentionality but their *telos* which orients and organizes the movement and the possibility of fulfillment, realization, and *actualization* in a plenitude that would be present to and identical with itself" ("LI," 193). It is certainly true that the essay questions the *telos* of writing but, as Derrida has been at pains to teach us, to question *telos* as "actualization in a plenitude" is also and always to question origins. Furthermore, the defensive clarity of this statement in "Limited, Inc" forgets, for the moment, the wedding of differance and intention, and it forgets their progeny: "irreducible absence." Not just in "Signature, Event, Context" does Derrida integrate intention with that "authorizing" nonconcept, but also in "Limited Inc." At the moment when he claims never to have invoked "the absence, pure and simple, of intentionality," he again defines intention as differance:

"Intention is a priori (at once) *differante:* differing and deferring in its inception" ("LI," 194). He has already written in "Signature, Event, Context" that the "first consequence" of displacing intention from its governing position is to reveal that the "iteration structuring [a text] introduces into it a dehiscence and a cleft [*brisure*] which are essential" ("SEC," 192). Since, in Derrida's thinking, it is not just the text which is "essentially" (that is, *in essence*) "cleft" but also the intending subject, then *both* subject and text suffer "this essential absence of intending the actuality of utterance, this structural unconsciousness, if you like, [which] prohibits any saturation of the context" ("SEC," 192). Unless we are to conclude that the "structural unconsciousness" is outside the play of textuality—certainly an untenable position in deconstructive thought—it can only be seen as another play of differance, which is to say as an "irreducible absence."

This is not a "pure and simple" absence, in Derrida's terms; it is an absence that cannot be realized in the "actualization of a plenitude" anymore than a presence can be. Yet it is "irreducible," and in that case intentionality "is not" in the same sense that the "I" is not. While Derrida is correct to remind Searle that he conserves intentionality in his essay, Searle is intuitively correct to question whether or not such a conservation is possible. The specific terms of Searle's argument—that intentionality plays the same role in writing as it does in speech—can be mastered by Derrida's "Limited Inc."[29] But the answer masters Searle only to the extent that we ignore the relationship between intention, differance, and the (erased) intending subject. It is difficult to reconcile Derrida's retention of a displaced intentionality with phrases such as "irreducible absence" and "essential absence," especially if one moves out of the frame of "Signature, Event, Context" and "Limited Inc" into other works such as *Dissemination.* It is even more difficult to find "the place" of the intention that Derrida wishes to (and must) retain when textuality itself disintegrates the intending subject, the "first consequence" of deconstruction. Having said in "Limited Inc" that "intention is a priori (at once) *differante,*" Derrida continues by noting once again that this situation eliminates the subject. For the "I" is the "proper name which suddenly finds itself removed. It can transform itself, at once, and change itself into a more or less

29. John R. Searle, "Reiterating the Differences: A Reply to Derrida," *Glyph,* I, 198–208.

anonymous multiplicity. This is what happens to the subject in the scene of writing" ("LI," 194). When the "I" is "removed," so is intentionality; there is no "place" within which it can be incorporated.

Nonetheless, intentionality must be embodied if language is to function, even if that singular "body" contains an "anonymous multiplicity." Only that "corporate" intention allows communication to happen. Thus Derrida must address Searle as "limited" and "incorporated" even though he chooses to treat him as an "anonymous multiplicity." The finest irony in Derrida's deeply ironic response to Searle is in the title of his essay. That title both acknowledges the limiting, incorporating force of intentionality and meaning and denies the power of that force in the ellipses that follow "a b c." Those ellipses reject closure, open up the "body" of the text, and allow its meaning to escape; it is limited *and* unlimited. The unlimited divisibility of the deconstructive "I" enables the philosopher to address a "Searle who is divided, multiplied, conjugated, shared" ("LI," 165). Ultimately, however, whether Searle is treated as the "singular" linguist or as the incorporated "Society with Limited Responsibility" which Derrida addresses, the intent to mean remains unscathed. It is incorporated in the form of a "signified meaning" that achieves enough "respite" and "rest" to stabilize Searle's text—at least long enough for Derrida to address it. Finally, he is not addressing either the linguist or the corporation but rather the phantoms of intention and meaning that have been incarnated, if only by the "shrill savage drapery of non-being."

The extent to which Derrida wishes to avoid phenomenological "nostalgia" and to deny "Heideggeran hope" for a masterword of presence is also the extent to which he must deny the operations of intentionality in language. His retention of intentionality, even as a displaced category, may reveal both nostalgia and hope in a deeply suppressed form. A rigorous implementing of deconstruction will not allow the intentional "I" to hold its coherence, and Derrida's repeated linking of intentionality and differance demonstrates the demands of his own system. Yet that system cannot operate without the very figure it must erase. The "I" may be a phantom, a radical self-haunting, but it cannot be perceived as the "irreducible absence" and still provide a "breathing space" for an intending subject. The ghost that haunts language in order to be embodied cannot be completely exorcised.

Insofar as Derrida attempts this exorcism, which must include the purification of language from the taint of the intending "I," he attempts to speak from "the other side of nostalgia." He attempts to orphan himself from the "purely maternal or paternal language" that has always grounded itself in a "master-name," in the single point of absolute self-presence which abides as a still point for the repose of meaning. His writing has undeniably been a "certain step of the dance" that has been able to skirt the edges of his "native country of thought," but that country has not quite been "lost." And it is not clear that he has completely escaped the "quest" for a proper word and that unique name which he has called "Heideggerean hope." For Derrida, too, performs a quest for the "right words," though this quest is genuinely quixotic. To expose the "dream" of presence as a mere effect of desire and differance, he "dreams" of a language that can operate without a firm ground, that can be entirely disseminative, a free play. He "dreams" of a language so "proper" to his thought that it cannot be considered conceptual, stable, or, in the most radical sense, "meaningful." He dreams a language of perfect "deincarnation," which completely rejects a "founding" word or a "contained" meaning. He needs words so "right" that they can carry the force of communication, which is to say, of intention and meaning, and still avoid the touch of presence which that force evokes.

Like Quixote's quest, Derrida's is both important and impossible: important for what it has shown concerning the inability of language to fully contain presence, impossible because a language that operates as pure dissemination and institutes the "I" as a "pure passageway," a simple conduit for the unceasing flow of meaning, would operate beyond comprehensibility. To find it would be to move beyond language altogether. Derrida has attempted to overcome this situation by naming and erasing his "non-concepts" in the same gesture; by "crossing out" the unique names that designate notions which he wants to appear outside of classical language; by attempting to disseminate those notions through multiple names so that they cannot serve as stable points of origin. Differance, however, demonstrates the impossibility of his project. It is a "classic" case of a found word becoming, irrevocably, a "founding" word. Though it is translated into "auto-affection," "supplement," "dissemination," "tracing"—all the unnameables that display existence as textuality—it is as forcefully conserved by them as it is displaced by them. It haunts them as the ground of their significance.

The words that "communicate" his thought, then, also undermine it. Yet the deconstructive edifice does not crumble any more

readily than the language of presence that is its scaffolding. For deconstruction's "dream" has revealed the interplay of presence and
absence which classical language concealed in its drive toward totality. In the act of trying to escape the "prison" of contained meaning, deconstruction has unmasked the fact that meaning as such *depends* upon a loss of presence that opens up the space of, and the
demand for, interpretation. It also has shown that presence cannot
by entirely evicted from language. Derrida, despite his passionate
search for words that might be appropriate to his thinking, has
known from the beginning that they must be "reappropriated" by
the language of presence if he wished to be coherent, and he certainly
understands the double meanings of that word. Coherence, as "un-
derstandability," demands coherence, as "the holding together
around a center" that stabilizes any structure. He has shaken that
structure, at least. For he has demonstrated that the still point that
secures language escapes the only system we have to seek it out.
"There is no name for it," Derrida says of differance. Yet we understand his statement because the "pure passageway for operations of
substitution" is not pure, because it remains haunted by "a singular
and irreplaceable intention" that flickers through the drifting drapery of the name that is "no name." That intentionality, that "I," is
exactly as Derrida has said, "moving between life and death." It is a
"phantom." But a phantom is not Derrida's "mere function." It inhabits the passageway; it institutes the ability of that passageway to
perform, even if the performance must be one of "substitutions."

   Jacques Derrida is a radically epitaphic writer: he evokes the invisible presence of meaning, of intention, of the subject because
there is no escape from those old ghosts, even in the writing that
declares them dead. He is epitaphic in the sense that all of his writing against the classical language of presence must be haunted by
that "dead" language in order to function at all. And he is a writer
of epitaphs in one more, very important, sense: for him, the self is
written into existence, it is auto-affection, an essentially epitaphic
gesture. Derrida's *L'ecriture* defers death but also announces it, carries it within its own tracing. If there is a masterword for Derrida,
that word is "death," and every major work he has written explores
the relationship between death and language. *Of Grammatology*
is exemplary. The work begins "What writing itself, in its non-
phonetic moment, betrays is life. It menaces at once the breath, the
spirit and history as the spirit's relationship with itself . . . it is the
principle of death and of difference in the becoming of being" (*OG,*

25). In the final moments of the book, Derrida is able to suggest that it is not just writing as inscription that carries death within, but language in general: "As always, death, which is neither a present to come nor a present past, shapes the interior of speech, as its trace, its reserve, its interior and exterior differance: as its supplement" (*OG*, 315). And at the "center" of *Of Grammatology*, the philosopher "names" the master-name himself: "For we have omitted the master-name of the supplementary series: death. Or rather, for death is nothing, the relationship to death, the anguished anticipation of death. All the possibilities of the supplementary series, which have the relationships of metonymic substitutions among themselves, indirectly name the danger itself, the horizon of all determined dangers, the abyss from which all menaces announce themselves" (*OG*, 183). For this thinker, existence is an ongoing writing, the "becoming of being," the play of differance—ongoing, that is, "until death. Death is the movement of *differance* to the extent that that movement is necessarily finite" (*OG*, 143). Differance, then, is Derrida's answer to Heidegger's call for "mortals" to "come into ownership of their own nature." In the nonconcept of differance, Derrida has "thought" that relationship and found that the "obliterated origin" of the self is the loss of the "I" to a language that, at the same time, constructs that self. As he writes in *Dissemination:* "The story that seems thus to be triggered off—for the first, but innumerable, time—then begins to function according to modalities in which death is affiliated with the (metaphor of the) textual machine. . . . All is lost and nothing is lost; you find yourself back without anything, yet steadier, quickened, cleansed, irrigated changed and deader" (*DN*, 292). The fact that Heidegger searches for the master-word "Being" (presence), and that Derrida announces that the master-word is "death" (nonpresence) spotlights immediately their differences. But it also establishes a certain link between the two, one that Derrida is still thinking through.[30] The connection between them lies in the shared perception that "life" is always implicated in the relationship between language and death.

This affiliation between life, language, and death is the dominant thematic concern of our best postmodern poet, John Ashbery. He explores it almost compulsively, from his earliest work to his latest. For Ashbery, as for Derrida, the achievement of full presence, of a

---

30. Derrida confirms this point throughout *Positions;* see particularly 51–55.

totality, can be known only as "my-death." Such a full presence is, literally, the "end of man." Ashbery's milieu, then, would seem to deny the possibility of lyricism altogether. For the meaning, the insight, that the lyric has traditionally offered depends upon the exposure of presence, of that still point which Wordsworth hoped to incarnate in his "spots of time," even though he knew it to be "far hidden from the reach of words." Ashbery, deprived of such hope, never attempts to "spot" time, to halt it in privileged moments of revelation. Yet he remains a lyric poet to the extent that such moments remain an overwhelming concern in his work and to the extent that we can define lyric as the formulation of a "self" by a "self" in language. Ashbery's "I" holds as a coherent point, but that "I" undergoes constant modification and is never still. It is, rather, a "turning point" (*TP*, 115), a forward-plunging "pivot" which perceives its world as a kind of "self-induced trance."[31] It can never forget that it is in constant motion, that at each moment "its new problematical existence will have already begun." It flies like a charged spark through the space of its finite time, exposing only the shape and light of its own energy as it seeks, accumulates, and loses meaning. His poetry is the tracing of the path that atom of energy takes.

Though Ashbery performs within Derrida's "new theater," then, his version of that theater differs in one crucial respect: the poet conserves the "I" as the energizing "living force" that the philosopher dissolves, and he does so by untethering it from the force of textuality as well as from the confinement of "englobed" presence. For him the theater of poetry remains the site of a performance given by an intentionality that inherently exists outside the text through which it performs. This deflection from deconstructive thought makes all the difference: it keeps the poet's work balanced just this side of a "lyric crash" that continuously threatens but never occurs. Because the "I" exists by living forward into its possibilities, it creates the "text" of its existence as an evacuated, but haunted and ongoing, "chronicle play . . . with the last act still in the dim future" (*TP*, 93). The pun in "chronicle" should not be overlooked: it demonstrates Ashbery's acceptance of time as *chronos* rather than *kairos*. As Frank Kermode has said, *kairos* suggests that time can be halted, demarcated into moments that allow the emergence of "a point in time filled with significance, charged with

31. John Ashbery, "Parergon," in *DD*, 55.

meaning derived from its relation to the end." Of this Ashbery is deprived, left only with chronocity, time as endless succession: "passing time or waiting time."[32] Episodic and sequential, the "I" is always performing, watching, and in the same moment leaving its own history behind. Rushing forward like Janus, perpetually on the threshold of an ending and a beginning, it looks both before and after. Forbidden the secure space of a stable present, it exists as desire and nostalgia, knowing that life itself is only "quickened by the onrushing spectacle" (*TP*, 94), but longing to join with the selves distributed into the acts that have been left behind. As a result

> we are like spectators swarming up onto the stage
> to be absorbed into the play, though always aware
> that this is an impossibility, and that the actors
> continue to recite their lines as if we weren't there.
> Yet in the end, we think, this may become possible;
> that is the time when audience and actor and writer
> and director all mingle joyously together as one,
> as the curtain descends a last time to separate them
> from the half-empty theatre.
>
> (*TP*, 94)

The longing for the moment when all of one's selves can "mingle joyously together as one" is not mastered by the painful awareness "that this is an impossibility" until "the end" when "the curtain descends a last time." Ashbery knows that what he longs for is not the death in oneness so clearly implied by the final curtain. "There is no point in looking to that," he continues:

> The apotheosis never attracted you, only those few
> moments in the next-to-last act where everything
> suddenly becomes momentarily clear, to sink again
> into semi-obscurity before the final blaze which
> merely confirms the truth of what had been
> succinctly stated long before.
>
> (*TP*, 94)

What he desires is not the lucid finality of death, not the end of movement and time, not the "final blaze." He desires temporal meaning itself, a "few moments . . . where everything becomes momentarily clear," a glimpse of "the truth of what had been succinctly stated long before." He wants to find meaning within the flow of time, within the movement that necessarily allows it "to

32. Kermode, *The Sense of an Ending,* 47.

sink again into semi-obscurity." Semi-obscurity is, at least, a *living* light. A dim, barely readable, momentary truth is preferable to the blaze of clarity that locks all into place, that confirms because it kills.

Ashbery's "I," then, is genuinely ambivalent. He may long for full presence, for the joyous oneness of momentary clarity, for the "few moments" in which the "I" could mingle with the meaning of its existence, but such a temporal pause seems far off. He finishes this section of *Three Poems* by saying that "there does not seem to be any indication that this moment is approaching" (*TP*, 94). Despite his desires, he understands that the loss is felicitous. At this point in the work he has already recognized that the "hope for better things to come" (*TP*, 89) has always been, at bottom, a hope for the pause in which a living union could occur. And he has discovered that "this place of joining was indeed the end" (*TP*, 90). Yet he cannot surrender his hope, choosing instead to reformulate it in a more diminished, but more livable shape:

> It has been an absorbing puzzle, but in the end
> all the pieces fit together like a ghost story
> that turns out to have a perfectly rational
> explanation. Nothing remains but to begin
> living with this discovery, that is, without the
> hope mentioned above. Even this is not so easy,
> for the reduced mode or scope must itself be
> nourished by a form of hope, or hope that doesn't
> take itself seriously.
>
> (*TP*, 90)

We must, he knows, live without the hope for the revelation of full presence that would provide unity. But, as he says, "this is not so easy" since it is hope that nourishes, that sustains the forward movement that is life itself. There are, he notes, other alternatives, "other and grimmer": that of "staying where you are and risking eventual destruction . . . or of being swept back . . . into a past drenched in nostalgia whose sweetness burns like gall" (*TP*, 91). He holds onto hope as a way of venturing life rather than risking "grimmer" deaths, knowing that, finally, all choices come to the same end.

Nonetheless it is, he goes on, "a choice we have to make," and Ashbery gambles on the reduced form of hope that "doesn't take itself seriously" but is absolutely necessary in order to nourish a life that can only be articulated "like a ghost story." "A ghost story nourished by a hope that doesn't take itself seriously" is as precise a description of Ashbery's poetry as one could wish. As one might expect, the hope he chooses, as "the other side of nostalgia" is what Derrida has identified as "the quest for the proper word and the unique name." It should not be surprising, then, that Ashbery's meditation on the privileged moment in *Three Poems* moves immediately from his resigned recognition that there is no "indication that this moment is approaching" to the statement that opens the next section: "Except that the silence continues to focus on you . . . everything around me is waiting just for me to get up and say the word, whatever that is" (*TP,* 94). Ashbery's attempt "to get up and say the word" is the subject of the next and final chapter of this study. For this postmodern poet writes the epitome of poetry as epitaph.

8

THE THING FOR WHICH THERE IS NO NAME

His case inspires interest
But little sympathy; it is smaller
Than at first appeared. Does the nettle
Make any difference as what grows
Becomes a skit? Three sides enclosed,
The fourth open to a wash of the weather,
Exits and entrances, gestures theatrically meant
To punctuate like doubled-over weeds as
The garden fills up with snow?
Ah, but this would have been another, quite other
Entertainment, not the metallic taste
In my mouth as I look away, density black as gunpowder
In the angles where the grass writing goes on,
Rose-red in unexpected places like the pressure
Of fingers on a book suddenly snapped shut.

Those tangled versions of the truth are
Combed out, the snarls ripped out
And spread around. Behind the mask
Is a still continental appreciation
Of what is fine, rarely appears and when it does is already
Dying on the breeze that brought it to the threshold
Of speech. The story worn out from telling.
All diaries are alike, clear and cold, with
The outlook for continued cold. They are placed
Horizontal, parallel to the earth,
Like the unencumbering dead. Just time to reread this
And the past slips through your fingers, wishing you were there.
                            —John Ashbery, "Man of Words"

There are no "tender fictions" available for John Ashbery. Closely affiliated with the postmodern thinking most powerfully represented by the work of Jacques Derrida, he cannot write innocently, as if words could contain meaning, as if poetry could incarnate a truth that could bring meaning unequivocally into being or reveal being as an achieved meaning. He cannot hope that his poems will stabilize a moment of understanding long enough for it to offer the sort of "epiphany" that George Herbert found annealed in his "Church Windows," or that William Wordsworth inscribed and read on the "stones" he called "spots of time." Yet just as Jacques Derrida continues to write meaningfully, to employ the "force of communication" in language that he insists is *not* communication, Ashbery continues to write poems out of the "desire to communicate / Something." This desire, however, is quite different from Wordsworth's hope to "enshrine" the "spirit of the past / For future restoration." Ashbery's "hope that does not take itself seriously" creates a poetry that depends entirely on the desire for meaning rather than on the presentation of meaning "enshrined." His poems "mean" but they can never quite "be," in MacLeish's sense of being as a "palpable" fullness. Ashbery's work performs; it acts out

> The extreme austerity of an almost empty mind
> Colliding with the lush, Rousseau-like foliage of its desire to
>   communicate
> Something between breaths, if only for the sake
> Of others and their desire to understand you and desert you
> For other centers of communication, so that understanding
> May begin, and in doing so be undone.
>   ("And *Ut Pictura Poesis* Is Her Name," *HD*, 45)

The poetry that erupts out of this "collision of an almost empty mind" with its "desire to communicate" is the poetry of pure intentionality. It is the representation of a "lush," singular, and living force which cannot be fully embodied by the words of a poem but wants to communicate "something between breaths." Poetry that conveys its meaning *between* breaths, rather than in the words it breathes, is inevitably "obscure"; it is, in fact, the performing of a semi-obscurity as the only possible mode of being for an intentionality that is always in flight.[1] "Understanding may begin" when one reads such work, but it will "in doing so be undone." It is as if Ashbery intended to deconstruct his poems in the act of writing them. For Ashbery, however, such writing is not evidence that meaning is nonexistent; rather, it evidences the interminable nature

---

1. "I'm attempting to reproduce in poetry, the actions of a mind at work or at rest," Ashbery says. "In the last few years I have been attempting to keep meaningfulness up to the pace of randomness . . . but I really think that meaningfulness can't get along without randomness and that they somehow have to be brought together." *CP*, 118–21.

of the meaning-making activity and of the drive to interpret that confirms the breathing, if obscurely "draped," presence of an "I." An understanding that could be "done" would, for him, be a "dead" understanding, for the mind must always undo itself so that it may continue to begin. This seems, at first, a strikingly deconstructive notion. His work does not, however, disintegrate the "I" in that undoing; it confirms the "I" as the generator and seeker of meaning. It is that which deploys words to show its own movement through them.

Wordsworth's attempt to preserve meaning in a privileged site, in poetry that behaves as an engraved stone, his desire to create a space which poet and reader could cohabit in a moment of understanding, depends upon his perception of the mind itself as an enclosed space. Within that space it seems possible for the mind to image itself and simultaneously to reflect upon those images. Such an act establishes an intense proximity between the thinking "I" and its self-representations, a proximity so close that the mind appears able to contain itself as a meaningful presence. For Wordsworth the mind's flight must culminate in a return to the single "point far hidden from the reach of words." It appears that he understands this movement as a "tender fiction" when it is externalized (as epitaph) and that he represses its fictional status in his poetry (as auto-affection), though we should remember that he never rested serenely in a repression that is, finally, an act of faith. He is able to sustain his hope for presence exactly insofar as he can sustain his belief that the "single point" remains a centered point, the "stone" buried at the core of his being. A persistent return to the buried point guarantees his sense of the mind as "self-haunted" and produces poetry which seems capable of enshrining meaning in words that are an object's "proper home." Wordsworth, then, feels that he can "make breathings for incommunicable powers" (*The Prelude*, III, l. 191) and that his haunted mind can throw light on its own meanings. Objects, including images of the self, can "through the turnings intricate of verse / Present themselves as objects recognized / In flashes, and with a glory not their own" (*The Prelude*, V, ll. 603–605). The contents of the mind, lit by the mind, can be revealed by words, and in the process they can reveal the presence of the poet as the bestower of "glory not their own." In this situation understanding does not come "undone."

However, Ashbery's vision of consciousness as "an extreme austerity," containing only the "lush" desire with which it collides, is a vision of an unsituated consciousness, "almost" empty of meaning as content. It is constantly in motion and exists as sheer longing.[2] It wants to be "filled" but is "full" only of the emptiness that is the living movement of desire. As he writes in "On the Towpath," "If the thirst would subside just for awhile / It would be a little bit, enough" (*HD*, 22). But the desire for an end to desire is not "enough" since, as he continues, "the ground is tentative" and "the sun fades like the spreading / Of a peacock's tail, as though twilight / Might be read as a warning to those desperate for easy solutions" (*HD*, 23). Ashbery resigns himself to the "between" state of semi-obscurity, instead of seeking Wordsworth's "glory." The spreading of a peacock's tail in this poem is analogous to the longing he describes in *Three Poems* for "those few moments in the next to the last act where everything becomes momentarily clear, to sink again into semi-obscurity" (94). It is the most one can hope for as a living moment of clarity, and one must accept its instantaneous "fading" into the "twilight" of understanding. A correct reading of the "semi-obscurity" of twilight confirms the fact that to remain alive is to experience the dispersal of clarity, of sunlight, even as one perceives it. The "warning" that "might be read" in twilight is that the sun "fades" within the momentary brightness of its "peacock's tail" and that the "solution" suggested by the glory of the sunset is always erased by the "scalp of night," a darkness completely detached from "the vacuous chatter / That went on, off and on, all day" ("On the Towpath," *HD*, 23). Nothing is permanent; like "chatter," everything is "off and on," in a state of endless movement and change much like the day itself. If there are no "easy solutions," it is because the mind itself is the movement of a question, not the stillness of an answer. It moves, unremittingly, out of the very moments it wants to retain. It moves even out of its own desire to stay in place, out of its own wish

> That these and other things could stay on
> Longer, though not forever of course;
> That other commensals might replace them
> And leave in their turn. No,
>
> We aren't meaning that any more.
> The question has been asked
> As though an immense natural bridge had been
> Strung across the landscape to any point you wanted.

2. Harold Bloom disagrees with this point. See "John Ashbery: The Charity of the Hard Moments," in *Contemporary Poetry in America,* ed. Robert Boyers (New York, 1974), 110–39.

The ellipse is as aimless as that,
Stretching invisibly into the future so as to reappear
In our present. Its flexing is its account,
Return to the point of no return.
("On the Towpath," *HD, 23*)

Ashbery's "I" can create a bridge to the object of its desire, "to any point you wanted," but it cannot possess that object. It can bridge the gap by "wanting," but the bridge is an "aimless" arc, an "ellipse" into a future that cannot bring the desired landscape into presence. Nor can it, in a Wordsworthian way, bring the self into presence by sending it on a detour through the landscape to find images that can bring it "home." The bridge of desire, "the insistent now," Ashbery writes, "always presents itself as the turning point, the bridge leading from prudence to 'a timorous capacity,' in Wordsworth's apt phrase, but the bridge is a Bridge of Sighs the next moment, leading back into the tired regions from whence it sprang" (*TP,* 115–16). The bridge reveals only its own invisible "stretching," a forward movement that is the only present one can know. The movement that bridges is also the movement that "tows" the "I" forward; the Bridge of Sighs is a sighing for the unattainable. Neither does the "towpath" lead back to an "original" self; it is that on which the self travels, knowing that only its movement, "its flexing," can "return to the point of no return." The return of desire to the point of no return is a "flexing," not a "reflexing," precisely because desire never relaxes, and since the "point" from which it projects is always moving ahead into the ellipse created by that flexing, it can never be the "same" point. It leads back into "tired regions," regions exhausted by the exit of an "I" which has already moved ahead of itself. Although it is modified by its own movement, the "I" never dissolves. It "holds" as the projection and return of desire, even if that return can never genuinely "arrive" where it began. "The voyage always ends in a new key" because we cannot return "to our own minds, a place that is not in any place, nowhere" (*TP,* 116, 67).

Consequently, though one may wish to hold meaning *in* the self with all the clarity and beauty of a "peacock's tail," or even to hold it just long enough to replace it with "other commensals," such a momentary fullness is denied by the nature of consciousness itself. "Commensals"—living things that inhabit others without harm to themselves or their hosts—cannot find a solid ground in a "place that is not any place," a "point of no return." Even a momentary

immobility, though much desired, is denied: "No, we aren't meaning that any more." We "mean" only the question (the quest) that
we are, a question/quest to which there is no answer except that
"its flexing is its account."

While Wordsworth, then, feels it is possible to speak "breathings
for incommunicable powers," Ashbery, speaking from a "point of
no return," must resort to locating meaning in the empty spaces
"between breaths." For the self, as desire, as "thirst," as a "question," cannot find its proper home in words without risking its
own death; it can only formulate itself between words that display
its quest, words that *seek* home: "That is the tune but there are no
words. / The words are only speculation. . . . They seek and cannot find the meaning of the music" (*SM,* 69). Ashbery's word
speculation, means, then, more than "mirroring"; it also implies
"questioning," and importantly, "gambling," a reckless investment
in words that cannot, must not, contain the "I," but must trace its
quest for meaning clearly enough to expose its nature, if only as a
"non-being." It is an investment in "semi-obscurity," in language
as a "twilight" medium which will "neither define / Nor erase"
such an entity but will allow it to be "seen by torchlight" in the
"savage drapery of non-being."

The endeavor to expose the "question of your being" as pure activity, as the process of "haunting" that cannot even be stabilized
into a "self-haunting," is risky indeed. When the images of the
self are consciously understood as never one's "own," because
those images can never return home, then the self is inevitably articulated as an exile from its "own" words. Wordsworth's "self-
haunted" mind, enclosing phantom-images that seem to generate
its self-presence, is exiled by virtue of that enclosure from nature.
Ashbery's "open mind," with "Three sides enclosed / The fourth
open to a wash of the weather, / Exits and entrances" ("A Man of
Words"), is obviously connected to the *world* by the bridge of its
desire and its intentional questioning. But, caught up in the endless
play of "exits and entrances," it is perpetually exiled from its own
representations, from the language it produces. As Ashbery writes in
"A Man of Words," "just time to reread this / And the past slips
through your fingers, wishing you were / There" (*SM,* 8).

Poetry that is only "the tune" seeking "the meaning of the music" is, undeniably, difficult for most of us to read.[3] The poet writ-

---

3. Ashbery's "difficulty" is notorious, though accusations of obscurity have less-
ened thanks to the efforts of critics such as Bloom and David Kalstone, who have
done much to teach us how to read the poet.

ing such work is also in a difficult position. A poet who works toward creating a "semi-obscurity" precisely because it seems to be the "right" sort of language in which to address and enact the question of "your being here," is denied "the easy solutions," the "commensals," revelatory of content. The difficulty for both reader and writer in such a context resides in the refusal of the poems to "position" either of them. The poems forefront the *movement* of consciousness through language, rather than the contents of consciousness that the words seem to represent. The words of Ashbery's poems behave like the bridge in "On the Towpath"; their "flexing" is their "account" of the poem. In Ashbery's work "flexing" is set against "reflection," making it extremely difficult for either reader or writer (and Ashbery frequently treats them as the same entity) to grasp the poem as content. The reader's problem is not that the poetry is impenetrable but that it remains virtually "open" at all points. Consequently, it refuses the closure of paraphrase that seems to expose understanding. If one keeps steadily in mind the poet's insistence that poetry is "performance," a "recital" in which conjugators transform "bleakness into something intimate and noble" (*TP*, 118), then one sees that paraphrase and the traditional sort of content-seeking analysis that criticism usually employs are not just inadequate for his work but are genuinely inappropriate. We must learn a new way of reading in the face of Ashbery's poems, a way that is a "flexing" *with*, rather than a reflection *on*, the words. We need, as the poet has said, to "learn to read in the dark" ("Litany," *AWK*, 81). We need to read by moving through the interpretive *spaces* opened up by the poems. The "torchlight" that Ashbery provides for his readers is his own conviction that poetry is best conceived as "something to be *acted out* and absorbed" (*TP*, 118). We cannot read Ashbery as only "listeners," absorbers of words uttered by "a man speaking to men," to borrow Wordsworth's phrase. Such an understanding of writing and reading depends (as much as Wordsworth's poems do) upon faith in the still point of return. But if "the past slips through your fingers" even as you are writing and reading, such stability cannot be found.

"A Man of Words" in *Self-Portrait in a Convex Mirror* is an exemplary lesson in "conjugation" for both reader and writer. The poem begins with an apparently simple statement, which suggests that an explanation, perhaps even some "autobiographical" development is about to follow: "His case inspires interest / But little sympathy, it is smaller / Than at first appeared." However, instead of a clarification of the nature of "his case," one encounters immediately two questions which are neither rhetorical, and thereby explanatory, nor answered:

> Does the nettle
> Make any difference as what grows
> Becomes a skit? Three sides enclosed,
> The fourth open to a wash of the weather,
> Exits and entrances, gestures theatrically meant
> To punctuate like doubled-over weeds as
> The garden fills up with snow?
>
> (*SM*, 8)

The leap from assertion into question and the sliding of one question into another remain confusing as long as one stays outside the poem as a listener waiting to absorb a content. If one yields to the sliding movement of the poem, however, and actually *asks* the questions, it becomes clear that they are examples of the kind of "interest" inspired by "his case," if not immediate explanations of the *nature* of that case. The first question interrogates the relationship between a poem (a "skit") and its source (the "nettle," a word that should be understood as both "provocation" and "prickly seed"), but what the poet means by "difference" is left suspended. The second question, though, begins to unravel "difference" by acting it out in the process of inquiring into the nature of the "skit." As the writer explores the possibility that the skit is not enclosed but "open to the wash of the weather," the "nettle" grows into the image of the "doubled-over weeds," and the place of performance becomes an "open-air" theater, a theater/garden.

In the process of questioning the connection between origin and production, then, the poet begins to expose them as different but interdependent. For the weeds produced by the nettle are the future source of the nettle itself. But this is not an entirely "natural" garden, it is a theater/garden where the weeds perform; they are "gestures theatrically meant to punctuate." Just as punctuation is an act that divides, interrupts, marks, and emphasizes the flow of language in order to establish meaning, the weeds are performative gestures that discern readable meaning in the accumulating snow. The question, then, appears to ask if the case of "a man of words" is such that his intent can seed and provoke "gestures" that mark and clarify meaning: are the gestures like the doubled-over weeds that uncover meaning in a falling snow whose weight they cannot bear but whose cold they will, ultimately, survive? In the act of *speculating* on "his case," the writer sees a rich, life-giving possibility. Questioning suggests that the mind, as well as the poem, is a theater/garden, a place for performance open to change, "the wash of weather," and that, when consciousness is "nettled," those provocations grow into gestures which mark significance on the influx of unpunctuated meaning that fills the mind like "snow."[4] If this is the case, then words, like weeds, may double over under the weight of "snow," may even be temporarily buried by that influx, but they will survive to produce the nettle which will, once again, perform its punctuation. And if this is the "case," the man of words remains alive in the performance of those words whose purpose is only to discriminate bits of meaning on the surface of a mind constantly filling up. The act of speculating, then, offers life to the poet, if not full mastery of the falling snow.

The poet's "case" proves to be more difficult, however, for the interrogation has suppressed a serious threat: one cannot continue endlessly to perform questions. At some point an answer begins to insinuate itself. And in Ashbery's work, answers are most often, as in "On the Towpath," no. At the moment the poet stops questioning the performance, the moment when "I look away," he discovers something more "natural" than theater but also more deadly. This move away from the performance of questioning into an assertion, an "answer," transforms the "gestures theatrically meant," the "doubled-over weeds," into "grass writing." The assertion evaporates the performance into an act of "reflection." No longer questioning and watching, the poet glances into the "density black as gunpowder." The shift in perspective produces fear, a "metallic taste in my mouth," and death, the vision of a "book suddenly snapped shut." When performance becomes "writing"—especially the ubiquitous and natural writing of "grass"—then a "man of words" becomes only marks in a book that can always be "snapped shut." Certainly the "grass writing" is a reference to Whitman's *Leaves of Grass*, the autobiographical inscription of that poet's own living performance. But Whitman's leaves are also, always, the "grass" that "covers all," the "beautiful uncut hair of graves."[5] In such records of living, "grass writing" appears as an answer to

4. Ashbery frequently metaphorizes *meaning* as "snow"—an image that suggests its infinite multiplicity, the idea that is "falls" all around us, and also suggests that it is transitory, steadily building up and melting away. For other examples see "Litany" (*AWK*, 116) and "The Skaters," in *RM*, 35.

5. Walt Whitman, "Song of Myself," in *Leaves of Grass*, ed. Harold Blodgett and Sculley Bradley (New York, 1968), 34.

the questions of meaning, as that in which "tangled versions of the truth," the truth of "exits and entrances, gestures theatrically meant," may be "combed out, the snarls ripped out / And spread around." But as a result one loses that "quite other / Entertainment," surrenders its liveliness to the "density black" of a "book suddenly snapped shut."

There is something inevitable about this loss; Ashbery's resigned sigh, "Ah, but this would have been another, quite other / Entertainment," suggests that the living performance of interrogation cannot be permanently sustained when one is a "man of words": "the story" is inevitably "worn out from telling." As one tells *about* it, the performance that remained alive as long as it was "open to a wash of the weather" is frozen into a "mask," closed into the form of a "diary" and

> All diaries are alike, clear, and cold, with
> The outlook for continued cold. They are placed
> Horizontal, parallel to the earth,
> Like the unencumbering dead.
>
> (*SM*, 8)

The diaries are a form of weather locked into place, permanently "clear" but also "cold." They are "placed" like coffins, "like the unencumbering dead." Clarity, as so often in Ashbery's thought, kills here, quite unlike the drift of snow which doubles the weeds but does not place them "parallel to the earth."

While Ashbery seems resigned to the movement of words from the living semi-obscurity of "snow" to the dead "clear and cold"—that is, from questioning to clarity—he is not entirely hopeless:

> Behind the mask
> Is a still continental appreciation
> Of what is fine, rarely appears and when it does is already
> Dying on the breeze that brought it to the threshold
> Of speech.
>
> (*SM*, 8)

If one remembers that in *Three Poems* the fact that a performance ends does not completely empty the theater, that "the idea of the spectacle as something to be acted out and absorbed still hung in the air" (*TP*, 118), then the importance of this ghostly "continental appreciation" emerges. The poem itself may become "grass writing," a "diary" that covers all, but the questioning intentionality, the "appreciation" of what "rarely appears," survives that death. It is because words cannot fully and permanently grasp that which is "already / Dying on the breeze that brought it to the threshold / Of speech," that the diary becomes, again, performance. "For we are rescued by what we cannot imagine," Ashbery writes in *Three Poems,* although "it is what finally takes us up and shuts our story" (104). We are saved by the passage of time that prevents the locking into place of a fully achieved imagination, by the very process of change—even if it, too, ultimately kills. Both poet and reader change in the time it takes to produce and perform this poem, and they are changed by virtue of their performance. Its inability to fully contain either the reader/writer or its own meanings keeps its "fourth side open to a wash of weather." As soon as "meaning is brought down to be with us . . . we have passed through" (*TP,* 34). Thus, the attempt to discover "what is fine and rarely appears" must be constantly repeated. Since every near appearance dissolves in the words that expose it, the words "nettle" consciousness into a rereading, into the sort of life-giving "recital" that Ashbery describes in *Three Poems.* Each repetition of the poem's process contributes to the passage of time and to the change in the reader/writer in such a way that no matter how many times one is "nettled" by the piece, each recital will be slightly "different," each reading will pass through the lively activity of interrogation and the dark angles of clarity that are "clear and cold," only to escape and begin again. "Just time to reread this / And the past slips through your fingers wishing you were there," the poet ends. While there is no denying the elegiac tone, the sense of loss, in these last lines, it is that loss of the past that prevents the entombment of the writer, that bestows the "time to reread this" and creates the necessity that one do so.

Though Ashbery seems, then, to have lost the "entertainment" that is open to "exits and entrances," his final line confirms that the poem as a whole is precisely that. The poem's enactment of "his case" shows that the "nettle," while it is not the same as the skit, makes a "difference" in that skit. Since it continues to exist "behind" the "mask" the skit becomes, it escapes the enclosure of the "diary" it creates. That which is "fine and rarely appears" claims its difference from its own writing, and because it is different, it defers death, the "death" of appearing fully, "clear and cold." The "case" of the reader, the other "nettle" required to activate the performance, also produces "difference" in words that seem to remain diary-like, unerasably the same. The reader, like the writer, suffers change, word by word, until at the end of the poem one feels the pressure of time (experienced as the pressure of interpretation) and succumbs gladly to the implied advice in the rush of words that suggest there is "just time to reread this." Yet no matter how many times the poem is reread, the intending "I" will create a difference in the performance and differentiate itself from it. For each word, rather than presenting the presence "behind" the mask, marks a moment when it, like the past, "slips through your fingers" and "what is fine" appears as "already / Dying on the breeze that brought it to the threshold / Of speech."

"A Man of Words," then, enacts the predicament of both poet and reader, and it does so as much through its temporal movement as through its contents, which are intended to facilitate that activity. It enacts the process of "speculation" in the double sense that Ashbery always intends when he uses that word. It "inspires interest" as a questioning which is also a watching, and that speculation generates a mirroring of both activities. Such mirroring, as "reflection," becomes the death-like "diary." For in the moment of reflecting, one "looks away" from poetry as performance and toward it as "writing." Yet both reader and writer escape the "diary" because Ashbery's work provokes a constant seeking after a fullness of meaning that is barely "brought to the threshold." Such meaning is exiled from the diary by virtue of the fact that it cannot be presented, that even its rare appearances are phantoms "already /Dying on the breeze" that brings it forth. The desire for meaning is the "nettle," the provocation and the seed, which is instantly transformed by the performance into "skit" and "weed." Its story may be only a mask, and it may be "worn out from the telling," but, as Ashbery writes in *Three Poems,* "this possibility of fulfillment creates the appetite for itself" (25), and that appetite for presence moves the poet and his readers out of the "clear and cold" weather into the snowy garden/theater of "recital." The poem becomes, again and again, a doubled-over weed, a "punctuation" in the process of meaning making that marks meaning but cannot stop its continual fall. The "nettle" makes a difference, then, because it is, itself, always different, whether it abides in the reader or the writer. And that difference matters, since it is difference itself that defers the death that threatens the "I" in its own "writing." In Ashbery's thought writing is always in danger of becoming a "diary"—that which seems to inscribe the "everyday glamor of a 'personal life'" but is really only the sign of life's mortality, of its actual vanishing point (*TP,* 23). It is always in danger of becoming "a permanent medium in which we are lost since becoming robs it of its potential" (8).

His self-conscious attempt to keep writing in a state of potential is one of the things that makes Ashbery's work seem so difficult, and it keeps his own position as a "man of words" precariously balanced. As David Kalstone has pointed out, this poet's work is certainly not autobiographical in any conventional or confessional sense of the word. Kalstone suggests, rather, that it is autobiography in the sense Wallace Stevens intended when he wrote that "it is often said of a man that his work is autobiographical in spite of every subterfuge. It cannot be otherwise . . . even though it may be totally without reference to himself."[6] Kalstone is extremely perceptive here, as he is throughout his extraordinary essay on "Self-Portrait in a Convex Mirror." Ashbery, however, presses Kalstone's (and Stevens's) sense of autobiography to even further extremes: the poetry is intended not just as a record of the mind's activity but as an extension of the mind's living, as a "writing-into-existence" of the mind that acts. "I'm attempting to reproduce in poetry, the actions of a mind at work or rest," Ashbery has said.[7] The word *reproduce* is a long way from a diary-like notation. The distance becomes clearer as the poet expands his statement by discussing the relationship of music to his work: "the importance of music to me is that it takes time . . . actually creates time as it goes along, or at any rate organizes it in a way that we can see or hear and it's something growing, which is another aspect of my poetry, I think; it's moving, growing, developing, I hope; that's what I want it to do anyway and these things take place in the framework of time" (*CP*, 120). This explains his proclivity for long poems where, he continues, "one is given much broader scope to work with and, as I said before, the time that it takes to write and the changes in one's mood and one's ideas enrich the texture of the poem considerably." The actual process of writing is "a continuing experience, an experience that continues to provide new reflections" (*CP*, 127). This revealing discussion of Ashbery's work culminates in his important final statement, which is about *Three Poems:*

> Somebody is being born; in other words at the end a person is somehow given an embodiment out of those proliferating reflections that are occurring in a generalized mind which eventually run together into the

6. David Kalstone, "John Ashbery: Self-Portrait in a Convex Mirror," in *Five Temperaments* (New York, 1977), 171. Kalstone's essay offers an excellent "reading lesson," a lesson in how to approach Ashbery's work. His understanding of Ashbery's work as *process* rather than as product, his sensitivity to the motivations and meanings of *Self-Portrait,* and his excellent discussion of the autobiographical elements of poetry in general have enriched my own responses to this poet.

7. See note 1.

image of a specific person, "he" or "me," who was not there when the
poem began. In "The System," I guess you might say that the person
who has been born as "he" has taken over in the first person again and is
continuing the debate. (*CP*, 131)

"Somebody is being born . . . and is continuing the debate"—Ashbery's need to keep writing in a state of active potential could not be
clearer. And it is also evident that he sees it as a self-creation that
occurs through the operations of language in time; the self created
instantly becomes a "he" through the proleptic force of the "I." In
Ashbery's "case," then, the work is autobiographical in a much
more radical sense than Stevens suggests; it creates the "act of the
mind" even as it records it. For in "The System" the "I" rarely appears, and when it does it quickly becomes another "he" left behind
by the "I," who returns in the first person only in "The Recital,"
which ends the whole work. It is an "autobiography" that inherently rejects any notation of a "personal life" and instead inscribes
the "extreme austerity of an almost empty mind." The embodiment of words reveals the mind's quest for a fulfillment that it cannot afford to find. Being alive is writing in a way that "actually creates time"; it is "continuing the debate," avoiding, even at the cost
of clarity, the "locking into place" that is "death-itself."

Ashbery's acceptance of this radical temporality and constant
change is, however, only one part of his story. For it "provides
some bad moments," he says, "all links severed with the worldly
matrix from which it sprang, the soul feels that it is propelling itself
forward at an ever-increasing speed . . . in the end the soul cannot recognize itself and is as one lost, though it imagines it has
found eternal rest" (*TP*, 70–71). The lost self is one of Ashbery's
deepest concerns, and his desire for self-discovery haunts, perhaps
even motivates, all of his work. It is the ultimate "nettle." We are,
he believes, caught in a "colossal trick," which has "filled up the
whole universe" and is "roiling the clear waters of reflective intellect, getting it into all kinds of messes that could have been avoided
if only, as Pascal says, we had the sense to stay in our room" (*TP*,
56–57). The "trick" is that the "I" is constantly drawn outside of
itself, out of its "room," by a desire that only seems to be a longing
for an "other," for a "point" on the landscape. It is really a desire *in*
the self *for* the self. The trick is productive, it has "filled up the
whole universe," but it sends consciousness on a fool's journey: the
"individual will . . . sallies forth full of ardor and *hubris,* bent on
self-discovery in the guise of an attractive partner" (*TP*, 57). The

self who "sallies forth" in desire looks in the wrong direction, has its "eyes averted from the truth," but there is no alternative since its "truth" is only the emptiness of its own desire for meaning. The misdirected journey creates a situation in which one cannot find "the reflection of one's own face" because "true reflective thinking has been annihilated." The denial of self-reflection is, however, the creation of life-itself, the "universal task" (*TP,* 57–58). Performing this life-creating task cannot alleviate the desire that lives by virtue of its performance: the end of desire is the end of life.

One remains, then, "bent on self-discovery" while traveling all the detours set up by the "colossal trick" of having to look outward rather than inward, forward rather than backward. "Propelling itself forward" is the only option of the living "I":

> if backward looks were possible, not nostalgia
> but a series of carefully selected views, hieratic
> as icons, the difficulty would be eased and self
> could merge with selflessness, in a true apprecia-
> tion of the tremendous volumes of eternity. But this
> is impossible . . . it can only result in destruction
> and even death.

> (*TP,* 71)

Truly a form of differance, Ashbery's consciousness differs from its own past, longs for a full presence that a "merging" with that past would offer, and defers "merging" as an avoidance of "destruction and even death." Like Derrida, Ashbery understands this desire for presence as "nostalgia" and yet, even though he rejects nostalgia, he cannot prevent the longing for some sort of self-representation that might provide self-presence. The lost soul cries out for recognition, "cannot recognize itself" in its representations, and continues to seek some form of embodiment that does not kill. In this moment, the poet suggests that such a form would be an "icon," a sacred representation that attains its sanctity by virtue of its ability to "embody" a living presence that is elsewhere. An icon might mediate between the past self and its lost "god." To establish such a figure, however, the poet would have to be able to discern which moment of his past contains a significance so primary that it can institute itself as an "iconic" moment. Such a "hieratic" view is impossible for a poet whose past seems to be distributed as equally significant (or insignificant) particles, as fragments. Without "backward looks" one cannot identify the particular fragment of one's self that would bestow full being. One is left only with "nostalgia," which always marks the loss of the past, not its restoration. It is not surprising that "the other side of nostalgia" evokes in Ashbery the gesture that Derrida attributes to Heidegger, a seeking for the "right words." Even this poet who characterizes himself as a "disabused intellect" (*TP*, 112), who knows that self-presence is death, remains "bent on self-discovery" and thereby participates in his own version of "Heideggerean hope."

> *You know now the sorrow of continually doing*
> *something that you cannot name, or producing*
> *automatically, as an apple tree produces*
> *apples, this thing there is no name for.*
>
> —John Ashbery, *Three Poems*

Ashbery's "hope that doesn't take itself seriously" is, in spite of his typically casual phrasing, complicated and powerful. In that hope lies every possibility for exploring the great question that initiates all others, the question that "revolves around you, your being here" (*TP*, 151). The self, exploring its own being, can hope for the self-discovery on which it is "bent" only through the otherness of words. Words are the "attractive others" which can bridge the gap between the poet and those equally attractive "points," the "landscape" he "wants" and to which he wants to "communicate / Something between breaths." The words and the other "points" are all implicated in the poet's endlessly detoured drive toward self-presence, a drive that must produce poetry in which "flexing is its account," where words operate in such a way that they avoid the tomb-like freezing, the immobility, of a "diary." For crucial to the project of self-discovery is "the opportunity of definitively clearing your name" (*TP*, 51). Yet that "clearing," that exposure of the "I," cannot be carved into a clarity that suggests any finality, an end to "moving, growing, developing." The clearing must not occur as "mummified writing" ("Litany," *AWK*, 8, 23, 68). The discovery of a cleared name, while much desired, offers its own sort of dangers, though the seeking of that name provides the basis of his poetry. Ashbery considers the problem explicitly in "Wet Casements," a poem "about" seeking the self through the other. "The conception is interesting," he says,

> to see as though reflected
> In streaming windowpanes, the look of others through

> Their self-analytical attitudes overlaid by your
> Ghostly transparent face.
>
> (*HD,* 28)

"The look of others," projected through an openness that is vulnerable to the changes of the weather—projected, that is, through "wet casements"—is always "the others'" attempt at self-discovery, their own "self-analytical attitudes." Thus, one's own face, reflected through their eyes, is reduced to a "ghostly transparent face," a face through which that look may *pass* as it attempts to return to its "point of no return." Such a process inevitably makes the "I" into a "you" and leaves both aspects of the self "drifting," "like a bottle-imp toward a surface which can never be approached, / Never pierced through into the timeless energy of a present" (*HD,* 28). The process will have "mentioned your name" as it was happening, the poet continues, but the passing reference is immediately lost as the name, only "overheard," is "carried away like an "epistemological snapshot" in a stranger's "wallet." When one realizes that the lost name is only a "snapshot" of the reflective process, not even of the poet's face, the extent of the loss is so complete that it is obvious that the name is utterly beyond retrieval. In the midst of this recognition, the poet discovers a passion much more intense than his initial "interest." Drifting as only a ghostly face and an "overheard" but lost name, he wants to find the name in order to "complete" himself:

> I want that information very much today,
> Can't have it, and this makes me angry
> I shall use my anger to build a bridge like that
> Of Avignon, on which people may dance for the feeling
> Of dancing on a bridge. I shall at last see my complete face
> Reflected not in the water but in the worn stone floor
>   of my bridge
>
> (*HD,* 28)

The important point here is that the hunger for one's own name is what generates the bridge of poetry. It is a hunger for the self which cannot be satisfied by the eyes of others who only abscond with the name in their own "bent toward self-discovery," and it is a hunger, finally, that cannot be satisfied in life. "This thing there is no name for," both the "I" and the poetry it produces, can achieve presence only "at last," and even then it does not find its name or its face but only its image: "my complete face / Reflected." And as al-

ways in Ashbery that "complete" reflection will not be found in the
moving waters that suggest life and refer to the "wet casements,"
but in the "death" of the completed "stone floor." "At last"—when
the bridge of words between the self and others is no longer "flexing" but finished—"I shall keep to myself," the poet writes with his
usual gentle irony, "I shall not repeat others' words about me." His
irony resides in the fact that such a future "at last" is a projected end
to the "interesting" process, which is literally a process of "conception," as he has said in his opening line. It is the only sort of "birth"
that the "I" can know: self-conception through a projection into
"the look of others." When one keeps to oneself, ends the repetition of desire, no longer repeats "others' comments," life, as well as
the poetic bridge, is finished. At that point words become "a permanent medium in which we are lost."

Ashbery, then, hopes for a self-presence in language that he
knows he cannot have. He wants a name "definitively" cleared, one
that can define the meaning of his being without resulting in "destruction or even death." As he suggests in "Wet Casements," if
one found such a name, one would have "pierced through into the
timeless energy of a present," a privileged moment of such power
that it would allow the "merging" of one's self into a coherence that
would have access to the "tremendous volumes of eternity." Ashbery speculates on the possibilities of such a moment repeatedly in
his work, nearly always in connection with death and the problem
of finding words adequate "to tell about it," words that will not in
the process of bringing it to the "threshold of speech" suggest that
it is "dying on the breeze." In *Three Poems* he articulates the privileged moment as "this impassive but real moment of understanding
which may be the only one we shall ever know" (76). It would, he
says, require "words that were not words but sounds out of time,
taken out of any eternal context in which their content would be
recognizable" (76).[8] Finding such words seems an impossibility,
for, like the Eliot of "Burnt Norton" to whom he refers so often
in this work, Ashbery understands that language operates only
in time.[9] The coherence of the privileged moment is, however,
wounded in an even more deadly way than by the cut that language

8. This moment in *Three Poems* serves as a kind of gloss on the closing lines of
"Self-Portrait in a Convex Mirror," where Ashbery writes of "cold pockets / Of
remembrance, whispers out of time" (*SM*, 83).

9. Eliot, *Four Quartets*: "Words move, music moves / Only in time; but that
which is only living / Can only die. Words, after speech, reach / Into the silence"
(180).

inflicts. Ashbery's description of its process in the more recent poem, "Litany" is instructive:

> There comes a time when the moment
> Is full of, knows only itself.
> Like a moment when a tree
> Is seen to tower above everything else,
> To know itself, and to know everything else
> As well, but only in terms of itself
> Without knowing or having a clear concept
> Of itself. This is a moment
> Of fast growing, of compounding myths
> As fast as they can be thrown off,
> Trampled under, forgotten. The moment
> Not made of itself or any other
> Substance we know of, reflecting
> Only itself. Then there are two moments
> How can I explain?
> It was as though this thing—
> More creature than person—
> Lumbered at me out of the storm,
> Brandishing a half-demolished beach umbrella,
> So that there might be merely this thing
> And me to tell about it.
> It was awful. And I too have no rest
> From the storm that is always something
> To worry about. Really.
>
> (*AWK*, 18–19)

The density of this passage is typical of Ashbery, but I will not unravel all of its implications. Here my concern is with the process, the manner in which the moment appears. It begins in perfect coherence; it is "full of, knows only itself." It appears by analogy, as a tree that "towers" (an indication of impending death and emptiness that will be examined in more detail shortly), and in this act of appearing it suddenly loses both its fullness and its comprehensive "knowing." Knowing now only "in terms of itself," it loses itself as its own content and is "*without* knowing . . . itself." This rapid shift from a flash in which it "knows only itself" to a second instance where it knows "in *terms* of itself" then initiates a "fast" process of "compounding" and forgetting, which confirms that the moment is no longer "*made* of itself." In its third instance, the moment now "without knowing itself" and "not made of itself" is reduced to "*reflecting* only itself." And reflection divides: "then there are two moments." The volatile movement of the moment in its act of appearing displays a steady disintegration of its integrity, a loss of coherence and full presence. It happens so quickly that the poet can only gasp, "How can I explain?" Even before the moment arrives in language it has become something other than itself and the poet is left feeling threatened, awestruck, and defenseless in the face of its arrival.

"It, or we, have been waiting all our lives for this sign of fulfillment," Ashbery writes, "now to be abruptly snatched away so soon as barely perceived. And a kind of panic develops, which for many becomes a permanent state of being, with all the appearances of a calm, reflective life" (*TP,* 73). The calm, reflective life that is really a frozen "panic" seems to be the only possible response to a movement from presentation to representation that happens so instantaneously that one cannot even frame the exact point at which "knowing itself" becomes knowing "in terms of itself." The longed-for "arrival" of the moment that is a "sign of fulfillment" is a "storm" that offers no respite or serenity, but only the "awful" burden to "tell about it." And that burden means "I too have no rest" and that the storm is "always something / To worry about. Really." How can one articulate a moment that moves from presentation to representation, to a reflection of itself, in the process of its performance? If the moment has "no rest," neither does the "I," and in Ashbery's work the two "entities" are always interwoven.

The "disabused intellect" is, indeed, "restless," and he is, for all his light touch, caught in a "serious" double bind. Longing for a moment of full understanding and self-presence, he understands, nonetheless, the "awful" impossibility of achieving it, and he knows the threat it bears within its own appearing. He also understands, however, the generative nature of that double bind, understands that the tensions and "anger" it creates are the life forces that produce his work. If that generative stress creates a certain "sorrow" in his poems, it is the sorrow of the exile longing for home—a longing that abides despite his knowledge that his arrival would mean death. For the "exile" is also a "refugee" fleeing from words that might "mummify," even as he "hopes" for words that can "definitively clear" his name. If the hope is not "serious," neither is the danger. The recalcitrance of language in the face of presence, its resistance to the full embodiment that intentionality desires, is what saves the writer from being contained. It denies the self the full discovery that would bring its meaning into being, but in the process it reveals being as that which lives itself out as "speculation."

Ashbery, then, needs the *resistance* of language to presence and, at the same time, needs to find a language that can yield to his intended meanings. His predicament is at least analogous to Derrida's and is certainly equally quixotic. But "better Don Quixote and his windmills than all the Sancho Panzas in the world," the poet writes (*TP*, 68). He takes up his burden of telling, his quest for the right words, with a joie de vivre that in no way undercuts the importance of his enterprise. His lightness is always pierced with an astringent slice of the dark. "The Ice-Cream Wars" exemplifies both Ashbery's "tone" and his predicament. It is one of many poems in which he treads lightly and intricately among bawdy sexual puns and comically cliched language only to arrive at a "deadly" serious ending.[10] I include the entire poem as much for the reader's delight as for clarity of reference:

> Although I mean it, and project the meaning
> As hard as I can into its brushed-metal surface,
> It cannot, in this deteriorating climate, pick up
> Where I leave off. It sees the Japanese text
> (About two men making love on a foam-rubber bed)
> As among the most massive secretions of the human spirit.
> Its part is in the shade, beyond the iron spikes of the fence,
> Mixing red with blue. As the day wears on
> Those who come to seem reasonable are shouted down
> (*Why you old goat!* Look who's talkin'. Let's see you
> Climb off that tower—the waterworks architecture, both stupid and
> Grandly humorous at the same time, is a kind of mask for him,
> Like a seal's face Time and the weather
> Don't always go hand in hand, as here: sometimes
> One is slanted sideways, disappears for awhile.
> Clouds appear above the lawn, and the rose tells
> The old old story, the pearl of the orient, occluded
> And still apt to rise at times.)
>   A few black smudges
> On the outer boulevards, like squashed midges
> And the truth becomes a hole, something one has always known,
> A heaviness in the trees, and no one can say
> Where it comes from, or how long it will stay—
>
> A randomness, a darkness of one's own.
>
>   (*HD*, 60–61)

10. Ashbery's attraction to "demotic" language is evident throughout his work. He explains: "I am interested very much in debased and demotic forms of expression. . . . They often seem so much more moving than something that is beautifully phrased and composed" (*American Poetry Review* [May/June, 1984], 30).

Almost certainly a response to "The Emperor of Ice-Cream," this poem engages the questions about the joy and mutability of the "melting" flesh and the fragile capacity of art in the face of death that intrigued Wallace Stevens.[11] Ashbery extends Stevens's brief but important reference to art as the embroidered sheet which covers a "cold" corpse into an ironic but rich speculation on the capacity for either the flesh or the word to embody the desire of the "I" for fulfilled meaning. The poem sets eroticism in a parenthetical relationship to the hunger for meaning in words, a gesture that expresses Ashbery's belief that longing for the other is a "detour" through which consciousness passes in its "bent toward self-discovery." It is important to notice, however, that the parenthetical sexuality is more than an explanatory interruption in the poem's central focus on language as a resistant surface. The parentheses also balance eroticism against art so that, though both may be as sweet and fragile as "ice-cream," they are bound together in an unresolved conflict. Hence, no emperor takes control in this poem, and both forms of embodiment remain at "war" not just with each other but with the kinds of death in which both are implicated. The poem suggests that the "Japanese text / (About two men making love on a foam-rubber bed)" is not the poem in process, the poem that is being "performed," but rather the text it "sees" and can only incorporate as an imbedded apposition, a complementary "second thought."

Although "it sees the Japanese text . . . As among the most massive secretions of the human spirit," this poem's "part is in the shade, beyond the iron spikes of the fence." Closed off from the sexuality that it "sees" but does not enact, this poem exists as a framing contrast, "A few black smudges / On the outer boulevards, like squashed midges." The poet *secretes* the Japanese text (which may be the sort of autobiographical reference that could turn the poem into a "diary"); it shrouds it as a parenthetical reference. The text in process covers sensuality with a kind of embroidered sheet that can reveal it only as that which is inaccessible to poetry's own workings. The doubleness of the word *secretions* is important here. As the releasing of one substance into another it suggests that the "human spirit" can discover parts of itself through sexuality. At the same time, the word suggests its opposite meaning, a hiding away. For the spirit that secretes itself is not contained

11. Harold Bloom has long been interested in Ashbery's relation to Wallace Stevens. See "John Ashbery: The Charity of the Hard Moments" and *A Map of Misreading* (New York, 1975), 203–206.

in that act. Finally, it remains hidden as other than that which it leaves behind. The spirit cannot "project" itself fully into another body, and the poet cannot "project" his meaning, or even the sensuality that it "sees," fully into the words of his poem. Yet the parenthetical method does not erase the "Japanese text," it exposes its presence elliptically as a possibility "left out." Announcing its absence is a way of making it known. It is placed carefully so that it leaves its trace in his text but cannot "fill" it. The body is "occluded," shut off from his words "*and* still apt to rise at times." But the form of its rising is as evanescent as "rapturous clouds" or the "rose [that] tells / The old old story."

On the other hand, the poem that is presented as "in process," the one that frames the parenthetical "Japanese text," is even less accommodating of permanence or the presence of meaning than the sexuality that contains spirit only as its "secretions":

> Although I mean it, and project the meaning
> As hard as I can into its brushed-metal surface,
> It cannot, in this deteriorating climate, pick up
> Where I leave off.

It is the resistance of language to his intention, to the intense desire operative in "I mean it . . . As hard as I can," that provokes the poet's glance into the "other" text, the Japanese text of sexuality that seems more accommodating than the "brushed-metal" of words. But when his exploration of that text shows that it, too, is partial, open to "time and the weather," and when the text can be seen as only a parenthetical reference to his intentions, then he turns again to the brushed metal. His projected meaning has, by now, exposed itself as only "a few black smudges / On the outer boulevards," as a blurred and dead "frame" closed off from intentionality as well as sexuality. The poem beyond the fence is as trivial as "squashed midges." Facing words that cannot fully articulate his meaning, cannot contain the "I," cannot "pick up / Where I leave off," and cannot even contain the sensual secretions of the spirit except by further secreting them, the poet falls from light irony to dark:

> And the truth becomes a hole, something one has always known,
> A heaviness in the trees, and no one can say
> Where it comes from, or how long it will stay—
>
> A randomness, a darkness of one's own.

Both sensuality and the attempt to project meaning into words are deprived of the fullness of being, ultimately producing a situation in which the "truth" of both is exposed as only a "hole." The "truth" is the truth of a self empty of all but its own desire; it is "a randomness, a darkness of one's own" that remains beyond flesh and words; it is the thing "there is no name for" that "no one can say."

Stevens's poem, with its resigned "Let be be finale of seem" and the dark irony of its final line, "The only emperor is the emperor of ice-cream," creates closure, if perhaps an unpalatable one. Ashbery would certainly agree that "be" is the "finale of seem," but he does not quite yield to Emperor Death, despite the powerful evocation of death in "the truth is a hole." He escapes that "finale" because nothing in "The Ice-Cream Wars" quite achieves being. His meaning, his intention, never achieves full containment, the embodiment that could prove mortal. It remains "beyond . . . the fence." Language never quite erases "seem" to "let be be." His words do not drape a substantial corpse whose "horney feet protrude," but only a nothingness that "one has always known" and "that no one can say." This refusal of the "name" is a refusal of death as much as a submission to the failure of language to incarnate the "thing itself." The "truth" escapes mortality, if only as a randomness and darkness, because that self is exiled from its language. Because the poem cannot "pick up / Where I leave off," the "I" *can* "leave" the poem, and it exits, in the end, as the truth that "no one can say."

As disturbing as the *nature* of truth may be in "The Ice-Cream Wars," it is important to note that Ashbery's careful phrasing and self-conscious use of line breaks affirm the *existence* of truth. As much as his "I" participates in the play of differance, the poet does not press that play to a genuinely deconstructive position wherein meaning and truth are purely products of language. There is still, for Ashbery, something "outside of the text," and that something demands a representation that can be, at least, semi-incarnative, that can reveal its "truth," if only as a "hole." Truth exists as "something one *has always*," and as "known," even if it cannot and must not be fully incorporated by words or located in a specific moment. As his poems demonstrate, the fact that the demand for self-representation cannot be satisfied perversely protects the being of truth, even as it frustrates its appearance. Even though or, better, *because* it is something "no one can say," it remains in the possession of consciousness as "one's own." Its unavailability is not an "effect" of the disseminative processes of language but of its exile *from* language. Intentionality, then, the "I mean it," does not disintegrate in its encounter with writing's resistance to its meanings; it uses that resistance to create a sort of friction that marks the movements of consciousness, its "entrances and exits." The "austerity of an *almost* empty mind" colliding with its only permanent occupant, its "desire to communicate" as a mode of self-discovery, remains a "singular and irreplaceable" life force. And that life force can only appear through words that attempt a definitive clearing of one's own name.

Ashbery's consciousness is neither Wordsworth's "full" point "far hidden" from words nor the "point" that Eliot avers (and so deeply desires) in *Four Quartets*.[12] Ashbery's point can never serve as a center for Eliot's "turning world." The idea of a fixed center is, he thinks, the result of "great fright." It is really only the "rigidity" of the mind itself, produced because it has

> focused on a nonexistent center, a fixed point when
> the common sense of even an idiot would be enough to
> make him realize that nothing has stopped that we and
> everything around us are moving forward continually
> and that we are being modified constantly by the speed
> at which we travel and the regions through which we
> pass, so that merely to think of ourselves as having
> arrived at some final resting place is a contradiction
> of fundamental logic.
>
> (*TP*, 74)

The characterization of the still point as "some final resting place" should not be overlooked here, for the "rigidity" of the mind occurs as a reflection of its own death: the nonexistent center generates "panic" disguised as fulfilled desire, a "calm, reflective life." It is the most dangerous detour the "I" can take in its quest for self-discovery. Those who focus on the "fixed point" are in the midst of a fatal self-deception: "they can think of nothing but themselves when all the time they believe that they are thinking of nothing but God" (*TP*, 74). They repress their knowledge of the "hole" that is

12. I am, of course, assuming the "traditional" understanding of Eliot's poem here, the reading that Ashbery clearly addresses in *Three Poems*. However, William Spanos's discussion of Eliot's work in "Hermeneutics and Memory: Destroying T. S. Eliot's *Four Quartets*" has shaken the received opinion of the work in important ways. Spanos directs his attention to the poem's process rather than its "statements" and, by focusing on its temporal movement, argues convincingly that Eliot shows the impossibility of achieving the "still point" that he wishes to claim as his center.

truth, the vital emptiness they "own," and substitute a notion "clear and cold" as death.

The nonexistent center is, in Ashbery's view, a delusory figure for timelessness. Since time bestows the only life we have, to be outside of time is deadly, even if it seems to offer eternity. On this point he seems close to Eliot's "Time the destroyer is Time the preserver" (*Four Quartets,* 195). But the two poets' visions of time are quite different. In the overt statements of his poem (though *not,* as William Spanos has shown, in its workings), Eliot asserts that his "still point" enables truth to appear in the light of understanding, the "light" that is "still / At the still point of the turning world" (*Four Quartets,* 177). Furthermore, he believes that a still point orders time into a fullness, a whole. Nothing could be further from Ashbery's assertion of truth as dark and random, as the "I" which is a moving point that intuits death within the light of the full understanding that it desires. Eliot's "still center of the turning world" posits a circular movement wherein "past and future are gathered." This is, Spanos has elegantly demonstrated, a willed "spatializing" of time, a figuration that promises that we can "arrive where we started / And know the place for the first time" (*Four Quartets,* 208). While Ashbery's "point of no return" exists as a seeker and gatherer of meanings (he has called the "I" an "insatiable researcher" [*DD,* 77]), it can never gather them into the "light" of fullness precisely because it cannot "gather" time. We exist, he says, "in the razor's-edge present which is really a no-time continually straying over the border into the positive past and the negative future whose movements alone define it. . . . We are appalled at this. Because its no-time, no-space dimensions offer us no signposts, nothing to be guided by" (*TP,* 103). The self exists *as* time, as this "continually straying" activity only defined by the future, which freezes the "no-time" of the present into the past, even in its "happening."

Consequently, when Ashbery paraphrases Eliot's famous lines, "In my beginning is my end. . . . In my end is my beginning," he does so, as he does with all references to Eliot in *Three Poems,* "in a different register, transposed from a major into a minor key" (*TP,* 93).[13] The words have a certain kind of correctness for him, but their accuracy must be understood in a new way. At the moment he thinks he has "come full circle," this poet discovers not an original

13. Eliot's desire to "spatialize," to frame being, is clearly demonstrated by these first and last lines of "East Coker."

understanding but "an intolerable mixture of reality and fantasy."
He finds that "this place of joining" is not an "end" that enlightens,
an end in the form of an answer. Rather, when one returns to what
"started you on the road" in the first place, one returns to that
"question of your being here" which always throws the "I" forward into its unknown future. And because we "are being modified
constantly by the speed at which we travel and the regions through
which we pass," that "end" is always different. It is "no new problem" but the "old problem," the question is resituated and changed
by passing time. An attempted return always fails to arrive; one
finds only that the self's "new problematical existence will have already begun," at the very moment one thinks one has come "home"
(*TP*, 107). When one returns to the "distribution center," he says in
"Fragment," one "returns to die." Yet one begins again for "in the
hollow thus produced," which is also "a cave of the winds," one
finds "ghosts of the streets / Crowding, propagating the feeling
into furious / Waves from the perfunctory and debilitated sunset"
(*DD*, 80). There is a fertility in a return that generates "propagating
ghosts," which can debilitate even this "end," this "sunset."

The desire for rest is powerful, and one can succumb to that
need. "If you have decided that there is no alternative," however,
you discover that "one must move very fast in order to stay in the
same place . . . you must still learn to cope with the onrushing tide
of time" (*TP*, 90). Furthermore, this "intolerable" vision of "reality
at odds with itself" always reveals the essential "restlessness" of the
"I," a revelation that reduces the illusion that one has come full
circle to "a zero" (*TP*, 91). The nothingness of this notion of time
as a "gathering" does not mean that it can be "banished" from the
desiring self, "anymore than physical matter can," Ashbery concedes. It does mean, though, that such "schemes" are ultimately exposed as deceptions, that "their nature, which is part and parcel of
their existence, is to remain incomplete and clamoring for wholeness" (*TP*, 91). In Ashbery's thought the "fixed point" is only a figure for the desire of the "I" itself—a desire that if satisfied brings
"destruction and even death." Such schemes are perpetrated by
"those dishonest counselors of many aspects" who are almost certainly past poets, especially Eliot, but who, more importantly, are
the counselors *within*. They are aspects of the desire and nostalgia
that create the "clamoring" of consciousness in the first place. That
"clamoring" is the "end" from which we must always, and repeatedly, "begin."

The "I," then, is thrown irrevocably and "fatally" into a trajectory of endless change which cannot promise either "arrival" or "return." Each discrete consciousness moves in its trajectory in a way that seems a "darkness and randomness of one's own." Yet *all* is not random. There are, Ashbery says, "two fixed loci of past and future" upon which "our very lives depend" (*TP,* 105). The beginning and ending of movement are known and certain: something "one has always" from moment to moment, and something that is "known" because it is lived. To be alive is "to be your breath, as it is taken in and shoved out" (*TP,* 5); it is to begin, end, and begin again every second. One may appear to be only "waiting" or "drifting"—metaphors for time and movement that appear everywhere in Ashbery's work—but one is always experiencing birth and death. We live, as he says in "Clouds," "with each day digging the grave of tomorrow and at the same time / Preparing its own redemption constantly living and dying" (*DD,* 68). The apparent discontinuity of this process is only a part of a greater whole which always threatens. We cannot "outsmart the sense of continuity" that this fluctuating but steady movement toward death creates. We do, however, want to evade the implications of fatality implied by the continual experience of death and, in a peculiar way, the very mundanity of the process assists our evasions. Because consciousness is, itself, a temporal process in which each moment dies and is reborn, because each day prepares "its own redemption," the ultimate savagery of the process is repressed. The finality, the unavoidable completion of that continuity "eludes our steps as it prepares us / For ultimate wishful thinking once the mind has ended" (*DD,* 68). The repetition of beginning and ending is so habitual that it creates the hope that mind can exist even beyond its death, the "ultimate wishful thinking." In this manner, time continues to redeem as it destroys, suggesting by its discontinuity that the mind cannot "end" and creating through its rhythms a necessary delusion that protects the self from the vaster continuity that *means* "my-death." The everydayness of the event is, then, both "alien and healthy, for death is here and knowable," yet it escapes full being. This "disabused intellect" knows, however, that "he shoots forward like a *malignant* star" (*DD,* 69, my emphasis), and like the "one who moves forward from a dream" in "Parergon" (*DD,* 55). His poetry, "the river of his passing . . . savage and mild with the contemplating," reveals "that the continuity was fierce beyond all dream of enduring," that our "undying joyousness" is "caught in that trap" (*DD,* 56).

The people who gaze upon the poet in "Parergon" turn their faces from the truth he exposes, but Ashbery, for all the comedy and "joyousness" of his work, never turns away from the death that, in the act of writing, he still manages to evade. The truth that is a "hole" of "one's own" is also the source of life and poetry. "Death is really an appetite for time / That can see through the haze of blue / Smoke rings to the turquoise ceiling." And "speculation / Raves and raves as on a mirror / To the outlandish accompaniment of its own death / That reads as life" ("Litany," *AWK,* 14). In writing, the poet's consciousness can

> disappear, like Hamlet, in a blizzard
> Of speculation that comes to occupy
> The forefront for a time, until
> Nothing but the forefront exists, like a forehead
> Of the times, speechless, drunk, imagined
> In all five shapes, and ever in one state
> Of repose, though always disclosed
> And disclosing, keeping itself like a chance
> In the dark, living wholly in a dream
> Sweet reality discovers.
>
> ("Litany," *AWK,* 44)

Writing poetry is "like a chance in the dark," the chance of being "disclosed and disclosing" while never being locked in "one state of repose." Though reality "discovers" this activity as a "dream," it is not a dream that lies. For as long as one continues to speculate, to the "accompaniment" of death, one is "Saying It to Keep It from Happening" —the title of his poem about the final "departure" that "will occur as time grows more open about it" (*HD,* 29). "Nobody lies about it any more," he asserts, since "we live / In the interstices, between a vacant stare and the ceiling, / Our lives remind us. Finally this is consciousness / And the other livers of it get off at the same stop" (*HD,* 29). Full being is death: "What is is what happens in the end," but while saying it one knows that "it's both there / And not there, like washing or sawdust in the sunlight, / At the back of the mind, where we live now" (*HD,* 30).

"Where we live now" is the no-time and no-place of a present, the emptiness of an interval that is only an idea where nothing, not the emergence of the self, that "thing of monstrous interest," nor the death of the self which is that same "event," can fully appear:

> it can never come about not here
> not yesterday in the past only in the

> gap of today filling itself as emptiness
> is distributed in the idea of what time
> it is when that time is already past.
> ("As You Came from
> the Holy Land," *SM, 7*)

As long as one keeps "saying," both the privileged moment and the deadly totality of such a moment are kept from "happening." It is only "speculation that comes to occupy the forefront for a time," and speculation is "the *chance* in the dark," the chance for being to exist as questioning and reflecting. Speculation, "never in one state of repose," is "disclosed and disclosing" because it is lived "in the interstices," in the spaces created by the movement of language that marks the intentional thrust of the "I." For Ashbery, that which discloses and is disclosed is no "irreducible absence," as Derrida would suggest. It is the "hollow" that is also the "cave of winds" with all of its "ghosts propagating," acting out desire. As long as one keeps writing, acting, speculating, death remains in the background:

> The tone is hard is heard
> Is the coming of strength out of night: unfeared;
> Still the colors are there and they
> Ask the question of this what is to be
> Out of a desert of chance in which being is life
> But like a paradox, death reinforcing the life,
> Sound under memory, as though our right to hear
> Hid old unwillingness to continue
> Or a style of turning to the window
> Hands directing the air, and no design sticks,
> Only agreement not to let it die.
> ("Sunrise in Suburbia," *DD, 49*)

The "tone" of the sunrise is "hard" because it resounds with that integration of death and life that Ashbery explores in "Clouds." The new day marks an end and a beginning that suggest the movement of time toward death. Death is the "hard" and "heard" tone; it is the "sound under memory." But it is also "reinforcing the life," since "our right to hear" represses any "unwillingness to continue" and generates the desire to turn to the window, to remain open to the influx of air. It generates intention, the desire to make meaning, to direct that air, even though "no design sticks." In a poem that serves almost as a commentary on this dense opening of "Sunrise in Suburbia," the meaning of "turning to the window" and "directing the air" is more fully disclosed and directly related to Ashbery's equation of poetry and music:

What is it now with me
And is it as I have become?
Is there no state free from the boundary lines
Of before and after? The window is open today

And the air pours in with piano notes
In its skirts, as though to say, "Look, John,
I've brought these and these"—that is,
A few Beethovens, some Brahmses,

A few choice Poulenc notes. . . . Yes,
It is being free again, the air, it has to keep coming back
Because that's all it's good for.
I want to stay with it out of fear

That keeps me from walking up certain steps,
Knocking at certain doors, fear of growing old
Alone, and of finding no one at the evening end
Of the Path except another myself

Nodding a curt greeting: "Well, you've been awhile
But now we're back together, which is what counts."
Air in my path, you could shorten this,
But the breeze has dropped, and silence is the last word.
("Fear of Death," SM, 49)

This beautiful and deceptively simple little poem plays with many of the issues explored in this chapter. The question of being with which the poem begins is explored as "performance," a flow of music created by "hands directing the air." The open window evokes the open mind and the "theater/garden" of "A Man of Words," but here the performing air "pours in" one "design" after another, a series of substitutions that suggest that "yes, it is being free again." Still, like the dawn that carries its own death, the freedom of air that has become music is immediately qualified The directed air is free, a random gift of endless change, but it is enslaved by its own continuity: "it has to keep coming." Music can exist only in time, never "free of the boundary lines of before and after." The freedom of the music-bearing air is further constrained by the poet's confession that "I want to stay with it out of fear." The poet stays with the air—which is to say with music/poetry—as a way of avoiding the fear of death so palpably exposed by the "merging" with myself that occurs at "the end of the path" where "we're back together." Since living is "to be your breath as it is taken in and shoved out," since it is a process of temporal beginnings and endings, the music that Ashbery makes "between breaths" has to "keep coming" even though it is not free from the "before and after." It has to "keep coming," to suffer that form of "boundary," in order to defer the arrival at the end of the path. "That's all it's good for," but for this poet that is everything. For the only "state free from the boundary lines" is death, and "silence is the last word" which incorporates all and must never be spoken. Language must continue to flow like air, to aim toward a meaning that is always its own future. "That is the tune but there are no words." The seeking for the right words must continue.

The "I" that lives "in the interstices" needs the boundaries of "before and after," but it is always facing away from its deserted past and toward its empty, projected future.[14] "He shoots forward like a malignant star," Ashbery writes in "Clouds," and he expands on that image in a startling way in *Three Poems*. In "The New Spirit" the "malignant star" becomes "Sagittarius," the archer of the heavens poised forever in the moment of the fully drawn bow, the moment of pure intentionality and fervent seeking. For Ashbery, Sagittarius is a far more appropriate "muse" than the traditional god of poetry, music, healing, and prophecy. Apollo has come to represent the still balance of fully achieved form, while the astronomical archer, half-man and half-beast, translated into the heavens at the pin-point moment when one cannot tell if the arrow has already been released or is just about to be released, is an exact figure for desire. The lustful hunter is also "the healer, caustic but kind" who sweeps away "the cobwebs of intuitive idealism" (*TP*, 42). With his bow drawn and looking eternally forward, this figure of the seeker "takes careful aim" toward "the promise of what remains to be fulfilled." But Ashbery is careful to note that this is "no shot in the dark it is an already realized state of potential" (42). The archer, whose state of being is a non-being, only a "realized state of *potential*," cannot have the fulfillment of desire but that lack of fulfillment is itself a "realized state," the only form of achieved self-definition that continues to offer life.

In the gorgeous closing lines of "The New Spirit" the archer's state of being is offered as the only viable alternative to a fulfillment of the desire for presence that brings death. At this moment in the poem, presence takes the form of a "tower," clearly phallic, full of

---

14. Several critics have been intrigued by Ashbery's "I." For two contrasting views, see John Koethe, "The Metaphysical Subject of John Ashbery's Poetry," in *Beyond Amazement: New Essays on John Ashbery*, ed. David Lehman (Ithaca, 1980), and Alan Williamson, *Introspection and Contemporary Poetry* (Cambridge, Mass., 1984), 116–48

light, and, at first, serene and seductive. It rises in a moment when
"the one of whom this is written remained motionless," full of despair: "There were no new stories" (*TP*, 42). In that moment, the
poet has stopped questioning and begun "looking for a sign, a portent." In looking for a portent, the poet has looked toward a "nonexistent center" and found a tower: "He thought he had never seen
anything quite so beautiful as that crystallization into a mountain of
statistics . . . everything and everybody were included after all . . .
into the broadest and widest kind of uniform continuum" (48–49).
The beauty of the wholeness has an anesthetizing effect that suggests he really can "remain immobile for a while." But the irrevocable movement of time saves him from the rest he both desires
and fears. The "light" of inclusiveness is defeated by the dark: "advancing swiftly with measured and silent steps . . . night again
erected with exact brilliance the very configurations he had been in-
voking" (49). The more exact "meanings" of night's stars, dying
and reborn daily and "shooting forward" despite their apparent stability, "seemed a sardonic construction put upon his words." In the
fading light of the sun, the tower is exposed as a dangerous pretense, and the crystal mountain seems, suddenly, a frozen and dead
representation of meaninglessness: "this horrible vision of the completed Tower of Babel" (49). Like all the towers in Ashbery—"the
many-colored tower of longing" in "On the Towpath," the tower
that "controlled the sky" in "These Lacustrine Cities" (*RM*, 9), and
Childe Harold's "Dark Tower" (*TP*, 92)—this one is a figure of immobilized desire, death.[15] The tower is the end of difference and deferral; consequently it is a "terror" that must be "shut out—really
shut out—simply by turning one's back on it" (*TP*, 50). Turning
away from completion toward potential is Ashbery's ultimate affirmation of "The New Spirit."

The "healer, caustic but kind" appears to rescue him from his
own vision, to remind him that he exists only as "a realized state of
potential" and that he must turn away from the Apollonian wholeness that is only "babel." Turning toward the empty future, "the
desert," the poet sees

> drooping above it the constellations that had
> presided impassively over the building of the

15. In an interesting reading of "These Lacustrine Cities," David Rigsbee notes
that the tower, which there emerged and "controlled the sky," is a symbolic displacement of desire (*Beyond Amazement*, 212).

metaphor that seemed about to erase them from the
skies. Yet they were in no way implicated in the
success or the failure, depending on your viewpoint,
of the project, as became clear the minute you caught
sight of the Archer, languidly stretching his bow,
aiming at a still higher and smaller portion of the
heavens, no longer a figure of speech but an act, even
if all the life had been temporarily drained out of it.
It was obvious that a new journey would have to be
undertaken.

(TP, 51)

The tower that had seemed so complete, seemed to include "all,"
has not even "implicated" the movements of the stars, the structure
of the universe that it had "seemed about to erase." It is no mountain now, but only a "metaphor," a dangerous "figure of speech"
from which the archer escapes entirely. The tower made of meaningless words cannot contain that which "is no longer a figure of
speech but an *act*." It cannot include the "new journey" that must
always be undertaken. The aiming archer, the intentional "I," may
preside over the building of the metaphor, but he always exists far
beyond it, "aiming higher." Sagittarius, perceived in the flash of
time between past and future but unable, in his stellar form, to relax
the bow, is "temporarily drained of life," but only temporarily. For
the mind is always in the act of emptying and filling itself: there is
always an aiming and an arrow being shot. Furthermore, the "I" is
not just the archer but also the arrow. In the process of moving
"you overlap once again with the one that thought you, sent you
speeding like an arrow into this pleasant desert. . . . Safe, out in the
open, and ready to start again" (*TP*, 29). The poet's intention, his
"aiming" toward a "higher" and therefore apparently "smaller,
portion of the heavens," overlaps with his poems, the arrows he
shoots. Yet like the arrows of Sagittarius, neither the "I" nor its
poems ever quite arrive at the meaning they aim for. Both are always "in a *realized* state of *potential*," which evokes the target but
never fully contains it. Ashbery's "difficult" style is, in part, a result
of his unwillingness to create work that might become that terrifying "last ceramic brick" that completes the Tower of Babel. Though
it would be "perfect in its vulgarity, an eternal reminder of the ad-
vantages of industry and cleverness," it would transform language
into a meaningless structure which, "as soon as it was not looked
at," would "cease to exist" (50).

    Keeping poetry in "a realized state of potential" is as much an

attempt to present the meaning of being and the being of meaning
as is MacLeish's famous "Ars Poetica." MacLeish's attempt, however, depends upon the "eye," fixed in a stable position at its window casement. Ashbery's depends upon an "I" untethered from its
own visions, one that looks away from the palpable but deadly
completion that MacLeish so much desires. "Ars Poetica" attempts
to erase time in favor of space; Ashbery's work attempts to keep
language as temporal as consciousness itself. His poetry, then, still
turns, like all lyrics, on the premise that it can evoke the meaning of
being as a kind of presence, although it cannot do so in any traditional sense of presenting the "I" as the content of a poem. His
poems are epitaphic in that they mark a "passing through" meaning
even as it occurs; they trace the path of an "I" which "overlaps"
with itself but is always "ahead" of that self. For him, poetry is the
inscription of an act, and an actor, that have been evacuated at the
moment of the writing. Such poetry traces the productive power of
an "I" that is always in the process of "acting-out." Poetry that
strives to be a "realized state of potential" is a poetry of sacrifice. It
surrenders fullness of being and of meaning in order to gain vitality
itself, and in the process it inherently deprives consciousness of any
privileged moments of complete coherence. It forbids self-presence
until the final moment of completeness, the victory of continuity
over time, the moment of death when one stops "writing." At that
point, differance will have finished the finite movement that has always been, "continuously," toward "my-death." One is then, at
last, framed "between bookends" ("De Imagine Mundi," *SM,* 35).

Yet Ashbery's inability to capture, or be captured by, the privileged moment does not, to his mind, mean that such a "pause" is an
illusion, any more than his inability to uncover the "I" suggests that
it is illusory. Rather, both are seen as realities (or better, as the same
reality) that are not available to language, even though only words
can "cloak" their invisible being into a visible "semi-obscurity."
Life depends upon this "semi-obscurity," and to capture the full
emergence of the moment in language would be to capture the finality of death: "the moment / Takes such a big bite out of the
haze / Of pleasant intuition it comes after. / The locking into place
is 'death itself'" ("Self-Portrait," *SM,* 76).[16]

The "haze of intuition" draws the self onward, provokes its

16. Ashbery's relation to the 'privileged moment' is discussed briefly by both
Bloom, "John Ashbery: The Charity of the Hard Moments," and Kalstone, "John
Ashbery: Self-Portrait in a Convex Mirror."

quest with "whispers of the word that can't be understood" ("Self-Portrait," *SM,* 75), the word that remains outside of human temporality, that "whispers out of time" ("Self-Portrait," *SM,* 83). The "whispered word" throughout Ashbery's work seems to promise self-presence, the fullness of the privileged moment; it is the name that one wants and cannot have. The seductive calling of the "whispered word," the desire for the advent of a privileged moment, and the longing for self-discovery in the "body" of one's own name are so densely interwoven for this poet that his work suggests that all of them coalesce into the same "event." They are all that "thing of monstrous interest" that seems always to be "happening" but "can never come about" ("Self-Portrait," *SM,* 7).

The question of whether poetry can, or should, articulate this woven "moment" has been with Ashbery from his earliest work, *Some Trees.* In that work the question of the privileged moment and the quest for the "lost words" are directly linked to the problematics of self-representation, a link that continues to hold throughout his poetry. Speculating in 1956 on a childhood picture, Ashbery perceives the photo of "my small self" as at best a warped fragment of the self who is presently writing. Instead of representing him, the photo seems to have captured "the sick moment / The shutter clicked," a moment in which, already, "I was wrong." That click of the shutter, which sickens the moment and wrongs the "I," is compared to language, which can give only a self-representation that distances and distorts. Still, he continues, the click of the shutter (obviously a "locking into place") and the word that substitutes for the thing itself are all we have, and they bear their own sort of truth:

> Still, as the loveliest feelings
>
> Must soon find words, and these, yes,
> Displace them, so I am not wrong
> In calling this comic version of myself
> The true one. For as change is horror,
> Virtue is really stubbornness
>
> And only in the light of lost words
> Can we imagine our rewards.
> > ("Portrait of Little J.A. in a
> > Prospect of Flowers," *ST,* 29)

After thirty years of seeking, Ashbery writes in a recent poem that the "lost words" still radiate the light of promise though they continue to withhold themselves from the seeker. In the face of the great question, phrased here as "Were we / Making any sense?"

and described again as "that thirst" he explored in *Houseboat Days,* words debilitate the intuition of meaning, which operates as a "setting" for one's performance. One may have an idea, but there are so "many ideas" that they create a "morass" of "good intentions" that are never fulfilled:

> they become a luminous backdrop to ever-repeated
> Gestures, having no life of their own, but only echoing
> The suspicions of their possessor. It's fun to scratch around
> And maybe come up with something, but for the tender blur
> Of the setting to mean something, words must be ejected bodily
> A certain crispness avoided in favor of a density
> Of strutted opinion doomed to wilt in oblivion.[17]

The incapacity of words relative to the "luminous backdrop," the "tender blur of the setting," puts the poet in a difficult position. Their "crispness" belies its "density" so that the poet needs a fully incarnative language. Yet words "ejected bodily" are not only imprecise but mortal: "strutted opinion doomed to wilt in oblivion." Consequently, the writer must search for words that are "not too linear / Nor yet too puffed and remote." Even if such words are found, they fall short of the intention toward meaning, causing one to fall back into "one's own / Received opinions," an occurrence that simply "redirects the maze, setting up significant / Erections of its own at chosen corners, like gibbets" (70). Ashbery displays a deep ambivalence here: though words bring order, that order is characterized as a gallows. Through them, he goes on, the landscape "becomes / at last / apparent," but it is only the "backward part of a life that is / Partially coming into view," and that is so distant that "the issue / Of making sense becomes . . . a far-off one" (70).

Ashbery goes on to suggest that the thirst for meaning can only be satisfied by a sort of mirage: "knowing can have this / Sublime rind of excitement, like the shore of a lake in the desert / Blazing with the sunset" (70). Nonetheless, like the fabled contents of a mirage, meaning does exist somewhere; the "hazy intuition," the "tender blur" is not "nothing," and it continues to stimulate the thirst that no mirage can satisfy. Thus, this fine poem, one of Ashbery's most beautiful, ends many pages later with a return to the question of meaning. It is, he says, "going to move still farther upward, casting / Its Shadow enormously over where I remain," even though "I can't see it" (89). Even though only the "shadow" of

17. John Ashbery, *A Wave* (New York, 1985), 69.

meaning can announce its existence, "yet the thirst remains identical, always to be entertained and marveled at" (89). The identical thirst, which holds in the face of change and loss, evidences the identity, the singularity, of the temporal "I" as it moves through time. The self may be modified by time, but that thirst, that questioning, that movement toward and in shadows remains the "same." It is the being which "you can neither define nor erase," which appears only as the "shrill savage drapery of non-being" that "stands out in the firelight" through the cloak of language ("Litany," *AWK*, 286). It continues, in its discontinuous way, to move into the distance, and it continues to see the "lost words" that might fully embody it until, as the poet says at the end of "A Wave," "it is finally we who break it off" (89).

In spite of his belief that the thirst for "the meaning of the music" is satiated only by mirages or the finality of "my-death," and in spite of his conviction that the "locking into place" which language enacts carries "death-itself" within, Ashbery does not write without hope. Poetry as performance, as an epitaphic endeavor that displays both the absence and the presence of an intending "I," poetry that does not delude itself into believing that it has captured self-presence in a privileged moment, is an exercise of hope against all the odds:

> no hope of completing the magnitude which surrounds us
> is permitted us. But this hope (which doesn't exist) is
> Precisely a form of suspended birth,
> Of that invisible light which spatters the silence
> Of our everyday festivities. A glebe which has pursued
> Its intentions of duration at the same time as reinforcing
> Its basic position so that it is now
> A boiling crater, form of everything that is beautiful for us.
> ("French Poems," *DD,* 38)

This "glebe," the speck of earth and "invisible light" that pursues its "intentions of duration," this "I," lives in the "interstices" by virtue of the "suspended birth" that is hope. Poetry, then, is born out of a hope "which doesn't exist" but nonetheless "is." It is a "state of realized potential" that motivates all writing, even the recording of trivia that produces the emptiness of a diary:

> What precisely is it
> About the time of day it is, the weather, that causes people
> to note it painstakingly in their diaries

For them to read who shall come after?
Surely it is because the ray of light
Or gloom striking you this moment is hope
In all its mature, matronly form, taking all things into account
And reapportioning them according to size
So that if one can't say that this is the natural way
It should have happened, at least one can have no cause for complaint
Which is the same as having reached the end, wise
In that expectation and enhanced by its fulfillment, or the absence of it.
("Grand Galop," SM, 17)

Hope, whether it takes the form of a "ray of light or gloom," may produce words that are only the fiction of "the way it should have happened." Yet "mature and matronly," an achieved state of creative potential, hope nurtures at least that much meaning. It creates the wisdom of knowing that one lives hope for its own sake, that it does not depend upon either "its fulfillment or the absence of it," since it is the "achieved state" of one's own being.

   Hope expresses itself in Ashbery's work as a "trying to tell you about a strange thing / That happened to me," which always becomes a discovery that, in the act of telling, the "strange thing" somehow "drifts away in fragments," escapes the words the poet finds:

                    It drifts away in fragments
And one is left sitting in the yard
To try to write poetry
Using what Wyatt and Surrey left around,
Took up and put down again
Like so much gorgeous raw material,
As though it would always happen in some way
And meanwhile since we are all advancing
It is sure to come about in spite of everything
On a Sunday, where you are left sitting
In the shade that, as always, is just a little too cool.
So there is whirling out at you from the not deep
Emptiness the word "cock" or some other, brother and sister words
With not much to be expected from them, though these
Are the ones that waited so long for you and finally left,
      having given up hope,
There is a note of desperation in one's voice, pleading for them
And meanwhile the intensity thins and sharpens
Its point, that is the thing it was going to ask.
("Grand Galop," SM, 19)

"In spite of everything" the words that "left, having / Given up hope" do come "whirling out at you" and, while there is "not much to be expected from them," the poet acts out his "case" by "pleading for them." The act of writing is an act of seeking which "sharpens" the question of being, the voice's "point" in the long run; seeking, itself, is "the thing it was going to ask." Ashbery completes this moment of his poem in the spirit of quiet hopefulness that is typical of his work. The "strange thing" can make its uniquely postmodern sort of appearance, not in words but in the traces it leaves behind, in "forgetting": "Still, that poetry does sometimes occur / If only in creases in forgotten letters / Packed away in trunks in the attic" ("Grand Galop," *SM,* 19). One cannot stop hoping for the presence of meaning, even if it is marked only as a crease in what we have forgotten, for "virtue is really stubbornness / And only in the light of lost words / Can we imagine our rewards."

Searching for meaning in the "light of lost words," that is, "continually doing something you cannot name," is for Ashbery the "life-itself" opposed to "death-itself" that the "locking into place" of self-portraiture seems to suggest. That such seeking produces "sorrow" does not prevent one's desire for self-discovery. It does mean that the creation and uncovering of a self must be undertaken in language that always evokes one's death even as it initiates life. When Ashbery writes his own "history" of "the growth of a poet's mind," *Three Poems,* he must erase "history" in order to produce potential. Consequently, the poem, while it constantly hints at the "personal life," is essentially an embodiment of a mind in action, not of its contents.[18] All three poems are investigative, speculative explorations into various possibilities for self-representation that collapse into an enactment of the *process* of speculation which is, ultimately, the only genuine form of self-representation available to this poet. In that process the poet oscillates so rapidly between questioning and reflecting that both activities become "one," very much as the various "systems" he explores are ultimately seen as "one." The "career notion" opposed to the "ritual" notion of existence, or the idea that "latent" happiness is an alternative to "frontal" happiness, for example, are finally presented as the "same." Mastered by the singularity of the investigating "I," their apparent

18. Kalstone notes the forefronting of consciousness over content in *Five Temperaments,* 210.

differences dissolve into the fact that "there is only one question" (*TP,* 80).

The questioning and reflecting activity is driven steadily forward by a single powerful force: a hunger for the self that can be uncovered only if one can find its "name." The book ends in an openness that insists on "recital," on a rereading that is a "return to the point of no return" *because* that name is never fully exposed. It remains, fortuitously, "buried." Unlike his great predecessor of *The Prelude,* this postmodernist believes that to find the word is to find it carved in a stone that marks only one's death, a death that bestows only totality without recompense.

The "truth" of being is not "all" for Ashbery; it is, as he says in the opening of *Three Poems,* the force that "divides all" (3). It is the act of mind which can speculate on itself only as the "you" it represents: "I am the spectator, you what is apprehended and as such we both have our own satisfying reality, even each to the other, though in the end it falls apart, falls to the ground and sinks in" (15). Truth is the "hole," the nothingness of one's own generative desire, the "cave of winds." And it is death· "There is a hole of truth in the green earth's rug / Once you find it you are as snug as a bug" (*DD,* 26). But truth is also one other great "hole":

> It all boils down to
> Nothing, one supposes. There is a central crater
> Which is the word, and around it
> All the things that have names, a commotion
> Of thrushes pretending to have hatched
> Out of the great egg that still hasn't been laid.
> ("Litany," *AWK,* 55)

The "boiling crater" that is "hope" in "French Poems" is exposed here as *also* the word, the omphalus of being. While it can be seen as "what it all boils down to," that crater has not yet given birth; it exists as sheer potential, and all the things that have names are merely "pre-tending" toward it. Since, however, the crater is also the grave, that is just as well. For the "task" of being, Ashbery writes in the opening of *Three Poems,* is to live out this doubleness:

> We must drink the confusion, sample that other,
> concerted, dark effort that pushes not to light, but
> toward a draft of dank, clammy air. We have broken
> through into the meaning of the tomb. But, the act
> is still proposed, before us,

it needs pronouncing. To formulate oneself around
This hollow, empty sphere. . . . To be your breath as
it is taken in and shoved out.

                              (*TP*, 4–5, Ashbery's ellipses)

For this poet the act of pronouncing is living, a formulation of oneself, it is the "continual pilgrimage" (*TP*, 5) toward both death and
the unborn word. Pronouncing the act, even though it contains the
"meaning of the tomb," is the writer's way of generating his life,
for "only the sound of the truth as it is broken off from your mouth
can kindle this apathetic valley that wants nothing better than to
lapse back into the scenery of its dull vegetation" (*TP*, 32). Even
though their sounds must be "broken off," the poet must have
words in order to prevent his own absorption into the earth. Though
truth is always fragmented by the names that are pretenses, only
through those broken sounds can life appear as "an open field of
narrative possibilities" (41) rather than as a diary kept by a "recording angel" (104). Speculative and incomplete, words that contain
only fragments of the whole create "stories" that are not "tales of
the past" but are "stories that tell only of themselves" from which
one's self has "vanished in the diamond light of pure speculation"
(41), vanished *so that* it can begin again. This is the only "system"
viable for a "disabused intellect" that hungers for self-presence even
though there is "a tragic flaw in the system's structure" with its
"draconian requirements of a conscience eternally mobilized against
itself in a shape that the next instant would destroy" (62).

   Living a process in which truth is "broken off" at the moment it
becomes speech has terrible dangers, Ashbery admits. It can produce a skepticism as deadly as that Tower of Babel which is the
doppelgänger of the boiling crater of the word. If we totally surrender the hope for meaning, for the full presence offered by a
privileged moment, an "impassive but real moment of understanding," then "we can be brought to doubt that any of this, which we
know in our heart of hearts to be a real thing, an event of the highest spiritual magnitude, ever happened." This, too, would be fatal,
for it would deafen us to "words that were not words but sounds
out of time," to the "unspoken message that motion could be accomplished only *in* time" (76). To doubt the existence of the crater
of the word that exists "out of time" is to destroy the possibility of
marking its "unspoken message" in words that *are* words, fragments of the truth broken off from the mouth. An absolute skepticism destroys the ability to formulate oneself as "names," as

"commotion" around this "hollow" that is a "confusion" of death and life. According to Ashbery, we must "correctly consider our-selves shut off from the main source" but, nonetheless, be "able to consider its traces in the memory as a supreme good" (77). He con-siders the necessity of "traces" in a remarkable paraphrase of Wordsworth's "Ode: Intimations of Immortality":

> The answer is in our morning waking. For just as
> we begin our lives as mere babes with the imprint
> of nothing in our heads, except lingering traces
> of a previous existence which grow fainter and
> fainter as we progress until we have forgotten
> them entirely, only by this time other notions
> have imposed themselves so that our infant minds
> are never a complete *tabula rasa,* but there is
> always something fading out or just coming into
> focus, and this whatever-it-is is always projecting
> itself on us, escalating its troops, prying open the
> shut gates of our sensibility and pouring in to
> augment its forces that have begun to take over our
> naked consciousness and driving away those shreds of
> another consciousness (although not, perhaps, forever
> —nothing is permanent—but perhaps until our last
> days when their forces shall again mass on the borders
> of our field of perception to remind us of that other
> old existence which we are now being called to rejoin)
> so that for a moment, between the fleeing and pursuing
> armies there is, almost a moment of peace, of purity
> in which what we are meant to perceive could almost
> take shape in the empty air, if only there were time
> enough, and yet in the time it takes to perceive the
> dimness of its outline we can if we are quick enough
> seize the meaning of that assurance, before returning
> to the business at hand—just, I say, as we begin each
> day in this state of threatened blankness which is
> wiped away so soon, but which leaves certain illegible
> traces, like chalk dust on a blackboard, after it has
> been erased, so we must learn to recognize it as the
> true form—the only one—in which such fragments of the
> true learning as we are destined to receive will be
> vouchsafed to us, if at all.
>
> (*TP,* 78 79)

"The answer" Ashbery suggests, in this breathless rush of words, is the relentless "fading out . . . coming into focus" process of consciousness as a vital state of potential, intent upon "seizing the meaning" of a privileged moment.[19] While that moment is defeated by time, the intuition that it can "almost take shape" leaves "illegible traces, like chalk dust on a blackboard," which we must learn to read. That dust is not truth itself but a "true *form*—the only one" that leaves "fragments of the true learning" for the mind to perform and absorb. We cannot do without what we cannot have, and words, "fragments," are a kind of "dust" that attempts to make its traces legible.

Like the privileged moment that exposes the "hole" of truth as a coalescence of desire, understanding, meaning, and death, truth as the buried word "is," even though it is not attainable. And if one tries "to seize the meaning of that assurance," the act of *trying* to seize bestows limited but real rewards:

> to have absorbed the lesson, to have
> recovered from the shock of not being able
> to remember it, to again be starting out
> from the beginning—is this not something
> good to you? You no longer have to remember
> the principles, they seem to come to you
> like fragments of a buried language you
> once knew.
>
> (*TP*, 86)

One does not have to "remember" principles that are built into the act of knowing itself. The inherent structure of consciousness is a "buried language," and its acts are the "fragments of a buried language" that "in the end . . . fit together like a ghost story . . . nourished by a form of hope that doesn't take itself seriously" (90). The hope that wants to find the cratered word is the same hope that wants to discover the self but must not "seriously" expect to do so.

---

19. In her essay "Fragments of a Buried Life" (*Beyond Amazement*, 66–86), Marjorie Perloff identifies this sort of "dream-work" and locates Ashbery's style in a "dream structure" wherein "the experience of dream is the *only* way of knowing we have" (73). Laurence Leiberman is also intrigued with the dream-like quality of Ashberian thought. See "Unassigned Frequencies: Whispers Out of Time," *American Poetry Review*, Vol. VI, No. 2 (1977), 4–18. Ashbery himself has said that "the dream aspect of my poetry has been over-emphasized. I think in fact that the conscious element in my poetry is more important than the unconscious element, if only because our conscious thoughts are what occupy us most of the day. . . . My poetry is really consciously trying to explore consciousness more than unconsciousness" (*CP*, 118). Obviously, I side with the poet in this case.

It lives by disinterring "fragments" of the "I," the word that always
escapes its words, so that its fragments reveal only its ghostly activity. And those fragments are, themselves, "ghosts" of the language that remains "buried." For Wordsworth, the "I" remains
hidden from words; for Ashbery, the "I" reveals itself through the
fragments it finds in seeking the hidden *word*.

The language of presence remains permanently lost, even though
"everything around me is waiting for me to get up and say the
word, whatever that is" (94), even though the poet's desire to possess it is so powerful that it seems as if "the trees and skies that sur-
round you are full of apprehension, are waiting for this word from
you that you have not in you" (95). In the intensity of his burden
and desire, it begins to seem that the word might have emerged already, without his knowing:

> You must have said it a long way back without knowing
> it. . . . And the word that everything hinged on is
> buried back there; by mutual consent neither of you
> examined it when it was pronounced and rushed to its
> final resting place. It is doing the organizing, the
> guidelines radiate from its control; therefore it
> is good not to know what it is since its results
> can be known so intimately, appreciated for what
> they are; it is best then that the buried word
> remain buried for we were intended to appreciate
> only its fruits and not the secret principle
> activating them—to know this would be to know
> too much.
>
>   (*TP*, 95)

The phrasing here returns one to the beginning of *Three Poems,*
where the poet has said that "we have broken through into the
meaning of the tomb. But the act . . . needs pronouncing." The act
that reveals the meaning of the tomb can only be death. But that
"word" has been purposely obscured, "said a long way back" and
never "examined." It is lost to the acting mind. Unquestioned, not
"acted out," the "meaning of the tomb" is itself rushed to its "final
resting place." Around its trace, consciousness formulates itself,
but it can do so only as long as it remains unspoken. For the act of
"pronouncing" and the act of dying must remain "still proposed,
before us." The word can carry life, merely *traced* with death, only
as long as the word remains "buried." Words that are only fragments of the word carry both life and death, the "found" word is

death-itself. The acting out of that meaning has generated all of *Three Poems,* this autobiography of "the austerity of an almost empty mind." Death is the "word that everything hinged on" but which must not be "examined" if life is to continue. "Its results can be known intimately," Ashbery writes in his wonderfully deadpan way, but in the act of writing/living "it is best, then, that the buried word remain buried." It is, finally, the evasion of mortality that generates the self and its writing, and "we were intended to appreciate only its fruits," these words, "not the secret principle activating them."

That the "secret principle activating" words is the unspeakable master-word, death, is evident nearly everywhere in Ashbery's work, as is the fact that for him writing is always a seeking for, and evasion of, that master-word. The word *death* never fully emerges in *Three Poems.* The questioning "I" continues its quest, continues writing itself into existence by moving speculatively between fragments of its reflections. Both poet and reader, coalesced in Ashbery's brilliant use of the word *you,* continue to "wait in anticipation" of an "inevitable reply," but the final "reply" to "the question of your being here," remains indefinitely if "temporarily delayed" (98).

The mind continues to act in its reading and writing, "living under and into this reply which has suddenly caused everything in my world to take on new meaning." The reply is never spoken, however; it never arrives. Instead, it is articulated as the "thread" of meaning woven unobtrusively into this text of the self (99). This is the "scarlet thread" that appears at the heart of Ashbery's long work, in the midst of his discussion of what one should "do" with that "impassive but real moment of understanding" which we know and want but which never arrives (74–78). The answer to the question of being, the unarticulated master-word, is available and desirable only through the traces it leaves as it withdraws from presence. Its "emanations" are useful only if we "weave them into the pattern of days." The thread/reply is "the identifying scarlet thread that runs through the whole warp and woof of the design" until the end of time, "until the meaning of it all flashes out of the shimmering pools of scarlet like a vast and diaphanous though indestructible framework, not to be lost sight of again" (77). Meanwhile, as "The Recital" makes clear, "any reckoning of the sum total of the things we are is of course doomed to failure" (113). The "scarlet thread" remains only part of the weaving of words "and there is still the urge to get on with it all" (111), the urge toward meaning as self-discovery. This living urge produces the nonclosure with which the book "ends." For what we are left with at the finish of this long quest for the buried word, for the "name" of the "I," is not the word itself but "an Idea of the spectacle as something to be acted out and absorbed" (118). And we are sent back to the beginning, to "recite," to continue by interpreting and performing.

Because the question of being *is* being, Ashbery sees existence as a radical incongruity, as an inconsistency of the self with the self which can become "congruent" only at death. Thus, any "man of words" is an "anomaly," that "anomaly" which in "Litany" is "the shadow of a whisper on someone's lips":

> You can neither define
> Nor erase it, and seen by torchlight,
> Being cloaked with the shrill
> Savage drapery of non-being, it
> Stands out in the firelight.
> It is more than anything was meant to be.
> Yet somehow mournful, as though
> The three-dimensional effect had been achieved
> At the cost of a crisp vagueness.
>
> ("Litany," *AWK,* 28)

The "crisp vagueness" of Ashbery's work, which has distressed so many readers, is "the cost" of incarnating a whisper as "a shadow on someone's lips." When words become "palpable," as MacLeish wanted, they are, he thinks, "like a fruit / That is too beautiful to eat" ("The Explanation," *HD,* 15). They leave consciousness malnourished and unable to "reappear in a completely new outfit" (15). "It would be tragic to fit / Into a space created by our not having arrived yet / To utter the speech that belongs there / For progress occurs through re-inventing / These words from a dim recollection of them, / In violating that space in such a way as to leave it intact" ("Blue Sonata," *HD,* 67). We should understand that his words, "these decibels," are a "kind of flagellation, an entity of sound / Into which being enters and is apart" ("The Skaters," *RM,* 34).

Language that allows both the entrance of being and its "apartness" remains an epitaphic language, a language that announces an absent presence. Although its "savage drapery" would probably seem to Wordsworth to be that language of the "counter-spirit" that he so feared, for Ashbery a language that behaves like a garment is the only option available for revealing a being that is, in its essence, the non-being of a state of potential. In attempting to write poetry that is "an achieved state of *potential*," Ashbery has pressed the epitaphic gesture to its furthest limits, allowing meaning to appear only in the "interstices." If his "crisp vagueness" became any more diaphanous, his work would fall into a lyric crash that would move it entirely out of the realm of poetry. He has not, however, gone beyond that limit, and he has made powerful and beautiful use of the postmodernist understanding of language as sheer representation. Yet he uses that knowledge in an incarnative way. He has said of *Three Poems* that "somebody is being born . . . is somehow given an embodiment." The play of differance, of representation, *is* embodiment for this poet. Representation, with all the gaps it creates, the distances between words and the thing–itself, with all of its potential for interpretive play and errance, is the most appropriate body for an "I" that is always differing and deferring the death of self-presence.

"Who has seen the wind?" Ashbery asks about consciousness in *Three Poems* (61). It is not to be found by "gazing into a mirror reflecting the innermost depths of the soul" (61). It is too quick, too multiple for that. Nonetheless,

> To be always conscious of these multiple facets
> is to incarnate a dimensionless organism like
> the wind's, a living concern that can know no
> rest, by definition: it is restlessness.
>
> (*TP*, 61)

We need, he says, to "produce the inner emptiness from which alone understanding can spring up, the tree of contradictions, joyous and living, investing that hollow void with its complicated material self" (63). We "arrive" then, with John Ashbery's work, at a moment when representation, *because* it cannot contain the truth, becomes the only appropriate "material" for incarnation. In an entirely "new key" Ashbery's work acts out Eliot's dictum: "Every phrase and every sentence is an end and a beginning, / Every poem an epitaph" (Eliot, "Little Gidding," V). It is, Ashbery writes, "as though all were elegy and toccata / (Which happens to be the case), / The guidelines" ("Litany," *AWK*, 27).

BIBLIOGRAPHY

Abrams, M. H. *Natural Supernaturalism: Tradition and Revolution in Romantic Literature.* New York, 1971.

————. "Structure and Style in the Greater Romantic Lyric." In *Romanticism and Consciousness,* edited by Harold Bloom. New York, 1970.

Adams, Hazard, ed. *Critical Theory Since Plato.* New York, 1971.

Alter, Robert. *The Art of Biblical Poetry.* New York, 1985.

The Anchor Bible Job. Translated by Marvin H. Pope. Garden City, N.Y., 1973.

Aristotle. *The Poetics.* Translated by S. H. Butcher. In S. H. Butcher, *Aristotle's Theory of Poetry and Fine Arts.* New York, 1951.

Ashbery, John. *As We Know.* New York, 1979.

————. *The Double Dream of Spring.* New York, 1976.

————. *Houseboat Days.* New York, 1977.

————. *Rivers and Mountains.* New York, 1977.

————. *Self-Portrait in a Convex Mirror.* New York, 1975.

————. *Some Trees.* New York, 1970.

————. *Three Poems.* New York, 1972.

————. *A Wave.* New York, 1985.

Augustine. *On Christian Doctrine.* Translated by D. W. Robinson, Jr. New York, 1958.

————. *The Confessions of St. Augustine.* Translated by Rex Warner. New York, 1963.

Barthes, Roland. "The Death of the Author." In Barthes, *Image, Music, Text.* Translated by Stephen Heath. New York, 1977.

————. *The Pleasure of the Text.* Translated by Richard Miller. New York, 1975.

Bloom, Harold. "The Breaking of Form." In *Deconstruction and Criticism,* edited by Harold Bloom, Paul de Man, Jacques Derrida, Geoffrey Hartman, and J. Hillis Miller. New York, 1979.

————. "John Ashbery: The Charity of the Hard Moments." In *Contemporary Poetry in America,* edited by Robert Boyers. New York, 1974.

————. *A Map of Misreading.* New York, 1975.

————, ed. *Selected Poetry and Prose of Shelley.* New York, 1966.

————, ed. *Shelley's Mythmaking.* Ithaca, 1969.

Browne, Sir Thomas. *Religio Medici.* In *Religious Prose of 17th Century England,* edited by Anne Davidson Ferry. New York, 1966.

Bruns, Gerald. *Modern Poetry and the Idea of Language.* New Haven, 1974.

Cameron, Sharon. *Lyric Time: Dickinson and the Limits of Genre.* Baltimore, 1979.

Coleridge, Samuel Taylor. *Biographia Literaria.* Edited by George Watson. New York, 1971.

———. "The Statesman's Manual." In *Critical Theory Since Plato,* edited by Hazard Adams. New York, 1971.

Colie, Rosalie. *Paradoxia Epidemica: The Renaissance Tradition of Paradox.* Princeton, 1966.

Culler, Jonathan. *On Deconstruction: Theory and Criticism after Structuralism.* Ithaca, 1982.

Curtius, Ernst. *European Literature and the Latin Middle Ages.* Translated by Willard R. Trask. New York, 1963.

Davidson, Harriet. *T. S. Eliot and Hermeneutics: Absence and Interpretation in The Waste Land.* Baton Rouge, 1985.

De Man, Paul. "Autobiography as De-Facement." *Modern Language Notes,* XCIV (1979), 919–30.

———. *Blindness and Insight: Essays in the Rhetoric of Contemporary Criticism.* New York, 1971.

———. "Intentional Structure of the Romantic Image." In *Romanticism and Consciousness,* edited by Harold Bloom. New York, 1970.

———. "Lyrical Voice in Contemporary Theory: Riffaterre and Jauss." In *Lyric Poetry: Beyond New Criticism,* edited by Chaviva Hosek and Patricia Parker. Ithaca, 1985.

———. "Shelley Disfigured." In *Deconstruction and Criticism,* edited by Harold Bloom, Paul de Man, Jacques Derrida, Geoffrey Hartman, and J. Hillis Miller. New York, 1979.

Derrida, Jacques. *Dissemination.* Translated by Barbara Johnson. Chicago, 1981.

———. "Limited, Inc a b c . . . ." *Glyph,* II (1977), 162–254.

———. *Margins of Philosophy.* Translated by Alan Bass. Chicago, 1982.

———. *Of Grammatology.* Translated by Gayatri Chakravorty Spivak. Baltimore, 1976.

———. *Positions.* Translated by Alan Bass. Chicago, 1981.

———. "Signature, Event, Context." *Glyph,* I (1977), 172–97.

———. *Speech and Phenomena and Other Essays on Husserl's Theory of Signs.* Translated by David B. Allison. Evanston, Ill., 1973.

———. "Structure, Sign, and Play in the Discourse of the Human Sciences." In *The Structuralist Controversy: The Languages of Criticism and the Sciences of Man,* edited by Richard Macksey and Eugenio Donato. Baltimore, 1970.

———. *Writing and Difference.* Translated by Alan Bass. Chicago, 1978.

Donato, Eugenio. "The Ruins of Memory: Archaeological Fragments and Textual Artifacts." *Modern Language Notes,* XCIII (1978), 591–606.

Eliade, Mircea. *The Sacred and the Profane: The Nature of Religion.* Translated by Willard R. Trask. New York, 1959.

Eliot, T. S. *Collected Poems, 1909–1962.* New York, 1963.

Ferguson, Frances. *Wordsworth: Language as Counterspirit.* New Haven, 1977.

Fish, Stanley. *The Living Temple: George Herbert and Catechizing.* Berkeley, 1978.

Foucault, Michel. *The Order of Things: An Archaeology of the Human Sciences.* New York, 1970.

Frye, Northrop. *The Great Code: The Bible and Literature.* New York: 1982.

Halewood, William H. *The Poetry of Grace.* New Haven, 1970.

Hartman, Geoffrey. "Antiself-consciousness and Romanticism." In *Romanticism and Consciousness,* edited by Harold Bloom. New York, 1970.

———. *Wordsworth's Poetry, 1787–1814.* New Haven, 1964.

Heidegger, Martin. *Being and Time.* Translated by John Macquarrie and Edward Robinson. New York, 1962.

———. "On the Essence of Truth." In *Martin Heidegger: Basic Writings,* edited by David F. Krell. New York, 1977.

———. *On the Way to Language.* Translated by Peter D. Hertz. New York, 1971.

———. "The Origin of the Work of Art." In *Martin Heidegger: Basic Writings,* edited by David F. Krell. New York, 1977.

———. *Poetry, Language and Thought.* Translated by Albert Hofstadter. New York, 1957.

———. "What Is Metaphysics?" In *Existence and Being,* edited by Werner Brock. London, 1949.

Hofstadter, Douglas R. *Gödel, Escher, Bach: An Eternal Golden Braid.* New York, 1980.

Hutchinson, F. E., ed. *The Works of George Herbert.* Oxford, 1945.

Johnson, Barbara. "Rigorous Unreliability." *Critical Inquiry,* II (December, 1984), 278–385.

Johnson, Thomas H., ed. *The Letters of Emily Dickinson,* 3 vols. Cambridge, Mass., 1965.

Kalstone, David. *Five Temperaments.* New York, 1977.

Kermode, Frank. *The Sense of an Ending: Studies in the Theory of Fiction.* London, 1966.

Krieger, Murray. *Poetic Presence and Illusion.* Baltimore, 1979.

Lacoue-Labarthe, Philippe. "The Caesura of the Speculative." *Glyph,* IV (1978), 57–84.

Lehman, David, ed. *Beyond Amazement: New Essays on John Ashbery.* Ithaca, 1980.

Leiberman, Laurence. "Unassigned Frequencies: Whispers Out of Time." *American Poetry Review,* Vol. VI, No. 2 (1977), 4–18.

Leitch, Vincent B. *Deconstructive Criticism: An Advanced Introduction.* New York, 1983.

Locke, John. *An Essay Concerning Human Understanding.* Edited by P. H. Nidditch. Oxford, 1975.

MacLeish, Archibald. *New and Collected Poems, 1917–1982.* Boston, 1976.

Martz, Louis. *The Poetry of Meditation.* New Haven, 1954.

Miller, J. Hillis. "The Critic as Host." In *Deconstruction and Criticism,* edited by Harold Bloom, Paul de Man, Jacques Derrida, Geoffrey Hartman, and J. Hillis Miller. New York, 1979.

————. "Deconstructing the Deconstructors." *Diacritics*, V (Summer, 1975), 24–31.

————. "The Still Heart: Poetic Form in Wordsworth." *New Library History*, II (Winter, 1971), 297–310.

Norris, Christopher. *Deconstruction: Theory and Practice*. London, 1982.

————. *The Deconstructive Turn*. London, 1984.

Packard, William, ed. *The Craft of Poetry: Interviews from the "New York Quarterly."* New York, 1974.

Peck, Charles, and Roger Ingpen. *The Complete Works of Shelley*. Vols. VI and VII of 10 vols. New York, 1965.

Plato. *The Collected Dialogues*. Edited by Edith Hamilton and Huntington Cairns. Translated by Lane Cooper. Princeton, 1953.

————. *The Republic*. Translated by B. Jowett. Garden City, N.Y., 1953.

Richardson, William J. *Heidegger: Through Phenomenology to Thought*. The Hague, 1967.

Riddel, Joseph. "From Heidegger to Derrida to Chance: Doubling and Poetic Language." In *Martin Heidegger and the Question of Literature*, edited by William Spanos. Bloomington, Ind., 1979.

————. *The Inverted Bell: Modernism and the Counterpoetics of William Carlos Williams*. Baton Rouge, 1974.

————. "A Miller's Tale." *Diacritics*, V (Fall, 1975), 56–65.

Rorty, Richard. "Deconstruction and Circumvention." *Critical Inquiry*, II (September, 1984), 1–23.

Schiller, Friedrich von. *"Naive and Sentimental Poetry" and "On the Sublime."* Translated by Julius A. Elias. New York, 1966.

Searle, John R. "Reiterating the Differences: A Reply to Derrida." *Glyph*, I (1977), 198–208.

Spanos, William. "Hermeneutics and Memory: Destroying T. S. Eliot's *Four Quartets*." *Genre*, II (Winter, 1978), 523–73.

————. *Repetitions: The Postmodern Occasion in Literature and Culture*. Baton Route, 1987.

————, ed. *Martin Heidegger and the Question of Literature*. Bloomington, Ind., 1979.

Starobinski, Jean. *The Invention of Liberty*. Translated by Bernard C. Swift. New York, 1964.

Stein, Arnold. *George Herbert's Lyrics*. Baltimore, 1968.

Summers, Joseph. *George Herbert*. London, 1954.

Tillyard, E. M. W. *The Elizabethan World Picture*. London, 1943.

Tuve, Rosemond. *Elizabethan and Metaphysical Imagery: Renaissance Poetic and Twentieth Century Critics*. Chicago, 1947.

————. *A Reading of George Herbert*. Chicago, 1952.

Vendler, Helen. *The Poetry of George Herbert*. Cambridge, Mass., 1975.

Wallerstein, Ruth. *Studies in Seventeenth Century Poetics.* Madison, Wis., 1950.

Warnock, Mary. *Imagination.* Berkeley, 1976.

Wasserman, Earl. "The English Romantics: The Grounds of Knowledge." In *Romanticism: Points of View,* edited by Robert Gleckner and Gerald Enscoe. Detroit, 1957.

———. *Shelley: A Critical Reading.* Baltimore, 1971.

Whitman, Walt. *Leaves of Grass.* Edited by Harold Blodgett and Sculley Bradley. New York, 1968.

Willey, Basil. *The Seventeenth Century Background.* New York, 1953.

Williamson, Alan. *Introspection and Contemporary Poetry.* Cambridge, Mass., 1984.

Wordsworth, William. "Note to Ode: Intimations of Immortality." In *The Norton Anthology of English Literature,* Vol. II of 2 vols. Edited by M. H. Abrams, et al. New York, 1974.

———. *The Prelude: Or Growth of a Poet's Mind.* Edited by Ernest de Selincourt. Oxford, 1975.

Zall, Paul M., ed. *Literary Criticism of William Wordsworth.* Lincoln, Neb., 1970.

INDEX

Autobiography: Augustine and,
140–41, 145–47, 153–54; Wordsworth and, 141, 142, 147–50,
153–54, 163–64, 172, 177, 178,
181, 188, 191–92, 198–99; De
Man's view of, 141–42, 171 n; definition of, 141–42; compared to
auto-affection, 142–45, 164, 171;
Coleridge and, 152–53, 156–60;
Ashbery and, 279–80

Bacon, Francis, 106
Barthes, Roland, 219–21, 224, 225,
233, 249, 252
Baudelaire, Charles, 7
Bible. *See* Book of Exodus; Book
of Job
Blake, William, 160
Bloom, Harold, 3, 39–40, 46–47,
288 n
Book of Exodus, 94, 108
Book of Job: King James translation
of, 64–65; Job's curse in, 66, 67,
71, 72; as language sacrifice, 66–67,
75, 79–80, 138; silence in, 66–67,
71–72, 79, 96, 213; failure of human language, 67–71, 76–77, 92,
93, 94, 102; Job's refusal to pray,
69–71; image of death in, 72–73;
inscription of words on rock,
73–76, 96, 112, 205; Elihu as poet/
priest, 76–79, 122; voice of God in,
78–80, 91, 95, 122; Job's desire for
language as bridge, 82, 205; compared with Herbert, 94–95, 96,
102, 109, 112, 122, 138, 205
Book of the World, 103–108, 175
Browne, Sir Thomas, 106
Burns, Gerald, 210

Cameron, Sharon, 212
Coleridge, Samuel Taylor: in *The
Prelude*, 148, 164, 191; autobiography and, 152–53, 156–60; definition of symbol, 152–53; subject/
object in, 156–59, 160 n; on consciousness, 159–60; on nature, 160;
on God, 160–61; on the origin of
spirit, 162; on imagination, 163,
165, 177; on life, 170

—works: *Biographia Literaria*, 152,
156–58
Colie, Rosalie, 137
Conrad, Joseph, 125
Curtius, Ernst R., 104

Deconstruction, 5–8, 219, 234, 235,
238–40, 252, 256, 258, 260–61
De Man, Paul: voice in lyric poetry,
2–3, 7; principle of intelligibility,
14; on Rousseau, 54–55; on Shelley,
55, 61; on autobiography, 141–42,
171 n; on Wordsworth, 189 n; on
language, 233–35, 239, 240; on
meaning, 253, 256
—works: "Shelley Disfigured," 55;
Blindness and Insight, 231
Derrida, Jacques: language as representation, 1, 3–9; modes of deconstruction, 8–10; on Heidegger,
9–10, 85, 217, 259, 260, 282; on
meaning, 9–10, 209 n, 250–54,
260, 268; on differance, 10, 11–12,
18, 82, 83, 89, 242–51, 257–58,
260–62; and metaphor of haunting,
13, 227, 256; on death and the
tomb, 15, 16, 103, 117, 177, 181,
261–262; on truth, 18–21, 63, 91;
on writing, 18–20, 74; on speech,
19–20, 60–61; on Plato, 23; on
Hegel, 31, 171 n; on the term *ontotheological,* 41; on quest for right
word, 63, 260–61, 266; on inspiration, 76; on silence, 82–83, 88,
98, 100; pyramid in, 83–84, 90; on
God, 84, 98, 106; on the self, 106,
218–19; on the abyss, 116; on auto-
affection, 142–45, 170–71, 188–89,
206, 218, 223, 224, 246–48; on representational thinking, 151; on cen-
tered/self-contained structure, 159,
210; on Rousseau, 167, 256; on
imagination, 177; and nature of
signs, 184; on hope, 205; on nostalgia, 205, 259–60, 281–82; on dissemination, 218–19, 221–25, 233,
235–39, 241–42, 244, 246, 249,
250, 252, 256; compared with
Barthes, 220, 221; machine metaphor in, 223–24, 226, 235, 240–44,

95*n;* "Jordan I," 95, 110; "Jordan
II," 95, 128–29; "Joseph's Coat,"
95*n;* "The Holy Scriptures," 95*n;*
"The Sonne," 95*n;* "The Thanksgiving," 95*n,* 109; "Deniall," 96;
"Assurance," 97; "Perseverance,"
97, 121; "Love III," 98; "The Collar," 101–103, 107, 112; "The Windows," 103, 132–34, 152, 205–
206; "Sepulchre," 107–108; "Good
Friday," 109–10, 126; "Death,"
111–12, 114, 124; "The Altar,"
112–13, 138–39; "The Sacrifice,"
113; "Church-Monuments," 113–
20, 122, 124; "Doomsday," 119,
124; "Love II," 121, 128; "Provi-
dence," 121–22; "The Glimpse,"
123; "The Temper," 123; "Decay,"
123–26; "Superliminare," 124, 126;
"The Sinner," 126; "Nature," 127;
"Aaron," 128; "Love I," 128;
"J E S U," 130–31; "Love-joy,"
131–32; "Christmas," 132; "The
Quiddity," 133; "Dulnesse," 134;
"Grief," 134–35; "Longing," 137;
"The Search," 137; "Church Windows," 268
Hermetic poetry, 210–11
Hirsch, E. D., 252
Hofstadter, Douglas, 236

Jauss, Hans Robert, 2, 3
Job. *See* Book of Job
Johnson, Barbara, 241

Kalstone, David, 279, 279*n*
Kermode, Frank, 198, 263–64

Lacoue-Labarthe, Philippe, 161–62,
170, 178, 208
Language: Derrida's view of, 1, 3–9,
98; Heidegger's view of, 1, 3–6,
8, 9, 98; death and, 1–2, 12–16;
Bloom's view of, 3; Miller's view
of, 3–8; Derrida's view of meaning, 9–10, 209*n,* 250–53; Derrida's
différance, 10, 11–12, 82, 83, 89,
242–51, 257–58, 260–62; Heidegger's dif-ference, 10–11, 12, 88;

Ashbery's view of, 13, 204–205,
226–33, 286–87, 287*n,* 290–91,
313–14; Plato's view of, 21–23;
Shelley's view of, 33, 35, 43–44,
47–50, 59–60; silence and, 82–87,
91, 93; Augustine's view of, 91–
92, 98–100, 103, 142, 150; Herbert's view of, 94–95, 97, 101–103,
109–10, 120–30, 132–39, 141, 150,
152, 205–206, 208–209; Wordsworth's view of, 141, 142, 154,
171, 172, 174–76, 182–87, 206–
209; Derrida's dissemination,
218–19, 221–25, 233, 235–39,
241–42, 244, 246, 249, 250, 252,
256; Derrida's machine metaphor,
223–24, 226, 235, 240, 241–43,
244, 251, 255; De Man's view of,
233–35, 239, 240. *See also* Deconstruction; Poetry; Structuralism
Leiberman, Laurence, 310*n*
Locke, John, 140, 154, 155, 157

MacLeish, Archibald, 212–16, 217,
233, 268, 301, 313
Marx, Karl, 235
Miller, J. Hillis, 3–8
Milton, John, 25, 82, 153

New Criticism, 234
Nietzsche, Friedrich, 235, 238
Norris, Christopher, 238, 239

Paul, Saint, 110
Perloff, Marjorie, 310*n*
Plato: on language, 21–23; on truth,
21–22, 39, 59, 63, 68; on writing,
22–23, 106–107; on speech, 23,
106–107; on poetry, 28, 29, 30, 32,
34, 38, 39; compared with Shelley,
38, 39, 59, 60; on absence of voice,
60; importance of, 90
—works: *Ion,* 21, 29, 30; *The Republic,* 21–22, 29; *Phaedrus,* 22–23
Poetry: definition of, 2; death and,
14–15; Ashbery's view of, 17,
226–30, 263, 273, 276–78, 279,
295, 297, 300–302, 314; truth and,
18; Plato's view of, 21–23, 28, 29,